GANDHI
and His
Ashrams

GANDHI
and His Ashrams

MARK THOMSON

www.popularprakashan.com

Published by
Asmita Mohite for
POPULAR PRAKASHAN PVT. LTD.
301, Mahalaxmi Chambers
22, Bhulabhai Desai Road
Mumbai - 400 026
info@popularprakashan.com

© 1993 Mark Thomson
First Published 1993
Second Edition 2024

(4546)
ISBN : 978-81-948714-5-3

WORLD RIGHTS RESERVED. The contents are original and copyrighted. No portion of this book shall be reproduced, stored in a retrieval system or transmitted by any means, electronic, mechanical, photocopying, recording or otherwise, without the written permission of the author and the publisher.

PRINTED IN INDIA
by Trinity Academy For Corporate Training Ltd.
Pune

For
Arun Gandhi

Publisher's Note

The 150th birth anniversary of Kasturba and Mohandas *Karamchand* Gandhi called for reissuing of some important books. *Gandhi and his Ashrams* by Mark Thomson is a very important contribution to Gandiana. Gandhi himself believed that Ashram was his major original contribution. He did not claim originality for Truth and Non-violence; these he pointed out were as old as the hills. Ashram was not a new concept in India but earlier it was largely oriented towards religious practices. Phoenix Settlement near Durban, Tolstoy Farm near Johannesburg in South Africa, as well as Satyagraha Ashram in Ahmedabad and Sevagram in Wardha, were centres of great activity. Sevagram was, in a sense the unofficial capital of India.

Gandhi and his Ashrams is much more than a description of those Ashrams. The author traces the history of events originating in these centres and is thus a history of these four eventful decades, from a very different perspective.

In this edition, fresh material has been added as postscript, not only by the author but also by Gandhi's granddaughter Ela Gandhi, great grandson Tushar Gandhi, and the eminent scholar Thomas Weber. This new edition should stimulate further thinking on the importance of Gandhi in the 21st century.

Mumbai
October 2019

Acknowledgements

This book derives from my Doctoral thesis, researched and written in India during the years 1978-82. The opportunity to live and study in India was made possible by a scholarship under the Commonwealth Scholarship and Fellowship Plan (CSFP). I would like to thank the Governments of India and Australia for this support.

The decision to leave my country for over four years in order to complete this work was made easier by the encouragement and support of my friend and teacher, Dr. Jim Masselos of the University of Sydney. His advice and assistance has been invaluable in producing this book.

I would like to thank all the Indian institutions and their staff that helped in obtaining research material. My host institution, the University of Bombay, and the Maharashtra State Archives were of assistance in this regard.

A number of Gandhian institutions were also a great help along the way. These included Mani Bhavan in Bombay, Sabarmati Ashram and the Gujarat Vidyapith in Ahmedabad, Sevagram Ashram in Maharashtra and the Gandhi Smarak Nidhi in Delhi. As I resided for short periods at the two ashrams and the Gandhi Smarak Nidhi, I would particularly like to thank these communities for their hospitality.

Several people have assisted in preparing and proofing the various drafts of the book and I thank them all. Above all, it would have been a much more unruly document without my father's proof reading and advice on the text.

Lastly, I would like to thank family and friends in India, Mauritius and Australia for their support and encouragement. I cannot do justice in words to the debt of gratitude I owe my wife, Carolie.

This new edition is dedicated to Arun Gandhi, the grandson of Mahatma Gandhi, who died on May 2, 2023, Kolhapur, India. Arun and his family were a great support to us as we negotiated life in Bombay (before Mumbai) as research students.

Contents

Publisher's Note	vii
Acknowledgements	viii
Introduction	1
1. Gandhi and Community : The Formative Years	4
2. The Phoenix Settlement and Tolstoy Farm : The Experiment Begins	37
3. The Satyagraha Ashram	91
4. The Village of Service : "India in a Village"	174
5. Conclusion	262
Postscripts	279
Introduction – Mark Thomson	281
"Gandhi Today" – Thomas Weber	284
"Phoenix Rising" – Ela Gandhi	287
"Sabarmati Ashram - A Fountain of Greatness?" – Tushar Gandhi	291
Bibliography	296
Appendix	307
Index	310

Introduction

Since Mohandas Karamchand Gandhi's death in 1948 his life and thought have continued to be the subject-matter of extensive study. The rich and diverse legacy he left behind has provided a seemingly inexhaustible source for research scholars. From the publication of the first biography of Gandhi in 1909[1] to the present day, his way of life and philosophy have been chronicled and analysed more extensively than any other twentieth century figure. By the time of his return to India from South Africa in 1915 he was already known around the world as an ascetic revolutionary.

The main body, of writings about Gandhi are in the form of complete biographies, brief biographical essays, personal memoirs, and articles and treatises on his moral, political, economic, social and educational thought, which he designated his philosophy of *satyagraha* or truth-force. As Gandhi became a figure of world renown, men and women who lived and worked closely with him in South Africa and India were motivated to write biographical accounts and personal recollections of their friend, colleague and mentor. However, apart from an exceptional few, the many early biographies suffer from unevenness and lack of focus, and are often more identifiable with panegyric than historical writing.

The best biographies have been written since his death, including the comprehensive study of the early and later stages of his life by Pyarelal,[2] Gandhi's secretary of many years, and books by Fischer, Nanda, Ashe, Payne, together with the small but excellent study by Woodcock.[3] In the preface to his penetrating biography Ashe highlights the need to define the paradoxical figure of Gandhi and demystify his ideas. This process has gone on unabated with detailed and scholarly studies of every aspect of his life and thought; looking at Gandhi the social, religious, economic and political theorist; evaluating Gandhi the statesman, educationist, revolutionary, socialist prophet and saint.

Despite this wide-ranging body of literature Gandhi's social experimentation in the ashrams or communities he established with his followers has been neglected. His pervading image in India and elsewhere remains that of charismatic leader and political revolutionary. This book is a contribution to the ongoing quest to rediscover the non-violent alternative. It tests the strength of Gandhi's claim that the ashrams were his finest achievements, and that the successes and failures of these communities were merely reflections of his own strengths and weaknesses. It is an attempt to understand the dynamics of his non-violent philosophy of action, firstly, as the foundation of his "experiments with truth" in the ashrams he shared with his followers, and, secondly, as the guiding principle underpinning his revolutionary programmes to realise a new individual and a new society.

In common with other treatises on the *satyagraha* philosophy this book adopts a biographical approach as a backdrop to the study of Gandhi's communitarian ideas and experimentation. His thought was inextricably bound up with his actions, and to study his theories in isolation from their practical dynamics is to deny the truth of Gandhi's claim that "my life is my message". The major sources were the correspondence and journalistic writings of Gandhi and his many colleagues and disciples who contributed in some way to the establishment and development of the Phoenix Settlement and Tolstoy Farm in South Africa and the Satyagraha Ashram and Sevagram Ashram in India. Whenever possible the material was supplemented by personal accounts of ashram life, interviews and questionnaire answers from people who at some stage had been intimately acquainted with ashram life. In addition, a large number of secondary sources were consulted.

Throughout the writing of this book the author was ever mindful that Gandhi, in the words of George Woodcock, "never set out to develop a fixed and final doctrine, but emphasised that his practice of *ahimsa* or non-violence was always experimental, that his political struggle like his personal life was part of a continuing quest for Truth as manifested existentially, a quest that could never end because human understanding was incapable of comprehending the Absolute."[4]

NOTES

1. Joseph J. Doke, *M. K. Gandhi : An Indian Patriot in South Africa* (Varanasi: A. B. Sarva Seva Sangh Prakashan, 1909).
2. Pyarelal, *Mahatma Gandhi : The Early Phase* (Ahmedabad: Navajivan Publishing House, Ahmedabad, 1965); *Mahatma Gandhi : The Last Phase* (Ahmedabad: Navajivan Publishing House 1966), and *Mahatma Gandhi : The Discovery of Satyagraha on The Threshold* (Bombay: Sevak Prakashan, 1980).
3. Louis Fischer, *Gandhi : His Life and Message for the World* (New York: New American Library, 1954); *The Life of Mahatma Gandhi* 2 Vols. (Bombay : Bharatiya Vidya Bhawan, 1951); B. R. Nanda, *Mahatma Gandhi, A Biography* (London: Unwin Books, 1965); Geoffrey Ashe, *Gandhi : A Study in Revolution* (London : Heinemann, 1968); Robert Payne, *The Life and Death of Mahatma Gandhi* (London The Bodley Head, 1969); and George Woodcock, *Gandhi* (London : Fontana / Collins, 1972).
4. Woodcock, op. cit., p. 10.

1

Gandhi and Community: The Formative Years

The ashrams Gandhi established served as laboratories where he and his colleagues experimented with non-violence as an alternative way of life. In these small monastic communities of men and women living according to absolute vows he sought to lay the ground-work for an egalitarian social organisation and economy, and to develop an education system that reflected the Indian genius. The ashrams provided economic and moral support as well as fostering the discipline and awareness necessary for their members to sustain grassroot civil disobedience. Gandhi saw the need in the tradition-bound, rigidly hierarchical Indian society, for a moral sanction able to inspire people to help themselves. He believed ashramic life, based on mutuality, simplicity and hard work, would nurture an asceticism that could be channelled through positive action to reform society. This chapter seeks to illumine some of the formative influences upon the development of his ashram concept.

Early Life

Mohandas Karamchand Gandhi was born on 2 October 1869, in Porbandar, a small coastal town in the Kathiawar Peninsula in western India. The Gandhis were Modh *banias*, a merchant caste, who were grocers traditionally. However, Gandhi's family had become hereditary Dewans or Prime Ministers of Kathiawar. The primary written source of Gandhi's experiences as a child and youth in the middle-class Hindu-Jain environment in Kathiawar during the 1870s and 1880s is his autobiography which was written many years later, as he was approaching sixty. There is little doubt that these early recollections were adapted to meet the moral needs and practical expediences of the period during which he wrote. Memories can connect past and present happenings and are an important part of the actuality in which they emerge. The book was written in serial form as a vehicle of self-appraisal and self-analysis, and as a moral and spiritual guide for his followers. Though many of the events described have most likely been distorted by memory, the book furnishes important insights into the phenomenon of Gandhi's development as a social and political activist and theoretician, and stands as a poignant study of the religious impulse in man.

Gandhi's parents were devout followers of Vishnu, the Hindu god who, it is believed, from time to time became incarnate to rehabilitate the world. His father was a righteous man who regularly went to the temple, heard religious discourses and towards the end of his life devoted much of his time to religious matters. Gandhi admired his father who clearly had qualities of leadership and was greatly respected in the community, but his mother had the strangest moral and spiritual influence upon him. She was a member of a small sect known as the *pranamis* who mingle Hindu and Muslim beliefs and practices. The basic tenets of the sect sought harmony among all faiths and simplicity of living. The latter involved vegetarianism, abstention from all stimulants, and periodic fasting, all of which his mother observed strictly. "The outstanding impression my mother has left on my memory is that of saintliness" recalled Gandhi, "she would take the hardest vows and keep them without flinching;"[1] Above all it would seem Karamchand Gandhi and his wife Putlibai bequeathed their son a heightened sense of morality and truth. Both had earned a reputation for honesty and wise counsel.

Gandhi revealed his rebellious nature at a young age. Though brought up in the lap of Hindu orthodoxy, the reformism of the *pranami* doubtless exercised some influence upon him. While he retained his attachment to certain ascetic forms of Hindu tradition, religious ritual had no appeal for him, and he was not afraid to break with tradition when his chosen path diverged. Erikson, in his psycho-analytical study of Gandhi, suggests that the childhood events Gandhi chose to recount in his autobiography in themselves reveal a man who "is early and painfully conscious of a special mission", and" "that he had to contain a superior energy which he later called truth-force and endowed with a discipline".[2] To overcome his shyness and timidity, for instance, he was encouraged by a school-mate to take up meat-eating. It was believed in certain reformist circles that the strength of the British was due to their meat diet. Gandhi thus broke the strict taboo of his community for a short period with a sense of patriotic duty, believing that to free India from the occupying power would require strong young men. He eventually gave up the "reform" because of the pain of lying to his parents.[3]

While Gandhi was not as a youth an especially devout Hindu, he was devoted to his parents. In their company he absorbed ideas that were later to provide him with a foundation on which to develop his own concepts. Tolerance towards all religions was a principle Gandhi learnt from them. They regularly visited temples of other sects and were themselves frequently visited by Jain monks. Organised under Mahavira in the sixth century B. C, Jainism had a strong appeal to the *bania* merchant communities of Gujarat. "Jainism was strong in Gujarat, and its influence was felt everywhere and on all occasions", wrote Gandhi.[4] Concepts such as *ahimsa* (literally meaning "absence of desire to kill") and the Jain doctrine of *anekantavada* (the many-sidedness of reality) may have been discussed within Gandhi's hearing. Though he was unaware of their impact, these early contacts with Jainism were probably instrumental in preparing his untrained mind later to accept the truth of the Jain teaching of the soul:

> Religion is not different sets of opinions. Religion is not just reading or memorising books known as scriptures or just believing everything said in them. Religion is the quality of one's soul and exists among men in a visible or in visible form. Through religion we are able to know our duties as human beings. Through religion we can recognise our true relationship with other living beings. It is obvious that this is not possible at all as long as we do not know our selves. Therefore, religion is that discipline of spiritual self-perfection through which we are able to know our own selves.[5]

Vaishnavites, Saivites, Jains, Muslims and Parsis were all welcome in the Gandhi household. During his father's three-year confinement to bed before he died Gandhi served as nurse. As his health deteriorated Karamchand became preoccupied with religion. On many occasions Gandhi was present in the sickroom, washing and massaging his father's feet and legs while friends and priests of different faiths read scriptures and discussed religion with his ailing father. A friend named Ladha, who purportedly had cured himself of leprosy by constantly chanting the *Ramanama* (or the name of Rama, an incarnation of Vishnu), would read the *Ramayana* to Gandhi's father. As a child Gandhi had taken comfort from an old nurse who suggested he repeat *the Ramanama* to quell his fear of ghosts and spirits. It was a superstitious rather than a devotional act, but this early experience accounts for his "enraptured" listening to Ladha. "That laid the foundation of my deep devotion to the *Ramayana*", he wrote.[6]

In terms of the two main currents of Hinduism in Gujarat, Gandhi was not attracted to the ritualistic, non-ascetic and caste-conscious tradition of the upper-class *Vaishnavas* worshipping Krishna (another incarnation of Vishnu). He disliked the "glitter and pomp" of the temple ritual and questioned the legitimacy of untouchabiliry. On the other hand, there was much in the worship of Rama that appealed to him; it had strong moral undertones, it was anti-caste, less ritualistic, more ascetic and a religion of the common people. Yet Gandhi was by no means convinced of the reality of God. Tolerance towards other religions had not enhanced his own faith in a divine being. On the contrary, he recollects that reading the *Manusmriti* (Laws of Manu, a Hindu lawgiver with divine sanction), particularly the story of creation, had turned him "somewhat towards atheism".[7]

Throughout his early life Gandhi had a predilection for moral teachings. From among the many plays he must have seen as a child he recalls the play of Shravana, which exemplifies heroic parental devotion, and the play of Harishchandra, which enshrines truth above all other values. The theme of truth as the expression of the Absolute in man occurs again and again in the account of his childhood and youth, suggesting that underlying his religious thinking was a moral sensitivity, a preoccupation with right action, with ethics. Truth became the focal point of his own unique philosophy of moral action.[8]

Pyarelal has suggested that the traditional Indian joint family, in which Gandhi grew up, provided him with an excellent preparatory training for community living and for understanding the subtleties of human relationships. Pyarelal equated the running of a joint family with managing a small kingdom with an an unwritten constitution; love and morality being the only sanctions available to the family head. Of necessity family members "develop the attitude of mutual help and regard, the capacity for give-and-take, and adjustment to one another's idiosyncrasies". To achieve harmony in this confined world, observed Pyarelal, "requires infinite patience, resourcefulness and knowledge of human nature", combined with a "meticulous regard for detail and perfection in performance of the littlest of the little things". Pyarelal believed Gandhi inherited many of these attributes from his father, and that the passion for ceaseless experimentation in community living as a part of his experiments with truth, the urge to live not only for mankind but in mankind and the time and care that he devoted in later years to the trivia of Ashram life had their seed in the tradition of the joint family that surrounded his early childhood.[9]

Much of Pyarelal's analysis is doubtless accurate. Yet he has drawn an idealistic picture of the extended family system and its efficacy in preparing children to "live not only for mankind but in mankind". The rules of conduct in a joint family are prescribed in sacred books and have been practised in India for centuries. Ideally, the individual is given a supportive framework and opportunity to be self-realised, and in return make an ongoing contribution to the maintenance of the family unit. The value of co-operation is given precedence over individualism for the good of the whole. However, in practice, it is not uncommon to find that individual members, and this is particularly true of female and junior male members, have involuntarily to suppress their own individuality.

Co-operation within the family is not based on the recognition of equality of status and the rights of its members, but, rather, as S.C Dube points out, on the recognition of four principles. These are respect for age, respect for position in the scale of kinship, superiority of the male and finally, the necessity of keeping certain matters confined to the responsible members of the family, or, at the most within the family.[10] Often members of the family are given very little responsibility in the management of the household or family affairs. In later years Gandhi learnt that Indian youth can be inhibited from making an independent and constructive contribution to society through fear of parental or family disapproval, and that as a result a valuable human resource can lie dormant.

Though the Gandhi household in Porbandar and later Rajkot may have been more enlightened than most, a number of customs followed placed undue pressure on the young man. Custom dictated his early marriage to Kasturba, and both suffered from the experience. In his autobiography Gandhi recalled his early introduction to sexual life as a source of guilt and shame which marred his spiritual and moral growth. He appears to have devoted himself to nursing his father during the early years of his marriage as a penance for his sexual excesses: "I was devoted to my parents. But no less was I devoted to the passions that flesh is heir to. I had yet to learn that all happiness and pleasure should be sacrificed in devoted service to my parents."[11]

The awakening of sexuality Gandhi experienced undermined his enjoyment of youthly pleasures and his marital relationship. His wife became, not an intimate companion, but an object of desire to be dominated. Gandhi was married early to comply with custom but his inability to reconcile an active sexual life with his sense of morality contributed to his later asceticism and ultimate alienation from the family.

The sometimes burdensome sense of filial duty that Indian children must accommodate is an aspect of the suppression of individuality characteristic of the joint family system. Gandhi's attitude to filial duty is apparent in a later letter to his seventeen year old son, Manilal, in which he discourages "fun and frolic" beyond the age of twelve, at which point the child must "go about with a full sense of his responsibility and make a ceaseless, conscious effort to develop his character".[12] Another example is the guilt that Gandhi felt at being absent from his father's room at the moment he died. Having served and comforted his father throughout that day Gandhi was relieved from duty by his uncle towards midnight. He went to bed, only to be disturbed a few minutes later by the servant informing him of his father's death. The fact that he was having sexual relations at the time left him with a sense of guilt and degradation.[13] In a biography of his grandmother, Kasturba, Arun Gandhi observed that many Indians live with a similar guilt because they were either absent from the death-bed of their parents or they feel they have deprived them of sufficient care and happiness.[14] The trauma of his father's death appeared to twist Gandhi's obsession for sex into a lifelong revulsion and sowed the seeds of his later renunciation.

Pyarelal's assertion that love and morality are the only sanctions available to the head of a joint family is also disputable. Economic factors can ensure that junior members of the family remain dependent on their seniors for their subsistence and education. As an expression of their gratitude and loyalty for the early support they are encouraged to assist the family in turn. Gandhi was allowed ultimately to study law in London because his mother and elder brothers believed him capable of qualifying for either his father's position as Dewan or Prime Minister of Kathiawar or for some other high official post. It was expected of him that he return to India on completion of his studies and support the family. Yet Gandhi's sense of his own special mission in life and strong faith in self-guidance encouraged him to break the confines of tradition and seek an alternative way of life.

When Gandhi later took a vow of poverty in South Africa and dedicated his life to service his family could not understand his motivations. Arun Gandhi asserts Kasturba was taunted by the family during her husband's early years alone in South Africa because he failed to live up to expectations. Though he more than repaid his financial debt to his brothers they were incredulous when he finally renounced all possessions, initially they believed he was depriving the family of earnings from his law practice out of personal greed. Kasturba was suspected of influencing her husband to disown the rest of the family. Gandhi's brother Laxmidas wrote to remind him of the "teachings of their father" and "his responsibility towards the family". Yet Gandhi's resolve was unshakable. He replied to his brother's complaint that he was following his father's teachings, and had enlarged his family to include the whole of humanity.[15] No doubt Gandhi learnt the value of restricted individualism and co-operative living in an Indian joint family, but he reinterpreted the familistic value of collective good to apply to society as a whole. He also revalued the traditional austerity and simplicity of *bania* family lifestyle. While adopting their simple style of living he went beyond the norm with his vows of celibacy and poverty. Unlike those who were frugal in the service of ultimate financial gain, his ends were ethical and religious.[16] Gandhi later defined "family" as an ever-expanding circle encompassing community, nation and the world.

In spite of Gandhi's unimpressive scholastic record it was felt that from among the male members of the family he alone had the

Gandhi and Community: The Formative Years   11

potential to reach a high official post, and restore the family to its former influential position. However, to obtain his mother's consent to the voyage to England, where he planned to study law, he had to take a number of vows. A Jain monk from whom 'his mother sought advice after her husband's death suggested three solemn vows that would ensure the young man's fidelity in the "strange" land; vows not to touch meat, wine or women. The other hurdle he had to negotiate before leaving India was his caste-elders' concerted opposition to his proposal. Before a general meeting of the caste Gandhi refused to be swayed by their arguments and unconcernedly accepted excommunication rather than bow to their judgement.[17] Though he may not have been consciously aware of the vital early influences absorbed in his familial environment, many of his early actions reflect the strong moral stance of his parents and the training they gave him, especially his preparedness to stand alone on the strength of a conviction, despite overwhelming opposition.

Student Days in London

When Gandhi sailed for England during September 1888 he had little knowledge of the world beyond Kathiawar. The period during which he studied law in London was one of intellectual ferment. The social and economic plight of the working classes in industrial society proved a catalyst for a wide-ranging debate on social alternatives. Socialists and anarchists vied with each other for prominence in radical activist circles. Societies such as Madame Blavatsky's Theosophical Society, the Vegetarian Society and the Anti-Vivisection Society sprang up to channel creative energies unleashed by the upsurge of humanitarian thought and activism. Gandhi joined the Vegetarian Society and was an associate member, briefly, of the Theosophical Society.

Vegetarianism often provided a doctrinal link, between the radical schools of social and religious thought challenging the capitalist ethos. These Western progressives were advocating vegetarianism at a time when many of their Hindu counterparts were denouncing it. They were a diverse group of intellectuals and activists who lived by the principle that vegetarianism was the only humane and morally defensible diet and the growth of their movement signaled an upsurge of interest in a return to the "simple life". The idea that a renewal of simple non-violent values would inevitably flow from an increase in vegetarianism profoundly influenced the thought of nineteenth century humanists such as Thoreau, Carpenter and Tolstoy. They denounced the excessive materialism of the industrial civilisation, and advocated a return to nature and a renascence of simpler values. Their ideas were given expression in a number of rural communities established in different parts of the world, organised around the principle of accommodating intellectual work and manual toil in a way of life in harmony with nature.

Gandhi was introduced to the ideas of vegetarianism through strict observance of his vow to remain vegetarian. Ironically, it was during a period in which he did everything possible, i.e. apart from eating meat, to present himself as an English gentleman. After suffering many embarrassments and even hunger at times due to an obstinate refusal to break the meat-eating vow, his difficulties ended when after much searching he discovered a vegetarian restaurant. From a display of literature in the restaurant's window he chose Henry Salt's *A Plea for Vegetarianism,* a rational defence of vegetarianism on a moral basis. He began a series of dietary exercises which initiated his "experiments with truth", and established the pattern of self-disciplinary measures that would characterise his later life.

Vegetarianism became for Gandhi much more than an individualistic practice. He interpreted it as a basis for mankind to attain a greater spiritual and moral unity.

> For me that was a great discovery in my search after truth ....
> I found that a selfish basis would not serve the purpose of taking a man higher and higher along the path of evolution. What was required was an altruistic purpose.[18]

His activities on behalf of the London Vegetarian Society, which made him a member of its executive committee, brought him in contact with many men and women who advocated a return to the simple life. A number of them lived on the basis of self-help: building their own cottages, designing and making their own clothes, footwear, furniture, and, above all else, growing their own food. English society labelled them "eccentric" but for Gandhi they were a source of inspiration, reinforcing his belief that a life in harmony with nature and society was the purest expression of truth and morality.

During this formative period in London, he revealed an ability to combine ascetic values with an active reformism. James Hunt suggests that "vegetarianism assumed the proportions of a religious sect for Gandhi, affording him fellowship, identity, and an ethic which (like Hinduism) quite naturally included dietary prescriptions".[19] Later in South Africa he encouraged expatriate Indians to express their unity with other vegetarians by joining the London Vegetarian Society. An early expression of his "this-worldly asceticism" was the idea that vegetarianism organised pragmatically could provide a bond and a supportive community that transcended national loyalties.

Alongside vegetarianism, another school of thought which aroused an interest in Hindu tradition was an outgrowth of the dynamic meeting between Eastern and Western currents of esoteric philosophy during the nineteenth century. In America the impact of Hindu beliefs on Western philosophy found its clearest expression, in the Transcendentalist movement. The Transcendentalists valued intuition above empirical experience. Gandhi no doubt was aware of Transcendentalist thought through his acquaintance with the writings of Salt and Carpenter, but he did not read the works of two luminaries of the movement, Emerson and Thoreau, until later in South Africa. It was not Transcendentalism but Theosophy that introduced Gandhi to the fount of wisdom at the heart of the Hindu tradition. Founded by the Russian emigre Madame Blavatsky to propagate her system of theosophy, emphasising the occult, the esoteric and the mystical, the Theosophical Society represented itself as an eternal religion expressing the fundamental truths of all religions. Its three declared objectives were :

> First — To form a nucleus of the Universal Brotherhood of humanity, without distinction of race, creed, sex, caste or colour.
> Second — To encourage the study of comparative religion, philosophy and science.
> Third — To investigate the unexplained laws of nature and the powers latent in man.[20]

The society's motto was, "There is no religion higher than Truth", but it was from Hinduism essentially that it derived its mystical and esoteric orientation.

Gandhi's first contact with Theosophy came in 1889 when two Theosophist friends sought his assistance in reading the Sanskrit original of the *Bhagavad Gita*. They had read Sir Edwin Arnold's verse translation of the Gita, *The Song Celestial* and wished to read the original. Gandhi felt ashamed that he had read the *Gita* in neither Sanskrit nor Gujarati, but he offered to assist them to the best of his ability. The following verses profoundly impressed him:

> If one
> Ponders on objects of the sense, there springs
> Attraction from attraction grows desire,
> Desire flames to fierce passion, passion breeds Recklessness;
> then the memory-all betrayed
> Lets noble purpose go, and saps the mind,
> Till purpose, mind, and man are all undone.

The theme of self-mastery as the basis for moral action struck a deep chord. He later described the *Gita* "as the book *par excellence* for the knowledge of Truth".[21]

Gandhi's friends encouraged him to read Theosophical literature and become an active member of the Society. He read works by Madame Blavatsky and Annie Besant, and was introduced to both at the Blavatsky Lodge, but the doctrines of Theosophy *per se,* particularly those concerned with the occult, had little appeal for him. He snared the society's faith that truth was the highest embodiment of religion and that all religions represent the same truth, but it was their praise of his own religion .that impressed him most. Just as he had discovered a theoretical basis for his observance of vegetarianism among the radicals of the Vegetarian Society, so too his interest in Hinduism was stimulated by approaching its doctrines from the Western viewpoint. "One of the most significant facts about the life and vocation of Gandhi," observed Thomas Merton, "was his discovery of the East through the West."[22]

During this period Gandhi began to learn more of other religions. He had developed a distaste for Christianity during his childhood.

In Kathiawar conversion to Christianity was associated with eating beef and drinking alcohol, and he was repelled by the proselytising efforts of missionaries bent on damning all other faiths as "heathen". A Christian friend in London convinced him that meat-eating and drink were not enjoined by the Scriptures, and suggested he read the Bible. Gandhi found he could only read the Old Testament "with much difficulty and without the least interest or understanding", but the new New Testament inspired him. He thought the Sermon on the Mount comparable to the *Gita*.[23] He began to attend church services, and from Nonconformists such as Charles Haddon Spurgeon and Dr Joseph Parker he learnt of a radical interpretation of Christianity that was neither dogmatic nor intolerant of other faiths, and imbued with the spirit of humanism.

Gandhi moved on the periphery of English society during his three years as a student in London, absorbing ideas from a wide range of sources, discovering the wisdom of the East through the eyes of the West. He associated with socialists, anarchists, radical Christians and feminists. They challenged the doctrines of individualistic rationalism. Many of them championed vegetarianism, the right to religious freedom and ideas of communality based on a return to a simple co-existence with nature. As an alternative to centralist systems, in which they saw labour as degraded and alienated from the factors of production, they proposed a decentralised social and economic system. They envisaged organic communities, self-governing and self-sufficient in the necessities of life, free to co-operate and associate with one another on the basis of mutuality.

However, it was not only the tenets of radical humanism that influenced the development of Gandhi's communitarian thought. He also came into contact with the ideas and values of a nineteenth century conservatism that sought to re-establish the "Social group as the central unit of theoretical inquiry and ameliorative action". Two conservative intellectuals had a marked influence upon Gandhi, Henry Summer Maine and John Ruskin. Their work provided "materials of a fresh and infinitely diversified veneration for community".[24]

The impact of Ruskin's ideas on Gandhi will be examined in the following section, for it was in South Africa that he read Ruskin's *Unto This Last*. He came across Henry Maine's work on comparative jurisprudence in the course of his law studies. Maine argued that the primitive village system of the Teutonic and Scandinavian countries was comparable with, and indeed similar to, the actual working system of the Indian village communities of the nineteenth century. The Hobbesian philosophy of individualistic rationalism had been founded on the idea that "mankind is nothing but a loose aggregation of beings, always ready to fight with one another, and only prevented from so doing by the intervention of some authority".[25] To the contrary, Maine argued, the Indian oral tradition of customary law could not have been preserved if man had not lived in organised, self-acting social groups from ancient times. With regard to man's predilection for war, he maintained that "Man has never been so ferocious or so stupid as to submit to such an evil as war without some kind of effort to prevent it", which he saw borne out by the number of "ancient institutions which bear the marks of a design to stand in the way of war, or to provide an alternative to it".[26]

Maine presented a picture of a village society composed of a large number of independent, communitarian groups, who traded, manufactured an cultivated on the basis of self sufficiency. With reference to the organisational and administrative infrastructure of Indian village communities, he argued that it would be "inappropriate to speak of a political superior commanding a particular course of action to the villages". The council of village elders (or *panchayat*) governed village society by virtue of its embodiment of customary law and usages, i.e., it merely declared what had always been.

> More than all, customary law is not enforced by sanction. In the almost inconceivable case of disobedience to the award of the village council, the sole punishment, or the sole certain punishment, would appear to be universal disapprobation. And hence the customary law of India would have to be called morality.[27]

Gandhi drew upon Maine's *Village Communities of the East and West* (1881) to establish the "wholesome character of pre-industrial Indian civilisation". He first cited it in his Open Letter to the Legislators of Natal in 1894, and later included it in the list of authorities he acknowledged in *Hind Swaraj*.[28]

Maine's work impressed upon Gandhi the idea that corporate ownership had been the norm rather than the exception in traditional Indian village communities. The conviction began to grow in him that India could prove to be an ideal environment in which to experiment with the type of simple, co-operative living envisaged by many of his London acquaintances. Maine also made pointed reference to the impact centralist policies of the British administration was having upon the organic structure of Indian society. In his view the introduction of centralised systems of industry, marketing, administration and legal authority, undermined the political and economic independence once enjoyed by the old organic groups, and significantly weakened the social control exercised by clan, village and caste. Though Maine accused the British administration of hastening the breakdown of the village community, he identified the growing individualisation of the old organic groups as the primary cause. As the communities grew larger and wider, social balance and the preservation of traditional law, and usage were undermined.[29]

In this sense Gandhi was heir to a Western interpretation of the village community that prevailed during the Victorian period. It depicted the village as a self-acting, egalitarian institution organised on the basis of collective ownership. Louis Dumont identifies three distinct periods in the development of the "village community" concept. The first is marked by the romantic descriptions of English administrators such as Elphinstone and Metcalfe, who described the village as a "little republic, self-sufficient, having its own functionaries, and surviving the ruin of empires". The second period of Victorian conception was typified by Maine's work.

> Finally, in the third period, Indian nationalists, relying on the descriptions and scruples of the British of the first period, constructed for themselves an idyllic picture of the village community as a secular and democratic institution — did it not have the assembly, the famous village panchayat? — which only the British ruined irremediably.[30]

The Western idealisation of the village community failed to take account of the omnipresence of hierarchy and dominance in the village system. It is the dominant caste or castes who control land usage, who have the power to grant work on the basis of patronage, and who commonly dispense justice by virtue of a monopoly of authority. Dumont observes : "The joint possession which, for Maine for example, gave the greatest strength to the 'village community' was in reality the joint possession by occupants of superior right, joint possession within the dominant caste or lineage."[31] It is necessary, however, to view Gandhi's later programme to rejuvenate India's villages, and his belief in the superiority of the ancient Indian civilisation over its modern form, in the light of his understanding of Maine's analysis.

Summing up Gandhi's years in London as a student, Hunt has written: "Thus Gandhi, suffering under the colonial mentality which led him to turn away from Indian ways and to adopt those of the west, was stimulated by this eccentric but lively group of Westerners to value his own heritage."[32] Above all else it appears that the idea of self-renunciation as the true basis for moral action had the strongest impression on his fertile mind. "My young mind tried to unify the teaching of the *Gita,* the *Light of Asia* and the *Sermon on the Mount."* He recalls, "That renunciation as the highest from of religion appealed to me greatly." He read Carlyle's *Heroes and Hero-Worship,* and was impressed by the Prophet Mohammed's "greatness and bravery and austere living".[33] In response to the doctrines of Theosophy and the radical Christians he sought a synthesis of the teachings of the major religions, the idea of self-renunciation his unifying principle. For the remainder of his life Gandhi sought to resolve the contradictions which become obvious when a spiritual asceticism is introduced into the realm of social and political activism. He left England the custodian of values that were in many respects alien to the majority of his countrymen.

A Karmayogi is Born

Gandhi's return to India in 1891 marked the beginning of an anxious period in his life. His mother had died, and the Gandhi family had long since lost their position of influence in Kathiawar. The responsibility lay on him to settle down and establish himself in the legal profession. He failed dismally in his attempts to do so in Bombay, and only just managed to support the family from the pittance he earned writing petitions and memoranda to present in the local courts of Rajkot.

A painful incident involving an English civil servant he had met earlier in London, and with whom he had had cordial relations, opened his eyes to the contrast between Britains at home and their colonial counterparts living abroad, governing an alien people. In his role as resident in Porbandar, Gandhi's English acquaintance became party to an investigation into certain actions of Gandhi's brother while the latter was secretary and adviser to the Rana of Porbandar. His brother asked him to intervene with the Englishman on his behalf. Reluctantly he went to the resident, who abused him for seeking to exploit their acquaintance in that fashion, and in the face of Gandhi's refusal to leave had him forcibly removed. Angered by the insult, Gandhi wished to proceed against the resident. He sought advice from the renowned Bombay barrister Sir Pherozeshah Mehta, and in return received his first lesson in the realities of British rule in India. Mehta informed him that he did not yet know either the British or life, and that to proceed against the English *sahib* would be to invite ruin. "This shock changed the course of my life", recalled Gandhi. He also began to see the corrupting effects of political patronage upon the administrations of the princely states: "This atmosphere appeared to me to be poisonous, and how to remain unscathed was a perpetual problem for me."[34]

In 1893 Gandhi seized an opportunity to remove himself from the unhappy situation. A Moslem trading house in Porbandar invited him to assist them in South Africa in a minor legal action against another merchant from Kathiawar. Gandhi left India in May of that year, an inexperienced and shy barrister. He returned twenty-one years later a seasoned activist with tried and tested techniques of action. South Africa during these years, was a country oppressed by discriminatory laws which relegated the black and coloured populations to slave status. For Gandhi, who became a leading activist in the struggle against these laws, South Africa was a laboratory in which he refined his early ideas and beliefs into a coherent philosophy of action.

Central to this philosophy was the idea that man becomes the source of his own salvation. In the Hindu tradition holy men commonly seek union with God either by *Bhakti-yoga,* the way of love and devotion, by *Jnana-yoga,* the way of knowledge, or by

Raja-yoga, a combination of love, devotion, knowledge and self-discipline. These are the quietist techniques favoured by seekers after spiritual truth in Hinduism. But in distant South Africa a *karmayogi* (one who seeks salvation through action) was born who interpreted the *Bhagavad Gita* gospel of selfless action into a powerful force for social, political and religious reform.

Settled life in Pretoria enabled Gandhi to renew his dietetic experiments and rekindle his interest in aspects of Theosophical and radical Christian thought. He was appointed an agent for the London Vegetarian Society in order to spread the "gospel" in South Africa, which he enthusiastically undertook both in spoken word and print. As he became familiar with the problems faced by the Indian community in the Transvaal and the Orange Free State, he also came into contact with a number of Christians, some of whom sought to convert him to Christianity. A Quaker who befriended him argued that though there may possibly be some truth in other religions, Christianity was the only true source of salvation for mankind. Gandhi discovered in Christian teachings much that appealed to him, but he could not accept that Jesus was the only incarnation of God the only Mediator between God and man, who had suffered and atoned for all the sins of mankind. He met a member of a Christian sect called the Plymouth Brethren who refuted the Hindu and Buddhist belief that the "ceaseless cycle of action" (i.e. *karma)* rules man's destiny. The Plymouth Brother argued that all man's attempts at improvement and atonement are futile because man can only find redemption from the inevitable burden of sin through faith in the 'great redemption' of Jesus. Gandhi replied: "If this be the Christianity acknowledged by all Christians, I cannot accept it. I do not seek redemption from the consequences of my sin. I seek to be redeemed from sin itself, or rather from the very thought of sin. Until I have attained that end, I shall be content to be restless."[35] Gandhi could not be swayed from his belief in the essential unity of all religions, and patiently resisted all efforts to dissuade him from his faith in Hinduism.

Unimpressed by the efforts of white South African Christians to convert him, Gandhi established links with Christians whose faith rested upon a radical interpretation of the Bible. One of these, Edward Maitland, was a founder of the Esoteric Christian Union and wrote a number of books in collaboration with Anna Kingsford in an attempt to reconstruct the basic principles of Christian faith and morality on a non-rationalistic basis. He sent Gandhi two of these books, *The Perfect Way* or *the Finding of Christ* and *The New Interpretation of the Bible*, both of which he liked as they "seemed to support Hinduism".[36] *The Perfect Way* sought to establish three positions:

(1) That the dogmas and symbols of Christianity are substantially identical with those of other and earlier religious systems.
(2) That the true plane of religious belief lies, not where hitherto the Church has placed it - in the sepulchre of historical tradition, but in man's own mind and heart; it is not, that is to say, the objective and physical, but the subjective and spiritual; and its appeal is not to the senses but to the soul.
(3) That thus regarded and duly interpreted Christian doctrine represents with scientific exactitude the facts of man's spiritual history.[37]

Drawing on ancient mystical traditions the Esoteric Christians gave expression to ideas not dissimilar from those propagated by the Theosophists. For them the true meaning and value of. asceticism was the attainment of spiritual perfection. By subjecting the body to self-denial and control it can be brought into harmony with the spirit, which can only derive sustenance "from substances the purest and most highly solarised, such as the vegetable kingdom alone affords". Vegetarianism, the simple outdoor life, and close communion with nature were regarded as essential aids to the attainment of perfection. The aspirant was emboldened to face absolute poverty and chastity "without fear and without desire save towards God". He was bound by vows of abstinence, prayer, meditation, watchfulness, self-restraint, fearlessness and voluntary poverty, until final victory over the body freed him from all vows: "He has undergone all his ordeals, and has freed his will. ... He is free of matter and will never again have a phenomenal body."[38]

In the wake of proselytising efforts to convince him to change his religion, the ideas of the Esoterics and Theosophists appealed to Gandhi's idealism. The mysticism of the Esoterics was derived essentially from Theosophy, both movements affirming the unity of religion and the validity of all ancient religious traditions. Fundamental to their affirmation was the faith that religious scriptures are allegorical guides to the inner world of the spirit. The Esoterics reaffirmed the teachings of Christianity as a further development of the doctrinal truths common to all religions, but they repudiated the orthodox view that the scriptures represent historical fact. Gandhi saw in these radical Christian ideas the essence of all the major religious teachings, confirming his faith in the universality of truth.

The religious philosophy of the Esoterics and Theosophists also concurred with the essence of "advice" Gandhi had earlier received from his Jain friend and mentor Shrimad Rajchandra. They had met on the day after Gandhi's return to India from London. A jeweller, Rajchandra was also a gifted intellectual and poet. During a time of uncertainty and inner turmoil in Gandhi's life the young Jain was a source of solace and inspiration. "In my moments of spiritual crisis he was my refuge", Gandhi wrote later.[39] Rajchandra's guidance awakened Gandhi to the profound truths of India's ancient religious traditions, not as abstractions seen from the viewpoint of the West, but as a living heritage and vital source for his own spiritual development. During a period when Gandhi was trying to reconcile the conflicting claims of Christian and Hindu doctrines he sent the jeweller three questions: "What is the soul?", "What is God?", and "What is liberation?" In reply Rajchandra expounded the Jain teaching of the soul, setting Gandhi's mind at rest with religious concepts that resolved the apparent conflict between the doctrines of the major religions, and convincing him these ideas were also inherent to the teachings of Hinduism.

> In the words of Shrimad Rajchandra, it is unnecessary in our work-a-day world for anyone to give up his own religion and adopt another in order to attain liberation. Everybody can attain liberation by following his own. For, liberation means complete freedom from all attachment and hatred and this is the common goal of all religions.[40]

Gandhi's association with Rajchandra and his Theosophist and Esoteric friends was an important source of inspiration during the early period of spiritual awakening in South Africa. These contacts banished all traces of the atheism he had toyed with in his youth, and confirmed his faith in Hinduism as the true path for his own spiritual quest. Gandhi's indebtedness to Edward Maitland further deepened. Through him he was introduced to the writings of Tolstoy, the prophet of simplicity, truth and non-resistance to evil by force, who was to have such a profound influence upon him.

Gandhi was indirectly familiar with the ideas of Tolstoy through his encounter with the vegetarian movement, but his reading of *The Kingdom of God is Within You* in South Africa opened his mind to the infinite potential of love and non-violence as powerful bases for personal action. He made an intensive study of Tolstoy's writings on religion, renunciation, voluntary poverty, community and vegetarianism. Later he corresponded with Tolstoy and became acquainted with several English Tolstoyans. During his stay in England in 1909 he visited the Whiteway colony of Tolstoyans, a group who experimented with communitarian living independently from the mainstream movement.[41]

Tolstoy argued that all institutions of the state were an abstract embodiment of violent and coercive authority, which those individuals with a highly developed consciousness of truth must selflessly resist. He proclaimed that "progress towards the welfare of mankind is made not by the persecutors but by the persecuted, that only goodness, confronting evil, conquers it in the end".[42]

> The sole meaning of human life lies in serving the world by promoting the establishment of the Kingdom of God. This service can be accomplished only by the recognition and avowal of the truth by each separate individual.[43]

Other works by Tolstoy that Gandhi read depicted the slavery of labour in an industrial civilisation, and the violence which underlies the structure of the state. Tolstoy declared the need for an ascetic programme to achieve a truly righteous society, sustained by vegetarianism, celibacy and other forms of self-control. In the face of the growing inhumanity of industrial civilisation Tolstoy repudiated the state and withdrew his support from the organised church. By way of outlining a code of righteous conduct Tolstoy formulated three replies to the searching question encapsulated in his book *What Then Must We Do?* :

> First : not to lie to myself; and — however far my path of life may be from the true path disclosed by my reason - not to fear the truth.
> Secondly : to reject the belief in my own righteousness and in privileges and peculiarities distinguishing me from others, and to acknowledge myself as being to blame.
> Thirdly : to fulfil the eternal, indubitable law of man, and with the labour of my whole being to struggle with nature for the maintenance of my own and other people's lives.[44]

It was a plea for social renewal through service, renunciation and mutuality.

The movement that began in response to Tolstoy's teachings led to the establishment of small experimental communities in several parts of the world. Agricultural colonies run along his guidelines were initially restricted to Russia, but subsequently the movement found support in North America, Britain, Palestine, the Netherlands and Bulgaria. From the late 1880s large numbers of his 'disciples' sought to reorganise their lives in keeping with his call to reject a society practising violence and exploitation. They endeavoured to live by their own labour, to live in harmony with nature, and to devote themselves to serving their fellowmen as expressions of a religious faith founded on the ideal of self-perfection.

Despite his concern for self-perfection Tolstoy repudiated the common notion that Christian scriptures relate only to personal salvation and not to public affairs. He deplored the isolationist mentality characteristic of Christian asceticism, believing that "to live a pure, holy life on a pillar or in a commune is impossible, because man is deprived of one-half of life-communion with the world—without which his life has no sense."[45] He became increasingly intolerant of attempts by his followers to develop a cult around his ideas and personality, and the problems faced by the numerous Tolstoyan settlements led him on occasion to doubt his own teachings. The quietist tendencies of many of his supporters derive from his teaching that man must surrender himself to the spirit of love in order to overcome evil; the only way to influence others was through the attainment of self-purification. He advised the "true Christian" to abstain from participation in the activities of the state, but he made no allowance in any of his writings for an organised form of non-violent activism against the legitimised oppression of the state.

Gandhi was certainly much impressed with the Tolstoyan idea of shaking free from the violence and coercion of the state and forming co-operative communities. His indictment of modern civilisation and the organised violence of the centralised state in *Hind Swaraj* is fully in keeping with the spirit of Tolstoy's teachings. In the trust deed of the Phoenix Settlement, which established the pattern of Gandhi's communal experiments, Gandhi acknowledged his indebtedness to the Russian sage by setting down the practice and propagation of Tolstoy's teachings as the main objective of the community.[46] But though he found in Tolstoy's elucidation of the Christian gospel of non-resistance much that was akin to the Hindu and Jain doctrine of *ahimsa,* Gandhi's translation of these ideas into a technique of direct action marked an original contribution more far-reaching in its implications than the pacifist teachings to which he had been exposed.

To distinguish the active form of non-violence he developed in South Africa from pacifist ideas, Gandhi conceived of the term *satyagraha* (or truth-force). Non-violence could suggest a negative form of action, and passive resistance could be associated with the defensive stance of the weak, but Gandhi conceived *satyagraha* as an instrument of the spiritually and morally strong. "Non-violence of my conception," he observed, "is a more active and more real fighting against wickedness than retaliation whose very nature is to increase wickedness."[47] In Gandhi's hands non-violence was forged into a formidable weapon. It implied not only an active refusal to commit a violent action but the will to suffer and serve selflessly in order to convert the opposition. He refined Tolstoy's idea of personal commitment to self-suffering as a means of humanising society.[48]

Gandhi did not believe social change was subject to factors such as "collective consciousness", "class struggle", or "the moral priority of any collective agency over the individual". His indictment of modern civilisation and his repudiation of the collectivist view of society, were predicated upon his faith that "the individual is the one supreme consideration".[49] In the democratic society of Gandhi's vision the individual was thus given priority, but if the all-round development of the individual was to be the highest value it could only be realised in a society where individual freedom was limited by the freedom and welfare of others. The Western doctrine of natural rights was in Gandhi's view a doctrine of unrestrained individualism or egoism, resulting in violence and the alienation of the individual from society. His individualism derived from the ancient Hindu concepts of *dharma* (natural duty) and *yajna* (selfless sacrifice).

> If leaving duties unperformed, we run after rights, they will escape us like the Will-o'-the-wisp. The same teaching has been embodied by Krishna in the immortal words, 'Action alone is thine, leave thou the fruit severely alone.' Action is duty, fruit is the right.[50]

Gandhi believed that the individual who orders his life upon an unshakable faith in duty, sacrifice, truth and non-violence, remains morally autonomous from collective agencies and is an unconquerable agent of social progress. *Satyagraha* was conceived by Gandhi as the only effective sanction against wrong-doing available to such an individual.

Tolstoy eloquently preached his doctrines of "Christian anarchism", but his ideas found their clearest expression in Gandhi's *satyagraha*. Similarly, he elaborated in action certain aspects of the thought of writers such as Ruskin and Thoreau. Their writings affirmed and strengthened his belief that self-renunciation and respect for the dignity of the individual are integral to non-violent action. But it is within the framework of his predilections, and in response to the situations he confronted in South Africa, that Gandhi found in the ideas of these western thinkers scholarly justification for his own conclusions. Far more than the authors themselves, he gave active expression to their ideas in a life of struggle against man's inhumanity to man.

The best example of Gandhi's reinterpretation and adaptation of another's ideas is his response to John Ruskin. Ruskin's insight into the evils of the political economy and the industrial system had little impact on the society of his time. His attack on the mainstream of economic thinking, his elevation of artisans to the level of artists, and his belief in the "chivalry of labour", were either damned or ignored by the press and power elites of the day. Yet his ideas had a considerable influence on the English socialist movement, particularly among the radical humanitarian circles Gandhi came in to contact with during his student days in London. Gandhi read *Unto This Last* in 1904, later remarking that it "captured me and made me transform my life".[51] He was inspired by what he read to establish the Phoenix Settlement in Natal that same year, "on principles of bread-labour and the responsibility of the community organisation to provide for the physical welfare of the worker who is its member".[52] Gandhi summarised Ruskin's teachings into three principles:

1. That the good of the individual is contained in the good of all.
2. That a lawyer's work has the same value as the barber's inasmuch as all have the same right of earning their livelihood from their work.
3. That a life of labour, i.e., the life of the tiller of the soil and the handicraftsman, is the life worth living.

He explained that the first of these he knew; the second he had vaguely realised; but the third had not occurred to him previously. Only the first of these principles is stated clearly in *Unto This Last*, but Gandhi argued that the second and third were contained in the first.[53] At a time when he was seeking to reconcile his life as a successful lawyer with his notions of simplicity, renunciation and social service, he found inspiration in Ruskin's work. Ruskin declared that human beings, "full-breathed, bright-eyed and happy-hearted", are the true wealth of society.

In his view the political economy fails to take the human soul into account in its theoretical model of the "economic man" ruled by the laws of supply and demand. "The largest quantity of work... will be done only when the motive force, i.e., the will or spirit of the creature, is brought to its greatest strength by its own proper fuel; namely, by the affections." Like the nonconformist Christian groups of the nineteenth century, Ruskin reaffirmed the fundamental principles of primitive Christianity. He denounced industrial civilisation as inhumane and anti-religion, and declared that he knew of "no previous instance in history of a nation's establishing a systematic disobedience to the first principles of its professed religion".

The investigation of a "science of becoming rich" was diametrically opposed to the tenets of the divine teachings, which denounce the love of money as the source of all evil and declare "mammon service" to be idolatory, "the accurate and irreconcilable opposite of God's service". For Ruskin the real science of political economy "is that which teaches nations to desire and labour for the things that lead to life; and which teaches them to scorn and destroy the things that lead to destruction". His alternative to the "Protestant Ethic", i.e., the pursuit or manifestation of salvation through the accumulation of wealth, was a call for people to leave the question of personal redemption to God alone, and to seek "not greater wealth, but simpler pleasure; not higher fortune, but deeper felicity; making the first of possessions self-possession; and honouring themselves in the harmless pride and calm pursuits of peace".[54] No doubt Ruskin's theme of self-renunciation for the common good impressed Gandhi; they shared a fundamental concern for the quality of life and a distaste for the economics of material accumulation.

Ruskin sought the "conversion" of the moneyed classes on the basis of the conservative idea that every right carries with it a corresponding duty. He rejected the socialist idea of a direct assault or, the rich and the subsequent division of their property, claiming that "division of property is its destruction; and with it the destruction of all hope, all industry, and all justice; it is simply chaos...." In the face of impending chaos Ruskin in fact appeared more concerned for the future security of the rich, than with the alleviation of poverty among the poorer classes. His attitude to the poor is patronising, insisting as he does that they can only find "redemption" through the good works of strong, wealthy men.

> The fortitude and intelligence which acquire riches are intended, by the giver of both, not to scatter, nor to give away, but to employ those riches in the service of mankind.... It is continually the fault or the folly of the poor that they are poor.... Put it at the worst, that all the poor of the world are but disobedient children, or careless cripples, and that all the rich people are wise and strong, and you will see at once that neither is the socialist right in desiring to make everybody poor, powerless, and foolish as he is himself, nor the rich man right in leaving the children in the mine.[55]

In many respects Gandhi was heir to this conservative idea. He maintained that each individual had the right to realise his full potential within society, which was only possible when one fulfilled the duty owed to society.

> Rights accrue automatically to him who duly performs his duties. In fact the right to perform one's duties is the only right that is worth living for and dying for. It covers all legitimate rights.[56]

Gandhi defended the traditional Hindu concept of *varna* (colour) whereby society is divided into the functional prototypes of *brahman* (priest), *kshatriya* (warrior), *vaisya* (tradesman) and *shudra* (labourer). He believed this established "certain spheres of action for certain people with certain tendencies, which avoided all unworthy competition".[57] Unification of non-violent society could not in his view be achieved by impractical social uniformity, but by the maintenance of the diversity inherent to the social system through respect for the dignity of the individual and provision of welfare for all. Gandhi and Ruskin shared a conception of social progress in which there was no place for violence, hatred and class conflict. Ruskin's perception of the role that should be played by the moneyed classes in society is echoed in Gandhi's later concept of trusteeship, which proposed that in order to avoid class war the owners of wealth in India should voluntarily convert themselves into trustees of their wealth.

Ruskin and Gandhi stood for the dignity of the individual, and both sought a renascence of moral values as the basis for all action. Yet, there were subtle differences in their view of an ideal society. Ruskin not only held the commoner to be inferior, but favoured an aristocratic hierarchy that denied the masses the right of controlling their own affairs on the grounds of incompetence. The authoritarian tendency discernible in Ruskin's conservatism finds its clearest expression in his assertion that an egalitarian social order is an impossibility:

> My continual aim has been to show the eternal superiority of some men to others, sometimes of one man to all others; and to show also the advisability of appointing such persons or person to guide, to lead, or on occasion even to compel and

subdue, their inferiors, according to their own better knowledge and wiser will.[58]

It is in the context of Ruskin's authoritarianism that Erikson observed the irony that Cecil Rhodes, Gandhi's "clearest philosophical and practical antagonist" in South Africa, had found in *Unto This Last* a sanction for his colonialist policies.[59]

While Gandhi concurred with Ruskin's view that people are born with different capacities, he did not interpret these differences in "value" terms such as "high" and "low", "superior" and "inferior". He knew that the realities of the caste-system were far removed from the caste-idealism of the *varna* concept. Any value inherent in the ideal had waned in practical terms by the development of an inflexible but fragmented caste structure, which precluded any form of egalitarianism. Gandhi's abhorrence of the peculiarly Hindu institution of untouchability, and his later programme to eradicate the caste-ideology of ritual purity upon which the institution is based, reflected his egalitarian approach to social problems.

The seeds of Gandhi's opposition to the inequities of caste were sown during his childhood and likely deepened as a result of his later contacts with the Theosophical movement. The theosophists began to draw attention to the plight of India's untouchable communities during the late 1800s, and one of the earliest schemes of uplift was the Olcott Memorial School opened by the theosophists for *panchamas* (as the untouchables were called) in South India, at Adyar, in 1894. However, Gandhi saw untouchability as implying much more than the ceremonial untouchability of those labelled as such. It became for him a symbol of the major malaise of Indian life. He saw that the city-dweller had come to think of the villagers as untouchable. He did not know them, he would not live with them, and if he found himself in a village he would want to reproduce city life there. In this aspect of his later work Gandhi would stress not only the socio-economic uplift of untouchables but of all suppressed communities:

> Untouchability is a hydra-headed monster and has affected every branch of society. And therefore we have become untouchable, one to another, so that there is no caste or section which does not consider itself superior to another section or

caste. There may be, there are, many other causes for it, but this superiority and inferiority complex is at the bottom of the communal trouble. Therefore the implication of this campaign is that we wish to achieve the brotherhood of man, which is unattainable so long as we believe that untouchability has divine sanction. It is, therefore, up to the caste-Hindus to consider and make their choice. They perpetuate untouchability, and they and Hinduism die.[60]

To remove the prevailing confusion over the true nature of *varna,* to cleanse Hinduism of its impurities, and as an expression of the dignity of all forms of work, Gandhi would later call on all Hindus to regard themselves as *shudras,* members of the lowest *varna:* "That is the only way to demonstrate the truth of Brahmanism and to revive Varnadharma in ifs true state."[61]

Another who influenced him was the Transcendentalist writer and philosopher, Henry David Thoreau. Gandhi's debt to Thoreau's "Essay on Civil Disobedience" has clearly been much exaggerated, for it was not until the former had conceived and put into effect the *satyagraha* technique of civil disobedience that he read the essay in a South African prison in 1907. Doubtless, he recognised a precursor in Thoreau, but Louis Fischer's description of Gandhi's Phoenix Settlement as a "Walden on the Veldt"[62] is perhaps a clearer indication of the significance of Thoreau's teachings for Gandhi.

Between 1845 and 1847 Thoreau went to live at Walden Pond in Concord, Massachusetts: "I went to the woods because I wished to live deliberately, to front only the essential facts of life, and see if I could not learn what it had to teach, and not when I came to die, discover that I have not lived."[63] As a determined individualist who was sceptical of organised movements, Thoreau did not join the Brook Farm experiment that attracted many of his Transcendentalist friends in nearby West Roxbury (1841-1847), and which became one of the more notable of many community experiments in North America during the nineteenth century. The Gandhian concept of an ashram is none the less not very far removed from Thoreau's idea in withdrawing to Walden. Though Walden was a place of retreat for Thoreau, it was a retreat imbued with the virtues of positive action; a search for truth through simplification of life-style and work of a constructive and soul-cleansing nature. "With respect to luxuries and comforts," said Thoreau, "the wisest have ever lived a more simple and meagre life than the poor." In a similar vein he has written:

> In proportion as he simplifies his life, the laws of the universe will appear less complex, and solitude will not be solitude, nor poverty poverty, nor weakness weakness. If you have built castles in the air, your work need not be lost; that is where they should be. Now put the foundations under them.[64]

In an examination of Thoreau's influence upon Gandhi and Indian intellectuals in general, Sujit Mukherjee has argued that *Walden* does not capture the Indian imagination because of the familiarity of its symbolism — "We have neglected to practise it, but we are told that the prescribed ideal of *vanaprasthashrama* — i.e., retirement to the forest for contemplation after acquiring education and living a full life — was in operation in India more than 2,000 years before Thoreau conceived of his withdrawal to Walden Pool. Thereau probably did not receive proper instruction in this ideal, because he actually went and did it — that too, without having first lived through the preceding phase of a householder's life. And what a let-down for Indian ideals that Thoreau should have returned from the forest!"[65] Though Gandhi did refer to the vow of *brahmacharya* (celibacy) he took in 1906 as an essential expression of his resolve to live the life of a *vanasprastha* (one retired from household cares), Mukherjee appears to have missed the main point altogether. Neither Gandhi nor Thoreau — the latter at Walden Pond, the former through the communities or ashrams he established during his life — intended their respective withdrawals from mainstream society as quietist exercises in contemplative activity. For both it was an opportunity to rejuvenate the spirit and cleanse the soul through self-reliance, constructive work and a simple life in harmony with nature.

Gandhi's ashrams were communalised expressions of the concept of withdrawal and renewal which had inspired Thoreau. Gandhi believed that the spirit of non-violence and truth-force could be best inculcated within the intimate communal environment of an ashram; the members acquiring the ability to communicate the spirit to others by attempting to apply the values of truth and non-violence in all their relationships and against all forms of coercion and conflict. But the ashramic life as conceived by Gandhi was by no means confined to an institutional structure. Rather, a pattern was established which enabled the individual to live in harmony with nature and fellow-man, based on self-reliance, creative activity and community service. To live such a life, Gandhi believed, was to conserve and rejuvenate the fundamental ties which have traditionally bound men and women together in organic communities. The constructive activities of individuals, whether performed collectively or independently, were seen by him as a visible link that indissolubly bound them to the community.

After two years at Walden Thoreau returned to society fortified by his experience, and confirmed in the belief that "no face which we can give to a matter will stead us so well at last as the truth", and that to avoid the life of "quiet desperation" endured by the mass of men, man must "cultivate poverty like a garden herb."[66] Similarly, Gandhi withdrew to his ashrams to refurbish his strength and spirit. Prayer, constructive work and simple living fortified him against the rigours of life outside his ashrams. Both Gandhi and Thoreau borrowed freely from a complex web of cross-cultural influences in order to give effective expression to their own ideas on society, politics, philosophy, morality and religion. Their clearest message to mankind was that man cannot realise his full potential in a life of material ease and passive acceptance of violence and oppression, but by constant striving on the path of non-violence, simplicity and truth.

Conclusion

The failings of modern civilisation had been brought into sharp focus for Gandhi through his understanding of alternative social philosophies and models in the West. None the less, he believed that the reconstitution of Indian society on a righteous basis must truly reflect the mentality and genius of India's heterogeneous people. By communicating the ideal of the *karmayogi* as the most-worthy of aspirations he imbued the work ethic with religious connotations far-reaching in its implications for the caste-ridden social structure of India. Fitting into the traditional pattern of the *sanyasi,* practising non-attachment in his search for truth, Gandhi brought his message of work as devotion to the masses of people by peripatetic teaching in South Africa and India. He awakened within many a consciousness of the power of positive action to influence men and the events that shape their lives.

On the other hand, the cross-cultural synthesis of communitarian and ascetic ideals Gandhi achieved indicated he was more of a universalist than a nationalist. It would appear, moreover, that the practical scheme of life he derived from Ruskin's *Unto This Last* owed less to Ruskin's work and more, as Ashe has suggested, to "an amalgam of Tolstoy, Edward Carpenter's Simple Life doctrine, the memory of Mariann Hill (sec Chapter 2), the theory of the ashram in Hindu religion, and the theory of corporate property in Hindu law (which had lodged in Gandhi's mind when he read Maine)."[67]

Gandhi believed in the essential unity of the divine spirit with all forms of life, a truth which he found in the teachings of all the major religions. For him Hinduism and Christianity were not basically different. His ashram concept is based on the ideas of withdrawal and renewal as well as the communal asceticism common to both religions. Gandhi's innovation was to imbue his activism with a similar asceticism. He believed that self-renunciation could be channelled through positive action to reform society and politics, without succumbing to the corrupting influence of power.

NOTES

1. *An Autobiography. The Story of My Experiments with Truth* (London : Jonathan Cape, 1966), hereinafter *Autobiography* p.4.
2. Erik Erikson, *Gandhi's Truth* (London : Faber & Faber Ltd., 1970), pp. 100-1.
3. *Autobiography,* pp. 16-20.
4. *Ibid.,* p. 18.
5. Cited in Stephen N. Hay, "Jain Influences on Gandhi's Early Thought", in Sibnarayan Ray (ed.), *Gandhi, India and the World* (Bombay : Nachiketa Publications Ltd., 1970), p. 21. —
6. *Autobiography,* pp. 27-8.
7. *Ibid.,* pp. 27-9.
8. *Ibid.* pp. 6,29.
9. Pyarelal, *Mahatma Gandhi — The Early Phase,* 2 vols. (Ahmedabad : Navajivan Publishing House, 1965), Vol. 1, p. 193.

10. S. C. Dube, "Indian Village: A Symposium", *Journal of Asian Studies,* XVI, No. 1, Nov. 1956; cf. N. V. Thirtha, "A Comparative Study of Gandhiji's Educational Ideas, and the Government of India's Basic Education Programmes — A Study in Values" (Stanford University, Ph. D. Thesis, 1959).
11. *Autobiography,* pp. 8-9.
12. Cited in Erikson, *op. cit.,* p. 118.
13. *Autobiography,* p. 26.
14. Arun Gandhi, "Kasturba" (Bombay : Unpublished Manuscript, 1980).
15. *Ibid.;* see also *Autobiography,* p. 222.
16. J. C. Masselos, "Gandhi and Tilak : A Study in Alternatives," in Ray, *op. cit.,* p. 83.
17. *Autobiography,* pp. 33-5.
18. Cited in Pyarelal, *op. cit,* p. 249.
19. James D. Hunt, *Gandhi in London* (New Delhi: Promilla & Co., 1978), p. 30.
20. These objectives appear at the beginning of each edition of *The Theosophical Society.*
21. *Autobiography,* p. 57.
22. Cited in George Woodcock, *Gandhi* (London : Fontana/Collins, 1972), p. 22.
23. *Autobiography,* p. 58.
24. Robert Nisbet, *The Quest for Community* (New York: Oxford University Press, 1953), pp. 25, 29.
25. P. Kropotkin, *Mutual Aid: A Factor of Evolution* (London : William Heinemann,4904), p. 77,
26. Henry Summer Maine, *International Law* (London: John Murray, 1888), pp. 11-13; see also *Village Communities of the East and West* (London : John Murray, 1881), p. 66.
27. *Ibid.,* pp. 67-8.
28. Hunt, *op. cit.,* p. 171; see also *The Collected Works of Mahatma Gandhi* (Delhi : Publications Division, Government of India, 1958), hereinafter CWMG, Vol. 1, 178 ff.
29. *Village Communities of the East and West,* pp. 112-3.
30. Louis Dumont, *Homo Hierarchicus* (London : Paladin, 1972), p. 204.
31. *Ibid.,* p. 205.
32. Hunt, *op. cit., p.* 34.
33. *Autobiography,* pp. 58-9.
34. *Ibid., pp.* 83-4.
35. *Ibid.,* pp. 102-4.
36. *Ibid.,* p. 114.
37. Cited in Hunt, *op. cit.,* p. 35.
38. Cited in Pyarelal, *op. cit.,* pp. 323-4.
39. *Autobiography,* pp. 74-5.
40. Cited in Pyarelal, *op. cit.,* p. 331.
41. CWMG, Vol. 9, p. 369; see also Hunt, *op. cit.,* p. 152.
42. Quoted in Earnest J. Simmons,Tolstoy(London:Routledge & Kegan Paul, 1973), p. 109."
43. *The Kingdom of God and Peace Essays,* cited in Hunt, *op. cit.,* p. 167.
44. *What Then Must We Do?* trans. (by Aylmer Maude (Oxford University Press, 1934), p. 329.
45. Cited in Simmons, *op. cit.,* pp. 460, 504; see also Pyarelal, *op. cit.,* pp. 673-4.
46. *Indian Opinion,* 14 September 1912.

47. Cited in Shriman Narayan, *Mahatma Gandhi. The Atomic Man* (Bombay : Somaiya Publications, 1971), p. 9.
48. *Hind Swaraj* (Ahmedabad : Navajivan Publishing House, 1938), pp. 131 -2; cf. Iyer, *op. cit.,* p. 271.
49. Cited in *Ibid.,* p. 114; see also pp. 115-6, 121.
50. *Young India,* 8 January 1925.
51. Cited in Woodcock, *op. cit.,* p. 24.
52. Joan Bondurant, *The Conquest of Violence* (Bombay: Oxford University Press, 1959), p. 155. A semi-anarchistic settlement had earlier been established along similar lines first in Tennessee and later in Georgia. Ruskin Commonwealth (1894-1901) was founded by the editor of the *"Appeal to Reason,"* its membership numbering at one time over 250, and comprising both socialists and anarchists.
53. *Autobiography,* p. 250.
54. *Unto This Last and Other-Writings* (London : Everyman's Library, 1968), pp. 119,161,168, 190-1.
55. *Ibid.,* pp. 186-7.
56. *Harijan,* 27 May 1939:
57. *The Modern Review,* October 1935, p. 413.
58. Ruskin, *op. cit.,* p. 160; cf. Bondurant, *op. cit.,* p. 156.
59. Erikson, *op. cit.,* p. 191.
60. *Harijan,* March 9, 1934.
61. *Ibid.,* Ma-xh 25, 1933.
62. Louis Fischer, *The Life of Mahatma Gandhi* — 2 Vols. (Bharatiya Vidya Bhavan, Bombay, 1955), Vol. 1, p. 67.
63. See Brook Atkinson's introduction to Thoreau's *Walden* (New York :Thomas Y. Crowell, 1966), pp. vii-viii.
64. *Ibid.,* pp. 16, 427.
65. Sujit Mukherjee, "Thoreau in India", in Eugene F. Timpe (ed.), *Thoreau Abroad* (Hamden Anchor Books, 1971), pp. 161-2.
66. Thoreau, *op. cit.,* pp. 8, 65, 433.
67. Geoffrey Ashe, *Gandhi, A Study in Revolution* (London : Heinemann, 1968), p. 131.

2

The Phoenix Settlement and Tolstoy Farm: The Experiment Begins

When Gandhi sailed from Bombay in April 1893 he had no idea his experiences in South Africa would set him firmly on the path to his later 'mahatmaship' and uncrowned leadership of the Indian people in their struggle against British imperialism. Through a series of discriminatory incidents, which he came to regard as marking the turning point in his life, the oppression of non-whites in South Africa was brought into focus. His indignation at white South Africans' treatment of him whilst on a trip from Durban to Pretoria spurred him to launch a campaign to awaken the Indians of Pretoria to the need to defend their rights. At a meeting of Indians called by him he explained that by conscious efforts to improve their habits and by learning English, the Indian community could integrate more easily into South African society and strengthen its position. The idea of linking self-improvement with the struggle to win one's rights became fundamental to his approach to civil disobedience.

His powers of leadership coming to the fore, Gandhi was soon thrust at the head of a small-scale mass movement, dedicated to non-violent agitation. Paralleling the Indian National Congress, he founded the Natal Indian Congress and organised petitions to the Natal Legislature and later to the British Colonial Office. He had a number of partial successes, and these heightened his determination to rid South Africa of discrimination against the Indian community. He was to remain in South Africa, with brief absences, until 1914, during which time he forged the political weapons he later utilised in the struggle against the British in India.

During these twenty years in South Africa Gandhi transformed himself from a prosperous Anglophile lawyer leading an agitational movement through legal channels, to a non-violent activist living a simple communitarian existence with his followers and prepared to sacrifice his life for the causes he believed in. Between 1904 and 1908 he began to give concrete shape to his doctrine of *satyagraha* which evolved in practice through a number of intermittent civil resistance movements he initiated from 1907 to 1914. Though the limited gains Gandhi realised for the Indian community in South Africa were later nullified by the racialist policies of successive white governments, his *satyagraha* movements did reveal the effectiveness of organised non-violent resistance against a more powerful opponent. The courage shown by Gandhi's *satyagrahis* in the face of repressive governmental action mobilised public opinion to such an extent that the inexperienced South African Government was considerably embarrassed. More importantly, they enabled the Indian community to win a significant moral victory.

"Gandhi was awakened to the nature of his destiny by situations that threatened the quality of his own life," observed Woodcock, "afterwards he devoted himself to defending the quality of the life of others."[1] He sought freedom for mankind to live in harmony and dignity.

The Monastic Ideal

A desire to experiment with communal living was already growing within Gandhi when he reached South Africa in 1893. He sought to interest his associates in the idea of establishing some type of small community once his law practice began to flourish. Until he was able to bring his family to South Africa he decided he would invite his workers and companions to live communally with him in his large and furnished house in Natal, but he soon discovered that a number of them took advantage of his generosity. He was not discouraged, and his assiduous reading of Tolstoy's works increased his desire to begin his own community. During his early years in South Africa Gandhi had begun to envisage the type of community best suited to the value system in which he believed. But it was an Order of Trappist monks living at Marian Hill near Pinetown, sixteen miles from Durban, that provided him with a functioning example of a micro-community living on the basis of voluntary poverty, self-renunciation and constructive work.

Gandhi had known of the vegetarian Trappists ever since he had read of this band of missionaries in Anna Kingsford's *Perfect Way in Diet* as a student in London. When he subsequently learnt that several Trappist settlements had been established in South Africa he was keen to contact them. In April 1895 the opportunity arose to visit their monastery at Pinetown. He published an account of the visit in *The Vegetarian* during the following month. He described the settlement as:

> a quiet little model village; owned on the truest republican principles. The principle of liberty, equality and fraternity is carried out in its entirety. Every man is a brother, every woman a sister.[2]

The population of the mission included one hundred and twenty monks and sixty sisters, both groups observing strict vows of silence and chastity, and twelve hundred native Africans, mostly children, who impressed Gandhi as being "patterns of simplicity, virtue and gentleness". Everything he saw at the settlement greatly impressed him. The males of the predominantly Zulu population were trained in the various workshops to be blacksmiths, tinsmiths, shoemakers, carpenters and tanners, whilst the girls joined the sisters in ironing, sewing, straw-hat manufacturing and knitting. The community had its own printing press, a flour mill worked by water power and an oil press. Without distinction of race all the men laboured in the fields where many varieties of tropical fruits and vegetables were grown. Efficient management of the workshops and farm enabled the settlement to be almost self-supporting.[3]

Gandhi was delighted with the pattern of life he saw at the Trappist settlement, later writing that any vegetarian meeting the "noble band" would be filled "with a spirit of love, charity and self-sacrifice". He went on to describe the Trappists as "a living testimony to the triumph of vegetarianism from a spiritual point of view". In the midst of the racism that permeated South African society Gandhi was overjoyed at discovering a multi-racial community devoid of tensions and prejudices. Though almost all were Germans, the Trappists made no attempt to impose their language on the African converts who received instruction in Zulu and English. In the simple surroundings of the mission everyone worked side by side, ate the same food and dressed in similar fashion :

> The most prominent feature of the settlement is that you see religion everywhere.... I know from personal experience that a visit to the farm...cannot but produce a lasting holy impression on the mind. ... It proves conclusively, to my mind, that a religion appears divine or devilish, according as its professors choose to make it appear.[4]

The Trappist pattern represented for Gandhi a dynamic and creative fusion of ascetic ideals with the practical concerns of service to and management of the community. In subsequent years he would hold up the model of the Trappists to his colleagues as an ideal mode of living, and as late as 1934 he recalled the Trappist pattern in defining the community ideal workers for untouchables should try to emulate. His conception of small communities of working men and women voluntarily devoted to self-realisation through the observance of absolute vows and service of the poor, is in many respects reminiscent of the monastic ideal of the Trappists and is in the tradition of monastic orders established on the basis of ideas espoused by Christian saints such as Basil, Benedict and Francis.[5]

Gandhi did not deny the personal value of introspection, meditation and communion with God as means of seeking spiritual enlightenment, but for him the path lay through service :

> Man's ultimate aim is the realisation of God and all his activities, social, political, religious, have to be guided by the ultimate aim of the vision of God. The immediate service of all human beings becomes a necessary part of the endeavour, simply because the only way to find God is to see Him in His creation and be one with it. This can only be done by the service of all.[6]

He argued that a value system based on truth and non-violence could not be upheld in society and politics unless social workers and politicians accept the monastic ideal of self-renunciation and introduce it into public life.

The Phoenix Settlement and Tolstoy Farm: The Experiment Begins

The association of industriousness with spirituality is by no means unique to the communal pattern of Western monasticism. It is also a salient feature of the ancient Vedic system of education. The *tapovan* (abode of austerities) of the ancient Indian *rishis* (teachers) were forest retreats where the teacher and pupil lived a life of austerity and spiritual discipline. The *tapovan* was the home of the teacher around which his pupils gathered. Life in the *tapovan* was an expression essentially of the teacher's ideals. The task of the pupil was to assimilate these ideals and the spiritual method of the teacher. Membership of these intimate social groups engendered feelings of belonging and of personal worth in the pupil, which enhanced the atmosphere of learning in the *tapovan*. An integral part of the pupils' daily regimen included tending the teacher's house and cattle.

> Tending the house was training the pupil in self-help, the dignity of labour, of menial service for his teacher and the student-brotherhood. Tending cattle was education through craft as a part of the highest liberal education. The craft selected is the primary industry of India.... The pupils received valuable training in the love of the cow and the industry of rearing cattle and dairy-farming, with all the other advantages it gave of outdoor life and robust physical exercise .... Therefore, the highest education was quite consistent with manual and vocational training to give a practical turn to human nature, and training to deal with objects and the physical environment.[7]

At the centre of the Vedic system was the concept *yajna*. Self-sacrifices as worship were not only the guiding principles of ancient Indian education, expressed by the pupil through the selfless performance of different classes of duties, but were the mainspring of all Hindu, Buddhist and Jain religious thoughts. It is the sacrifice that leads to religion and it is religion that leads to the Absolute, explained R. D. Mookerji in his study of ancient Indian education.[8]

In the account of his visit to South Africa early in 1914 Charles Freer Andrews, who became one of Gandhi's most intimate friends, saw in the stark simplicity of the Phoenix Settlement an embodiment of the *tapovan* ideal of *Aryavarta* :

The simple ashram in the forest: the *guru* and the *chela* living their lives apart: themselves close to nature, and living content with nature's simplest gifts.[9]

Indeed Gandhi's concept of ashramic education did not differ significantly from the Vedic ideal. However, his revaluation of the *yajna* concept was not limited to sacrifices performed to facilitate personal development, but encompassed all service undertaken in the cause of community and national development. The principles he associated with ashramic life were "rigid simplicity", "perpetual continence", "detachment from the world", "voluntary poverty", and above all else, "formation of character with a view to self-realisation". He insisted that all members of his ashrams enjoy equal status, and he interpreted his position as head of the respective communities in a way comparable to that of the *rishi* of ancient times in his *topavan*. He saw himself as the parental head of an extended family rather than the superior of an institution.

Whilst Gandhi derived profound inspiration from his knowledge of Christian monasticism, his appeal to the Indian people lay rooted in a Hindu expression of "this-worldly asceticism". He sought to awaken the masses to their own social, cultural and economic traditions, revalued in a dynamic way and purged of all inequities, as means to redress the oppressive social and economic conditions under which they laboured.

Gandhi was not alone in his attempts to refurbish Hinduism as a vehicle for social progress. A religious renaissance had begun in the nineteenth century, inspired by the teachings of Ramakrishna, a mystic who believed the true path to self-realisation was the service of God in man. He did not live to form a society on this principle, but his belief in the unity of all religions, his denunciation of the love of money, and his work on behalf of the poor, inspired many young men to seek a life of self-renunciation and service.

Ramakrishna's chosen successor was Swami Vivekananda. He organised the disciples of Ramakrishna after the seer's death, shaping them into an ascetic order dedicated to social service. The Ramakrishna Order undertook charitable work, opened schools for untouchables, and worked for the uplift of women. Vivekananda taught that a Hinduism rid of superstition and imbued with a social conscience, was the key to national rebirth. He sought to awaken a national consciousness, based on a common understanding of the tenets of Hinduism. "I cannot believe in a religion that does not wipe out the widow's tears or bring a piece of bread to the orphan's mouth", he said.[10] Though he was unable to meet Vivekananda, who died in 1902, and read only one of his books, Gandhi's bid to introduce a religious asceticism into politics was certainly in keeping with the spirit of Vivekananda's efforts to activate Hinduism on a national basis. Gandhi later acknowledged that he and the Ramakrishna Order worked essentially in the same spirit:

> Wherever I go the followers of Ramakrishna invite me and I know their blessings are on my work. Ramakrishna Sevashrams (people's service centres) and Hospitals are spread throughout India. There is no such place where their work is not being carried on a small or large scale. Hospitals arc opened and the poor are given medicine and treatment .... I pray to God to increase such Sevashrams. I hope such people will join them who are pure and who have love for India. Let them do the work inspired with the love of India.[11]

A secular approach to communal asceticism was the Servants of India Society founded by Gopal Krishna Gokhale in 1905. Gokhale was a graduate of Fergusson College in Poona, a charitable institution run by the Deccan Education Society. He was the most eminent among a group of western-educated moderates who increasingly sought social and political reform during the latter stages of the nineteenth and early twentieth centuries. Gokhale's Society consisted of volunteer workers and intelligentsia living on a subsistence wage, who renounced office-seeking and approached community service as a vocation. Their activities included relief work among famine victims and the poverty-stricken, and the promotion of trade unionism.

During Gandhi's years of struggle in South Africa he forged strong links with Gokhale. Though he was initially sympathetic to the aims and aspirations of the Servants of India Society, Gandhi later questioned the wisdom of their support for Western education and the direction in which it was leading India. In a letter to his cousin Maganlal in 1901 he lamented Gokhale's involvement with the Society, which he argued, was "simply an indifferent imitation of the West". By retaining servants, by spending large amounts of money on the maintenance of buildings, and by accepting only English-educated graduates into their midst, the Society, in Gandhi's view, merely compounded the tendency amongst India's elites towards slavish imitation of Western civilisation.[12]

The Phoenix Settlement

During 1903 a small group of people began to form around Gandhi, people who were to eventually assist him with his plan to establish a co-operative community. He had not been particularly satisfied with an earlier attempt in Durban to live communally with a number of his English and Indian acquaintances, but the experience had not quenched his desire to continue experimenting along these lines. At a time when his law practice was flourishing in Johannesburg he forged several lasting friendships with Europeans who shared many of his ideals, and particularly his passion for vegetarianism. He joined a group of Christians and Theosophists called the Seekers' club, with whom he frequently read the *Bhagwad Gita*. Unlike the Durban Christians he had met earlier, the group had no desire to convert Gandhi to anything. They valued his contribution to their discussions as a Hindu. Indeed he criticised members of the group when their conduct failed to correspond with the Theosophical ideal of brotherhood.

Gandhi's awareness of the difficulties associated with an attempt to live according to high spiritual ideals led him into a period of introspection. He began memorising the *Gita* in order to assimilate its teachings, but his public activities interrupted his study. Nonetheless, it became for him a "dictionary of conduct" to which he referred daily for solace and guidance. Concepts such as "non-possession" and "equality" captured his imagination. But with an understanding of these ideas came the realisation that a marked change in his attitudes and the circumstances of his life was necessary if he was to have an opportunity to realise these ideals. In pursuit of a radical change, he allowed his life insurance policy to lapse and notified his brother that in future all of his resources "would be utilised for the benefit of the community".[13]

The example of the Trappists reaffirmed for Gandhi the need of promoting vegetarianism as a basis for improving the quality of living. He made it a political catchword and tried to alert all communities in South Africa to the dangers inherent in flesh-eating. The commercial farming of fruit and vegetables was largely controlled by Indians, mainly vegetarians, who wanted to ensure a regular supply. Gandhi argued that wholesale adoption of vegetarianism would lead to the decentralisation of society because many more farmers would be required. He claimed that the problem of overcrowding in the cities would be solved and a much larger population could easily be supported. In the account of his visit to the Trappist monastery at Marian Hill he wrote:

> The whole of the Republic, although the soil is very fruitful, remains a desert of dust. And if the gold mines could not be worked from any cause, thousands of men would be thrown out of employment and literally starved to death. Is there not here a great lesson to be learnt? The flesh-eating habits have really tended to retard the progress of the community and, indirectly, to create division among the two great communities which ought to be united and work hand in hand.[14]

Though South Africa was particularly suitable for the practice of vegetarianism Gandhi's propaganda had little impact. White South Africans were generally sceptical of his claims. The whites had little interest in this type of agriculture, but they resented the success of the Indians. Undeterred, Gandhi called on interested people to start the "patriotic" work of spreading the "gospel" of vegetarianism, and establishing fruit and vegetable farms wherever it was economically viable. He insisted that good ethics be linked to good economics, and that farms begun along these lines become "real centres of vegetarianism".[15] Many years of struggle ensued before Gandhi had an opportunity to set up his own settlement, farm and newspaper, but he never forgot the example of Mariann Hill.

In 1903 Gandhi began *Indian Opinion* as a means to serve and consolidate the Indian community. The succession of meetings and events which culminated in the founding of the Phoenix Settlement began when Madanjit Vyavaharik (co-owner of *Indian Opinion,* with Gandhi) learnt of an outbreak of plague in the vicinity of

Johannesburg while canvassing subscribers and collecting subscriptions. On two earlier occasions, once in India and again in Durban, Gandhi had revealed his highly developed sense of social responsibility by undertaking sanitary work when plague was feared. Similarly, he and his co-workers plunged into aiding the sick during the Johannesburg outbreak.

Gandhi addressed a scathing letter to the press accusing the Municipality of Johannesburg of negligence and responsibility for the outbreak. The letter, as he recalled later in his autobiography, attracted the attention of three men whose friendship he came to value most highly: Henry Polak, Rev. Joseph Doke and Albert West. West, whom Gandhi had been regularly meeting at his favourite vegetarian restaurant, became alarmed upon reading the letter. He promptly offered to help in nursing the patients, but instead Gandhi convinced him to take charge of the *Indian Opinion* press at Durban.[16]

Shortly after establishing himself in Durban, West informed Gandhi of the precarious financial position of the journal. The news disturbed Gandhi but brought his ideas concerning communal living sharply into focus. The night he left Johannesburg to investigate the problem in Durban he was given Ruskin's *Unto This Last* at the station by Henry Polak, another friend he had met at the same vegetarian restaurant and who also expressed an interest in his work after reading the hostile letter to the press. The dramatic effect Ruskin's book had on Gandhi has been referred to earlier. He determined that "the logical consequence of *Unto This Last* could only be a kind of agrarian communism".[17] On arrival in Durban he proposed that *Indian Opinion* be run on a co-operative basis, and that a farm should be purchased to house the press and its staff, each of whom would be given a plot of land on which to live. The workers would receive an advance payment each month and the remainder of the total profits divided amongst them at the end of each year. The workers were also to be given the option of purchasing their plot of land from the co-operative at the actual cost price.[18]

Gandhi appealed to the workers to join him in *"a* novel and revolutionary project", which would sharply reduce the cost of publishing *Indian Opinion* and greatly improve the quality of their lives. "Living under such conditions," said Gandhi, "and amid the beautiful surroundings which have given Natal the name of the

The Phoenix Settlement and Tolstoy Farm: The Experiment Begins 47

Garden Colony, the workers could live a simpler and more natural life, and the ideas of Ruskin and Tolstoy be combined with strict business principles." In an atmosphere of mutual tolerance, dedication and "brotherly combination between the Europeans and the Indian workers" he foresaw the two racial groups having an educative influence on each other. With the possibility of daily working hours being reduced each worker would have the opportunity of becoming his own agriculturist and enjoying the attendant advantages:

> The English workers could belie the taunt that the Englishman in South Africa would not cultivate the soil and work with his own hands. He had here all the facilities for such work, without any of the drawbacks. The Indian worker could copy his European brothers, and learn the dignity and utility of healthy recreation as distinguished from constant, slaving toil for miserable gains.[19]

While West was keen to participate in Gandhi's idealistic scheme (though he claims a certain amount of wishful thinking encouraged him), the majority of the press workers were unimpressed with the plan. The co-owner, Vyavaharik, was openly hostile to the proposal. He considered it foolish and warned that *Indian Opinion* would collapse if Gandhi persisted. He did not wait to see the outcome, but relinquished his share of the press to Gandhi as repayment of a financial debt and returned to India. West recalls that "a good many otherwise friendly Indians strongly disapproved of the scheme and were not at all helpful".[20]

However, they persisted. One hundred acres were purchased in the picturesque valley of the Piezang river, situated two and a half miles from Phoenix station and fourteen miles from Durban, on the North Coastline to Zululand. The initial investment was one thousand pounds sterling but by the time the settlement was established it had cost Gandhi five thousand pounds.

Gandhi's decision to retain the name of Phoenix for the settlement reflected the experimental nature of his community work. In reply to a suggestion that the name of the settlement be changed to mirror its Indian orientation and Gandhi's involvement in the work, he indicated his firm belief in the universality" of the community experiment at Phoenix.

"I wish that my name is forgotten, and only my work endures. The work will endure only if the name is forgotten.... The word *math* or ashram has a particularly Hindu connotation and therefore may not be used. "Phoenix" is a very good word which has come to us without any effort on our part. Being an English word, it serves to pay homage to the land in which we live. Moreover, it is neutral. Its significance, as the legend goes, is that the bird Phoenix comes back to life again and again from its own ashes, i.e., it never dies. The name Phoenix....serves the purpose quite well for we believe that the aims of Phoenix will not vanish even when we are turned to dust.... At present our whole structure and behaviour are those of the bird Phoenix."[21]

The idea of farming in an isolated area, attending to the press work in their spare time, and all for the small sum of three pounds per month, was not a particularly attractive proposition for those in search of a comfortable living. West observed that the scheme might never have started if practical matters such as trade union rules and minimum wages had been duly considered.[22] Yet immediate obstacles were overcome, and in response to Gandhi's enthusiasm the nucleus of a small community began to take shape, including West, the machinist, Govindaswami, and Gandhi's cousin, Chhaganlal. Gandhi tried to persuade a number of relations and friends who had come from India to join the community, but with little success. With the exception of Maganlal Gandhi (Chhaganlal's brother) those who agreed initially soon returned to a life of business and comfort. Maganlal was to play an important role in the future development of Gandhi's constructive work. "Maganlal Gandhi left his business for good to cast in his lot with me, and by ability, sacrifice and devotion stands foremost among my original co-workers in my ethical experiments", wrote Gandhi. "As a self-taught handicraftsman his place among them is unique."[23]

During October and November 1904 the transfer from Durban to Phoenix took place. Work on the construction of a shed for the press began when a wealthy philanthropist, Parsee Rustomjee, donated corrugated iron sheets and other building materials. With the aid of some Indian carpenters and masons, who had worked with Gandhi during the Boer War, the press shed, was erected within a month. Living and working conditions were very

The Phoenix Settlement and Tolstoy Farm: The Experiment Begins 49

difficult. "The place, uninhabited and thickly overgrown with grass, was infested with snakes and obviously dangerous to live in."[24] All the workers camped out in tents. Though preoccupied with his legal practice in Johannesburg Gandhi stayed and worked with them whenever possible. One of his early suggestions was that mud huts with thatched roofs would be suitable for the settlement, but not surprisingly his colleagues were unenthusiastic and vetoed the idea. No one could match his fervour in such matters. "His bent was naturally towards the ascetic and not towards the aesthetic," recalled Millie Polak, "and it must be admitted that this tendency and his constant practice of the hard and simple life stood him in good stead when he had to endure the discomfort and privation of prison life. He could abjure his followers so to live in times of peace that they might be able to endure hardship in times of struggle."[25]

Issuing the first number of *Indian Opinion* from Phoenix proved to be one of the earliest tests of endurance Gandhi and his co-workers faced. A major problem was to remove the printing plant, with its heavy machinery and type, from Durban to Phoenix. The road was rough, and three rivers, over which there were no bridges, had to be negotiated. In true pioneering spirit, using four large farm wagons, with spans of sixteen bullocks each, the task was managed in a day. In keeping with his "new-found gospel of handicraft and manual labour" Gandhi had hoped to work the press with hand-power, but West, with his experience of heavy machinery, insisted on the necessity of a power source. For this purpose an oil-engine was installed, but as an alternative arrangement if it should fail west designed a hand machine with a driving wheel on a strong wooden frame. By means of a handle four persons could operate the printing machine. This contraption (dubbed "The Wheel") soon proved its worth.[26]

As a further precaution against power failure they reduced the format of *Indian Opinion* from daily newspaper size to foolscap. Apart from improving the style, in case of emergency single pages could be printed on a small treadle machine. These were timely precautions. When all was in readiness on the first night of production the engine would not start, despite the efforts of West and an engineer. Furthermore, there were too few hands to keep the hand wheel operating, an exercise which was heavy work requiring a number of men working in relays. West was loathe to wake the carpenters sleeping on the press floor, but Gandhi did not hesitate to ask for their assistance. Unhesitatingly they agreed, reviving the spirit of the press workers. West sang a hymn and all vigorously joined in the work throughout the night. In the morning the engine started immediately, to the delight of everyone. For Gandhi the failure of the engine had come as a test of their determination to be self-reliant.[27]

As a result of his insistence on self-help the paper continued to be published regularly in an atmosphere of co-operation. Later the engine was dispensed with, and for a time two donkeys were utilised to turn the printing wheel. The arrangement did not satisfy Gandhi, and for a few hours on printing day the services of four strong Zulu girls were hired. Every able-bodied man took his turn at the handle and the paper continued to be "ground out" in the same spirit of that first eventful night.[28] When funding from other sources, including Gandhi's law practice, dried up towards the end of 1909, he was determined that Phoenix would continue to publish at least a one-page issue of *Indian Opinion* and arrange for its distribution. At the same time the domestic situation at Phoenix became strained. Children of gaoled *satyagrahis* had been billeted there and the responsibility of caring for them placed additional pressure on the settlers. Again Gandhi appealed to his colleagues to treat this period of struggle and hardship as an opportunity to test their spiritual mettle and devotion to service:

> It is out of our ignorance that we believe we get our bread because of our efforts. It is best if one realises that he who has given us teeth will also give us food for chewing....It is the duty of those who have devoted themselves to Phoenix to improve the life there and do their best to develop *Indian Opinion;* for through *Indian Opinion* we have been imparting education and doing public good. We need not be disheartened if some of us in Phoenix do not put in their best, waste our resources or are quarrelsome. He who knows better should put in double the effort to make good the deficiency.[29]

Gandhi's preoccupations with the *satyagraha* campaign kept him away from the settlement more than he wished. On one occasion he was in London trying to secure some guaranteed status for Indians as part of the negotiations for the unification of South Africa. In his absence the responsibility for rejuvenating the beleaguered community fell to Maganlal Gandhi. As an expression of the spirit of sacrifice necessary to ensure the survival of the settlement, Gandhi asked Maganlal to declare his intention to live and die at Phoenix if necessary even though no one else remained. "The others will catch your spirit, provided it is born of your steadfast mind and not of arrogance", he wrote to Maganlal. "Be quite sure that its echo will definitely be heard."[30] It is a measure of the settlers' loyalty to Gandhi and their devotion to the Indian cause that Phoenix and *Indian Opinion* survived the crisis. "Though Phoenix was never entirely stable," observed Ashe, "it survived as a community and grew more gracious."[31]

After the press was set up and functioning smoothly the next priority was to provide accommodation for everyone. There was no uniformity of approach to the problem. Each settler chose his own plot and with the assistance of the obliging carpenters erected a building according to personal requirements. Four of the original group, for instance, opted for a flat-roof style of house, which enabled them to sleep out on top when the weather was hot. Unfortunately these constructions could not withstand heavy rain — water leaked under the flat iron sheets and through the wooden ceilings, causing flooding in the rooms and considerable inconvenience for the inhabitants. Notwithstanding the sometimes difficult living conditions the settlers persevered — "The houses soon took on the appearance of a neat little colony". Wild grass was cleared from around the houses, gardens planted and an area levelled to make a courtyard.[32]

Prabhudas Gandhi (Chhaganlal's son) recalls that his father and uncle (Maganlal) were given four acres of land in three different plots. On the largest plot they built a large square room and nearby, a small room for a kitchen. The rooms had raised wooden floors as a safeguard against damp, rain water and the ubiquitous snakes and mice: "The rooms had proper arrangements for the draining away of rain water and had wide glass windows so that these huts were as airy and convenient as any well-built houses."[33] Gandhi's own dwelling quarters consisted of a living-room, two small bedrooms, a tiny kitchen and a shower which had been designed so that the occupant pulled a string and got sprinkled by a watering-can through a hole in the roof. On the roof of the bungalow a simple kind of adjustable windscreen was constructed to shield roof-sleepers from the frequently strong winds. This type of experimentation with simple technologies enriched life in all Gandhi's communities. Another example of the settlers' ingenuity was John Cordes' steam bath. A German who had come to Phoenix from Rhodesia where he had lived for some years, Cordes had great faith in the healing properties of water. He designed a steam cabinet for his place and in conjunction with a cold hip bath and warm towels, "treated" anyone who came to him.[34]

Over the years the number of settlers swelled gradually. Though Gandhi was rarely there, he housed Kasturba, their sons and a nephew, Gokuldas, at Phoenix for quite long periods. Soon after the press had been set up Gandhi returned to Johannesburg where he informed Polak of all that had occurred under the influence of Ruskin's *Unto This Last*. Polak was excited and asked to join the scheme. Gandhi agreed with pleasure and Polak, after resigning from *the Transvaal Critic* (of which he had been sub-editor), arrived at Phoenix to assist Herbert Kitchen, an English Theosophist who took over the editorship of *Indian Opinion* when Mansukhlal Nazar suddenly died. As he had been unimpressed with the Phoenix scheme, Nazar had insisted on maintaining an office in Durban and editing the weekly from there. The new arrangement with Kitchen and Polak living at the settlement and sharing the editorial duties, was more acceptable to everyone. Polak shared West's flat-topped bungalow. The pair of bachelors cooked their own food and shared a simple life together. This early period in their lifelong friendship did not last long, however, for under Gandhi's influence both their living arrangements and bachelor status soon changed. Polak clearly revelled in life at Phoenix and was very popular there due to his ease and sociability, but Gandhi needed his services at Johannesburg in the law practice. He acquiesced to Gandhi's request, later signing articles with a view to qualifying as an attorney.[35]

Ever influencing the lives of his closest associates whether friends or relatives, Gandhi persuaded both Polak and West to marry. Polak agreed to marry his fiance of several years, Millie Graham, who arrived in South Africa during December 1905. On the other hand, West had been considering a visit to his home in England. The Zulu "rebellion" (1906) almost disrupted these

The Phoenix Settlement and Tolstoy Farm: The Experiment Begins 53

plans, but Gandhi insisted he should go and return with a wife if possible. "Phoenix was the common home," wrote Gandhi, "and as we were all supposed to have become farmers, we were not afraid of marriage and its usual consequences."[36] West returned engaged to an old friend, Ada Pywell, whom he later married at Phoenix in June 1908, the ceremony taking place in Cordes' bungalow. A little later he was joined by his sister and mother-in-law. The latter was nearly eighty and in poor health when she arrived in South Africa, but the subtropical climate gave her renewed vigour (she lived to be ninety five). Mrs. Pywell, or "Granny" as she was known to Gandhi and the settlers, helped the women of the settlement with their sewing and knitting and her cheerfulness was a constant source of inspiration. Ada West gave lessons in music and organ playing to students of the nearby Native Institute, and also helped Cordes and Chhaganlal Gandhi to manage the press office.

It seemed as though the Polaks' marriage set a precedent everyone sought to follow. Encouraged by Gandhi, the Indian settlers also sent for their families from India, and Cordes sent for his small son (Willie), who had been born of a negro woman in Rhodesia. "Phoenix thus developed into a little village, half a dozen families having come and settled and begun to increase there."[37]

During the early South African years Gandhi's ideas concerning celibacy *(brahmacharya)* had not fully matured. He quite probably considered the marriage of his bachelor friends would have a settling influence upon them, which would in turn stabilise the fledgeling community at Phoenix. In the early stages of their marriage the Polaks became members of the Gandhi "joint family" in Johannesburg, which frequently consisted not only of blood relatives but friends, co-workers, employees and political associates.

Gandhi's attempts to orient life in his household towards simplicity and self-sufficiency had begun in Durban as early as 1897. To reduce expenditure he had washed his own clothes and cut his own hair. In the light of Ruskin's teachings the Johannesburg household was managed on the same principles guiding the Phoenix experiment: manual work, self-help and simple living. A handmill was introduced to grind flour for the preparation of unleavened wholemeal bread, which Gandhi thought "would ensure more simplicity, health and economy". Every morning Gandhi, the Polaks or the children joined in the task of grinding the flour. It was never compulsory work for the children, but Gandhi believed it provided them with beneficial exercise, and fondly recalled their doing the work cheerfully and conscientiously. The children were required to assist the employed servant with his work, and everyone attended to cleaning the lavatory closet. "The result was that none of my sons developed any aversion for scavenger's work," observed Gandhi, "and they naturally got a good grounding in general sanitation."[38] The boys were also given the responsibility of nursing anyone who became ill, though this was rare at Johannesburg. Gandhi was convinced that the main aim of education was character-building, and nowhere is the tendency to mould the lives of those closest to him more clearly expressed than in his determination to educate the children according to his own beliefs. Of vital concern both at Phoenix and Tolstoy Farm was the education of the settler's children, and for this reason his educational ideas and experimentation will be examined more closely later in the chapter.

In the years preceding the Zulu rebellion Gandhi was anxious to resolve the paradoxical character of his life-style. The problem centred on how to reconcile the value system embodied in the life of poverty at Phoenix with the career of a successful barrister, public activist and spokesman for the Indian community. Outwardly he lived the settled life of a benevolent and resourceful patriarch, deciding vital questions for his friends and relatives, and generally exercising an extraordinary influence on all who knew him. Not only did he contribute a large proportion of the material published in *Indian Opinion,* but personally subsidised the weekly from his own substantial earnings (between £4,000 and £5,000 per annum). As the "incongruously conducted paper gained in readership and public esteem" his reputation as a dedicated lawyer and champion of the oppressed Indian community was greatly enhanced. The circle of Westerners under his influence was also widening. Most notable were a German Jewish architect, Hermann Kallenbach, and a Baptist minister, Joseph Doke, both of whom provided invaluable support to Gandhi during the *satyagraha* struggles in South Africa. Yet, in the midst of all the esteem he attracted as a result of his public activities, inwardly his mind seethed with a moral dilemma: "Thus, with the laudable object of quickly realising the ideals at Phoenix, I seemed to be going deeper and deeper into a contrary current, and had not God not willed otherwise, I should have found myself entrapped in this net spread in the name of simple life."[39]

After the establishment of Phoenix Gandhi became increasingly preoccupied with the question of translating the teachings of the *Bhagavad Gita* into action. Intensive study of the Christian gospels and the writings of Maitland and Tolstoy, lengthy discussions with his Theosophist and radical Christian friends, and a renewed faith in Hinduism, had all coalesced to enhance his understanding of the great religious poem. Gandhi expressed a faith in the Gita's ideal of non-possession quite early in his career as a public worker. For instance, in 1901 he decided not to accept a large number of expensive gifts given to him in gratitude for services rendered to clients and the community in South Africa. Though he faced staunch opposition from Kasturba, he argued that acceptance would compromise the ideal of selfless service.[40] During a period of spiritual introspection in 1903 an extensive examination of the Gita led him to rgalise that non-possession meant that those seeking salvation should become like "trustees" of the community. Though they may control great wealth and possessions, ownership must be completely renounced.

One of Gandhi's biographers has claimed that he ruled *Indian Opinion* and the Phoenix Settlement in an authoritarian fashion; indeed, that he was "like a baronial lord" who left no one with "any illusions about who owned the press and the farm".[41] In the light of Gandhi's beliefs this assertion appears untenable. Doubtless he wielded enormous influence over his colleagues by virtue of his charismatic personality and a refined technique of moral persuasion. He also expected those who joined him in working for the community, to live a life of austerity and manual labour, but the suggestion that he flaunted his ownership of everything relating to the Phoenix experiment and dominated his co-workers is not borne out by the available evidence. Notable features of Gandhi's character were his generosity and kindly treatment of people. Moreover, though he strove to cultivate the virtues of non-violence, celibacy and non-possession, the Gita ideal of *samabhava* (equability) came naturally to him.[42] His enigmatic ability to transcend the narrow confines of social and religious barriers and factional politics appears to stem from this aspect of his personality.

This is not to suggest that Gandhi had no failings, but the writer wishes to highlight the inadequacy of certain emotive criticisms introduced into the narrative of several of his Western biographers, which appear to stem from differing cultural perspectives. Some writers "accuse" him of being domineering and insensitive to the needs of his family, and of obstinately refusing to heed the advice of his friends.[43] He did tend to treat his family as a mere extension of his own austere nature. Kasturba and the boys sometimes suffered from his refusal to allow them to express their own individuality. The eldest son, Harilal, particularly believed that his father's attitudes to life and education severely handicapped his own development. The fact remains that repression of individuality is fundamental to the Indian joint family system, and the word of the family head is law. Perhaps it was unfortunate for his wife and sons that Gandhi was such an unusual man, with a penchant for renunciation, spiritual striving and community service. Doubtless his inability to distinguish between his private and public life caused his family considerable anguish. Yet a case could be argued that Gandhi's wife and children did benefit both morally and spiritually from his awareness of the emptiness of materialistic values and that he acted in his sons' best interests by refusing to educate them under a system that would have resulted in their alienation from India's religious and cultural traditions and from the bulk of her populace.

The other point of concern here is Gandhi's domination of the communities he established and the political struggles he inaugurated. Again, certain Western writers have referred to his sometimes overpowering self-righteousness and unshakable belief in the correctness of his own judgment as essentially negative aspects of his character.[44] There is evidence to suggest that as a result of this tendency the various causes he served devotedly may have been at times harmed. However, it is important to realise that a charismatic the leader attains his authority and consolidates his "legitimacy" by constantly proving his personal strength in life. The initiators of "utopian" movements throughout history have invariably led their followers by virtue of their superior vision and personal example. No doubt there is an inherent weakness in this form of authority. The leader is usually deserted, or his ideas routinised, by his following as his control over them wanes.

The problems associated with this style of leadership have been identified by Max Weber in his essay, "The Sociology of Charismatic Authority". He distinguishes two aspects of a technique to counteract the harmful effects upon a movement which accompany the waning of such a leader's authority. Firstly, emphasis on rational discipline eradicates personal charisma and stratification by status groups. "Those who obey are not necessarily a simultaneously obedient or an especially large mass, nor are they necessarily united in a specific locality. What is decisive for discipline," argued Weber, "is that the obedience of a plurality of men is rationally uniform."[45] Much of the stress Gandhi laid upon self-renunciation and purity of service was perhaps in recognition of the effectiveness of rational discipline. However, it is true that he placed less emphasis on this question in South Africa than later in India, where he was concerned that his followers cultivate rational discipline in their lives.

The second aspect of the technique identified by Weber is that the cultivation of self-discipline in those devoted to a charismatic leader can be utilised to shift that devotion to a common cause or "rationally intended success".[46] Gandhi's supporters in South Africa were asked to discipline themselves by adhering to the principles of truth and non-violence in all their dealings with one another and in the successive struggles with the government. Though the rallying point of these struggles was the immediate problems confronting the Indian community, Gandhi encouraged his followers to regard their experience as preparation for the greater struggle that lay ahead in India. The common focus of all his activities in South Africa, whether it be the operation of *Indian Opinion*, the Phoenix Settlement and Tolstoy Farm, or the *satyagmha* campaigns, was to refine a technique of action to alleviate the plight of India's poor. In the context of his ultimate objective Gandhi wrote in 1908 :

> There is an obvious reason why the first duty of the whites and of the Indians living in Phoenix is to serve the Indian community. Indians must, of course, serve India. If instead of doing that anyone were to claim that he was dedicated to the service of mankind as a whole, it would be nothing more than a pretence... The whites who have joined us were formerly

engaged in their own avocations. There was no need for them to offer their services to the white community. Wishing to renounce their selfish pursuits and devote themselves to the service of others they decided to join the journal.... Those who have chosen to settle in Phoenix wish to educate themselves and to extend the benefits of their education to the entire Indian people.[47]

Gandhi's asceticism and charismatic authority were thus integral to his envisaged plan to improve the quality of life of his countrymen. He sought to realise the Absolute through service, and all other concerns, family or otherwise, were subordinated to that ultimate goal.

However, prior to 1906 he was concerned that his life-style was not sufficiently in accord with his ideals. The role of urbane barrister and householder had become incompatible with his desire to exercise restraint and self-control in all matters. He recognised that absolute dedication to service would require the harnessing of all his energies and that furthermore, his co-workers would have to exercise similar restraint. "In order to do justice to their mission," wrote Weber, "the holders of charisma, the master as well as his disciples and followers, must stand outside of routine occupations, as well as outside the routine obligations of family life."[48]

In pursuance of the Gita ideal of renouncing "objects of the sense" Gandhi had since 1900 pondered the virtues of *brahmacharya* (celibacy), and began a succession of haphazard experiments in this regard.[49] He was impressed with the Indian proverb that "as a man eats, so shall he become". He decided to abstain from many types of food, at times living on fruits and nuts alone. Not unlike the early hermetic Christians, he included fasting as a vital element of his ascetic regimen. In his view, however, to realise the Gita ideal, mere abstention was not enough. It was necessary to negate the craving for sustenance altogether. His efforts to subject the body to the discipline of the mind left him close to death on occasion, but he was undeterred :

> For the seeker who would live in fear of God and who would see Him face to face, restraint in diet both as to quantity and quality is as essential as restraint in thought and speech.[50]

When he did fall ill his dislike for medicines and love of simplicity spurred him to seek alternative treatments. His predilection for tending the sick and serving his fellow-man quickened his desire to experiment with simple nature cure remedies that would be accessible to the poorest man. Beginning with himself and his family, he also encouraged the settlers to join him in these self-disciplining experiments and nature cure therapies.[51] Yet, despite these measures to reconcile his ascetic ideals with his life as a public activist, Gandhi remained dissatisfied.

1906 marked the turning-point in Gandhi's struggle to resolve the dilemma. Early in that year the killing of a tax collector by a Zulu chieftain (Zululand had been annexed by the British in 1887) had sparked off a succession of violent disturbances. The Natal government mounted a punitive campaign to suppress what it termed the Zulu "rebellion". Still believing in the "benevolence" of the British empire, Gandhi volunteered to form an Indian Ambulance Corps, just as he had done during the Boer War. The brutalities and sufferings he witnessed during the campaign of suppression greatly distressed him. Sympathising with the plight of the Zulus he resolved to devote all his energies to serving humanity. At the same time he decided that he could no longer allow the responsibilities and pleasures of family life to sway his resolve: "In a word, I could not live both after the flesh and the spirit. On the present occasion, for instance, I should not have been able to throw myself into the fray, had my wife been expecting a baby. Without the observance of *brahmacharya* service of the family would be inconsistent with service of the community. With *brahmacharya* they would be perfectly consistent."[52]

On his return to Phoenix — Kasturba and the boys lived there for the duration of the "rebellion", the Johannesburg household having been broken up — he informed Chhaganlal, Maganlal, West and other settlers of his intention to take a final vow to observe *brahmacharya* for life. His reasoning appealed to them, and though they alerted him to the difficulties of the task, several agreed to observe the vow. As usual Kasturba was not consulted, but she complied with his decision without argument. Though initially she may have been sceptical of her husband's motivations, it certainly improved relations between them. No longer so domineering towards her, Gandhi welcomed a new-found independence of thought and action and began to value her support and loyalty.

Gandhi's motives for taking the vow were complex. His intolerant and ill-informed views regarding sexual relationships and his insistence on the 'evil' nature of all sexual responses have been extensively "analysed" by Western writers, most particularly by Erikson. It is difficult to gauge to what extent Gandhi's long struggle to repress his sexuality stemmed from childhood experiences such as his early marriage to Kasturba or the traumatic guilt associated with being absent from his father's deathbed. Perhaps it is sufficient to recognise here that self-denial of ordinary pleasures is fundamental to the ascetic mentality as it is expressed in many religious traditions.[53]

The Hindu idea of seeking God by cultivating the virtues of equability and desirelessness particularly appealed to him. However, it is unusual for a married man to take the vow at the early age at which Gandhi adopted it. He was thirty-seven. His determination to mortify the flesh and the passions, and his belief that dietetic control and fasting are linked to sexual continence, was reminiscent of certain Indian yogic practices and the eremitical practices of early forms of Christian monasticism. In the case of these traditions, however, the privations experienced as a result of extreme forms of abstinence are usually also associated with social renunciation. Yet, the effect of the vow on Gandhi was to heighten his social consciousness in preparation for the struggles that lay ahead. He experienced a spiritual cleansing which broke with the past and became the mainspring for his belief that strict abstinence[0] was an essential discipline for those prepared to sacrifice themselves to the cause of truth and non-violence. In addition to these reasons, another incentive to take the vow was Kasturba's poor health. She had almost died earlier from internal haemorrhage, and although she had undergone a gynaecological operation, performed without anaesthetic because she was too emaciated, she nevertheless remained anaemic. It was feared that another pregnancy would endanger her life.

The early hopes that Phoenix would develop into a health, agricultural and educational centre *par excellence* were thwarted by a number of factors. Among these were the demands of running the paper, the severe disruptions caused by the political struggle, during which many settlers served terms of imprisonment, and ultimately the departure of Gandhi from South Africa in 1914. Initially everyone had been optimistic that the income derived from *Indian Opinion* and the produce of the farm would not only be sufficient to support the community but would enable each settler to realise substantial savings, since the profits accruing from the enterprise were to be divided equally. Those who joined the scheme with this intention were soon faced with the harsh realities of Gandhi's concern that service to the Indian community would be the principal aim of the experiment. The salaries of those connected to the journal were fixed according to their needs, which varied, depending on the size of the worker's family and such things as the amount of extra expenditure incurred travelling about the country in the interests of the journal. Gandhi insisted that any extra income earned from the journal or from donations would be spent on public work.

In 1912 the ownership of Phoenix and *Indian Opinion* was passed from Gandhi to a board of trustees, and the management objectives of the settlement were precisely laid down. It was decided to discontinue job-work and publishing advertisements, as it was felt these practices were inconsistent with the charitable objectives of Phoenix.[54]

The time available for the settlers to earn a living from the land was also much reduced. In practice the normal working hours of the majority were devoted to press work. The problem was compounded for those settlers who spent lengthy periods in prison during the *satyagraha* campaigns. Nevertheless, their gardens were attended to in spare time, which eventually enabled the settlement to be self-sufficient in fruit and vegetables. Though the settlers advised and assisted one another the agricultural experiment remained uneconomical due to a lack of co-ordinated joint farming. Each settler cultivated a separate plot, growing the crops thought to be most suitable. Their energies were also diverted into unremunerative work such as the maintenance and extension of houses, and the building of a library and school. Though a builder was contracted to do the brickwork for the school and library, all the timber construction was done by the settlers, including a very high roof. "We did not mind doing the work — it was a pleasure," recalls West, "but while we did carpentry, we were not cultivating the soil."[55]

Another problem which dampened the spirits of the novice farmers was the high incidence of damage to crops by roaming mules and donkeys. Due to the variable nature of the settlers' incomes the destruction was all the more disheartening. For many years the land remained without proper fencing, but eventually this was resolved by planting protective hedges. Referring to all the unforeseen problems that arose in the course of life at Phoenix, Millie Polak has written:

> The ideals and theories that had sounded so right and reasonable in the study, or read so well in books, had a chance of being put to the test at Phoenix, and, as might be expected, were often found impracticable when applied to the hard facts of life.[56]

Drinking water shortage, "primitive" sanitary arrangements, fear of snakes and spiders, and dislike of the very simple food and accommodation provided at Phoenix, all played heavily on Millie Polak's mind. She often remonstrated with Gandhi over the imposition of what she believed were unnecessary austerities at Phoenix and was very relieved when her husband shifted back to Johannesburg. After Kitchen's retirement and departure from Phoenix Polak took over as editor of *Indian Opinion,* the Rev. Joseph Doke deputising during his absences. Due to his wife's dislike of life at the settlement they continued to share Gandhi's small and sparsely furnished house in Johannesburg (which had replaced the large house given up at the time of the "rebellion"), visiting Phoenix several days a week to complete the editorial work. Mrs. Polak was content with this arrangement. She and Gandhi continued their spirited discussions on wide-ranging issues such as the role of women in society and celibacy in marriage, the upbringing of children, diet and the non-killing of poisonous animals.[57]

On the whole, however, the majority of settlers were not so disillusioned with life at Phoenix as Mrs. Polak. Friendly relations were enjoyed with the Zulus inhabiting the surrounding hills, who would often call on their way to and from the railway station and sparsely stocked general store (situated close to the station) for a drink of water or to purchase fruit from the settlers. The wife of a Negro squatter living nearby across the river assisted the women with washing and cleaning, and a short distance from Phoenix lived an Indian woman who acted as midwife when the

The Phoenix Settlement and Tolstoy Farm: The Experiment Begins 63

wives of Indian settlers gave birth. West recounts that for the birth of his two children he cycled the fifteen miles to Durban to call an Indian doctor. He and his mother-in-law acted as nurses on both occasions.[58]

Life at Phoenix was always much enriched when Gandhi was able to spare time away from his legal and political activities to be there. His good humour, love of simplicity, capacity for self-sacrifice and preparedness to serve anyone requiring guidance or assistance, on many occasions inspired men, women and children of otherwise average ability and with no special talents to rise above their "normal mental and moral stature to heights of great sacrifice and bravery".[59] Whilst at the settlement Gandhi was continuously active, meeting with the regular stream of visitors to his house or delighting in the performance of simple acts of service, such as cooking meals, doing domestic work, cutting hair, nursing the sick and attending to the needs, whether serious or trivial, of the community children.

Though the school building would have been a suitable meeting place for the community, Gandhi's large living room remained the centre for social activities. It was the hub of religious life at Phoenix. Evening prayer meetings were held there and every Sunday the community always joined together for what West termed "a united spiritual exercise." Jews, Hindus, Muslims, Parsees and Christians all participated in the "service", which was a blend of religious teachings and spiritual songs from the East and the West. As no particular religion was given a superior position, the service each Sunday reaffirmed the universal bonds of love and truth upon which the community had been founded. Passages from the *Bhagavad Gita and* the New Testament were read, English hymns were sung, and Gujarati *Bhajans* (sacred songs) would be chanted by those who knew the language. A small hymn-book, printed and bound at the Phoenix Press, and containing eighteen hymns from many sources, had been specially arranged for the "universal service".[60]

Perhaps the "finest moment" of Phoenix came in 1913, when the settlers became the mainstay of the third and final *satyagraha* campaign. The experience confirmed the truth of Gandhi's claim that life at Phoenix was essentially geared to prepare families for the rigours of *satyagraha*. At the conclusion of the second campaign discipline at Phoenix became extremely severe, and an understanding was reached with all eligible male pupils and their parents that those who chose to remain at the settlement must be prepared to join the struggle.

When the agitation began over the government's action in passing a law ruling all marriages not celebrated according to Christian rites invalid, only one family held aloof. The activities of the Phoenix *satyagrahis* became the focal point of the struggle. Since it was illegal for Indians to cross from Natal into the Transvaal Gandhi sent a group of sixteen settlers — twelve men and four women, including Kasturba — ostensibly to make their way to Tolstoy Farm (which was in the Transvaal), but in reality to court arrest at the border. With their arrest the struggle was vigorously renewed. Hundreds of volunteers suffered imprisonment, and when the indentured labourers on the sugar estates in Natal decided to strike in sympathy with the *satyagrahis,* approximately two thousand marched to Phoenix squatting on the ground near the press. This posed a formidable problem for those who remained behind at Phoenix to manage the affairs of the press and community, including a number of boys under sixteen years of age.

Despite the ever-present danger of raids by the police, the settlers worked day and night to provide welfare and distribute the food sent from Durban tor the striking labourers by the Indian Association. To strengthen discipline among themselves the Phoenix workers decided to observe strict vows until such time as their friends and elders were released. They served the labourers and the families of the *satyagrahis* without distinction, cooked meals, washed clothes, minded the younger children, and scavenged for all. In reference to their contribution to the *satyagraha* struggle Gandhi wrote in the Golden Number of *Indian Opinion* published in 1914:

> Although they and the others who managed the affairs of Phoenix stayed out of prison, they did better work than those who went to gaol... The Indian community can never truly measure the services that the Phoenix workers rendered to it at that time.[61]

The passing of the Indian Relief Bill by the Union Parliament in June 1913 marked the end of the eight-year-old *satyagraha* struggle. A little over one year later Gandhi and Kasturba departed from South Africa for the last time. The Phoenix settlers had been forewarned of this eventuality as early as in 1912 during the visit of Gokhale, the renowned Indian philanthropist and public activist. He had confided in West his hope of convincing Gandhi to return to India as soon as a settlement of the Indian question in South Africa could be reached. He foresaw Gandhi playing an active role in the national Independence movement. In a farewell speech to indentured Indians at Verulam in Natal, Gandhi assured the meeting that his departure did not mean assistance would no longer be available at Phoenix for those in need. He advised them that Chhaganlal Gandhi and West would continue to render assistance to anyone free of charge. "If Phoenix ever failed them and wanted a farthing from them," said Gandhi, "then they should shun Phoenix."[62]

West recalled that Gandhi's departure came as a serious blow to the aspirations of those who remained behind at Phoenix. Several of the settlers and Gandhi's sons sailed direct to India where they were accommodated in Rabindranath Tagore's Shantiniketan *ashram* and were later joined by Gandhi and Kasturba during 1915. For three years following the "exodus" of Gandhi and his family from Phoenix West and several other settlers continued to publish *Indian Opinion* on the terms set down in the Phoenix Trust Deed of 1912. They acted as advisers in matters arising out of the Relief Act, and struggled to maintain the agricultural experiment.

In time it was decided that an attempt to make Phoenix totally self-supporting was necessary as financial help could no longer be accepted from the Passive Resistance Fund. Working day and night for months West and Ragoo Govindoo (known as "Sam" by the settlers) ploughed extra land and planted crops of corn and fruit, attending to the press work for four hours each afternoon. Droughts and floods wreaked havoc on their efforts, destroying crops and rendered the land unworkable for long periods. When acres of bananas and citrus fruits failed it was realised that the soil was infertile; only pineapples flourished in the stony ground. Through correspondence Gandhi confirmed the settlers' opinion that agriculture was unlikely to become economically viable. "If we could adopt the standard of living of a Negro or Indian agriculturalist, live in a hut, and leaving the world aside, and the education of our children, scrape a few handfuls of food from the ground, it might be possible, but we could not bring ourselves to do it", observed West.[63]

It was also decided that the principle of refusing advertisements in *Indian Opinion* and printing of jobs as a source of income should still be adhered to. In a letter to West during 1917 Gandhi expressed his thoughts concerning the future of Phoenix: "My view is that if you can turn *out Indian Opinion* only by removing to town, you should suspend publication. I do not like the idea of your competing for jobs or ads. I think that when that time comes we shall have outlived our purpose. I would rather that you sold out Phoenix and you and Sam were engaged in some other independent work. If you can make of Phoenix something without the paper I should like the idea. But if you cannot even eke out a living from agriculture at Phoenix, Phoenix should be sold."

Gandhi was now deeply involved in the Indian Independence Movement, and his thoughts concerning the future of *Indian Opinion* and Phoenix reflect a hardening of his nationalistic attitudes. In reply to Gandhi's letter West expressed disappoint-ment at the change hed detected in Gandhi's approach to the South African situation. West recalled that his own outstanding ideal

> was to serve as a link between the Indian people and the European. That was the kernel of my ideal. Throughout the various changes at Phoenix I have never lost sight of it. All such questions as food reform, living by means of agriculture etc. were a part of the scheme of bringing the two sections together. But in all our understanding we agreed that *Indian Opinion* was to be the real agent by which the ideal was to be spread abroad and it was always recognised that the paper was indispensable and especially the English columns. When you say, therefore, that you would like the idea of our making something of Phoenix without *Indian Opinion* I think you have waived an important principle, the chief motive for my connection. Your suggestion that only Gujarati could be published in case Mr. Sam and I left, seems to be born of your newer ideals developed in India. To think that such a paper would fulfil the purpose for which we have worked so long is to my mind an entirely mistaken idea.[64]

In lieu of this West and Govindoo felt they were left with

little alternative but to retire from Phoenix and earn a living in Durban. Gandhi agreed to lend them the jobbing plant and paper stacks for this purpose. They discussed the proposition of working in Durban and helping to manage *Indian Opinion* from there with Manilal Gandhi who had been sent from India some months earlier. He was not enamoured of their ideas, but accepted the position. West offered to continue editing the paper from Durban, informing Manilal he could qualify for the managership within six months. The arrangement was acceptable to both parties for many months, but when Manilal rejected an editorial article from West, he discontinued his editorship. As soon as Govindoo and West began to make a success of their business they returned the jobbing plant to Phoenix.[65]

The press was now fully controlled by Manilal, but he soon realised that without the financial backing *Indian Opinion* had received from its inception it would have to be closed down. He informed Gandhi that the paper would have either to accept advertisements and do job printing or receive funding from other sources. Gandhis response was similar to the answer he had given West. He replied that he had not sent Manilal there to conduct a business but to render public service. In his view *Indian Opinion* had served its purpose. It had brought into being several Indian newspapers, which all served the public in some way. He advised that the paper should cease publication and the Phoenix land be parcelled out.[66]

Manilal did not heed his father. He began to do job printing and accept advertisements, continuing to publish the paper until his death in 1956. His wife, Sushila, carried on editing *Indian Opinion* until 1961 when failing health and a lack of funds forced her to cease publication. It is possible that Gandhi relented on the question of closing the paper because spokesmen of the Indian community in South Africa, aware of its value as an effective mouthpiece of world renown, argued for its continuation. What ever the case, the services it provided after the departure of Gandhi from South Africa are perhaps best summed up in the editorial of the final issue on 4 August 1961 :

> Not only did the journal seek to secure to the Indian people political and economic rights due to them as a tax-paying part of the population, but it also sought to chart out a new way of

life based on what had become a passion with Gandhiji - Truth ... In recent years the journal has tried to present to the people of emergent Africa the teachings of Mahatma Gandhi. It has put forward the case for *satyagraha* as a weapon which the people of Africa can use in their struggle. In addition it has tried to attend to the immediate affairs of the Indian people themselves thus serving both a broad and a narrow horizon ... and while there is a sense of grief that something which has served for 58 years should come to an end there is at all times the challenge of the following from the *Bhagavad Gita* : "For to the one that is born death is certain and certain is birth for the one that has died. Therefore, for what is unavoidable, thou shalt not grieve."[67]

Life for the Gandhis who remained in South Africa was never one of ease or comfort. Sushila Gandhi was born into a wealthy family of strict orthodox Hindus who became devout followers of Gandhi. She recalls that her family home came to reflect the Satyagraha Ashram in Ahmedabad (see Chapter 3). Spinning and weaving were household routines and everything worn was made from *khadi* (hand woven cloth). After her marriage in India to Manilal, whom she had never met before their wedding day, the couple returned to Phoenix Sushila helped in the press, setting Gujarati type. In 1930 they were recalled to India to assist with the mass civil disobedience movement (the work at Phoenix was entrusted to a friend). After a year spent in prison during the *satyagraha* campaign Manilal returned with Sushila to South Africa, where their life's work was centred and where all their children (Sita, Ela and Arun) were born.

For many years Manilal and Sushila were primarily concerned with publishing *Indian Opinion,* but during the early 1950's efforts were made to attract funding for a school to provide education for the large numbers of Indian children deprived of this opportunity. Manilal wrote to prominent members of the Indian community all over South Africa, and followed this up by visiting personally many recipients of the letter.

To begin with Sushila improvised classes for the children in part of the old house once occupied by Gandhi (both the old press building and house were torn down during the 1950's because of extensive white ant damage to the structures) but within a few months the numbers swelled from five to two hundred. However, a favourable response to the request for money led to the establishment of a school dedicated to the memory of Kasturba Gandhi. By the early 1970's five hundred children, both Indian and African, were being educated there. It was later jointly managed by the Department of Indian Affairs and the Phoenix Settlement Trust. Arun Gandhi recalls that at one time the South African Government threatened to close the school because the area was designated as an African area, while the majority of pupils were Indian. The authorities may also have been sceptical of the type of education imparted at the settlement, perhaps fearing the dissemination of radical ideas regarded as dangerous to the "apartheid" regime. Arun, a journalist resident with his family in Bombay, was fortunate in meeting an English-speaking South African politician on a visit to India and persuading him to take up the cause of Phoenix. The authorities subsequently tolerated the activities of the settlement.[68]

In addition to the child education scheme a small adult education programme was also begun during the 1950's among the black farm labourers working the one hundred acres of farm land owned by the settlement. Initially only five or so of the labourers took up the offer extended to them by the Gandhi family, but the numbers rapidly swelled until approximately sixty Africans were seeking to take advantage of the opportunity. Arun Gandhi recalls that he and his sisters were involved in the teaching. When asked whether this was not too much responsibility for a fifteen or sixteen-year-old boy, he replied that by virtue of the circumstances of the Gandhi family in South Africa responsibility devolved upon the children at a young age. Indeed he remembered the teaching as an enjoyable experience.[69] Programmes of education and consciousness-raising among the Indians and Africans continued to develop over the years. Summer schools or camps were held every year, where children of all races gathered to learn the teachings of Gandhi and to exchange ideas. Writing in 1981, the daughter of Manilal and Sushila, Ela Ramgobin, indicated that due to the pressures exerted by the regime in South Africa "the success of these programmes cannot be gauged nor details revealed as essentially they remain confidential".[70] A medical care centre was also added to the activities of the Phoenix Settlement. Doctors from Durban agreed to participate in the medical scheme and rotate their services on a schedule basis. The Centre had a full-time staff of Africans and Indian nurses who assisted the doctors in the clinic and supervised the twelve-bed hospital.

For many years the affairs of the Phoenix Settlement Trust, including a library and museum, were administered by a committee, which included members of the Gandhi family. Sushila Gandhi retired after a life of active service to the Indian and African communities in South Africa. The hopes and uncertainties of the future for Phoenix were summed up by her in an interview published during 1971:

> The future is uncertain. Unless a miracle happens, I shall be the last Gandhi to work here at the Settlement.... You ask whether I would have chosen the "hard life" had I known what was in store for me. Oh yes, I most certainly would have. It has been a wonderful life. And you know hardships cease to be difficult if they are accepted and just lived day by day. I must confess that I do not see eye to eye with all the teachings of the Mahatma. But I do believe in the spirit of all he did and said. And I have tried to live in this spirit. The Ministry of Community Development wishes to use our estate as a buffer between two areas of a planned housing scheme — Indians on the one side, Africans on the other. I cannot say what will happen. My prayer is that the way will open for us in this work. We could pay teachers a little but not very much. I see that as a possible future for Phoenix. Who knows, like the mythical bird, this settlement may yet rise again to its former life and usefulness. The spirit is still here.[71]

Tragically, the Phoenix Settlement was destroyed by fire in the 1980s during a period of inter tribal fighting. Whether Phoenix can rise "like the mythical bird" from the ashes of South Africa's "apartheid" system will depend on the efforts of the many people dedicated to its reconstruction.

Tolstoy Farm (1910-1913)

Tolstoy Farm was established as a corollary to the Phoenix Settlement scheme. During the second *satyagraha* campaign against the Asiatic Registration Bill (referred to as the "Black Act" by Gandhi and his followers), which was designed both to prevent Indians who had left the Transvaal during the Boer War from returning and to prevent any future Indian immigration, the mainstay of the resistance movement were poor Indians residing in the Transvaal. The majority had to leave their families practically without any means of support during the time spent in prison. As a solution to this problem Gandhi saw the need for a "sort of co-operative commonwealth" in the Transvaal after the pattern of the Phoenix Settlement; a community where *satyagrahis* and their families would work to support themselves, and in the process learn to live a new and simple life in harmony with nature and one another. To facilitate the plan Kallenbach bought a farm of about eleven hundred acres, twenty-one miles from Johannesburg, and offered it to Gandhi and the *satyagrahis* rent-free on 30 May 1910, with the proviso that the settlers withdrew on the termination of the struggle.[72]

Gandhi was not only determined to imbue this experiment with the same binding spirit of co-operation that held the settlement at Phoenix together, but he also hoped to avoid whatever shortcomings had handicapped the Phoenix project. At Tolstoy Farm the emphasis was on communal living in every sense. Accommodation was shared, and instead of each settler cultivating a separate plot of land, it was decided that the entire acreage would be cultivated jointly to ensure more efficient production of larger crops, and to enhance the co-operative spirit of the exercise. Gandhi viewed the experiment as an excellent opportunity to inculcate simple, non-materialistic values within the Indian community in South Africa as a whole: "They will have on the farm, a noble life in place of the unclean and monotonous ways of town life. Moreover, what they will learn on the farm will prove useful for a lifetime. Indeed, we have said in the past that the Indian community would be well rewarded if it were to take to agriculture and would be saved the anxieties incidental to business. We have to pay a heavy price for not recognising this best of occupations."[73]

Tolstoy Farm was so named by Kallenbach himself. He had a great faith in the Russian's teachings and for some time had sought to embrace the ideals of simplicity, manual labour and self-renunciation in his own life-style. Erikson observes that Kallenbach, a German Jew, may have been aware of the *Kibbutz* movement which at that time, under Tolstoyan influence, was setting up

Jewish settlements in Palestine. The main difference of course was that men and women were housed separately at Tolstoy Farm.[74]

A vital factor in the success of the Jewish Independence movements in Palestine was the creation of a dynamic rural economy, based on small agricultural settlements, in which members, united together in a spirit of religious brotherhood, performed all tasks and exalted the dignity of labour. Similarly, in each of the communities Gandhi established, the life-style was rural-oriented on a non-exploitative basis and the members were enjoined to exemplify the dignity of "bread-labour". He later maintained that if all men would only strive for self-sufficiency by the performance of enough physical labour to produce their daily needs wants would be minimised and food would be simple. Rather than live to eat, the poor of the world would begin to know the joy of eating to live. In 1935 he -explained that those who took up the practice of labouring for bread would "derive the greatest relish from the productions of their labour, improve their health and discover that many things they took were superfluities".[75]

Kallenbach chose a suitable farm for the site of Gandhi s second community. The soil was fertile and nearly one thousand fruit trees — including oranges, peaches, apricots, figs, almonds and plums — already grew there. This was a valuable source of income and food for the *satyagrahis* when the trees were in season. Two wells and a spring ensured a steady supply of water. As the spring was five hundred yards from the settler's quarters the water was fetched on carrying poles.

The question of providing accommodation for the settlers did not present any great difficulty. Apart from a small house built by the previous owner, which accommodated six persons, all construction was done by the settlers themselves. With the assistance of Kallenbach as architect, several Indian carpenters who offered their services free of charge, and a number of African labourers, two buildings were put up to house the men, women and children. In addition a separate house was constructed for Kallenbach, as well as a school building and a workshop for carpentry and shoemaking. Stones for the foundations were available on the farm but had to be rolled quite a distance to the building site.

The initial work was done by six Indians and Kallenbach, who all lived and ate together in the original house. Before long the number of settlers increased considerably, including about forty young men, two or three, old men, five women, and between twenty to thirty children. After about two months of living in tents the motley crowd were all housed in the new structures of corrugated iron and wood. Gandhi's high hopes for the experiment were coming to fruition. "This is a very important venture," he said, "its roots go deep; it is up to the *satyagrahis* who settle there to make it bear sweet fruit by the way they live."[76]

As the population of the settlement swelled so too its requirements grew. Gandhi called on Indian tradesmen and fruit and vegetable dealers to supply goods to the farm free of charge or at reduced prices. He asked the Indian community as a whole to support the Tolstoy Farm project in the same ennobling spirit of sacrifice displayed by the carpenters. The message was clear— support for the farm would ensure that the *satyagraha* campaign was successfully waged and brought to an earlier conclusion. By minimising the costs of maintaining the *satyagrahis* on the farm a core of activists could continue for a longer period if necessary. It was a technique Gandhi was lo use very effectively in the civil disobedience movements in India. He saw that a heterogeneous group of people trusting in him and the principles of truth and non-violence, living together, working together, and prepared to sacrifice themselves in the *satyagraha* struggle symbolised a unity and strength capable of rousing people to rebel.

The *satyagrahis* at Tolstoy Farm observed a strict daily regimen. No servants were employed except for several African labourers who were hired to help with building construction, and later occasionally on the farm. From cooking and scavenging to teaching the children, all daily tasks were carried out by the settlers themselves. Though there were Christians and Muslims amongst the *satyagrahis,* meat was not eaten, partly in deference to Gandhi's strong belief in vegetarianism, and partly for reasons of economy and simple organisation. The severity of the pattern was reminiscent of ordered life in certain Christian monastic orders :

> The time as well as the number of meals was fixed. There was to be one single kitchen, and all were to dine in a single row. Everyone was to see to the cleaning of his own dish and other things. The common pots were to be cleaned by different parties in turn. I must state that *satyagrahis* lived on Tolstoy Farm for a long time, but neither the women nor the men asked, for meat

(even the children readily accepted this vegetarianism). Drink, smoking, etc. were of course totally prohibited.[77]

Gandhi and Kallenbach set the example of renunciation and discipline that permeated the Tolstoy Farm community. From 1910 to 1913 they carried out many dietetic experiments and fasted regularly. Though Hindus normally allow themselves milk and fruit when fasting, as this was Gandhi's normal diet, he took nothing but water during a fast. His attitudes towards diet, and sex hardened : "The concupiscence of the mind cannot be rooted out except by intense self-examination, surrender to God and, lastly, grace. But there is an intimate connection between the mind and the body, and the carnal mind always lusts for delicacies and luxuries. To obviate this tendency dietetic restrictions would appear to be necessary. The carnal mind, instead of controlling the senses, becomes their slave, arid therefore the body always needs clean non-stimulating foods and periodical fasting."[78] On occasion he fasted as a form of moral penance for what he believed were "transgressions" committed by settlers, whether adults or children.[79] Unable to conceive of any boundary between public and private morality he tried to expiate the wrong-doings of others by taking responsibility for their actions upon himself. It bound the community and his ever-increasing circle of disciples and supporters more closely to him.

The young people and children at Tolstoy Farm were encour-aged to follow one another's religious observances. During the Muslim *Ramzan* fast, for instance, they all agreed to join Gandhi in observing the fast. "The result of these experiments was that all were convinced of the value of fasting," he observed, "and a splendid *esprit de corps* grew up among them." A large proportion of the settlers responded to Gandhi's arguments and began to observe partial or complete fasts. Recalling that some of his friends faltered in their experiments, Gandhi noted in his autobiography that "fasting is futile unless it is accompanied by an incessant longing for self-restraint". The *Bhagavad Gita* remained his constant source of inspiration in matters of bodily discipline:

For a man who is fasting his senses
Outwardly, the sense-objects disappear,

The Phoenix Settlement and Tolstoy Farm: The Experiment Begins 75

Leaving the yearning behind; but when
He has seen the highest,
Even the yearning disappears.[80]

The watchwords of the Tolstoy Farm community were industry, economy and self-sufficiency. Unused to the rigours of rural life, the settlers struggled in cold, hot and wet weather conditions to improve their quality of life. As Kallenbach knew something of gardening it became obligatory for those not engaged in the kitchen, young and old, to devote some time to this pursuit. Of course, the young did the bulk of the work, digging pits, felling timber and carrying loads. Ample exercise, nourishing, regular food and clean air and water kept the settlers, and especially the children, in good health. When illness did strike neither a doctor was called nor drugs used, but at all times Gandhi persevered with nature cure therapies such as earth and water treatment, fasting and changes in diet. One of the rules laid down was that anyone who had to conduct business in Johannesburg on behalf of the community must travel by third class rail, and to discourage settlers from going to the city unnecessarily it was also stipulated that pleasure-seekers must travel there and back on foot. In fact many acquired the habit of walking as a result and greatly benefited from the exercise, but most importantly precious money was saved by this one rule. Gandhi would often rise at two o'clock in the morning, walk the twenty-one miles into Johannesburg, attend to his law practice and other concerns, and walk back by evening. To ensure that money was not squandered in the city simple provisions were made available to day travellers. An iron handmill was purchased to grind wheat for home-baked wholemeal bread and groundnuts for butter. Marmalade was made from oranges grown on the farm.[81]

Gandhi recalled that all the settlers accepted these disciplines cheerfully: "It would have been impossible to have a single settler if force had been employed. The youngsters thoroughly enjoyed the work on the farm and the errands to the city.... No more work was given to them than what they willingly and cheerfully rendered, and I never found that the work thus done was unsatisfactory either in quantity or quality."[82] Despite the large number of settlers, the farm was kept very clean. All rubbish was buried in trenches, all waste water collected in buckets and used to water the trees, and all food refuse and excreta was covered in earth pits and later utilised as manure. These methods were not only hygienic but afforded a rich supply of organic fertiliser for the farm. Later, in India, Gandhi launched an extensive propaganda programme to teach the villagers the necessity of efficient sanitation and hygiene, and ways in which such practices could improve their crops. The settlers also made their own furniture, clothes and sandals, Kallenbach went to the Trappist monastery near Pinetown to learn sandal-making. All wore trousers and shirts made out of coarse blue cloth and fashioned after a gaol uniform, which were suitable for labouring. The food served was simple vegetarian prepared in Indian style and eaten with wooden spoons made at the settlement.[83]

In Gandhi's reminiscences of the Tolstoy Farm experiment Kallenbach figures prominently. He had lived a life of ease until meeting Gandhi, and some Europeans regarded his determination to follow the austere pattern set by his Indian friend as foolishness. In fact he was the mainstay of many settlement activities such as sandal-making, carpentry, gardening and tending the fruit trees. Each morning he would engage settlers to assist him in his task, and due to his affable nature everyone enjoyed working with him. After learning that certain types of snakes protect field crops from rodents and other vermin Kallenbach made an extensive study of snake lore. He taught the settlers to distinguish different varieties, and though the farm was infested with snakes they avoided killing them unless absolutely necessary.

Gandhi and Kallenbach had frequent discussions on religion. Both believed in the duty of carrying out in practice every principle they were convinced of intellectually, and eagerly joined one another in dietetic experiments and regular fasting. When Gandhi read that Indian dairymen resorted to cruel methods to extract milk from their cows he and Kallenbach gave up cow's milk. Though Gandhi was never convinced that a purely fruit diet was best for man, he had no doubts as to its religious value. "Medically there may be two opinions as to the value of this diet," he writes, "but morally have no doubt that all self-denial is good for the soul."[84] Before retiring at nine o'clock every night the settlers would join Gandhi in reading from the *Bhagavad Gita* and other religious scriptures, to pray and to sing devotional songs in

English, Hindi and Gujarati. This daily gathering reunited the community in the same spirit of devotion and brotherhood which had marked its inception : "The settlers learned to look upon one another as members of the same family; the *satyagrahis* secured a pure place of refuge; little scope was left for dishonesty or hypocrisy."[85]

The ordered pattern of life at Tolstoy Farm was in many ways akin to the discipline of monastic "rule". However, Gokhale's experience at the settlement during his tour of South Africa in 1912 indicates there may have been more pride than humility in the asceticism of Gandhi and his followers at times. Gandhi was keen that Gokhale should see the Tolstoy Farm experiment, but during his brief visit he became ill. He was forced to suffer the hardships of settlement life whilst in poor health. Yet, he found this more tolerable than the excessive attention and concern showered upon him by Gandhi and the *satyagrahis*. It was Gokhale's practice in India never to permit anyone to wait upon him except a servant There were no servants at the settlement but he was upset with the settlers' concerned ministrations. He complained: "You all seem to think that you have been born to suffer hardships and discomforts, and people like myself have been born to be pampered by you. You must suffer today the punishment for this extremism of yours. I will not let you even touch me. Do you think that you will go out to attend to nature's needs and at the same time keep a commode for me? I will bear any amount of hardship but 1 will humble your pride."[86] Gokhale bore everything cheerfully, but allowed no one to serve him in any way, except to bring food.

By March 1911 it was apparent that the second *satyagraha* campaign was almost over. There were no plans to continue the settlement after the end of the struggle, but Gandhi had no desire to abandon Tolstoy Farm without first compensating Kallenbach for the expenditure he incurred in subsidising the experiment (he had spent some £600 on buildings alone). He wrote to Maganlal Gandhi of his decision to remain at the farm: "My struggle will not be over when our *satyagraha* struggle ends. It is as it should be. That I shall have to stay on at Mr. Kallenbach's farm is something not expected. I shall get plenty of experience even from that; and who knows, it may be for my good."[87] A number of settlers remained with Gandhi to work on the farm and tend the fruit trees. His educational and disciplinary experiments continued unabated. The austerities he began to practise at Phoenix had become a way of life at Tolstoy Farm.

After the Farm was eventually closed in 1913 many of his pupils joined Phoenix and played an important role in the final *satyagraha* struggle: "The training imparted in Tolstoy Farm proved to be of great use in this last fight. The mode of life accepted by the *satyagrahis* on the Farm became an invaluable asset in the struggle. It was copied and improved upon in Phoenix."[88] In his recollections of this period Gandhi doubted whether the political struggle could have been maintained for eight years without the extra funds and moral support the Tolstoy Farm experiment attracted. As a symbol of unity, sacrifice and strength he believed the experiment had proved invaluable.[89]

During a trip to South Africa, in 1968, some friends helped Erikson to find Tolstoy Farm. Nobody in the vicinity had heard of Gandhi, and it was only with some difficulty that they found the farm, which was at that time occupied by an Afrikaner farmer and his family. With regard to Kallenbach, a person of that name told Erikson on the telephone that there had once been a "wealthy eccentric" in the family.[90] The Indian community acquired the original building of the farm as a memorial to Gandhi.

The Educational Experiments — A Non-Formal Approach

Gandhi's educational theory and practice played a most important, but controversial role as the integral link between all his manifold concerns. After many years of piecemeal experimentation his ideas evolved into a coherent and consistent philosophy. His primary objective was to develop a practical means of providing all Indians with the minimum education necessary to understand the complexities of their environment, and to be self-sufficient within that environment.

Gandhi believed that the main aim of education was "character-building" and he found in the writings of Tolstoy, Ruskin, Emerson and Thoreau much that confirmed his belief. For instance, addressing a gathering on the nature of scholarship in 1837, Emerson said: "The one thing in the world of value is the active soul. This every man is entitled to; this every man contains within him, although in almost all men obstructed, and as yet unborn. The soul active sees absolute truth and utters truth.... Of course, he who has put forth his total strength in fit actions has the richest return of wisdom.... Character is higher than intellect. Thinking is the function. Living is the functionary.... I hear therefore with joy whatever is beginning to be said of the dignity and necessity of labour to every citizen."[91]

Tolstoy too laid much stress on manual activity as an essential expression of religious faith and a sound basis for spiritual development. But the direction Gandhi's educational thought would take ultimately is most clearly indicated in Ruskin's preface to the first edition of *Unto This Last*. In its germinal stage Gandhi's concept of self-supporting education was indistinguishable from Ruskin's suggestion that "any man, or woman or boy, or girl, out of employment, should be at once received at the nearest school and set to such work as it appeared, on trial, they were fit for, at a fixed rate of wages determinable every year." Ruskin also proposed that training schools associated with "manufactories and workshops" should be set up for boys.[92] Common to Gandhi and all these thinkers is the idea that education, to be practical and effective, cannot be divorced from manual work.

Though Gandhi had shown an inclination to teach prior to his life in South Africa, it was in his own household in Durban and later in Johannesburg that he first began to give practical expression to his views on education. The first lessons he taught his children were concerned with voluntary work and the dignity of labour rather than literary education. He refused to allow the boys to be educated under the prevailing formal educational system, which he argued was of little use and did not produce men and women capable of fulfilling their duty to society. He always regarded character-building as the principal aim of education and the foundation upon which any subsequent learning rested. This meant that "under ideal conditions, true education could be imparted only by the parents, and that then there should be the minimum of outside help".[93]

Gandhi's children did not share his insight into the damage caused by adherence to an alien system of education. They resented being deprived of an opportunity to receive an English literary education. An Indian friend once offered to pay the cost of educating one of Gandhi's sons in England. The offer was refused and another boy sent from Phoenix, contracted tuberculosis soon after reaching England and was forced to return home. Though Harilal was the only son to break away from his father's influence (and probably as a consequence suffered from guilt for the remainder of his life) the evidence suggests that all the boys were frustrated and dissatisfied with the education they received. Nirmala Gandhi, wife of the third son, Ramdas, in an interview with Ved Mehta during the 1970s, said: "Poor Ramdasji, he always blamed Bapu for not giving him any formal Western education to speak of — Bapu did not believe in it. He thought all types of work, big or small, were equally worthwhile. In fact, he thought that running a kitchen was more important than teaching at a university, since the universities supported British rule. Poor, poor, Ramdasji.... Later on, Bapu sent him back to South Africa, where he really belonged."[94] In retrospect, it would appear that Gandhi's sons were the victims of their father's extraordinary role in contemporary history, rather than of his neglect.

On one occasion, at Phoenix, Harilal complained bitterly to Millie Polak: "My father was properly educated; why can't I be?" She sympathised with him, and repeated Gandhi's arguments by way of explanation. "That is all very well," Harilal replied, "but my father could not do the work he is doing if he had not been educated, and I want to be too."[95] Both the Polaks remonstrated with Gandhi over his apparent failure to give his sons a "proper education", and his insistence that whatever instruction they did receive should be in the Gujarati medium. In this context Albert West also disagreed with Gandhi's views. Though he understood that scholastic education was unnecessary for the formation of character, he was confused by Gandhi's determination to have his way on the question of his sons' education.

In 1920 a friend of West, who was also a co-worker with Gandhi during the Rowlatt *satyagraha (1919),* wrote to him from London, criticising Gandhi's methods: "He does not seem to me to realise what a very imperfect thing is the human nature which is his material for constructing a better scheme of things, and to my mind he makes the fatal mistake, which the greatest teachers have always avoided, of supposing that everyone is immediately capable of attaining the Kingdom of Heaven." West recalls that many of those who worked in close association with Gandhi in South Africa at times observed the same thing — "And yet we loved him in spite of it, or rather, because of it".[96]

When Gandhi first wrote down his views on education in *Hind Swaraj* (1909) he asked that the pretension of learning many sciences be abandoned and that ethical education be given more priority. He also saw dangers to Indian culture and society inherent in the use of English as the medium of instruction. The thoughts of the renowned educationist and activist, Paulo Friere, are pertinent to Gandhi's belief that adherence to the British system of education amounted to an acceptance of cultural, in addition to political and economic imperialism:

> Education as the exercise of domination stimulates the credulity of students, with the ideological intent (often not perceived by educators) of indoctrinating them to adapt to the world of oppression.... Nor may a revolutionary society inherit these methods from an oppressing society .... one does not liberate men by alienating them.[97]

To counteract the tendency towards acculturation evident amongst India's elites during British rule Gandhi felt that Indians desperately needed a universal language with which to identify. "if we can do this we can drive the English language out of this field; through our slavery the nation has been enslaved and it will be free with our freedom", he wrote.[98] Using strong language Gandhi later reiterated in his autobiography, his opposition to the use of English: "It has always been my conviction that Indian parents who train their children to think and talk in English from their infancy betray their children and their country. They deprive them of the spiritual and social heritage of the nation, and render them to that extent unfit for the service of the country."[99]

Gandhi's first experiment with education in a school environment was at Phoenix. Several months after the establishment of the settlement Gandhi described the scheme to Gokhale and claimed that the community was patterned after the Fergusson College in Pune, a charitable institution run by the Deccan Education Society. Though it is a moot point to what extent Phoenix was fashioned after Fergusson College, Gandhi wanted" Gokhale's support for *Indian Opinion* and the settlement. He informed Gokhale enthusiastically of his intention to open a boarding school on the grounds of Phoenix, "second to none in South Africa", primarily for Indian children but open to any child able to board. To assist his scheme he asked Gokhale to send two or three graduates with an aptitude for teaching, "who bear a blameless character and who would be prepared to work for a mere living".[100]

The modest development of the Phoenix school that did take place was a far cry from these ambitious plans. The grandiosity of the envisaged scheme indicates that even at this early stage of Gandhi's career as a public worker he was preparing to spread his "gospel" on a large scale. He exhorted young Indians in South Africa to dedicate themselves to educational work as a labour of love; to prepare for a long and strenuous struggle; and to be not only content with poverty, but to train themselves for the vocation.[101] In reply to a youth who wished to join Phoenix after the end of the second *satyagraha* campaign in 1911, Gandhi outlined the strict regimen followed by pupils there:

> In, Phoenix 1. you will have observe *brahmacharya;* 2. you will be under a vow of scrupulous regard for truth; 3. you will have to do chiefly manual labour, i.e., work with the hoe and shovel 4. if you intend to add to your book learning, please forget all about it."Whatever addition comes naturally or because circumstances demand it will be welcome; 5. you should make up your mind that our duty is to strengthen character rather than acquire book-learning; 6. you should embrace absolute poverty. You should think of joining Phoenix only if you would and can do this. You should tell yourself that life there will grow harder as the days pass and know that this is for your good.[102]

In the early days of Phoenix the school was conducted in the house of Cordes, the German Theosophist from Rhodesia. The original class consisted of the Gandhi boys and several children, of non-indentured Indians, who lived in huts about one mile from Phoenix. Chhaganlal Gandhi taught arithmetic, Maganlal Gandhi took Gujarati lessons, Cordes gave lessons in English, and other settlers contributed whatever they could in haphazard fashion. The various *satyagraha* campaigns swelled the number of pupils considerably as Gandhi took the responsibility for educating the sons of gaoled *satyagrahis*.

During the second phase of the *satyagraha* struggle two or three boys from the cities were billeted with each family at Phoenix.

Though this situation only lasted for between eight to ten months it placed a severe strain on the financial resource and social harmony of the settlement. While the boys were reasonably well-behaved, it remained that they were unaccustomed to the hardships of life at Phoenix and found it difficult to settle down. Among the boys were Muslims and Christians, and though the Hindu families were encouraged to ensure that the guest students were not treated as outsiders, Prabhudas Gandhi recalls that his family members, for instance, despite their efforts to reconcile the presence of non-Hindus in the household, did not achieve emotionally the ideal set before them by Gandhi. After Gandhi's departure for London in 1909 the experiment of lodging students with settlement families was terminated and never renewed.[103]

Yet, the educational experiment did progress. During the last phase of the *satyagraha* struggle money was raised to build a school; children of civil disobedients" again stayed at Phoenix; and sickly children from poor Indian families in the cities and towns were nursed back to health and received schooling whilst at the settlement. "If the first note was simplicity, the second was universal brotherhood," wrote Andrews, "for here distinction of creed and race and colour had been resolved in a higher synthesis which was wonderful to witness .... No one was a servant in Gandhi's household, or rather all were servants of one another."[104]

The system of education at Phoenix was erratic. The teachers and the text-books were frequently changed and Gandhi was rarely able to lend his guiding hand to the experiment. For as long as Cordes remained at Phoenix (he later left for India to pursue his interest in Theosophy, and died at Sevagram *Ashram* in 1960) he was principal of the school. In accordance with the aim of strengthening the moral character of the pupils, attention was paid to the simultaneous development of mind and body, but in contrast with Gandhi's approach Cordes was a strict disciplinarian.[105] The children were required to spend three hours at school, two hours on agriculture, two hours in the printing press, and, time allowing, to read their lessons at night When Gandhi could spare the time he would discuss religion, important events, people and books with them as they did manual work.

The Indian children were required to speak in their own language at home and to spend time learning other Indian languages. Gandhi would impress upon them the importance of ancient Indian culture, but though he wanted the children to live a life of extreme simplicity and to identify themselves with the very poor, he nevertheless encouraged them to "take full advantage of modern science in work, in the fields, in the home and elsewhere."[106] Each day would thus involve instruction in general and literary knowledge, various techniques of creative work and a great deal of physical exercise.

Gandhi never compelled or coerced the children to do anything, and believed that they should neither be insulted nor humiliated for any reason. To ensure that they developed as responsible members of the settlement nothing of import was kept from them, and when they presented themselves to him in the evening after the chores were finished he would praise their efforts and offer further encouragement. In reply to his son Manilal's anxious queries with regard to further education Gandhi summed up his attitude to the Phoenix experiment:

> First of all, we shall have to consider how we can realise the self and how serve our country. After we do this, we can explain what Phoenix is. For realising the self, the first essential thing is to cultivate a strong moral sense. Morality moans the acquisition of virtues such as fearlessness, truth, *brahmachanya* and so on. Service is automatically rendered to the country in this process of cultivating morality. Phoenix is a great help in this process. I believe that it is very difficult to preserve morality in cities where people live in congestion and there are many temptations. That is why the wise have recommended solitary places like Phoenix. Experience is the real school... Phoenix is not perfect but we wish it to become so. ...The school is a means to achieve our end. If it breaks down, we shall know that we are not yet fit for that kind of work.[107]

This answer may not have consoled the boy but it is a clear indication of Gandhi's faith in the ancient ashramic educational system of *aryavarta* and his determination to make Phoenix or some future community the fundamental experiment of his life.

Political activism would always remain secondary to constructive service offered through the dynamics of non-violence. During all the political agitations Gandhi always had the presence of mind to attend to the problems of social construction work.

Yet, his resolve to reconcile social service with an active political life on occasion caused him considerable anguish. It is ironical that while he yearned to be able to concentrate his efforts on community service, his sons longed for more opportunity to express their own individuality.[108]

The Tolstoy Farm community founded in 1910 and disbanded in 1913, proved to be an ideal laboratory for Gandhi's educational experiments. "Tolstoy Farm was a family in which I occupied the place of the father," wrote Gandhi, "and that I should so far as possible shoulder the responsibility for the training of the young."[109] The routine of the children on the farm was divided between attending classes (Kallenbach and Pragji Desai assisted with these) and contributing to the maintenance of the farm. As at the Phoenix Settlement manual work was combined with instruction on a daily basis, but Gandhi took this one step further at Tolstoy by introducing vocational training to give "all-round development to the boys and girls". Although at this stage there was no attempt to educate the children through the medium of a specific handicraft, Gandhi enabled each child to become self-supporting by supplementing their education with vocational training. Their ages ranging from six to sixteen, the children had on an average eight hours of manual training per day, and one or, at the most, two hours of book learning."[110]

An added dimension of the Tolstoy Farm experiment was the decision to hold co-educational classes, and indeed to encourage the boys and girls to do everything together. Gandhi had an implicit faith in the essential "purity" of children. Whenever an incident occurred to shake this faith he would accept responsibility, and fast as penance for the offence. He continued to believe in the benefits of co-education, but to guard against moral lapses he would ensure that a more stringent regimen was followed in later years.

The activities which the young contributed their energies to at Tolstoy Farm included general labouring, cooking, scavenging, sandal-making, simple carpentry and messenger work. But Gandhi did not recommend manual activities merely because they were materially productive or remunerative. In addition to productive crafts, manual work of a purely constructive nature was also essential for the maintenance and development of community life. The contribution of work such as sweeping, scavenging and water fetching was seen to be invaluable to the psychological, social and moral well-being of an integrated community. Gandhi's objective in this context was to inculcate the ideals of social service and citizenship through all the activities of children from the earliest formative years.

Conclusion

When Gandhi left South Africa in 1914 his ideas and ideals had a strong foundation in experience, and the pattern his life would subsequently follow lay firmly rooted in the inspiration and knowledge drawn from the twenty-one years spent in an alien land.

During the South African years he had refined his asceticism, setting the standards of austerity he would in future expect his followers to maintain. Gandhi had not fully adopted the religious way of life at Phoenix, but at Tolstoy Farm his spirituality permeated community life. At Tolstoy he was at a physical and spiritual peak, which Pyarelal believed he never reached again in India. He was developing ideas and putting them into practice at a greater pace then previously and, in Pyarelal's words, "was like a blazing meteor".[111]

Tolstoy Farm was a home for *satyagrahis* and in future Gandhi's communities would play a vital role in his political campaigns. They provided moral and economic support to active *satyagrahis* and were an ideal training ground for potential *satyagrahis.* At Phoenix and Tolstoy Farm he was experimenting with ideas formulated during his student years in London and early years in South Africa. The two communities had developed as an expression of his main aims, and on the basis of the asceticism fostered at Phoenix and Tolstoy Farm he waged a series of non-violent campaigns against the South African Government with some success.

His antagonism towards modern materialistic civilisation which had begun during his student days in London, had grown in South Africa. In 1909 he had set out the issues which most concerned him in *Hind Swaraj,* a short polemical tract which he called "a severe condemnation of modern civilisation",[112] In essence the message was that modern civilisation, of which the British Raj was but an expression posed a severe threat to Indian society. The Raj could only be combated through true self-rule, achieved not by social or political violence, but by a renascence of the highest ascetic values of personal renunciation and non-violent action. Gandhi had reached such a position as a result of his growing disenchantment with the British Empire and with Western civilisation in general.

Increasingly, Gandhi stressed his idea of *satyagraha* as a means of returning to the natural condition of man. The approach permeated his thought and action. For him *satyagraha* had become not merely a political technique of rebellion but an alternative medium of education and way of life. Moreover, he had come to believe that this way of life could only reach its zenith in India.[113] Yet how this was to work out, he was still unsure when he departed from South Africa for London in 1914:

> "There was, and there would be, much vanity in his poverty, much conceit in his humility, and much stubborn persistence in his helplessness, until he would find a leverage to make for himself and for the destitute Indians—out of poverty, humility and helplessness a new strength and a new instrument."[114]

NOTES

1. Woodcock, *Gandhi*, pp. 28.9.
2. *The Vegetarian*, 18 May 1895 ; CWMG, Vol. 1, pp. 180-6.
3. *Ibid.*
4. *Ibid.*
5. Cf., N.B, Workman, *"Monasticism"*, Encyclopedia of the Social Sciences; Dom E. C. Butler, "Monasticism", *The Cambridge Medieval History* (London: Cambridge University Press, 1911), Vol. 1; also Robert Nisbet, *The Social Philosophers* (St. Albans: Paladin, 1976)
6. *Harijan*, 29 August 1936.
7. Radha Kumud Mookerji, *Ancient Indian Education* (London : Macmillan & Co., 1951), pp. xxvi — xxx.
8. *Ibid.*, p. 16.
9. C. F. Andrews, "Mr. Gandhi at Phoenix", *Modern Review*, Vol. XV, no. 5, May 1914, pp. 563-4.
10. Cited in Ashe, *op. cit.*, p. 131.
11. CWMG, vol. 40, p. 144.
12. Gandhi to Maganlal Gandhi, 27 January 1910, *Ibid.*, vol. 10, pp. 138-9.
13. *Autobiography*, pp. 220-2.
14. *The Vegetarian*, 18 May 1895, CWMG, Vol. 1, pp. 180-6.
15. See Pyarelal, *op. cit.*, p. 548.

16. *Autobiography,* pp. 245-6.
17. Ashe, *op. cit.,* p. 83.
18. *Indian Opinion,* 12 December 1904.
19. *Ibid.*
20. Albert West, "In the Early Days with Gandhiji", *The Illustrated Weekly of India,* 3,17 & 31 October, 1965.
21. Gandhi to Maganlal Gandhi, 24 November 1909,CWMG, Vol. 10, p. 69.
22. West, op. cit.
23. *Autobiography,* pp. 250-2.
24. *Ibid.,* p. 251.
25. Millie Graham Polak, *Mr. Gandhi: The Man* (Bombay : Vora and Co., 1949), p. 67.
26. West, *op. cit.,* see also *Autobiography,* pp. 252-4.
27. *Ibid.*
28. Polak, *op. cit.,* p. 40.
29. Gandhi to Maganlal Gandhi, 27November&2Decernberl909, CWMC, Vol. 10, pp. 81-2, 87.
30. *Ibid.*
31. Ashe, *op. cit.,* pp. 84-5.
32. Prabhudas Gandhi, *My Childhood with Gandhi* (Ahmedabad: Navajivan Publishing House, 1957), p. 39.
33. *Ibid.*
34. West, op. cit.
35. *ibid.,* see also *Autobiography,* pp. 254-5.
36. *Ibid.,* pp. 257-8.
37. *Ibid.,* pp. 258-9; see also West, op. cit.
38. *Autobiography, p 259*
39. *Ibid.,* pp. 255-56.
40. *Ibid.,* pp. 183-5.
41. Robert Payne, *The Life and Death of Mahatma Gandhi* (London: The Bodley Head, 1969), p. 149.
42. *Autobiography,* p. 231.
43. For example, see Ashe, *op. cit.,* pp. 88-9. The author has written : "Too many admirers of the saints have slid over this difficulty. Can you let down people who love and trust you, in the name of integrity? Can you sustain your own hand of virtue out of the generosity of people who disagree? Can you turn somebody else's cheek? Apart from a few scattered words of regret, Gandhi seldom admitted that he saw any dilemma ...how to obey the uncompromising command, and live with it, yet live with other people too. With one's wife and children, for example." See also Payne, *op. cit.,* pp. 186,188.
44. For example, see. Payne, *op. cit.,* pp. 188-9, 249-53.
45. In H. H, Gerth and C. Wright Mills (eds), *From Max Weber, Essays in Sociology* (London : Routledge and' Kegan Paul, 1948), pp. 253-4.
46. *Ibid.*
47. *Indian Opinion,* March 10, 1908.
48. Gerth and Milk, *op. cit.,* pp. 248-9.
49. *Autobiography,* p. 74.
50. *Ibid.,* p. 228.
51. *Ibid.* pp. 174,177,224-8; see also M. K. Gandhi, *Key to Health and Nature Cure* (Ahmedabad : Navajivan Publishing House, 1948 and 1954 respectively).

52. *Autobiography,* p. 264.
53. Gandhi received affirmation for his beliefs in the writings of Tolstoy and Thoreau. For example, see *The Writings of Henry David Thoreau — Early Essays and Miscellanies* (New Jersey : Princeton University Press, 1975), p. 275.
54. *Indian Opinion,* 10 December 1907 & 4 September 1912; see also West, *op. cit.*
55. *Ibid.*
56. Polak, *op. cit.,* p. 41.
57. *Ibid.,* pp. 37-8, 41-50, 63-7.
58. West, *op. cit.*
59. *Ibid.*
60. *Ibid.;* see also Polak, *op. cit.,* pp. 108-10.
61. *Indian Opinion,* Golden Jubilee No., 1914.
62. West, *op. cit.*
63. *Ibid.*
64. Albert West to Gandhi, 3 March 1918, S. N. 7605.
65. West, *op. cit.*
66. *Ibid.*
67. *Indian Opinion,* 4 August 1961.
68. Arun Gandhi, Interview held in Bombay, 26 February 1981.
69. *Ibid.*
70. Ela Ramgobin (daughter of Manilal and Sushila Gandhi) to R. M. Thomson, 21 April 1981.
71. Fay Goldie, "Last of the Gandhi', in South Africa", *The Illustrated Weekly of India,* 3 October 1971, pp. 19, 21.
72. 'Satyagraha i.n4 South Africa", CWMG, Vol. 29, p. 188, hereinafter "Satyagraha in South Africa", later published by Navajivan Publishing House, Ahmedabad (1938).
73. *Indian Opinion,* 11 June 1910.
74. Erikson, *op. cit.,* p. 210.
75. *Harijan,* 29 June 1935.
76. *Indian Opinion,* 18 June 1910.
77. "Satyagraha in South Africa", p. 190.
78. *Autobiography,* p. 275.
79. Cf. *Ibid.* pp. 285-7; also Polak, *op. cit.,* pp. 107-15.
80. *Autobiography,* p. 278.
81. See "Satyagraha in South Africa".
82. *Ibid.,* p. 191. "
83. *Ibid.*
84. *Autobiography,* p. 274.
85. "Satyagraha in South Africa".
86. *Ibid.*
87. Gandhi to Maganlal Gandhi, March 9, 1911, *CWMG,* Vol.10, p. 446.
88. *Indian Opinion,* Golden Jubilee No., 1914.
89. "Satyagraha in South Africa".
90. Erikson, *op. cit.*
91. Ralph Waldo Emerson, "The American Scholar", in Nissim Ezekiel (ed.), *An Emerson Reader* (Bombay: Popular Prakashan, 1965), pp. 175,178,179,180.
92. Cited in M. S. Patel, *The Educational Philosophy of Mahatma Gandhi* (Ahmedabad: Navajivan Publishing House, 1953).

93. *Autobiography,* p. 278.
94. Ved Mehta, *Mahatma Gandhi and His Apostles* (Middlesex : Penguin Books, 1977), pp. 51-2.
95. Polak, *op. cit.,* pp. 53-4.
96. West, *op. cit.*
97. Paulo Friere, *The Pedagogy of the Oppressed* (Middlesex: Penguin Books, 1972), p. 52.
98. *Hind Swaraj or Indian Home Rule,* cited in Ram K. Vepa, *New Technology, A Gandhian Concept* (New Delhi: Gandhi Book House, 1975), p. 245.
99. *Autobiography,* p. 261.
100. Gandhi to G. K. Gokhale, 13 January 1905, CWMG, Vol. 14, pp. 332-3.
101. *Indian Opinion,* 23 December 1905.
102. Gandhi to Raojibhai Patel, 29 November 1911, CWMG, Vol. 11, p. 191.
103. Prabhudas Gandhi, *op. cit.,* pp. 48-50.
104. Andrews, op. cit., p. 565.
105. Prabhudas Gandhi, *op. cit.,* pp. 55-6.
106. *Ibid., p.* 68.
107. Gandhi to Manilal Gandhi, 24 November 1909, CWMG, Vol. 10. p. 7G.
108. See Gandhi to Manual Gandhi, 27 September and 22 October 1909, *Ibid.,* Vol. 9, pp. 435-6, 495.
109. *Autobiography, p. 27S.*
110. *Harijan,* 18 September 1937.
111. Pyarelal, Interview held in New Delhi, 30 November 1981.
112. *Hind Swaraj* (Ahmedabad: Navajivan Publishing House, 1938), p. 16.
113. See *Indian Opinion,* Golden Jubilee No., 1914.
114. Erikson, *op. cit.,* pp. 152-3.

3

The Satyagraha Ashram

On the voyage to Bombay from London in 1915 Gandhi no doubt had a presentiment of the stormy path his life in India would follow. He voiced his uncertainty in a letter to Albert West: "I have been so often prevented from reaching India that it seems hardly real that I am sitting in a ship bound for India. And, having reached that, what shall I do with myself? However, 'Lead kindly light, amid the encircling gloom, lead Thou me on'. That thought is my solace, and may it be yours in the darkest moments."[1] Yet by the time of his arrival in India Gandhi did have some idea of where he was going. He outlined the main objective of his proposed programme of work in an interview with the *Madras Mail*. On the advice of this Political mentor, Gokhale, he had decided to avoid involvement in political matters for one year to familiarise himself with the realities of the Indian situation. He was however, determined to continue the Phoenix experiment.[2]

Though ostensibly fashioned after the traditional pattern of an ashram, i.e., a place of spiritual retreat, Gandhi clearly envisaged a much wider role for his community. It would train young men and women to be "ideal" servants of the country. Self-realisation would be the ultimate goal, but rather than the traditional quietist withdrawal from all social concerns, active involvement in social service would be the means. The concept appeared inherently contradictory to many, but to Gandhi, armed with his interpretation of the *Bhagavad Gita* as a doctrine of selfless action and consciousness of the immense problems facing the Indian people, there seemed no other recourse.

By orienting his proposed scheme towards rural society and "service to the motherland" Gandhi sought from the outset to identify with the struggling masses living in India's 700,000 villages. It was this ability never to dissociate himself from the people at large that distinguished Gandhi from the moderate school of politicians who dominated the arena of public activity accessible to Indians during his years in South Africa. Western educated, and maintaining only tenuous links with the great mass of the Indian people, such men were mainly concerned with consolidating a position of influence in their own localities. The Muslim League leaders and extremists such as B. G. Tilak and Aurobindo Ghose were exceptions, but beyond a limited circle of influence the average Congressman was uninterested in, and detached from the aspirations and concerns of the vast majority of his countrymen.

> Rarely did they have access to networks of local power or resources for leadership which would have enabled them to mobilise wider sections of society: even if they had, this would have been a course fraught with danger for them in their position of isolated success.[3]

For the remainder of his life Gandhi would repeatedly state that a *sarvodaya* society could not be realised without first paying attention to the man at the bottom of the social ladder. Social and economic exploitation of the poor must be removed. The *swaraj* (self-rule) of his vision was thus a "poor man's *swaraj*" in which the necessities of life were to be enjoyed by the weakest people in society. He stressed the need for the regeneration of the villages, with the removal of hunger and poverty as the main challenge.

In a famous speech at Benares Hindu University in 1916 Gandhi voiced many of his radical views and drew the attention of the Indian public to the plight of the villages. He declared that the salvation of India could only come through the peasant.[4] By championing the interests of groups such as labourers, peasants and the really poor in the villages, whose problems did not normally come within the purview of established politicians, he revealed the extent of untapped political resources in the country. His intention was to awaken the masses to his simple, non-violent technique of direct action, as a means of redressing all manner of wrongs. Local action to achieve the social and economic uplift of the downtrodden would be one objective, but more important in Gandhi's view was the need to arouse within the people a consciousness of the need to help themselves.

The Satyagraha Ashram 1915-1933

During the unsettled period in Gandhi's life, before the establishment of the Satyagraha Ashram in Ahmedabad, the group of relatives and co-workers from Phoenix who had departed from South Africa ahead of him in 1914 had been living at Rabindranath Tagore's Shantiniketan Ashram in Bengal. Shantiniketan was an experimental school founded on ashramic principles by Tagore at the turn of the century. It had a hundred and twenty-five students when the Phoenix party arrived in 1914. They were accommodated in a small compound, where they lived and worked. Under Maganlal Gandhi's direction they were expected to enhance the quality of life at their host institution by cultivating self-discipline and self-sufficiency and by service to other members of the ashram. Special emphasis was placed on agricultural work, particularly planting and maintaining of fruit trees, and the performance of tasks ranging from cooking and scavenging to the production of copra and ground-nut oil.

Gandhi expected his followers to set an example of simple living, creative manual work and tolerance towards others; the latter especially so in the light of the caste distinctions which operated in Shantiniketan at the time. In short, they were to follow the pattern of life established at Phoenix and Tolstoy Farm. Gandhi had written to them earlier:

> Personally, I have always felt, and it now appears that there is no institution today in the world to excel Phoenix in its ideals or its way of life. If there is any, the civilised world had not heard of it. I am happy that all of you have the same impression.[5]

He had been prepared to meet the expenditure incurred by the Phoenix group during their stay at Shantiniketan from the Satyagraha Fund set up during the days of struggle in South Africa, but Tagore welcomed the opportunity to accommodate Gandhi and his party and bore all the expenses.

When Gandhi and Kasturba arrived at Shantiniketan they were given a hearty greeting and shortly afterwards Tagore invited Gandhi to take over supervision of the ashram school programme.

Gandhi decided not to interfere with the pattern of teaching, but he did bring about a complete change in the daily regimen of the teachers and pupils. Initially he engaged them in a discussion of self-help: "I put it to the teachers that, if they and the boys dispensed with the service of paid cooks and cooked their food themselves, it would enable the teachers to control the kitchen from the point of view of the boys' physical and moral health, and it would afford the students an objectlesson in self-help."[6] Though one or two teachers remained unconvinced the experiment was successfully launched with the support of Tagore, who told the students, "the experiment contains the key to *swaraj*".[7]

To allow Gandhi a free hand in implementing his ideas Tagore withdrew from Shantiniketan for a short period to stay in another of his ashrams, Sriniketan. The servants and kitchen staff were given leave and the residents took over the manual tasks previously performed by them. Everyone joined in enthusiastically for the first few days but it was apparent after some time that certain members suffered from exhaustion due to overwork. The new system clearly hampered the method of teaching followed at Shantiniketan. Simplicity of living was the cornerstone of student life at the ashram, but the austerities introduced by Gandhi reduced the time and energy available for teachers and pupils to pursue literary interests and such extra-curricular cultural activities as art, music and dancing, all of which were specially emphasised by Tagore.[8] It was obvious to Gandhi that Shantiniketan could not become another Phoenix, and he hastened his search for a suitable location for his ashram.

The death of Gokhale in February 1915, unexpectedly brought to an end Gandhi's brief stay at Shantiniketan. Gokhale had been keen that Gandhi join the Servants of India Society on his return to India, and he no doubt appreciated Gokhale's support of his proposal to establish a community after the pattern of Phoenix. An account had been opened in the Society's books to provide him with funds for the proposed ashram and whatever public expenses he might incur in the course of his work.[9] However, with his influential benefactor gone Gandhi realised he could no longer expect to rely on funding from the Society.

Though a good deal of common ground existed between Gandhi and the Society, his unequivocal opposition to Western education and modern civilisation in general left members of the society uneasy, and perhaps a little afraid that he might set about dismantling the system to which they owed their own position of influence. In fact, disparities between the aims and aspirations of Gokhale's Society and Gandhi's vision of a free India had been evident some years before Gandhi returned to his homeland: "I do feel that the aims of Phoenix as well as the way of life there surpass those of the Society", he wrote to Maganlal in 1910. "What we are doing here is the real thing; what goes on in Poona is, leaving aside the motive, unreal."[10]

Gandhi had clearly been content to remain detached from the Society, and the sharp division amongst its members as to whether they should admit him in the light of his somewhat controversial views, convinced him that he should withdraw his application to avoid mutual embarrassment. He advocated the ascetic ideals which inspired the establishment of Phoenix and Tolstoy Farm, but the object of the Society was "to equip men to take part in every movement of modern life, educational, political and economic". The differences were irreconcilable, as Gandhi explained to V. S. Srinivasa Sastri, who succeeded Gokhale as President of the Society: "Whilst there is possibility of cooperation when we are working independently I can see that I would, as a member, become a disturbing factor. The methods of the society as such are so totally different from mine in many respects. Our common discipleship would constitute an indissoluble bond though we would be following out Mr. Gokhale's work from different viewpoints."[11] Gandhi tempered his early criticisms of the Society in later years, describing the Poona headquarters in his autobiography as a "place of pilgrimage".[12]

After withdrawing his application to join the Society, Gandhi set about fulfilling his promise to Gokhale by touring India and observing the current social and political situations. At the same time, he refrained from specific political comment on what he saw, confining himself to general remarks on the reform of the individual and society. After a trip to Calcutta and Burma he attended the Kumbha Mela, a religious festival held at Haridvar in northern India every twelve years. The Servants of India were sending a large volunteer corps for service, and Gandhi was invited to send the Phoenix party to assist them. Their experience at Shantiniketan had shown him that scavenger's work would be one of his and his co-workers' special functions in India. Led by

Maganlal Gandhi the Phoenix group took the responsibility for the disposal of excreta and cleaning of the festival area, while Gandhi spent the greater part of his time holding discussions on religion and other subjects with numerous people who called on him. He was surprised by the extent to which his reputation had preceded him to India, and bemoaned the excessive attention showered upon him as a result. "I felt as though I was between the devil and the deep sea" recalled Gandhi, "where no one recognised me, I had to put up with the hardships that fall to the lot of the millions in this land.... Where I was surrounded by people who had heard of me I was the victim of their craze for *darshan*."[13]

Gandhi was unimpressed with what he saw of religious fervour at Haridvar and determined to atone for the conduct around him. The feeling that he must purify himself was compounded by the lavish entertainment he had received from various hosts since returning from South Africa. To him it seemed that without imposing severe restrictions on himself he received more service than he gave. He vowed that without exception he would not eat more than five articles of food during any one day, and would never eat after dark. Thoughtless defecation on the roads and banks of the river assailed his senses at Haridvar. Everything he witnessed at the places of pilgrimage along the sacred river confirmed his belief that India was in a state of rapid moral and spiritual decay. "But the Haridvar experiences proved for me to be of inestimable value," he wrote, "they helped me in no small way to decide where I was to live and what I was to do."[14]

After leaving Haridvar Gandhi and the Phoenix party moved further up the river Ganges to Hrishikesh, a small place of pilgrimage for devout Hindus. Here he met and talked with a number of prominent religious men, including Acharya Ramadevji and Mahatma Munshiramji at his *gurukul* (religious school). Among the many questions discussed with them was the need to introduce instruction in manual skills into the curriculum of the *gurukul*. In answer to a *swami* confused by his decision not to wear the distinguishing sacred thread of the Hindus around the neck, Gandhi said, "I will not wear the sacred thread, for I see no necessity of it, when countless Hindus can go without it and yet remain Hindus. Moreover, the sacred thread should be a symbol of spiritual regeneration, presupposing a deliberate attempt on the

The Satyagraha Ashram

part of the wearer at a higher and purer life. I doubt whether in the present state of Hinduism and of India, Hindus can vindicate the right to wear a symbol charged with such a meaning. That right can come only after Hinduism has purged itself of untouchability, has removed all distinctions of superiority and inferiority, and shed a host of other evils and shams that have become rampant in it."[15] He now felt it imperative that he establish a permanent settlement somewhere as a practical expression of his ideas and ideals.

The Satyagraha Ashram was founded on 25th May 1915 at Ahmedabad, the erstwhile capital of Gujarat. Several alternative sites for the ashram had been suggested to Gandhi by friends including Haridvar, Vaidyanathadham (near Calcutta) and Rajkot, but he "had a predilection for Ahmedabad".[16] Friends there volunteered to make funds available for the ashram and a house for Gandhi and his followers. Moreover, Gandhi felt he could be of most service to India by working in his home province and communicating through his mother-tongue. Ahmedabad also had other attractions. It was an ancient centre of handloom weaving, and thus an appropriate location for his proposed scheme to revive hand-spinning and weaving. Ironically, the city was also a major growth centre of mill-made cloth, an industry introduced and financed by wealthy Indians on the British pattern which threatened to destroy all remnants of artisan spinning and weaving.

Another irony is that funds for the Ashram were made readily available by capitalists from Bombay and Ahmedabad. Gandhi's communitarian beliefs could hardly have appealed to big-business, but perhaps these businessmen envisaged grasping political power for themselves by patronising the Gandhian programmes. Communists later argued that the Ashram and the constructive work programme that grew out of its activities was a capitalist fraud designed to capture the national independence movement by exploiting a man greatly revered by the Indian people.[17] By the end of 1925 merchant and industrialist friends of Gandhi had donated approximately two hundred thousand rupees to the Ashram for the land and buildings alone, and were paying not less than eighteen thousand rupees per annum for its upkeep. Gandhi always maintained that they did so in the hope that he was developing the characters of the men, women and children who lived there.[18] However, it is clear that Gandhi's *swadeshi* campaign posed no immediate threat to vested interests of the moneyed classes *perse*. On the contrary, the sales of products made in Indian factories received a boost in the wake of Gandhi's propaganda. In the case of cotton mills, Gandhi accepted they would function side by side with the production of *khadi,* but that ultimately one would have to give way to the other. He believed that the mills would eventually be unable to compete with *khadi* once it was produced in every village. He explained to Birla — the Marwadi industrialist and supporter of Gandhi — in 1932, "for the time being people like you can have both the activities at the same time provided the ideal is kept: before the public in order to assert the truth".[19] He regretted his inability to do without their support, and admitted that the guarantee of monetary aid greatly undermined the spirit of sacrifice upon which Sabarmati was theoretically based. Yet he never discouraged benefactors.

The first site of the ashram in Ahmedabad was in Kochrab, a small village near the city. A barrister in Ahmedabad, Jivanlal Desai, offered to let his bungalow there to Gandhi and his parry of about twenty-five men and women. The first question to be settled was the name of the a shram. Among those suggested were "Sevashram" (abode of service), "Sevamandin" (temple of service), and "Tapovan" (abode of austerities). Gandhi liked "Sevashram" but discarded it as it did not emphasise the method of service to be employed in the ashram. He thought "Tapovan" was pretentious and that it would be presumptuous to call themselves *Tapasvis* (men of austerity), even though austerity was fundamental to their asceticism. They settled on "Satyagraha Ashram", as it conveyed both their goal and their method of service :

> Our creed was devotion to truth, and our business was the search for and insistence of truth. I wanted to acquaint India with the method I had tried in South Africa, and I desired to test in India the extent to which its application might be possible.[20]

In order to regulate the conduct of the Ashram Gandhi decided to formulate a code of rules and observances. A draft Constitution was printed and circulated among Gandhi's friends, who were invited to express their opinions on it. Not only did he hope to arouse their interest in the proposed activities of the Ashram, but that moral and material support from them would also be forthcoming. Gandhi defined an ashram as "a community of men of religion".[21] He believed it was not only an essential part of his own well-being, but essential to the practice of *satyagraha*. "Religion" was not used here in the context of theological or ritual dogma, but in the sense that all the activities and aspirations of the institution should be based on an unshakable faith in the principles of truth and non-violence.

At Kochrab there were no servants and the members were expected to follow a strict regimen of vegetarian food, manual labour, social service, celibacy, prayer and sleep. At Gandhi's behest the ashramites took nine vows, which amounted to a demanding code of asceticism: Truth-telling, non-violence, celibacy, control of the palate, non-stealing, non-possession, refusal to use foreign cloth, fearlessness, and acceptance of untouchables. "The vows were to be observed in an intelligent and creative way," observed B. R. Nanda, "they were not intended to be mechanical formulae, but as practical aids to moral and spiritual growth. They may appear to be platitudes, but nevertheless they embodied ancient truths which were none the less valid for not having been realised by the common run of mankind in workaday life."[22]

The vows were far from being an expression of Hindu orthodoxy. On the contrary, they challenged many of the basic precepts of caste and religious ideology. For instance, the traditional interpretation of *ahimsa* denied the right to put a suffering animal out of its misery. When Gandhi later permitted at the Sabarmati Ashram the mercy killing of a calf suffering from an incurable disease, his action was condemned in orthodox circles.[23]

A number of the vows, including those of truth, non-violence and chastity, were of universal application. Others, particularly the vow to eradicate untouchability and to practise fearlessness, were oriented towards a caste-ridden Indian society dominated by an alien government. Though Gandhi affirmed what he saw as the good and true of traditional Indian civilisation, he was deeply concerned about ridding it of aberrations such as child marriage, religious prostitution, animal sacrifice and untouchability. He also argued that the social and religious unification of the people was essential to the formation of a co-operative economy based on self-sufficiency. Not until Indians were free of the burden of racial prejudice and division on the basis of religion and caste could they hope to achieve self-rule. Moreover, in his view the traditional dichotomy between manual and intellectual work was harmful, as he explained in *Harijan* : divorce of the intellect from body-labour had made us perhaps the shortest-lived, most resourceless and most exploited nation on earth.[24]

He sought to break down caste ideology and remove the factors of alienation existing between the villager and the city-dweller, and between the manual and intellectual worker.

> I want to bring about an equalisation of status. The working classes have all these centuries been isolated and relegated to a lower status. They have been *shudras* and the word has been interpreted to mean an inferior status. I want to allow no differentiation between the son of a weaver, of an agriculturalist and of a school master.[25]

No caste distinctions were tolerated in the Kochrab and Sabarmati Ashrams and every member, child and adult alike, was required to contribute to the maintenance of the Ashram and to devote a certain amount of their time each day to the constructive work activities that gradually developed. These later included a spinning and weaving department, a cow-shed and a large farm. Gandhi clearly stated that the guiding principle of the Ashram's educational pattern was character-building, and that the children would be "constantly weaned from wealth hunger". One of the central proposals was to set up a National School within the Ashram to provide an education that would incline the pupils to remain in the Ashram on completion of their studies in order to serve their country. It was planned to have the students board at the Ashram and to discourage any involvement with family or activities which might disrupt their studies during the period spent there.

Reaction to Gandhi's proposals concerning the Ashram ranged from unreserved support to angry denunciation. Sadhu Magalnath from Hrishikesh praised the concept, and a correspondent from Madras welcomed the Ashram as embodying the spirit of *aryavarta*. Others could not come to terms with the severe austerity of the Ashram regimen, nor with the mandatory vow of celibacy.

The Satyagraha Ashram

The severest critics came from the ranks of the western educated, who rejected Gandhi's general condemnation of modern civilisation as shortsighted and irrational.[26]

However, the issue which generated the greatest controversy concerned the admittance into the Ashram of an untouchable family. Gandhi's action put the vow to accept untouchables to the test sooner than expected and threatened to disrupt his plans. Earlier he had informed his supporters in Ahmedabad of his intention to admit an untouchable to the Ashram, provided he met the other requirements, as soon as the opportunity arose. A *vaishnava* (devotee of Vishnu) friend had replied self-complacently, "Where is the untouchable who will satisfy your condition?"[27] As Ahmedabad was considered to be a stronghold of *Sanatana dharma,* which holds the caste system as one of the unchanging foundations of Hinduism, it was appropriate that Gandhi should begin his programme to undermine the orthodox ideology from there. In fact he had thrown down the gauntlet to the *sanatanists* in 1915 during a striking speech at Mayavaram in the Madras Presidency just prior to founding the Ashram. He had declared that *swadeshi* (the principle of using only articles of indigenous make) and the removal of untouchability would be his main concerns.[28]

Gandhi's move to admit a Gujarati Dhed (then considered untouchable caste) family into the Kochrab Ashram unequivocally associated the small community with a programme to uplift the disadvantaged classes of India, and the resultant controversy brought a great deal of notoriety on his shoulders. The admission of the family also brought open rebellion from Kasturba and another woman. In response to Kasturba's complaints Gandhi told her to leave the Ashram if she could not accept the situation and assured her they could part as friends. He seemed delighted with the turn of events. He was beginning to challenge some of the iniquitous beliefs of orthodox Hinduism at the heart of one of its oldest strongholds. It also afforded him an opportunity to demonstrate the efficacy of *satyagraha as* a technique of direct action. When supporters who had previously provided monetary aid withdrew their support in protest he spoke of shifting the Ashram to an untouchable area and living on whatever could be earned from manual labour. "It would mean much even for my staunchest co-workers", he told a friend. "It is of importance to me because it enables me to demonstrate the efficacy of passive resistance in social questions and when I take the final step, it will embrace swaraj ..."[29]

The family of Dheds, consisting of Dudabhai, his wife Danibhen and their daughter Lakshmi, bore the brunt of abuse during the furore over their admission. One instance occurred over the use of the well. The man employed by the owner of the bungalow to lift water became afraid that water from the buckets used by the Ashram would pollute him. He began cursing the Ashramites and molesting Dudabhai. Gandhi sought to pacify the man using the gentle *satyagraha* technique of winning over an opponent by suffering: "I told everyone to put up with the abuse and continue drawing water at any cost. When he saw that we did not return his abuse, the man became 'ashamed and ceased to bother us."[30]

Other pressures were exerted on the Dheds by the members of the Ashram themselves. The atmosphere was tense as funds dried up and the caste-Hindus of Ahmedabad threatened to boycott the Ashram. The prejudices Prabhudas Gandhi had seen expressed by members of his own family and other Indian families when boys of different religious faiths had been billeted at Phoenix were now surfacing again. The women of the Ashram were indifferent, if not openly hostile to the family who suffered many minor insults. Yet Gandhi's determination ultimately prevailed. After some time Kasturba became attached to the baby girl, who was later adopted by Gandhi. The precarious financial situation of the Ashram was alleviated unexpectedly by a donation from a wealthy textile magnate, Ambalal Sarabhai who became a close friend of the Gandhi family as well as a generous supporter.[31]

The Dhed family's perseverance set an example to the Ashram community, which, as a family, faced the problems arising out of the experiment and overcame them. For Gandhi it represented an important breakthrough in his programme to undermine the dehumanising ideology that human beings were impure by birth and that human function and aspiration could only be determined by caste.

> The admission of this family proved a valuable lesson to the Ashram. In the very beginning we proclaimed to the world that the Ashram would not countenance untouchability. Those who wanted to help the Ashram were thus put on their guard, and the work of the Ashram in this direction was considerably

simplified. The fact that it is mostly the real orthodox Hindus who have met the daily growing expenses of the Ashram is perhaps a clear indication that untouchability is shaken to its foundation. There are indeed many other proofs of this, but the fact that good Hindus do not scruple to help an Ashram where we go to the length of dining with the untouchables is no small proof.[32]

In themselves, these words from his autobiography served as useful propaganda for the removal of untouchability. It was written in the early 1920s during quiet periods of rest in the Ashram and during his confinement in Yervada Gaol, Poona, for the part he played in the Rowlatt Satyagraha and subsequent non-co-operation movement. The work was first published as a serial in Gandhi's journals, *Young India* and *Navajivan* (Gujarati).

Early in 1915 Gandhi had informed C. F. Andrews that he did not anticipate an occasion for *satyagraha* for five years, but a number of the young men and women being trained as *satyagrahis* in the Ashram would be called on to serve their country before then. Though Gandhi had attracted much attention and presented himself as a public figure during his year of voluntary probation, he had yet to establish himself as a public activist of national standing. In many ways the speech he delivered at the opening of Benares Hindu University on the evening of 16 February 1916, changed the situation. The unpalatable home-truths with which he confronted the dignitaries and the crowd attending the special occasion left no doubt that his was a new and persuasive voice of rebellion. "We may foam, we may fret, we may resent, but let us not forget that India of today, in her impatience, has produced an army of anarchists", he told the stunned gathering. "I am myself an anarchist but of another type."[33]

Suddenly people all over the country wanted to know what type of anarchist Gandhi actually was. He received a rush of invitations to make speeches, to open schools, and to attend conferences. On these occasions he rarely referred to politics but spoke in generalities on a wide range of subjects, including character building, the Ashram, hand-weaving, diet and the pursuit of truth and non-violence. Clearly he preferred to wait for an opportunity to explain his concept of non-violent "anarchism" by means of positive action. Meanwhile the Ashram was his retreat, where he collected his thoughts and devoted his energies to the concerns of the community. With moral authority as his only sanction he ruled the Ashram not so much as the head of a monastic community but as the patriarch of an extended family.

An opportunity to apply the *satyagraha* technique on a larger scale arose in 1917, a year which not only marked an important stage in the development of Gandhi's work programme but also saw the re-location and re-structuring of the Ashram. In response to a request by Rajkumar Shukla, a peasant from Champaran in Bihar, Gandhi visited the north Indian district to investigate the grievances of the villagers in the face of exploitation by British indigo planters. Though he had declared the uplift of India's villages to be his main concern his knowledge of rural problems was limited at this stage. He did not waste this chance to experiment at the village level.

Gandhi's experiences with the Champaran peasantry were a revelation to him. He was now convinced that work of a permanent nature would be impossible without proper village education. Everywhere he went in Champaran, due to dietary deficiencies and insufficient clean drinking water people were suffering from some form of ailment, Many were lame and prematurely senile, and many suffered from goitre. When some dirtily dressed women caught his attention on one occasion, he asked Kasturba to discover the reason for their condition. One of the women explained that she owned only one *sari* and therefore could not wash it. Gandhi was appalled by their lack of resources, ignorance and sheer idleness, and resolved to tackle the problem through the education of the children.

In consultation with his co-workers Gandhi decided to open primary schools in six villages. One of the agreements reached with the villagers was that they should provide the teachers with board and lodging and Gandhi and his colleagues would see to other expenses. As the parents became involved with the programme the schools were transformed into community projects. This approach significantly broadened the base of Gandhi's activism and sowed the seeds for the comprehensive village welfare schemes he launched during the 1920s and 1930s.

The expansion of his work into the massive field of village regeneration also required more money. Gandhi sent two circular letters from Champaran to sympathetic friends, setting out an exposition of the Ashram's aims and aspirations in general, and an outline of its activities as support for the renewed quest for monetary aid. The categories of expenditure listed were boarding and lodging expenses for the pupils staying in the Ashram, hand-weaving, the National School, the propagation of Hindi and Gandhi's social and political activities. Donors were assured that careful accounts were maintaine for all categories, and that copies would be circulated annually among supporters of the Ashram.[34]

The major problem in setting up the education scheme in Champaran was finding suitable teachers. It was difficult to attract local teachers who not only met Gandhi's exacting requirements but were also prepared to work either for a subsistence allowance or without remuneration at all. However, when he issued a wider public appeal for volunteer teachers there was a good response. Some came from as far away as Bombay and each school was staffed with men and women to avoid alienating any of the villagers. In addition to teaching duties the volunteers improved village sanitation and offered rudimentary medical care. Armed with only three drugs (quinine, sulphur ointment and castor oil) the volunteers, including women from the Satyagraha Ashram, treated thousands or people. For anything too complicated they consulted a doctor sent to Champaran at Gandhi's request by the Servants of India Society. The doctor made regular rounds of the villages, attending to the sick, organising the cleaning of wells, and teaching the villagers improved drainage and scavenging techniques. The scheme drew mixed responses from the villagers, some of whom helped as well as they could, whilst others were either hostile or apathetic. Gandhi discovered that volunteers without an academic background were more accustomed to village ways, did not alienate the people and thus attained the best results.

At Champaran Gandhi's concept of basic education, which he placed before Indian educationists for their scrutiny many years later in 1937, began to take concrete shape. In a letter to the District Magistrate of Champaran he set out the aims of the educational programme:

> In the schools I am opening, children under the age of twelve only are admitted. The idea is to get hold of as many children

as possible and to give them an all-round education, that is, a knowledge of Hindi or Urdu, and through that medium, of arithmetic, rudiments of history and geography, a knowledge of simple scientific principles and some industrial training. No cut and dried syllabus has been yet prepared, because I am going along an unbeaten track. I look upon our present system with horror and disgust. Instead of developing the moral and the mental faculties of the little children, it dwarfs them. In my experiment whilst I shall draw upon what is good in it, I shall endeavour to avoid the defects of the present system. The chief thing aimed at is contact of the children with men and women of culture and unimpeachable moral character. That, to me, is education. Literary training is to be used merely as a means to that end. The industrial training is designed to give the boys and girls who may come to us an additional means of livelihood. It is not intended that on completing their education, they should leave their hereditary occupation, namely agriculture, but make use of the knowledge gained in the school to refine agriculture and the agricultural life.[35]

Gandhi's approach was an unequivocal rebuttal of the prevailing English-oriented system of education and an announcement to British officialdom of his intention to develop an alternative to meet the educational needs of village India. Though the work in Champaran declined when Gandhi and his co-workers left the area, the experiment crystallised many of his ideas concerning education and laid the foundation for further research. "The volunteers had come for temporary periods, I could not secure any more from outside, and permanent honorary workers from Bihar were not available," recalled Gandhi. "The few months' work in Champaran, however, took such deep root that its influence in one form or another is to be observed there even today."[36]

During one of Gandhi's brief visits to the Kochrab Ashram at the rime of the Champaran struggle, it was decided to seek a new location. Plague had broken out in Kochrab and despite strict adherence to the rules of cleanliness set down for the Ashram, Gandhi thought it impossible to ensure the well-being of the children. Ashram activities were not oriented towards village work at the time and the ashramites had no means of alleviating the surrounding insanitary conditions. With the assistance of a merchant in Ahmedabad, Punjabhai Hirachand, an alternative site was found in the vicinity of Sabarmati Gaol, three or four miles to the north of Kochrab on the banks of the Sabarmati river.

The site appealed to Gandhi for several reasons. As "gaol-going" was an expected outcome of *satyagraha* he thought the choice of a site in the vicinity of a gaol most appropriate. Furthermore, he knew that the sites chosen for the construction of gaols were generally clean. Another attraction was the open ground of the site, providing space for simple buildings to house the ashramites, now numbering forty. In South Africa and at Kochrab Gandhi had favoured locations for his communities that were neither too far nor too near a city. The pattern later was to change with the establishment of the Sevagram Ashram adjacent to a small village in Central India, but the Sabarmati location conformed to Gandhi s ideal.

It is also significant that the Sabarmati river and the area in which the Ashram was established have a unique place in Hindu mythology. A little to the south of the Ashram land is an old temple dedicated to Dadhichi Rishi, a saintly sage who is believed to have had his ashram on the site chosen by Gandhi. The legend, with which Gandhi was familiar, had it that in order to defeat the *asuras* (demons) the Vedic God Indra, the Lord of Heaven, approached Dadhichi to beg of him a rib from his body, with which to forge a mighty weapon. The sage granted the request and sacrificed his life by a long fast. Indra transformed the rib he sought into Vajra (the Thunderbolt) and defeated the *asuras* in battle. Like the *rishi* of mythology, on a number of occasions Gandhi too was prepared to sacrifice himself by fasting, indeed it became one of the most effective weapons in the *satyagraha* arsenal.

The ashramites faced many difficulties during the period before the setting up of a permanent settlement at Sabarmati, and these were compounded by Gandhi's absence. He was preoccupied with the work in Champaran, and though the inspiration for the removal and the choice of a new site had been his, the responsibility of setting up and consolidating the new ashram fell to Maganlal Gandhi. The monsoon was about to break and provisions had to be brought from the city four miles away. The early stages of lie Sabarmati Ashram were in fact reminiscent of the hardships associated with the setting up of Phoenix and Tolstoy

Farm. The ashramites lived under canvas and utilised a tin shed for a common kitchen. The land was infested with venomous snakes which, as in South Africa, they avoided killing unless absolutely necessary.

The hardships were endured and the Ashram took shape under the supervision of Maganlal. Simple structures of mud brick, tiles and wood, which was thickly painted with coal tar to seal it, were erected, including, in time, a school building, a dining hall and kitchen, a library, and the *Vanatshala,* in which handlooms were installed. Initially Gandhi lived in the latter structure, but later he and Kasturba moved to 'Hridyakunj', built adjacent to the rise of the river bank, which included a small central hall, three rooms, a small kitchen and store room. Kasturba had one of the back rooms, while Gandhi utilised the hall and the front room with a verandah facing the river. As the need arose new buildings were constructed and extensions made to existing structures. Gandhi insisted on good latrines and urinals, and a quick-drainage sewage system. It was also decided to lay down broad roads which gradually linked all the component parts within the Ashram. To facilitate the work Gandhi advised Maganlal to arrange for the colection of stone, gravel and other building materials, in whatever quantity they were available.

Maganlal played a vital role in the running and development of the Ashram. Whenever Gandhi was caught up in the whirl of politics, the onerous task of managing the community and its activities fell on Maganlal, which placed heavy demands on him. He frequently wrote to Gandhi in his absence requesting advice and seeking moral support for decisions he had made that were unpopular with other ashramites. At one point when Maganlal was faced with wholesale dissatisfaction among the ashramites as a result of the hardships experienced during the setting up of the Sabarmati Ashram, Gandhi wrote to remind them of their obligation to suffer for the good of the country :

> We should always be prepared for death and live without fear. To teach one to live such a life — that is the aim of the Ashram. You are all doing something great indeed. It is an excellent thing to live in tents and put up with hardships. If we had stayed on in the bungalow, we would have had to hang our heads in shame. Living in tents you are all getting beaten into shape. You

are being educated. You are setting an example. You are learning to fight it out with Nature.³⁷

During the periods Gandhi spent in the Ashram he was undisputed head of the family, but in his absence the problems of managing the heterogeneous community were brought into sharp focus. The motley crowd at the Ashram variously included little children and octogenarians, graduates of Indian, American and European universities, deeply religious men and sceptics, simple farmers and Sanskrit scholars. Among them were Pandit Khare, a musician who conducted the morning and evening prayers, in later years, Imam Saheb Bawazeer, the only permanent Muslim member of the Ashram who remained there with his family till his death in 1932, Pandit Totaram Sanadhya, a deeply religious man and an expert farmer who subsequently took charge of farming, and Surendranath Gupta a diligent worker who joined the Ashram in 1916 and remained until its closure. The Ashram was a human laboratory in which Gandhi experimented with himself and others, and where he and the other residents attempted to put his communal ideals into practice. Because of his total commitment to Gandhi's activities in South Africa, Maganlal Gandhi had received no formal education, and he did not possess Gandhi's ability to maintain a level of harmony and co-operation among the group. Ashramites complained to Gandhi of his quirk temper and a tendency to display partiality in his decision-making.

Over the years Gandhi had come to rely heavily on Maganlal's utter devotion to him and capacity for work. To avoid undue pressures being exerted on the Ashram when the time came to challenge the British administration, it had been decided early in 1918 to transfer everything, including Ashram premises and donations, to Maganlal's name. Though he was instructed by Gandhi to consult the other inmates and the teachers of the National School in all matters, all responsibility for the future of the Ashram and interrelated activities was vested in him.³⁸

Complaints against Maganlal placed Gandhi in an awkward position. On one occasion, faced with full-scale withdrawal from the Ashram in protest over Maganlal's style of management, Gandhi sought to explain that the fate of Maganlal and the Ashram were inextricably bound together. In an address to the ashramites he reaffirmed his belief that Phoenix had been his finest creation in South Africa, and declared that he would ask the Indian people not to judge him by the *satyagraha* campaigns but only by the Ashram. In Maganlal's defence he said: "Beside him Polak is a mere child; the blows that Maganlal has endured, Polak has not. Maganlal has offered all his work as sacrifice, not for my sake but for the sake of an ideal. It is not for me he is slaving; he is wedded to an ideal.... It boils down to this, that I cannot run the Ashram after sending away Maganlal. If I send him away, I would be the only one left in the Ashram. For the task we have undertaken, Maganlal, too, is fully needed. I have yet to see a better man than he.... You must take it as proved that I am bad to the extent that Maganlal is bad."[39]

Gandhi told the ashramites to desist from voicing their complaints to outsiders and thus bringing the institution into disrepute. During the periods he was staying in the Ashram they were free to take some liberties but whilst he was away he insisted that they all make a special effort to conduct themselves in a worthy fashion and follow his instructions stringently. He was clearly worried by criticisms received from outside parties who held that the conduct of the Ashram represented "a soulless soul-force" and that its severe discipline had "made it merely mechanical."[40]

The crisis over Maganlal's behaviour passed, but wranglings among the residents continued. The shortcomings of many people attracted to the Ashram were a constant source of worry for Gandhi. He had hoped to attract self-motivating people to his Ashram. The realisation that a large proportion of his followers were inspired by him alone distressed Gandhi. "The first principle which emerges is that to be attached to a person apart from his work is blind attachment," he told them in 1918, "it is from the whole lot of us that the worth of the Ashram will be judged."[41]

Despite internal problems, the ashramic life at Sabarmati remained an important point of reference in Gandhi's efforts throughout the 1920s to develop a faith in sacrificial work among the masses. Though his belief was that India could go a long way towards realising the *sarvodaya* ideal if the people would voluntarily discipline themselves by undergoing training in non-violence, he stressed that the work towards the political goal would be best left to those qualified in the field. Instances of violence during the first national civil disobedience struggle

(1922) revealed the difficulty of controlling the masses recently awakened to a consciousness of their political power. He explained that civil disobedience was for those saturated with the spirit of truth and non-violence and who were ready for the utmost sacrifice. However, he argued that the whole nation could contribute to the revolutionary struggle through any activity of a constructive nature.

Gandhi urged all Indians to use the gifts that God had given them to the best advantage by making themselves efficient instruments of service. To facilitate their efforts, from 1920 his *sarvodaya* doctrine acquired a coherence of thought and action which he formally embodied in a fourfold constructive work programme. The initial elements of the programme were Hindu-Muslim or communal unity, removal of untouchability, the promotion of *khadi* (homespun cloth) and ether village industries. These were added to over the years and came to include prohibition, village sanitation, child and adult education, uplift of women, education in hygiene and health, propagation of national language, cultivating love of one's own language, and cow protection. Gandhi believed the programme should be as comprehensive as possible since freedom would not be won and consolidated without the stabilisation and perfection of the non-violent technique of action. By the end of 1929 he had established or reorganised twenty organisations to carry the message of non-violence to the cities and villages.

The programmes of work implemented under the auspices of these organisations were often determined by the results of experiments undertaken in the Ashram. The development of the *khadi* industry was a case in point. The central role assigned to the Ashram in the early years of the *khadi* programme was to demonstrate the viability of cloth production as work to supplement village incomes. Experiments were carried put in all areas of *khadi* workmanship. Systemized spinning and prayer were common activities which brought the residents together in a daily affirmation of the communal spirit Gandhi hoped the nation would emulate.

Though the Ashram did experiment with agriculture, Gandhi supported Maganlal's efforts to maintain the project only to the extent that it raised funds for the Ashram expenses. From 1918 he insisted that the *khadi* programme be given top priority. To engage all available hands in this work, labourers were hired to tend the crops. His rationale was that while India did not lose large earnings to other countries because of agriculture, the destruction of the handloom industry amounted to an annual loss of millions of rupees. "We should drop or curtail, one by one, those of our activities which we think others are likely to take up; and pay more attention to those in which others have less faith, or none, but which are all the same essential. Spinning is one such activity", he wrote to Maganlal in 1919.[12]

A factor which later contributed to Gandhi's decision to limit the constructive work activities of the Ashram was the criticisms he received from within the Ashram itself. One member felt the Ashram had not attracted sufficient people with either the ability or the capacity to manage a wide range of activities. Gandhi was sent a letter of criticism in Nadiad during a bout of severe illness in 1918. Though extremely ill at the time his reply is typical of his capacity to attend to the problems of his colleagues, his willingness to experiment and his preparedness to admit mistakes:

> There is bound to be some breaking of things in the course of an experiment. Out of all this the real thing will emerge. But only he who goes searching for it will secure it.... You stated one side. I have given the other, the ideal. Both are true. One man of character can tilt the balance on the side of virtue. I should like you to acquire that strength of character and use it. We must, to be sure, correct mistakes where we find them, and wind up what we cannot manage. I did this in South Africa and Champaran, and will do so here if necessary.[43]

To facilitate the decentralisation of the constructive work programme, and to establish "national schools" at the regional level, ashrams after the pattern of Sabarmati were founded all over India. Gandhi had received suggestions from co-workers that ashrams should be established in each province of India. However, many people failed to understand that an ashram was not merely an institution, but an organic growth nurtured and sustained by dedicated workers. Gradually the number of ashrams swelled throughout the 1920s as men and women with the requisite strength of character and dedication to Gandhi's ideals came forward to establish and manage them. The ashrams and the services they offered were regarded as common property of the Indian people. Similarly, the ashramites were enjoined to regard their time and energy as belonging to the nation. With reference to one such ashram established by C. Rajagopalachari near Pudupalayam in south India, Gandhi told a gathering of villagers in 1925: "The Ashram is public property. You have a right to see it at any time you like. It is in your midst. And so long as you find that its activity is a helpful activity and serves your district, it is your bounden duty to help it in every way."[44]

Other well-known ashrams included Jugatram Dave's Ashram in Veddchi, Vallabhbhai Patel's Ashram in Bardoli, both founded in the Surat District of the erstwhile Bombay Presidency, J.B. Kripalani's Gandhi Ashram in Benares, and Vinoba Bhave's Satyagraha Ashram in Wardha. Situated predominantly in rural areas, these offshoots of the Satyagraha Ashrarn (the total number is not known) were often more effective than Sabarmati in communicating Gandhi's teachings to the villagers. Due to inexperience there were instances of wastage — for example, on unnecessary buildings — but on the whole the ashrams operated more efficiently and economically than Sabarmati where there was a degree of wastage of human and monetary resources.

The ashram established on 14 January 1921 at Wardha in Central India by Ramniklal Modi and subsequently taken over at Gandhi's behest by Vinoba Bhave — who had been a member of the Kochrab Ashram and who was later described as the "spiritual heir" of Gandhi—earned a reputation of some renown. Gandhi would hold it up to the Sabarmati residents as a model community and an embodiment of his ideals *par excellence*. Addressing the Wardha ashramites after a ten-day visit in 1925, he said:

> Ashrams like this one are established so that such a way of life incomplete harmony with *dharma* may prevail everywhere. I have, therefore, always cherished the hope that these ashrams will serve as instruments for raising the country and teaching and spreading true *dharma*. I do not worry whether that hope will be fulfilled in the present or after many generations — it is sufficient for us that we go on doing our duty along the path we have chalked out for ourselves.[45]

In contrast to Sabarmati, Gandhi found Wardha Ashram to be a peaceful, harmonious community. The members respected the rules and performed their tasks diligently. All wore *khadi* produced in the Ashram and the yarn spun and cloth woven were uniformly of excellent quality. He attributed the obvious differ-ences between Sabarmati and Wardha to several factors. The number of inmates at Wardha was much smaller, and they had the added advantage of constant guidance and inspiration from Vinoba Bhave, who rarely left the Ashram and who carried on, with his work in an independent fashion. In an admission of his own responsibility for the problems faced at Sabarmati Gandhi wrote in 1927, "Sabarmati has no one mind uncontrolled by outside force to charge it as Wardha has". In his view another contributing factor was the relative stability of the work programme at Wardha. At Sabarmati the ashramites were expected to adjust to regular changes in their regimen, in order to accommodate new activities and experiments, but at Wardha the activities were more regulated to ensure discipline and to consolidate the work done.[46] Moreover, it appears the Wardha Ashram was not hampered in its operation by the sychophantic individuals often attracted to Sabarmati.

Gandhi's attempts to rationalise his neglect of Sabarmati were unconvincing. He was frequently absent from the Ashram for long periods, attending to the many concerns of his political and non-political work. His guiding spirit and voluminous correspondence alone were not sufficient to inspire many ashramites to maintain the high standards of behaviour expected of them. Though Gandhi's concept of ashramic life did not differ significantly from the Vedic ideal, under the Vedic system "the pupil's membership of the family of his guru constitutes a constant stimulus to the ideals to which he is dedicated, while it also operates as a protective sheath, shutting out unwholesome influences".[47]

It is the word "constant" that highlights the main flaw in the method employed at Sabarmati, and which indicates the contradiction in Gandhi's contention that his was a parental role in the Ashram. An essential part of good parenthood and good education is consistent and stimulative interaction between the parent and child, between teacher and pupil.

It is ironic that though, in Gandhi's view, community service

The Satyagraha Ashram

should take precedence over the various political struggles he instigated as chief architect of the national freedom movement, in many respects his preoccupation with the political affairs of the nation had a disruptive influence upon the Ashram and undermined the development of constructive work in general. It was impractical to expect Maganlal Gandhi, and later his successor Chhaganlal Joshi, a Bombay sociologist, who were made Gandhi's proxies in the Ashram, to provide the level of inspiration and guidance so essential to the smooth functioning of the diverse community. In the face of criticisms from without and within Gandhi revealed his frustration with the experiment. On one occasion, in reply to the head of an ashram who had advised him to remain at Sabarmati and endeavour to perfect its operation, Gandhi said : "I would love to do it. The external political activity is not of my seeking. I, therefore, cannot give it up of my will. If God desires that I should develop the Ashram by being in it, He will make my way clear. If it is a real organic growth, I know that it will continue to make progress whether I am in it or outside. After all, if any such institution has to depend upon one man's existence on earth, it has to perish with him, but if it is to be of a permanent character, it must depend for its existence upon its own independence and internal vitality."[48] Thus at times no would deny the importance of his role in the Ashram, but on other occasions would lament his inability to devote more time to its running. Whatever his thoughts were, there is no doubt that he was discontented with its progress. "If I was to lay the foundation of the Satyagraha Ashram today, I would organise it differently in the light of my experience to date", he said in 1925.[49]

The Ashram's valuable contribution to the development of Gandhi's constructive work programme was always overshadowed to some degree by the problems that plagued the small community. He was alerted to the superficiality of community spirit at Sabarmati as early as in 1918, when his nephew Prabhudas complained that the Ashram, in Gandhi's absence, appeared lifeless. Gandhi replied, "It would be a sad state of affairs, indeed, if it were my physical presence alone which lent the Ashram its life, for the mere body is bound to perish."[50] Yet his nephew's assessment was accurate.

The level of harmony attained at Phoenix and Tolstoy Farm, where Gandhi's European and Indian followers largely put aside differences of custom, religion and class to achieve a remarkable unity of spirit, proved elusive at Sabarmati. He lamented the loss of his South African confidants in a letter to Sonja Schlesin in 1919:

> I must plough the lonely furrow. It often makes me sad when I think of all my helpers in South Africa. I have no Doke here, I have no Kallenbach.... No counterpart of Kachalia or Sorabji. Impossible to get the second edition of Rustomji. Strange as it may appear, I feel lonelier here than in South Africa. This does not mean that I am without co-workers. But between the majority of them and me there is not that perfect correspondence which used to exist in South Africa. I do not enjoy the same sense of security which you all gave me there.[51]

India was not South Africa. Clear-cut issues had confronted the Indian community in South Africa, but in India specific programmes of action were undermined by the over-riding factor of a rigidly hierarchical caste system. Strict adherence to the concept of ritual purity, with its attendant prejudices and intolerances, seriously handicapped Gandhi's attempts to imbue the Ashram and related community programmes with a spirit of egalitarianism. In his view caste ideology sapped the moral and spiritual resolve of the people. The tolerance, spirituality and creativity which had once pervaded Indian society had degenerated into apathy, bigotry, indiscriminate imitation and idleness. The same mentality constantly threatened to spillover into the Ashram. To guard against it required a consistently firm hand, which Gandhi found himself unable to provide: "I do not possess that power by which my words once uttered would have an immediate and permanent effect. I have to be near the persons all the time. I wish I could stay at the Ashram for a long time and supervise the work there. But God does not allow me to fulfil that wish."[52]

Despite Gandhi's assurance to the contrary, Maganlal was relieved too infrequently of total responsibility for the Ashram management. The severe strain on Maganlal not only impaired his judgment at times but began to damage his health. Three months prior to Gandhi's return to the Ashram in May 1925, after serving a prison sentence of twenty-two months for his role in the first national civil disobedience movement, he told a group of co-workers in Borsad that "running an Ashram taxes one's spiritual

The Satyagraha Ashram

resources more agonisingly than discharging the duties of a Viceroy ever does".[53] Of course he was referring to his own difficulties in conducting the Ashram, but he could have been speaking on behalf of his long-suffering cousin.

In 1926 Gandhi decided to retire from public life for one year in order to rest and attend to the affairs of the Ashram. It was the longest period he had spent at Sabarmati since its inception. His decision at this time to register the Ashram under a trust deed and transfer the management to a committee of trustees — Jamnalal Bajaj, Revashankar Zaveri, Mahadev Desai, Imamsaheb Bawazeer and Chhaganlal Gandhi — significantly lightened Maganlal's work-load, but it appears his health was already irreparably damaged. Whatever the case, Maganlal Gandhi died during April, 1928. His death was a crushing blow to Gandhi and seemed to hasten the decline of standards within the Ashram.

Numerous eulogies bore witness that the "soul of the Ashram" had indeed departed.[54] But perhaps the most perceptive tribute came from Vallabhbrur Patel, who wrote to Gandhi in his forthright manner: "No one's equalled his, and he was the only person who made an incessant effort to carry out entirely all your principles. You sowed the seed of *khadi,* but it was he who from its germination watered and nursed and tendered it with watchful care. For me his help was invaluable in connection with public work in Gujarat.... It has often occurred to me that today your principles are not making sufficient headway in the country because your co-workers are so imperfect and it almost seems that you should be born again with all your co-workers to complete your mission."[55] Gandhi could take little comfort from these remarks. Maganlal had never been an effective substitute for Gandhi in the Ashram, but his capacity for work had been an inspiration to dedicated residents. Mahadev Desai observed that Maganlal was in this sense "the noblest representative" of Gandhi at Sabarmati.[56]

Toward the end of his life Maganlal had left Sabarmari to devote his energies to constructive work in the villages. Based on Gandhi's vision of an ideal village, Maganlal began constructing a model village in Kheda District and working with untouchables; activities that were close to Gandhi's heart and in which he had ultimately hoped to involve all adult members of the Ashram. With reference to Maganlal's dedication to the Ashram and all it stood for C. F. Andrews wrote :

> All the vigorous simplicity of the Ashram he practised in his own person. No one kept more true and faithful to its ideal than he did. He never relaxed its rules in his own favour for a single moment. Even in times of illness he practically tried to keep his own life up to the Ashram standard.... The Sabarmati Ashram ideal is not an easy one to practise in its entirety, and it would have been easy for one, with so many responsibilities as Maganlalbhai upon his own shoulders, to have eased a little his own personal burden of strict fulfilment.... Few realised at what cost this was done and how unceasing was his sacrifice.... His love for the untouchables was nothing less than a passion. One of my last happy memories of him was a day in the flooded area in the Kheda district, where he was building the new model village. I watched him that day dealing with all sorts and conditions of men and women; and my mind went back to similar scenes of tenderness I had witnessed during the Satyagraha struggle in South Africa.[57]

Whenever there was an opportunity to remain for a period in the Ashram Gandhi invariably found his time taken up with writing, discussing political strategy with senior Congressmen and receiving a regular stream of casual visitors, the majority of whom came merely to take *darshan* and meet the Mahatma. He realised that stability would be achieved at Sabarmati only if he could give the community his uninterrupted attention, but his role in national affairs prevented this. He discouraged people from seeking him out without an appointment, but to little effect.[58] During his year of 'rest' in 1926 he performed his daily spinning *yajna*, gave classes on his interpretation of the *Bhagavad Gita* and *Ramayana* and evening talks on subjects arising out of the everyday life of the ashramites. In addition, he edited *Navajivan* and *Young India* and attended to his visitors and correspondence.

His advice was constantly sought on the various concerns of the ashramites. Maganlal's successor, Chhaganlal Joshi, and the management committee rarely took a decision without first consulting him. He found their utter dependence frustrating. In 1928, after a period during which he took up the chairmanship of the managing committee, he dissociated himself from the committee.

"I am not on the committee because I do not wish to remain on committees", he told a gathering. "Now I do not wish to take work by means of authority—with iron hands—but through love, by touching your heart. By not remaining on the committee I want to show others who are on it that their responsibility is not less."[59] However, he had little faith in this strategy. Experience had shown him that in the case of Sabarmati his stature was such that there was little or no means of devolving authority: "The virtual control of the Ashram however still remains with me and will continue to do so, so long as I continue to deserve the affection of my comrades."[60]

Gandhi was placed in a difficult position. On the one hand he claimed that the strengths and weaknesses of the Ashram were no more or less than expressions of his own temperament, and that he was incapable of building anything better.[61] On the other hand his energies were divided between such a multiplicity of roles as to make it impossible for him to ensure that this was indeed true. He acknowledged the contradictory nature of his stance: "The Ashram is my most important creation, but I always remain away from it. I see, thus, that I am myself untruthful in my conduct. Is it strange, then, that there should be theft and immorality in the Ashram."[62]

Letters received by Gandhi from people seeking information or admission to Sabarmati revealed the extent of the misconceptions held by the general public as to the ideals of the community and the rigours of life there. Many Europeans regarded Gandhi as a saint to be worshipped and unquestioningly followed, and a number of these sought to become his disciples.[63] The most notable was the Englishwoman, Madeleine Slade, who was re-named Mira Ben by Gandhi. The daughter of an admiral, she had been introduced to Gandhi's ideas through the writings of Remain Rolland, the French novelist, musician and pacifist. Rolland considered Gandhi a saint and his enthusiasm for the "Apostle of India" (as he referred to Gandhi) infected the young woman. She wrote to Gandhi, requesting that he allow her to become an assistant. He tentatively accepted, doubtless reassured by her willingness to spend a year learning to spin and subsist on a vegetarian diet before coming to India. From the moment of their meeting at Sabarmati in November 1925, Mira became one of Gandhi's most loyal, hard-working devotees and regular companions. She cleaned latrines, learnt to spin and card, and gradually became proficient in Hindustani. Her relationship with Gandhi was unusual, alternately harmonious and discordant. Her excessive devotion to him distressed Gandhi on occasion, but he held up her dedication to work as an example to others. During separations Mira and Gandhi corresponded profusely. He found her unreserved opinions and perceptions useful. She was largely unimpressed with Sabarmati and the bulk of the ashramites, and kept Gandhi informed of her misgivings when she was there. Like Gandhi, she found the selective ashram at Wardha more in tune with his ideals and told him so.

However, as a rule, Gandhi discouraged overseas applicants who sought to make a long-term commitment to him. He also did his utmost to remove misconceptions held by Indian applicants. Several wanted to join in order to pursue literary or philosophical studies. One wished to send a delinquent child to Sabarmati for rehabilitation, and yet another advised Gandhi as late as in 1925 to establish a society of servants along the lines of the Servants of India Society, which must have particularly pained him.[64] Yet, despite his efforts to discourage unsuitable applicants, at Sabarmati rule violation, laxity and petty bickerings remained the norm. As a result it was decided in June 1928 not to admit any new members to the Ashram, except under special circumstances,[65] but this did not resolve the internal situation. By the end of 1929 Gandhi's patience was clearly exhausted:

> Our Ashram is not an asylum for the infirm and the crippled. There grown-up men and women have come together inspired by a certain ideal.... If those who have thus voluntarily come together do not observe the rules which they themselves have made and if we tolerate that, I think we are traitors to *dharma* and society.[66]

The behavioural lapses at Sabarmati were innumerable, but there were areas of particular concern to Gandhi. One was the maintenance of the common kitchen, which for him symbolised communal harmony and unity. In reality the kitchen issue crystallised the underlying tensions running through the community. Initially the kitchen had been variously managed by Maganlal Gandhi, Vinoba Bhave, Chotelal Jain and Gandhi himself, but later the Ashram women were given the responsibility. The task was assigned to them not because it was part of their traditional role in the home, but in order to break down the ingrained prejudices within their ranks to working and eating alongside members of different religions and castes. Gandhi was particularly concerned to awaken the women of India to a consciousness of their personal strength and social responsibility. He explained to the Ashram women: "My idea is this: A man should remain a man and yet should become woman; similarly a woman should remain a woman and yet become man. This means that man should cultivate the gentleness and the discrimination of woman; and woman should cast off her timidity and become brave and courageous."[67] He taught them that work in the kitchen, cleaning latrines, in fact the performance of any manual labour by way of service to others, was the purest form of *yajna*.

The women were slow to assimilate his teachings. For many years it was found impossible to run a common kitchen managed by them. Separate kitchens were operated, ostensibly for the sake of convenience but actually because of lack of co-operation among the women. Many of the women refused to undertake sanitary work and were irregular in their attendance at prayer sessions, which Gandhi described as a "hotchpotch of something Eastern and something Western". He later admitted to Mira[68] that he too failed to enter into the spirit of devotion at prayer times, and agreed with another European woman who described the prayer meetings as "formal" and "soulless". The formality of the prayer sessions was compounded by the practice of calling a roll at the completion of the evening session in order to register the daily spinning tally of each ashramite.[69] A number of the women clearly felt alienated by these proceedings, which were far removed from the traditional Hindu form of worship.

At Sabarmati there were educated women and relatives of Gandhi who were dedicated to his ideals, but there were also a significant number who had merely accompanied their husbands. Often they had no notion of the aims and aspirations of the Ashram. These women presented Gandhi with a real challenge, particularly as his conviction grew that the women of India held within their grasp the "key to *swaraj*". He believed all they needed was the right encouragement and direction. From 1926 he corre-sponded regularly with the Ashram women during his absences, reproving when necessary, encouraging them at all times, and devoting progressively more of his time and energy to their education.[70]

Gandhi was at ease in the company of women, and inspired in many a sense of their own strength and dignity as individuals. The women at Sabarmati never fulfilled his high expectations, but his faith in their potential was sustained by a measure of success. Ashram women had been in the forefront of Gandhi's community work from the time of the Champaran struggle. The example they set was revolutionary, especially in Bihar which was a stronghold of the *purdah* system. Many of the ashrams subsequently established all over India were managed by women. Gandhi's ideas and activities had created a new dimension for their involvement in community work and political activity. Pyarelal recalls that though many young men lost direction during the various *satyagraha* campaigns the bulk of the women remained non-violent.[71] In her foreword to Gandhi's *Women and Social Justice,* Amrit Kaur has written:

> In his own institutions and programme of work he has paid equal attention and given equal place to girls and women There is an air or freedom and self-confidence in the girls and women who have lived with him or been under his care whether in Sabarmati or Sevagram or elsewhere, which is a joy to behold and rarely visible in Indian society elsewhere.... The Spinners' Association the child of his creation which is perhaps nearest his heart, is in essence a women's association.[72]

Several women at Sabarmati managed the Ashram store for a period, many became involved in flood relief operations, and the majority contributed in some way to the *khadi* programme. Towards the end of the 1920s the community kitchen was resur-rected by the women, but on condition that they be allowed to prepare both spiced and unspiced food. Gandhi's interpretation of the vow to control the palate did not allow for the use of spices, but it was a concession he was willing to make for the sake of communal harmony. However, the divisive practice of operating separate kitchens continued, and it proved difficult to disperse with employed labour in the common kitchen.

Despite the tendency of the Ashram women to form cliques and

The Satyagraha Ashram

quarrel among themselves, ultimately many did contribute in varying degrees to the maintenance and development of the Ashram work programmes; and by so doing contravened orthodox customs and rules laid down for women. To some extent Gandhi's gentle methods of persuasion thus bore fruit but he was far from satisfied with the progress of the Ashram women. However, women were subsequently to play a vital role in many areas of the Gandhian developmental and political programmes as a result of his educational efforts in the Ashram and elsewhere.

A disruptive factor at Sabarmati was the high incidence of rule violation. Vows pertaining to Ashram observances such as control of palate, non-possession, non-stealing were frequently broken, but it was Gandhi's insistence that all members of the Ashram, young and old, married and unmarried, observe *brahmacharya* which aroused the greatest controversy. His reliance on vows stemmed from his belief that absolute principles could not be upheld in either society or politics unless an ever-increasing body of community servants accepted ascetic ideals as the basis for all their actions. In this sense absolute vows became matrices of self-discipline and 'self-purification. By strict observance of vows Gandhi sought to demonstrate to his followers and society at large that active involvement in society and politics did not preclude the pursuit of personal salvation, provided service was the sole aim of social and political activism. Gandhi had declared early in his career that he would attempt to introduce a religious asceticism into society and politics. "Most religious men I have met are politicians in disguise," he remarked to Polak on one occasion, "I, however, who wear the guise of a politician, am at heart a religious man."[73]

The central question here is whether Gandhi correctly assumed that the way of total detachment and sublimation was valid for everyone seeking to serve society. He warned against the taking of vows that were beyond one's capacity, but he did not explain how one was to measure this. The failure of many residents at Sabarmati to observe their vows appears to indicate that without the requisite detachment and strength of character an individual's taking of absolute vows can be self-defeating. Such failure can lead to either self-abandonment and dissolution or rigidity of response and dogmatism. C. F. Andrews told Gandhi that it was especially wrong to encourage immature and growing people to take absolute vows: "Verbal consistency may be only a lower form of truth, not truth itself. It may even overshadow the truth and obscure it. For life is always a growth into something new and unexpected and original."[74] After recognising the impediments to spiritual and moral growth which could arise out of "formal and mechanistic consistency", Gandhi failed to foresee that many of his followers were either unprepared or unsuited for the arduous discipline of observing absolute vows. They often did so merely out of blind obedience to him, and tended to respond to different situations with a ritualised consistency that undermined their personal development.

Many ashramites found themselves unable to sustain their vows when unforeseen circumstances arose, and this, at times, left them beset with feelings of guilt and unworthiness. Violation of the vow of *brahmacharya* was a common problem. An inherent contradiction is discernible in Gandhi's unyielding insistence on rigid observance of celibacy at Sabarmati, a community made up of married couples as well as young men and women and children of both sexes.[75] The rule of celibacy is commonly associated with monastic life, and a community of celibates usually of the same sex. Doubtless Gandhi had before him the memory of the Trappist monastery in South Africa when he set down the pattern of life to be followed in his communities. At Pinetown men and women lived together under strict vows of silence and celibacy, but the Trappists had undergone extensive training and rigorous discipline in preparation for their final vows, which were taken only after a heightened consciousness of their import and value had been reached. This was clearly not the case at Sabarmati. On the contrary, many residents seemed not to have understood Gandhi's axiom that marriage meant dissipation of energy and division of loyalty.[76]

Gandhi soon learnt the difficulty of communicating his *brahmacharya* ideal to men and women freely intermingling beyond the confines of traditional obligation and custom. In several cases the only alternative available to him in order to avoid a public scandal was to arrange the marriage of the offenders. He approached these marriages with his usual pragmatism: "Though the regulations of the Ashram are strict, we are unable to enforce discipline. It is not easy to impart training in *brahmacharya* to young persons. Not that older folk are able to observe *brahmacharya* strictly.... We can't use force on the young people whom we keep in the Ashram. It happens sometimes that marriages cannot be avoided."[77] He treated the occasions as learning experiences, to be celebrated with the utmost simplicity and promoted in the columns of *Navajivan and Young India* as examples worthy of emulation.

In the case of the marriage of his third son, Ramdas, the bride and groom consecrated the ceremony by fasting, performing tasks such as spinning, cleaning the well basin, cleaning the cowshed and watering the trees, all of which symbolised their unity with the whole of creation, and finally, reading a chapter from the *Bhagavad Gita*. On this occasion the couple were of different castes and Gandhi declared that it was his hope no more marriages would be held at Sabarmati between parties belonging to the same caste: "It behoved people in the Ashram to take the lead in this respect, because people outside might find it difficult to initiate the reform." He emphasised that the Ashram countenanced marriage only to the extent that it served as an instrument of restraint rather than of indulgence.[78]

Yet another situation of this kind was tragically resolved when an ashramite committed suicide rather than face the consequences of his sexual relationship with another member of the Ashram. In addition he had embezzled money from the Ashram accounts.[79] In many respects Gandhi's myopic attitude to marriage and sexual relations undermined the stability of the Ashram and the constructive work programme in general. He unfairly expected young men and women to sublimate their sexual urges merely by taking a vow, the practice of which was confined usually in the Hindu tradition to male ascetics able to live as hermits away from the company of women. Evidently many potentially dedicated community workers were confused and disillusioned by Gandhi's precept that human beings could choose sex or service, but not both. He assumed his own view of sexuality to be a universal truth and could not accept that for people of different temperaments asexual relationship could be ennobling and lead to an awakening of social consciousness.

The vow of *brahmacharya* was also responsible for other areas of conflict at Sabarmati. It must be realised that Gandhi's experiments with co-education and the emancipation of women were revolutionary in their Indian setting. The women of the Ashram were encouraged to "break the shackles" of the traditional *purdah* system and to set an example to other women by realising their strength and independence. The young were advised to differ from their parents should their conscience warrant it. Such aspects of Gandhi's teachings, and the ease with which men and women, boys and girls, intermingled at Sabarmati, outraged the sensibilities of orthodox elements in Indian society. He was accused of alienating children from their parents by having them take vows such as *brahmacharya* and non-possession before they were old enough to appreciate their implications. He was criticised for allowing so much freedom between the sexes, and of inciting others by the habit of placing his hands on the shoulders of girls in the Ashram.[80] These and similar accusations made him extremely cautious on the question of *brahmacharya*.

Measures taken to stem the tide of orthodox opposition to the *brahmacharya* experiments occasionally had adverse effects upon the Ashram. For instance, it was found that the rule of *brahmacharya* had to be relaxed in order to attract capable teachers to the Ashram. This led to the division of the community into two sections, the teachers' quarters and the Ashram proper. The division was inevitable in the circumstances but further high lighted the contradictions in Gandhi's approach. An "us and them" attitude developed that "poisoned the Ashram atmosphere".[81]

Though the boys and girls at Sabarmati were quartered in different sections of the Ashram it was perhaps inevitable that what Gandhi euphemistically referred to as "errors" would occur. When he discovered in 1925 that a number of residents, children and adults, regularly transgressed the *brahmacharya* rule he undertook a fast as penance. However, it is doubtful whether his method of vicarious punishment profoundly changed the ashramites' attitude to *brahmacharya*. Indeed several of his closest associates criticised his taking upon himself the sins of those around him. For instance, Sarojini Naidu asserted that "it is only the personal and not the vicarious repentance of a man that brings him redemption and pardon."[82]

Gandhi tried in vain to rejuvenate the ancient system of ashramic education, whereby the pupils left their parental homes and lived with their preceptors as *brahmacharis*. Few in the Ashram understood the implications of his experiments, and he openly admitted that the innovations he incorporated into the traditional system were fraught with risks.[83] It would appear

The Satyagraha Ashram

that he attempted too much too soon, and thereby greatly diminished the effectiveness of his experiments.

During 1928, in response to misgivings he had about the direction the Ashram was taking, Gandhi decided to introduce several changes. Because of the difficulties experienced in observing the rules with a strictness implied by the name Satyagraha Ashram, it was changed to "Udyog Mandir" (or "Industrial Temple"). A number of the Ashram work programmes were broken down into various departments within the Mandir, each with a separate management, and some ceased. It was a measure of Gandhi's dissatisfaction with progress at Sabarmati that the original Ashram was divested of its external activities, merely retaining the open prayer ground as "its most life-giving activity". Though it was generally agreed that the rule of *brahmacharya* should be more strictly enforced, in other areas such as the common kitchen the rules were relaxed. Those who felt they could not accommodate the new changes were asked to leave.[84]

The whole exercise represented Gandhi's attempt to put his own home in order in the face of long-standing internal and external criticisms which showed few signs of lessening. "The name Satyagraha Ashram has so many sacred associations," he told the public, "that only the hope of reverting to it intact has reconciled us to the change of name to the extent indicated."[83] If indeed he was convinced of this possibility after a period of reconstruction and reinvigoration, he was mistaken. Several incidents in the subsequent year destroyed whatever hopes he had of restoring Sabarmati as a dynamic symbol of national unity and community service.

What distressed Gandhi most was the revelation that his cousin, Chhaganlal Gandhi, who had been intimately associated with his community work since the establishment of the Phoenix Settlement in South Africa, was found guilty of petty larcenies over a number of years and had saved the massive sum of ten thousand rupees. The *Bombay Chronicle* reported that in the light of Chhaganlal's thirty years of service, Gandhi was perplexed by these lapses; "the working of the law of Karma is inscrutable".[86] Another of the incidents involved Kasturba, who it was learnt had retained a number of cash gifts over the years for her personal use, which under the rules of the Ashram amounted to theft. She offered due penitence for what was termed an "aberration". The third incident concerned the seduction of a widow in the Ashram by a young man living there. Gandhi decided to reveal these incidents to the general public, much against the advice of Chhaganlal Joshi who feared their exposure would lead to a cessation of money donations and that departments of the Ashram would be forced to close.

As was his habit Gandhi claimed corruption in the Ashram to be merely the reflection of the wrong in himself. It was a method he employed again and again to temper the attitudes of those critical of the Ashram and its members :

> If those who believed in me and the Mandir desert us after these revelations it will serve two purposes at a stroke. Both they and myself will be extricated, from the false position and I would welcome the relief and the lightening of my burden it will bring me. If all good men in the Mandir left it in disgust the problem would again be readily solved. Equally handy would the solution be if all bad men left the Mandir. Lastly, if I could bring myself to flee from the Mandir that too would be a solution. But life's riddles are not solved quite so easily. None of these things will happen.[87]

From this point life at Sabarmati began to deteriorate rapidly, many ashramites leaving in the wake of the scandal. Gandhi persevered, but in spite of his claim that the Ashram was purer for these revelations, he gradually distanced himself from its operation and appeared to prepare for its ultimate closure. He wrote to Chhaganlal Joshi: "I know that you find it difficult to stand alone. Do not believe that the dairy, or... even the weaving factory, should run in any circumstances. I have made it my profession in life to break up homes and have felt no wrench in the heart at any time while doing so... I shall... feel no wrench in the heart in breaking up this Ashram and building a new one."[88]

The Salt March

The proudest moments for Gandhi's communities in South Africa were realised in the throes of civil disobedience, which had proved to be the "acid test" of Gandhian asceticism. The extent to which Gandhi and his disciples had cultivated non-violence and discipline in their lives was revealed for all to see during stressful periods of the *satyagraha* campaigns. He was certainly satisfied with his followers' performance in South Africa. Similarly, the Salt Satyagraha of 1930 brought credit to the Sabarmati community, and substantially erased much of the stigma of corruption and immorality that had become attached to the Ashram. While in many respects the Ashram had proved a hindrance to constructive work, in the sense that the demands of running the institution kept workers from devoting more time to constructive activities, the *satyagraha* campaigns at Bardoli in 1928, the Salt Satyagraha and subsequent civil disobedience campaign would have been impossible without the support of the Sabarmati Ashram. Gandhi foreshadowed this role in a speech to the ashramites one month before the Dandi March began:

> In the Ashram itself, you have enjoyed yourselves to a certain extent, but enjoyment is worthwhile only when you show your mettle and sacrifice yourself when the time comes. You must now convert the Ashram into a lamp of sacrifice. Those who feel themselves weak or unable to join the fight must quit the Ashram. Once you have plunged yourselves into battle, if you retread, it will be a blemish on you and a blot on the whole fair name of India.[89]

Workers from Sabarmati had taken part in previous *satyagraha* campaigns such as the Champaran struggle, the Ahmedabad mill strike and the Bardoli movement. Explaining the role of the Ashram to Motilal Nehru, who had questioned Gandhi's preoccupation with its development, he claimed that the majority of workers involved in the Bardoli Satyagraha owed their preparation in one way or another to the influence of Sabarmati.[90] Bardoli, an area in south Gujarat, had been first mooted as a suitable location for mass civil disobedience in 1922. On that occasion the idea was abandoned owing to outbreaks of violence in other parts of the country. In 1928, when Bardoli was to have its periodical settlement of land revenue, and the Government wished to raise the revenue by about twenty-five per cent, the people called for a public inquiry into conditions before the increase was levied. The Government refused and the people responded, with the assistance of Gandhian workers, by organising and successfully carrying through a no-tax campaign.

At Bardoli the Ashram had been involved indirectly in the struggle, providing support in the conduct of the campaign, but in 1930 Gandhi mapped out a direct role for his community. Toward the end of 1929 the Congress had sanctioned a renewal of civil disobedience and instructed its members and supporters to withdraw from the legislatures and cease payment of taxes. The task of initiating the *satyagraha* campaign and shaping its course devolved primarily upon Gandhi. Initially the question of which issue to focus attention on perplexed him. After six weeks of careful thought and planning at Sabarmati he laid out his course of action in an extraordinary letter to Viceroy Irwin. He outlined the grievances of the nation against British rule and then revealed his plan should the Viceroy refuse to negotiate on "the immediate removal of these evils"

> But if you cannot see your way to deal with these evils and if my letter makes no appeal to your heart, on the eleventh day of this month I shall proceed with such co-workers of the Ashram as I can take, to disregard the provisions of the Salt Laws... It is, I know, open to you to frustrate my design by arresting me. I hope that there will be tens of thousands ready, in a disciplined manner, to take up the work after me.[91]

On the Dandi March seventy-eight men from the Ashram were given the opportunity to prove their worth to the *swaraj* cause. Prior to their departure they were reminded by Gandhi of their vows and pledge to sustain the Ashram way of life whatever the cost: "This fight is no public show; it is the final struggle — a life-and-death struggle. If there are disturbances, we may even have to die at the hands of our own people." On 12 March the marchers, whose names and personal particulars were published in *Young India,* formed into a column inside the Ashram grounds and began their walk to Dandi, two hundred and forty-one miles to the south. "We are marching," Gandhi told them, "in the name of God."[92]

The twenty-four day march was a triumph for Gandhi's grass-roots activism. At sunset and sunrise he held prayer meetings in the open, and for an hour each day the ashramites spun and wrote their diaries. In the wake of the column the local administration in many *talukas* collapsed, as three hundred and ninety village headmen resigned their posts. The number of marchers swelled to thousands, including businessmen and numerous women. The attention of the world was suddenly focused on Gandhi and his motley crowd of *satyagrahis*. On reaching Dandi he symbolically broke the Salt Laws by illegally gathering some salt, and thereby launched a massive non-co-operation campaign, including the wide-scale manufacture of illegal salt and measures that had been adopted in 1921 such as boycott of shops selling liquor and foreign cloth. Many Ashram women played a vital role, organising picket lines and setting a courageous example in the face of police action.

As the movement increased momentum Gandhi was arrested and thousands of *satyagrahis* were beaten and imprisoned, among them many ashramites. He was overjoyed to learn of the ashramites' contribution. He wrote to one of the women members: "How fortunate you are. You got beaten and were also awarded a jail sentence. All of you have upheld the honour of the Ashram and brought glory to your sex."[93] He was referring to an incident that took place on 21 January 1931. A baton charge was made upon a procession of women and girls led by members of the Ashram, who had organised a meeting in protest against an earlier beating of a young girl from Sabarmati. Though neither the procession nor the meeting was prohibited, the police struck with force. Gangabehn Vaidya, an old widow who was head of the women's section at Sabarmati and a member of the Managing Board, was beaten, and left drenched in blood.[94]

For Gandhi it represented a vindication of his methods and ideals:

> The Ashram women have immortalised themselves and the Ashram. Our prayers and the vows of self-discipline have borne fruit. Other women also have shown such courage....But I have formed the impression that the special merit of the sacrifice made by the Ashram women lies in the religious spirit which inspired it.[95]

Throughout the Salt Satyagraha and the subsequent non-co-operation campaign Gandhi placed special emphasis on the role of women in the work programmes. The women who remained behind at Sabarmati were anxious to join the struggle. To console them Gandhi explained that all Ashram activities were interconnected, and that sanitation work and spinning were equally important as picketing. "For the solution of these problems contains the key to the solution of bigger problems," he told one of the women," as in the body, so in the universe."[96] To facilitate the uplift work among women in south Gujarat several women from Sabarmati established the Anavil Ashram in the Surat District.

At the time of the Dandi March Gandhi and a number of ashramites had vowed not to return to the Ashram before India attained *swaraj*. Those who did not accompany him to prison settled in villages they had passed through on the march and offered their services to the people. The constructive work done during the political struggle in many respects laid the foundation for the concerted village programme launched by Gandhi in the early 1930s. The ashramites had come a long way from the time when they were afraid to venture into the villages.

While Gandhi was in Yervada Gaol which he referred to as "Yervada Mandir" the bond between himself and the ashramites was sustained through a series of letters, in which he discussed at length the various Ashram observances.[97] After his release from prison in January 1931 he visited the Ashram on a number of occasions, and settled for a period in a nearby bungalow. He was accused of breaking his vow not to return to Sabarmati but dismissed this as fatuous criticism.[98] In one sense he created an awkward situation for himself by taking the vow before India gained her freedom. No doubt at the time of the Salt March he was relieved to have an opportunity of dissociating himself from the Ashram. However, during the struggle the ashramites performed creditably, and renewed his faith in the worthiness of the Sabarmati experiment. But now he was unable to settle there without attracting the attention of a host of critics. The problem was compounded when a number of residents who had also taken the vow were allowed by him to re-settle in the Ashram. He refuted the suggestion that they had returned because life was easier inside the Ashram.[99]

The halcyon days following his release from detention soon ended as he was drawn back into the political arena. The ashramites were left somewhat directionless while he attended to the problems surrounding the Gandhi-Irwin Settlement and the subsequent Round Table Conference in London. "I am not living in the Ashram, either physically or mentally," he wrote to Chhaganlal Joshi, "and therefore, think very little about it.".[100] The Conference failed to achieve anything of substance. One week after his return to India on 28 December 1931 he was again ensconced in Yervada Gaol, and remained there until May 1933. He kept up a steady stream of correspondence with ashramites, particularly Prema Behn Kantak, who had taken up responsibility for the women's section, and Narandas Gandhi, who had replaced Chhaganlal Joshi as Secretary of the Managing Board. When the Government allowed him to select prospective visitors from Sabarmati who in his opinion were "non-political", he replied: "If by political are meant those who have been heretofore imprisoned as civil resisters or are believers in the doctrine of civil resistance then there is no non-political inmates in the Ashram."[101]

The population of the Ashram had considerably diminished by 1932. There remained a few adults to supervise the children and the surviving industrial activities. Gandhi was primarily concerned that rules continued to be observed and standards maintained. He received innumerable queries from the members concerning the function of the Ashram and their role in it, all of which revealed the extent of misconception among his followers concerning the ideals he stood for. Yet Gandhi was resigned to the failings of the Ashram and seemed satisfied that it served its purpose: "I derive some satisfaction," he wrote, "from the thought that every one of the three Ashrams which I have established served or has served its immediate aim."[102]

Gandhi continued to proffer advice on every aspect of Ashram life. He wrote to the ashramites of ideal situations and received in turn reports that expressed confusion and conflict. Mira Behn was particularly vehement in her criticism of behaviour in the Ashram, believing it to be rife with "deception and unnaturalness". "I have the impression that nowadays the Ashram is being run by force", she wrote to Gandhi, "this force has produced a fine outward appearance it is true, but underneath how much bitterness, backbiting and hypocrisy one finds."[103] Among other things Gandhi learnt of a general laxity towards the daily spinning *yajna,* the occasional failure of inmates to observe the rule of *brahmacharya* and the unsettling influence of certain dominant personalities.[104] Though he denied that his intention was to disband the Ashram at the earliest opportunity, there are indications that he was considering the step.

Shut away from political activities Gandhi began to devote more of his thought to village work and the uplift of India's disadvantaged communities. In an effort to encourage ashramites to spread out into the villages and take up *khadi* work and promote the removal of untouchability, he explained that the ashramic pattern was not confined to Sabarmati and its many offshoots, but could be duplicated anywhere provided the Ashram rules were observed. He requested ashramites who had left Sabarmati to inform him of the difficulties they encountered in observing the rules. "Those who live outside the Ashram but follow its rules really live in the Ashram itself," he wrote to Narandas Gandhi. "On the other hand those who live in the Ashram but follow its rules unwillingly and only in their letter, and who in their thoughts live outside the Ashram, do not really live in the Ashram."[105] To facilitate the organisation of village workers on a national basis, he also asked Narandas Gandhi to prepare a register of persons who had received training at Sabarmati from the time of its establishment.

During September 1932 Gandhi undertook a six day fast (known as the "Epic Fast") to discourage untouchables under the leadership of Dr. Ambedkar from seeking separate political representation. Ambedkar, the spokesman for the untouchables at the Round Table Conference, had favoured the British plan which envisaged that the fifty or sixty million untouchables should have their own electorate distinct from the Hindus. Gandhi believed this would be divisive, counter-productive and perpetuate the status of the down-trodden classes. While he argued for the re-absorption of the untouchables into the caste system, Ambedkar's view was that untouchability would remain so long as the ideology of caste continued to permeate Indian society.[106]

Gandhi claimed that the aim of his fast was essentially to draw attention to the oppressive conditions under which untouchables suffered. Tagore described the fast as Gandhi's ultimatum "against that deep-seated moral weakness in our society."[107] Indeed, the fast proved to be effective. As news reached the masses that Gandhi was rapidly fading, many temples all over the country were opened to untouchables, and significant numbers of *brahmins* dined with scavengers, street cleaners and leather workers. In addition, roads, wells and schools hitherto closed to untouchables were opened to them.

It was by no means a wholesale revolution, but the progress made convinced Gandhi of the need to absorb himself and his followers in the mammoth task of rehabilitating untouchable communities. With regard to the role of the Ashram in this work he wrote: "Even if the whole Ashram gave up its other activities and plunged into this movement of self-purification, I would not regard that sacrifice as too big."[108] He now stipulated that all ashramites be trained for anti-untouchability work. New volunteers were sent to Sabarmati for a period in order to familiarise themselves with the method of service adopted in the villages and to make contact with experienced workers.[109] The Ashram children were also encouraged to contribute their energies to the campaign. Gandhi suggested that on Sundays they visit untouchable communities in the vicinity of Sabarmati to offer their services and to set an example of industriousness and good behaviour to their untouchable peers.[110]

It appeared that Sabarmati would be given a new lease of life, but this was not the case. A spate of incidents during the early months of 1933 revealed the extent to which the Ashram had drifted from its moral and spiritual moorings. It was discovered that two ashramites in whom Gandhi had considerable confidence as *brahmacharis* had entered into a sexual relationship. The revelation distressed him. "You see how my hopes arc being reduced to ashes", he wrote to Prema Behn Kantak.[111] He had readily admitted the risk in expecting young people to observe an absolute vow of celibacy, but he responded irrationally on this occasion. He warned the Ashram children that friendships with the opposite sex were unnatural, and that "impure desires" should be confessed before their elders. Narandas Gandhi was informed that the "guilty" parties were to be treated as "sick" persons to be nursed back to health.[112] Gandhi's ignorance of the nature of sexuality is apparent in these exhortations. He was not familiar with Freudian theory and appeared to have no knowledge of the danger inherent in the repression of natural urges. It is likely that by focusing so much attention on the question of sublimation of sexuality he inadvertently made many young people conscious of their sexual desires.

The Ashram was beset with petty animosities, jealousies and suspicion, but Gandhi's self-righteous faith in the moral and spiritual authority of his "inner voice" was unshakable. "Truth will stand," he wrote to Mira, "even if the Ashram is reduced to ashes and all my idols are broken to pieces."[113] Reports received subsequently were even more unsettling for him. Hiralal Sharma, a naturopath admitted to the Ashram during the early months of 1933, found several ashramites to be suffering from venereal disease. He also observed that a slavish mentality prevailed at Sabarmati. Earlier Prema Behn Kantak had complained to Gandhi that the rules were too rigid and that he was responsible for allowing self-indulgent men to reside there. On the other hand, Sharma claimed that Prema Behn exerted an undue influence upon many ashramites, including Narandas Gandhi, and was responsible for destabilising the community. Attempts were made to discredit Sharma, but the evidence suggests that much of his criticism was valid. Duncan Greenlees, an Englishman who had volunteered for anti-untouchability service, was appalled by an incident in which an old man accused of theft was beaten with sticks by ashramites, and he described Narandas Gandhi as a "mere businessman."[114] Moreover, he concurred with Sharma's view that the Ashram regimen was followed slavishly. Gandhi defended Narandas, remarking that he found Greenlees to be unintelligent and Sharma to be untruthful and impolite.[115]

However, notwithstanding his defence of Narandas, Gandhi began a twenty-one day fast of self-purification on 8 May 1933, and encouraged the ashramites to do likewise.[116] The Government released him from prison on the first day of the fast, afraid of the repercussions should he die in custody. He fasted with relative ease, but conditions at Sabarmati continued to deteriorate. Several of the oldest members of the Ashram had left after the Dandi March, and work in the various service departments had been greatly reduced. The closure of Sabarmati was now inevitable. He wrote to Narandas Gandhi, "from the beginning it has been assumed that the Ashram may have to sacrifice itself one day in this manner".[117]

Though the closure was due primarily to internal problems, Gandhi believed the move would be useful as political propaganda. In July he claimed the Government was planning to take possession of Sabarmati. There is no evidence of this, but since the Ashram had refused to pay revenue dues for two years the Government seized certain goods from Sabarmati and sold them in lieu of payment. In the light of this action it was feasible that the authorities may have planned to seize the remaining property. Gandhi announced the disbandment of Sabarmati and the decision of the ashramites to court arrest in sympathy with the thousands of *satyagrahis* and villagers who had suffered as a result of governmental action during the civil disobedience movement. In a letter to the Government he suggested that the Home Secretary take possession of the land, buildings and crops, and make beneficial use of them.[118] Moneys and articles belonging to benefactors were to be kept in trust by responsible friends of Gandhi. The stock of khadi and contents of the workshop were transferred to the All-India Spinning Association, and the cows and other cattle came under the auspices of the Goseva Sangh (see below). Explaining these developments to the press, Gandhi said: "The disbandment of the Ashram would mean that every inmate would constitute a walking ashram, carrying with him or her the responsibility for realising the Ashram ideal, no matter where he is situated."[119]

In contravention of Government orders Gandhi marched with the departing ashramites, which led to a further short imprisonment, but the Government did not respond to his offer concerning Sabarmati. After consulting his closest colleagues and wealthiest benefactors he decided that the Ashram should be converted permanently into a colony for Harijans (the name Gandhi gave the untouchables, which means "children of God").[120] The new proposals drew a mixture of reactions. One correspondent argued that Sabarmati should be left to fall into ruins. Though many of Gandhi's supporters were bewildered by the disbandment, they generally approved of the new scheme. To dispel misconceptions concerning his attitude to the changes Gandhi published a short reply to the numerous queries he received: "I see nothing wrong in the Ashram inmates being without a permanent abode and living anywhere contented with whatever comes their way. When everything is over, we may set up another Ashram; that is the only proper course for us."[121]

Sabarmati never regained its early dynamism nor was its role as an ashram revived. Several Harijan families came to live there, and they were joined by a number of non-Harijans involved in the educational and developmental institutions that grew out of the original work departments of the Ashram. Initially the management of Sabarmati was handed over to the Harijan Sevak Sangh, an organisation founded in 1933 to promote and organise the service of untouchables, but as the activities of the different institutions expanded it was found necessary to form separate trusts.[122]

Shrouded in greenery, the original Ashram is today a quiet haven amidst the noise, dust and bustle of the rapidly growing city of Ahmedabad. Once a semi-rural area, Sabarmati is now surrounded by urban development. Many of the early buildings, i.e. those not set aside for the museum, still hum with the sounds of Gandhian activities, but a sense of corporate unity is missing. Each institution has its own management hierarchy, and functions in its own way, apparently unconcerned with the affairs of the other institutions that dot the Sabarmati landscape. No doubt Gandhi would be saddened to find the Ashram transformed into a museum and shrine; a static symbol whose purpose is primarily to inspire national sentiment in the many visitors. Every corner of Sabarmati is permeated with this sentiment, but the meticulously maintained original buildings, the well-trimmed lawns and hedges, and museum and library all tend to obscure the *raison d'etre* for the establishment of Sabarmati as a vehicle for national service.

The Work Programme

In South Africa Gandhi had read Romesh C. Dutt's *Economic History of India* (1902-1904), which held that one of the major factors contributing to the increase of poverty in India under British rule was the deliberate destruction of indigenous cottage industries and handicrafts. For instance, by monopolising the marketing of cloth in Bengal from the eighteenth century the East India Company virtually enslaved the artisan weavers of Bengal. Whilst the Company's profits from the cloth trade were enormous, the weavers were increasingly forced to engage in farming to supplement their meagre income. As Bengal owed much of its prosperity to artisan and peasant manufactures, the policies of the British led to the growing impoverishment of village society. This pattern was also repeated in other parts of India. "Direct coercion practised by the administrative and police bodies of the East India Company," observes V. I. Pavlov, "and the binding of artisans through the Company's buyers-up and brokers was also common practice in other regions occupied by the British."[123]

However, unlike Dutt and other radicals, Gandhi did not see the industrialisation of India under state ownership as a panacea for the damaging effects of British economic imperialism. For him the crux of the problem was what to do for a country where masses of people were denied the basic necessities of life because they were idle for four to six months each year. Soon after the Ashram was permanently settled he was arguing that if India was to prosper she would have to be self-sufficient in cloth. This would involve a programme aimed at inducing the villagers to supplement their slim resources by utilising the usual hours of idleness by hand-spinning, hand-weaving or any of the other occupations which contribute to the manufacture of *khadi*. His intention in this context was clear as early as in 1909 when he stated in *Hind Swaraj* that he wished to reintroduce the pre-British economy in Indian villages, where the "ancient and sacred handlooms had an honoured place".[124] In fact he had planned to introduce handloom weaving into the programme of instruction at Phoenix, but the idea never came to fruition.

Gandhi was not the only commentator of the day who saw the dire need to revive India's waning village industries. The principle of *swadeshi* had first been utilised as a political weapon during the agitation over the partition of Bengal in 1905. Surendranath Banerjee, a journalist, and twice President of Congress, had rallied grass-roots support for the agitation with his call to boycott British goods and the instigation of a "Buy Indian" campaign; and in 1906 Congress endorsed *swadeshi* and passed its first resolution demanding *swaraj*. However, during the agitation in Bengal unscrupulous mill-owners and merchants in other parts of India, particularly in Bombay and Ahmedabad, took advantage of the ensuing demand for Indian-made cloth by forcing up the price and fraudulently marketing foreign cloth as *swadeshi* cloth. The mill-owners argued that it was simply the law of supply and demand, a fundamental principle of capitalist economics, which Ruskin damned in *Unto This Last* as unethical and irreligious.

To nullify the effects of such business practices Gandhi

conceived of *swadeshi* as implying not merely the use of national products, but the use of local products in preference to those that come from a distance. He argued that such an approach mirrored the ancient village system wherein the artisan and handicrafts-man made their product for the local populace and normally marketed the surplus in nearby villages. "*Swadeshi* is that spirit in us which restricts us to the use and service of our immediate surroundings to the exclusion of the more remote", he proclaimed. By implementing this doctrine he maintained that every village would be almost self-supporting and self-contained, exchanging only such necessary commodities with other villages as were not produced locally.[125]

Another to display an awareness of the problems confronting village people as a result of the destruction of village industries was Professor Latthe. In a paper published in 1915 "The Development of Village Industries Through Co-operation" he observed that India was essentially a country where village and cottage industries had prospered until recent times. He claimed the only way crafts and industries such as agriculture, handloom weaving, oil pressing, sugar making and leather manufactures could be revived was through co-operation on a sound economic basis. Lathe cited the case of the handloom industry, which had managed to survive despite crippling competition from foreign and local mill cloth because of the huge demand for coarser kinds of cloth among the poorer classes. As handlooms were admirably suited to supply this type of cloth he called for the ready availability of cheap raw materials and loans to village producers, together with the introduction of improved looms.[126]

Gandhi began his programme to rejuvenate hand-spinning and hand-weaving on a similar basis. Research into the possibilities of simple reforms in the traditional handloom industry became a priority of the Sabarmati Ashram. Another aim was to wean educated youth away from their obsession with government and professional occupations, and encourage in its stead an interest in the handloom industry as a patriotic service to their country. In Gandhi's view the craving for work modelled essentially on the British pattern had led to severe dislocation and alienation among India's educated elites.

A further thrust of Gandhi's scheme involved assistance to those who had abandoned weaving through inability to derive sufficient income from the work. By the end of September 1917 the Ashram had sponsored five such families, each of whom had agreed to revert to weaving when the Ashram offered to supply all their yarn requirements. The woven cloth was collected by ashramites who paid the weavers cash at the market rate. Initially interest-free loans were made to the weavers to purchase yarn, which was subsidised by donations from supporters of the Ashram. In the early stages Umar Sobani, a mill-owner and friend of Gandhi, provided the slivers of cotton, but subsequently the Ashram acquired the services of a carder. As the cloth received from the weavers was sold without difficulty on a strictly cash basis, the loss of interest on the initial loan was minimised. During the formative period of the programme the Ashram refrained from any further contact with the weaving families, but it was planned to use this channel of communication gradually to gain their trust and improve the quality of their lives.[127]

During the mill strike in Ahmedabad in 1917, soon after the Charnparan *satyagraha,* the weaving programme at Sabarmati gained momentum. Gandhi's involvement with the mill labourers' agitation over their demand for higher wages represented an important phase in the succession of events that led to his leadership of the national freedom movement. It was also a catalyst in the development of the *swadeshi* movement.

The first handloom had been set up at the Kochrab Ashram and a weaving expert employed to instruct the residents. However, as the weaver did not teach anyone the full technique Maganlal Gandhi used his natural talent for mechanics to master the weaving process. Others were taught the art and in due course more looms were required, and a building to house them. At the time of the strike the Sabarmati weaving shed was under construction and provided a useful source of alternative employment for many of the striking labourers. Within a short time the shed was complete and the Ashram ready to expand its weaving programme.

Gandhi's intimate contact with both mill-owners and workers during the Ahmedabad disturbances furnished a wealth of knowledge concerning the industry. Moreover, the Ashram resolution to wear only hand-woven cloth made from Indian yarn heightened the group's awareness of the difficulties faced by handloom weavers. Initially the Ashram was unable to satisfy its own cloth demands. From direct contact with weaving families they learnt the extent of handloom production, the difficulties of obtaining yarn, and of the fraudulent practices of certain mill-owners. They also became aware of the harsh living conditions suffered by the weavers as a result of growing indebtedness.

Gandhi's decision to introduce spinning into the Ashram programme stemmed in the main from two discoveries. Firstly, he learned that all fine cloth woven by the weavers was from foreign yarn, since Indian mills did not possess the technology to spin fine yarn. Secondly, by using and propagating cloth woven from Indian mill yarn he realised that the Ashram inadvert-ently became an agent for the spinning mills. Obviously as these mills increased their capacity to weave their own yarn, the handloom weaver was being phased out of the industry.

He widened his search for a skilled spinner. His own efforts were unrewarded, but Ganga Behn Majmudar, a widowed philanthropist he had met at the Broach Educational Conference in 1917, discovered a number of people in Vijapur in the Baroda State prepared to dust off their old wheels and resume spinning, provided they were assured of a regular supply of slivers and a market for their yarn. To begin with Gandhi relied on the mill slivers provided by Umar Sobani, but he realised that this was no more justifiable than using mill yarn. However, the resourceful Ganga Behn also found a carder and trained several youths to make slivers from the carded cotton. Gandhi secured donations of cotton from Bombay business-men, and weavers from the area were recruited into the scheme, with the result that the first *khadi* production centre was established at Vijapur.

These developments encouraged Gandhi to concentrate his efforts on the promotion of *khadi*. Maganlal was sent to Vijapur to learn the art of spinning. He quickly mastered the technique and within a short time had introduced modifications to the old spinning wheel design. His version of the wheel began to be manufactured in the Ashram and the quantity of *khadi* produced by the ashramites rapidly rose. Gandhi sought further donations from his wealthy supporters to expand the work, including the installation of sixteen looms and the provision of accommodation for approximately one hundred and fifty people in the Ashram.[128]

The ashramites ceased wearing clothing manufactured from mill yarn, and launched a propaganda programme to promote the use of *khadi* as a symbol of national integration and freedom.

Gandhi argued that *khadi* was the most practical of cottage indus-tries since it required little capital, the implements could all be manufactured in the villages, and there was no shortage of indig-enous skill in their use and manufacture. In response to the misgivings of certain mill-owners he explained that it was not his intention to have the spinning wheel compete with, or attempt to displace, any existing industry. His claim was that *khadi* offered an immediate, practicable and permanent solution to the prevailing unemployment and underemployment in rural India.

Gandhi was concerned that the Ashram remain in the forefront of *khadi* work. Women in Ahmedabad and adjoining areas, some of whom were untouchables and many of whom were previously either unemployed or wage labourers, were encouraged by the Ashram propaganda to take up spinning and weaving. However, Gandhi became anxious because the Ashram was not sufficiently prepared to meet the growing demand for *khadi*. Responding to letters received from friends, relatives and ashramites he would frequently reiterate his faith that *khadi* was the essence of *swadeshi* and that all their efforts must be concentrated on its production and promotion. In a letter advising the widow of his nephew Gokuldas to join the Ashram he writes, "It is my conviction that any man on woman who produces cloth for the people will have earned the highest *punya*.[129]

As Gandhi himself was perpetually under public scrutiny he learned to spin and did so daily. Moreover, he was adamant that the Ashram supply him with *dhotis* made from hand-spun yarn. His earliest definition of *swadeshi* cloth did allow for the production of hand-woven cloth from mill-yarn, but as the volume of hand-spun yarn increased and his attitude to the mill industry hardened he instructed the Ashram to limit its propaganda and production to hand-spun and hand-woven cloth alone. "Besides, the more experience I gain, the more I realise that machinery will keep us in permanent slavery," he told Maganlal, "and I find that what I said about it in *Hind Swaraj* is literally true."[130]

Towards the end of 1919 the Ashram was preparing to market *khadi* on a large scale. *Dhotis* and *saris* were being manufactured in marketable quantities and Gandhi sent workers all over India to seek out weavers and people prepared to spin. Marketing arrangements were settled with the old swadeshi store set up in Bombay during the Partition of Bengal agitation and with many weaving factories. Gandhi explained to the ashramites that anyone expecting to earn more than a bare living out of spinning and weaving should leave the Ashram.

He used his journalistic ability to full advantage in promoting the *khadi* cause through the columns of *Young India* and *Navajivan,* both of which were edited and published from Ahmedabad.[131] The reader was told that the Ashram derived no profit from the scheme and that extra earnings were either used to cover losses in the initial stages of the programme, reinvested in the scheme, or used to reduce the price of *khadi* received from districts where the cost of production was higher than elsewhere. Since the weavers were not paid a uniform rate throughout the country the Ashram subsidised those who received substantially less than others. It was found difficult to introduce standards regarding the width, quality or the price of *khadi,* but Gandhi asked his sympathisers to be patient and to view their support of the scheme as a service to the poor.[132]

By politicising the swadeshi issue Gandhi hoped to develop an organisational infrastructure that would reach into every corner of India. The thrust of his propaganda was multi-directional. Those with anti-British sentiments were appealed to on the basis of patriotism. To attract devout Hindus to the scheme the use and production of *khadi* was imbued with a religious significance. Gandhi referred to the adoption of *khadi* as recognition of the purity of community service and the need to foster a revolution in one's life. In his view the performance of such service represented a devotional offering to God that set the devotee firmly on the path to salvation.

The thick and rather coarse fabric, which Jawaharlal Nehru described as the "livery of freedom", soon became the uniform of the *swaraj* movement. At the Nagpur Congress in 1920 the passing of a resolution concerning the promotion of *khadi* was a measure of the extent to which Gandhi had begun to dominate the political arena. By concentrating political activity in the areas of *khadi* promotion and the removal of untouchability he hoped to link the politically neglected villagers with the aims of Congress. He observed in his autobiography that by passing the *khadi* resolution Congress had "established a living bond of relationship with the 'skeletons' of India".[133] He warned Congressmen in 1921 that they "must cease to be a debating society of talented lawyers who will not leave their practice", and throw themselves whole-heartedly into the promotion of *khadi* as a practical service to their country. In a climate of political, economic and cultural oppression he argued that the country had no faith in law courts implementing imperialist legislation nor debating assemblies that were corrupt and ineffective.[134]

Gandhi was convinced that the masses were ready to take up production of *khadi,* but were handicapped by a shortage of experts prepared to train them in their villages. Though his exhortations induced many Congressmen to involve themselves in the *khadi* scheme, it was apparent that the majority merely paid lip service to the *swadeshi* concept. Moreover, in order to encourage businessmen to observe the boycott of British-made goods during the first national non-co-operation campaign following the Rowlatt Satyagraha (1919) it was evident that more than the expedient support of opportunist Congressmen was required. In 1921 he optimistically announced that *swaraj* was attainable within a year if the nation as a whole took up *khadi* work. However, before the year had run its course the impossibility of reaching the objective left him disillusioned and frustrated :

> I know that the real work is to inspire Congress workers themselves with faith in the spinning wheel... The masses have that faith, but they want backing, they want expert training. Everyone is there to exhort people to do the spinning, but none to do it himself .... The degradation of India torments me so much that if India refuses to be emancipated, resurrected by the end of the year, that torment may consume me ...[135]

To induce clothiers to sell nothing but the home made product and to ensure foreign cloth and machine-spun cloth were not fraudulently sold as *khadi,* much depended on the willingness of the middle classes to insist that they be supplied with the local cloth irrespective of the price or the quality. In an effort to popularise it among the middle classes, exhibitions and competitions were held in many urban centres around the country during the non-co-operation campaign. A wide range of *khadi* products were displayed and the latest spinning wheel designs and techniques demonstrated.

Yet despite the massive propaganda programme the villagers and the middle classes on the whole remained apathetic to the concept. Gandhi appeared to overestimate the potential effectiveness of his propaganda and the willingness of the middle classes to engage in *khadi* work. Though many people took up spinning and weaving, including many Congressmen, as the quantities of marketable cloth rose the tendency was to rely on the Ashram to supply spinning wheels and to market the finished product. However, the situation demanded the total decentralisation of the industry, such that by stages each province, each district, each *taluka* and ultimately, each village should be self-sufficient in the production of the cloth and the manufacture of wheels.[136]

Khadi simply could not compete with mill produced cloth. It was more expensive than the mill product, it was not as durable, and was harder to clean. Gandhi accepted that there were many problems associated with the scheme, but he unrealistically continued to expect the middle classes to support *khadi* merely on a patriotic basis: "The incentive to use *khaddar* must be national for the middle-class people, and they are expected to put themselves to inconvenience in order to popularise it."[137]

Toward the mid-1920s the ever-present danger of factional rifts within Congress had convinced Gandhi that the aims and ambitions of politicians were not conducive to the promotion of social and economic reforms. In order to secure the autonomy of the programme he formulated the idea of the All India Spinners' Association, its primary objective being to popularise the spinning wheel and to step up production of *khadi* in the villages. A call went out for volunteers to assist in the task of decentralisation.

With a minimum of prior training, Gandhi believed that a dedicated band of village workers could bring about the necessary transformation in every village in India.[138] The ideal worker he envisaged would expect nothing from the villagers, barring clean water, so as to avoid becoming a burden on the village; he would humbly go among the people, not to order them and instruct them, but to set an example through service, even though he might receive nothing but abuse in return. In reality few workers met the ideal. There were many cases of village workers adopting a position of superiority in their dealings with the villagers. "Though we enlisted ourselves as workers," observed Gandhi, "we have become persons who take work from others."[139]

In the face of growing criticism of the *khadi* programme Gandhi's village workers were often anxious to attain quick results. However, there was a danger that expressions of impatience and frustration towards the villagers would alienate them and reduce their willingness to co-operate :

> Idleness has taken possession of the poor, because they have lost all interest in living. They will begin to take interest only after we have worked in their midst for a sufficiently long time. We may wait for full effect even for ages if we are satisfied that our way is the only way of solving the problem of the masses. It is because of our unbelief and impatience that often we run from remedy to remedy, nothing takes root and the position goes from bad to worse.[140]

Critics of *khadi* pointed to the failure of the programme to capture the imagination of the people and unite them in a national cause. *Khadi* was an effective economic symbol but many were of the view that it did not sufficiently inspire the masses to seek political freedom. One correspondent put it this way to Gandhi: "I fail to understand your criminal apathy towards the political aspirations of the country. You don't go to the root cause of the dramatic failure of the non-co-operation movement. You will confess that it failed due to the insufficiency of teaching or the principles of *ahimsa* to the masses.... Logically then, the most momentous task at present, which ought to attract your attention, must be of preaching and propagating the principles of *ahimsa* .... Why then so much stress on an insignificant item, namely production and consumption of *khaddar?* This must have its place, but it must not devour others in the non-co-operation programmes."[141]

Gandhi did not agree, and those in Congress who supported his view that no changes should be made to the non-co-operation programme came to be known as "No-Changers". They were motivated primarily by loyalty to Gandhi who was in gaol until 11 January 1924. However, Congress leaders who favoured concentrating the energies of the freedom movement on political agitation in the legislatures were in the ascendancy. These politicians, including C. R. Das and Motilal Nehru, came to be known as the "Swarajists".

Gandhi decided not to oppose the Swarajists and advised the No-Changers to adopt a neutral stance towards legislative work. On his release from prison he withdrew from Congress activities in order to concentrate on work at the regional level, and to allow himself more scope to develop the Ashram's role in constructive work. He advocated the disbandment of the Congress controlled All India Khaddar Board, its functions to be replaced by the All India Spinners Association (AISA). The proposal was accepted by the All India Congress Committee in September 1925. In justifying his stance Gandhi declared: "No Congress can possibly resent a change in extension of popular liberty. What is more, the change, in my opinion, is in accordance with the requirements of those who have hitherto been identified with the Congress. For them, perhaps, it does not go far enough. I should be sorry if such is the fact. ... I have always held that the National Congress should have no wrangling within its ranks and that there should be no unseemly attempt to capture Congress."[142]

Gandhi was now in a position where he would not be in danger of compromising, and thus sacrificing, his principles to retain political power:

> Whatever special qualities I may possess ... I shall be able to exercise more efficiently by remaining detached from and untroubled by, than holding, office. So long as I retain the affection and confidence of the people, there is not the slightest danger of my not being able without holding office to make the fullest use of such powers as I may possess.[143]

Another reason for remaining outside the Congress organisation was to ensure support for his political objectives from young radicals who accepted Jawaharlal Nehru's leadership but might have been unwilling to accept his own.

From 1925 to 1929 Gandhi moved around India promoting the constructive work programme and consolidating support for community work. To the thousands of villagers who swarmed to his meetings in the Indian interior he was a saint. They knew little of the political situation or modern civilisation, but many had begun to worship him as an incarnation of God.[144] He found the cult of personality growing around him repugnant, and was distressed to learn that some of his co-workers were encouraging the villagers' superstitions. He ordered them to desist,[45] and endeavoured to channel the people's devotion to him into something constructive. He called on people to purge Hinduism of social evils such as

The Satyagraha Ashram

child marriage, temple prostitution and untouchability, and to take up the spinning-wheel.

Gandhi hoped to awaken the educated classes to the need for an extensive uplift programme among India's disadvantaged communities. Addressing the Madras Social Service League in March 1925, he said : "I very much fear social service that is generally rendered in our towns takes the form, as Gokhale would say, of recreation; whereas if it should be effective and valuable for the people whom we serve and for the nation, it should be the chief part of our daily business. Social service that savours of patronage is not service."[146]

His obsession for *khadi* bewildered the British and the educated urban Indians, but they had not witnessed the poverty and degradation of village people as he had. Throughout the 1920s the ashramic life at Sabarmati remained an important point of reference in his efforts to inculcate a faith in sacrificial work among the masses. *Khadi* work retained its position of preeminence in the affairs of the Ashram, as the spinning wheel continued to represent for Gandhi a dynamic symbol of social and economic progress and national integration.

In April each year, during the annual Satyagraha Week (later renamed National Week) which Gandhi instituted to commemorate the cause of national freedom,[147] spinning marathons were held in the Ashram. Prizes were awarded on the basis of endurance and quality of the yarn spun. Exceptional quantities of yarn and cloth were manufactured at these times, since the wheels and looms operated day and night. The children especially revelled in the atmosphere of excitement generated during the National Week. In 1927 one of the boys recounted his experiences during a marathon spinning session in a letter to Gandhi: "I began to lose courage in the eighth hour. The hands refused to work, my head reeled. Much against my will I left the wheel and lay down on my back; but I could get no peace. Suddenly the thought of the Jallianwalla Bagh, the anniversary of which we are celebrating, came to me and with it the picture of those that lay bleeding in the Bagh for over twelve hours untended. Then my fatigue left me and with a bound I was at the wheel again."[148] With their zeal and extra strength such efforts from the Ashram youth were not uncommon.

However, in 1928, "the practice of having some wheels running day and night during the whole week was practically discontinued, it being thought that the process ultimately became a feat of physical endurance rather than one of spiritual advance".[149] As a concession to tradition Gandhi did allow three boys to ply the wheel for twenty-four hours on the last day. Each year he would describe with unconcealed glee the achievements of the Ashram during the National Week in the columns of *Young India* and *Navajivan*. For him the failings of the Ashram seemed insignificant during this week of unflagging purpose which epitomised the kind of selfless action he hoped the nation as a whole would emulate.

By the mid 1920s the role of the Ashram in producing cloth had widened considerably. Initially only the children had spun during a regular period, their yarn being every day noted in a register, but to enhance production the practice was extended to include all members. In association with the Gujarat Vidyapith (a national teacher training college launched by Gandhi in 1920 close to the Ashram) and the AISA, training programmes were begun to instruct national school teachers in all the processes of cloth production, including carding, ginning and the maintenance of accounts. The shortage of teachers trained to teach crafts necessitated the rapid expansion of these programmes.[150]

To facilitate the instruction of teachers and pupils in every aspect or *khadi* production acres of cotton were cultivated on the Vidyapith and Ashram land. In 1928 Gandhi founded the Khadi Seva Sangh which, in conjunction with a Rural Education Scheme begun at the Vidyapith, was intended to organise a vanguard of workers well-versed in all aspects of this work. A *Khadi Vidyalaya* was conducted at the Ashram for candidates selected for admission to the Sangh. After undergoing a rigorous training these workers were sent out to inspect the work done at established institutions and schools, to train teachers in their own localities and to establish rural schools wherever possible.[151]

Despite these developments the attitude of the Indian public towards *khadi* was generally unenthusiastic. Clearly the work could not be hurried and there was no question of making the adoption of spinning compulsory in schools whilst public opinion was unfavourable. Moreover, without the support of the public it was difficult to secure suitable marketing facilities for the schools and to expedite the decentralisation of the teacher training programmes. In retrospect, even had the public responded with enthusiasm to the *khadi* propaganda, it is doubtful if substantial benefits would have accrued to the poor in the villages while the bulk of India's cotton growing tracts remained in the hands of large land-owners. When it is considered that "hand to mouth" conditions prevailed among the poor in these areas,[152] it is not surprising that radical groups who conceived of the freedom movement in terms of a class struggle against capitalist exploitation became frustrated and impatient with Gandhi's methods.

In 1928 Jawaharlal Nehru outlined to Gandhi his misgivings with regard to the efficacy of *khadi* work :

> Khadi will grow slowly, and if war comes it will grow very fast, but I do not see how freedom is coming in its train. As I mentioned before our *khadi* work is almost wholly divorced from politics and our *khadi* workers are developing a mentality which does not-concern itself with anything outside their limited sphere of work. This may be good for the work they do but little can be expected from them in the political field.... I think that western or rather industrial civilisation is bound to conquer India, may be with many changes and adaptations, but none the less, in the main, based on industrialism. You have criticised strongly the many obvious defects of industrialism and hardly paid any attention to its merits. Everybody knows these defects, and the Utopias and social theories are meant to remove them. It is the opinion of most thinkers in the West that these defects are not due to industrialism as such but to the capitalist system which is based on exploitation and others. I believe you have stated that in your opinion there is no necessary conflict between capital and labour. I think that under the capitalist system this conflict is unavoidable.... You have advocated very eloquently and forcefully the claims of the *Daridranarayana* — the poor in India. I do believe that the remedy you have suggested is very helpful to them and if adopted by them in large numbers will relieve to some extent their misery. But I doubt very much if the fundamental causes of poverty are touched by it. You do not say a word against the semi-feudal *zamindari* system which prevails in a great part of India or against the capitalist exploitation of both the workers and the consumers.[153]

Nehru did not go so far as young radicals who believed Gandhi had outlived his usefulness to the political struggle, but his views echo the sentiments of rising socialist elements in the freedom movement, dissatisfied with the Mahatma's over-riding concern for non-political constructive work.

A further criticism of Gandhi's approach was that the total commitment to *khadi* work at Sabarmati handicapped the development of other activities required for the resuscitation of the villages. On one occasion Mahadev Desai, Gandhi's secretary and loyal companion, criticised what he believed was an unnecessary emphasis on spinning in the Ashram. In his view the preoccupation with *khadi* hampered the overall development of the Ashram. Gandhi's response was typical : "I may not give up the spinning wheel, because I have come to regard spinning as a form of *yajna*.... The results of the spinning wheel *yajna* are a matter of faith. Has anyone observed personally that our spinning ends the poverty of the poor? But my faith tells me that it does."[154] Mahadev, like Jawaharlal Nehru, was no doubt unconvinced by such remarks, but Gandhi, while broadening his reform programme over the years, remained true to his faith in *khadi*.

However, several ashramites were usefully employed in other areas of work such as the cow-protection programme. *Like khadi* it was begun fo. practical economic reasons, but also invested with a special religious significance; an activity linking the secular with the spiritual. From earliest times the basic livestock of the peasant were cattle, used for ploughing, transport and food. The inviolability of the cow developed slowly, but over the centuries worship of the living animal, not as representative of a deity but in its own right, became a salient feature of Hinduism.[155] Training in the rearing of cattle and dairy farming was an important part of the foundation of the highest knowledge for which the teacher or *rishi* of ancient India was renowned.[156]

Gandhi's conception of cow protection included cattle breeding, improvement of the stock, humane treatment of bullocks, and the establishment of efficient dairies and tanneries. He first became involved actively with this work at Champaran, but there it failed to take root due to his preoccupation with the peasants' agitation. The Ashram programme, during the first decade, was confined to the maintenance of large numbers of cattle, which were kept for ploughing, for the manure they provided, and for their milk. However, by 1926, both a tannery and a dairy were operational. Gandhi sought expert advice on the management of these projects, and ensured that sufficient funds were allocated for their development. He explained to Maganlal that the projects should be assessed "not from the economic angle but in the light of the social and spiritual benefits to the Ashram".[157]

To promote cow protection work nation-wide the All-India Cow Protection Association was founded at Sabarmati in 1927, but due to lack of public response it was disbanded a little over a year later. The failure of existing cow societies to respond to Gandhi's request for information and monetary aid was a measure of the neglected state of the cattle industry. It pained him that an animal sacred to the Hindus should be so ill-treated. Cows were tortured to extract the maximum milk, bullocks were left to waste away once they had outlived their usefulness to the farmer, or ended up in the slaughterhouses of Bombay and other large cities, and dead cattle were unhygienically disposed of by illiterate tanners with little knowledge of the potential worth of a carcass.

Though the general public remained disinterested, substantial monetary help from supporters enabled Gandhi to continue the cow protection programme. Towards the end of 1928 the Go Seva Sangh (Cow Service Society) was founded. In association with the Ashram project its objective was to carry our extensive experimentation ways to increase the milk yield of cows, to improve cattle rearing and breeding techniques, and to systematise the tanning of hides and the hygienic disposal of carcasses on a sound economic basis.

The main thrust of Gandhi's scheme was to communicate the findings of these experiments to the villagers, and ultimately to assist in the establishment of dairies and tanneries on the Ashram pattern to serve the rural population. However, he had no illusions as to the resistance within the villages to his proposals :

> There was a time when appropriate changes could be effected in our civilisarion and people accepted the need for changes. As long as these conditions of progress were accepted, so long, we can say, our civilisation was living. Now we believe that whatever is written in a book which is published *as shastra and* which finds its way into our hands is the lord's word and cannot be altered in any way. We must get out of this horrible mental death. We can see with our own eyes that there have been changes in our ways of thought and life in every age. Accepting this truth,

cultured workers should enter the villages with confidence in themselves. It is necessary to accept certain general principles; there will be differences in the methods of implementing them. The general principle is that we should produce or make whatever we can in the villages themselves.[158]

Apart from the apathy and suspicion of the villagers and the educated classes towards Gandhi's proposals, the work was handicapped by conditions within the Ashram itself. The difficulty was not shortage of labour. On the contrary, the ashramites favoured the dairying and tannery experiments, the latter involving creative work such as the manufacture of small leather goods. The problem was that too many of them sought cow protection work merely to avoid more onerous duties such as spinning and sanitary work, thus reducing the efficiency of not only the dairy and tannery projects but the overall work programme. It was symptomatic of a general decline in standards of work and discipline which disrupted all the activities of the Ashram in the latter part of the 1920s.

An educational scheme was planned to train students in the field of cow protection and a school was begun, but the programme faltered due to the instability of the Ashram. In 1929 the management of the dairy was made independent of the Ashram to insulate the work from the problems plaguing the community. The project was still funded from the Ashram budget, but the rules for running the dairy were made the responsibility of its manager, who was free to employ men of his own choice. However, he was expected to continue the supply of milk to the Ashram, and selected ashramites were allowed to continue working on the project provided they met their other obligations. The dissociation of the dairy from the Ashram at a time when the disbandment of Sabarmati appeared imminent reveals Gandhi's determination to consolidate and develop the cow protection programme.[159]

Gandhi was aware of the importance of agriculture to a dynamic economy, but he encouraged Maganlal Gandhi's farming programme at Sabarmati only in so far as it enabled the Ashram to be self-sufficient in fruit and vegetables. He was more concerned to promote the benefits of fruit orchards than develop new techniques of farming.[160] Another reason for limiting farming at Sabarmati was the poor quality of the soil, which Gandhi had an expert analyse in 1917. Potash was in small quantities and there was an absence of phosphates. The soil was suitable for fruit culture, but inadequate for grain crops.[161]

However, the decision to cultivate cotton in the late 1920s expanded the Ashram's involvement in agriculture. The students of the Vidyapith and the Khadi Vidyalaya were the mainstay of the project; practical instruction in the science of cotton growing and optimum use of the fibre formed an essential part of their training.[162] However, the cotton grown was not of good quality. A less publicised area of agricultural experimentation at Sabarmati was bound up with the sanitation programme. Gandhi had begun experiments in burying human excreta and converting it to manure at Phoenix. The work was continued at the Ashram, and was later enhanced by a study of organic farming techniques made by an American disciple of Gandhi, Richard Gregg.[163]

Though Gandhi encouraged these developments he restrained ashramites from devoting all their energies to the work. In his view the Ashram should restrict its activities to work that comple-mented farming and enriched the quality of village life. Experiments with bread making and bee-keeping were begun, and in 1926 production of an animal powered well-lift invented by an agricultural graduate was started. Gandhi enthusiastically promoted the invention as "a boon to cultivators", but though he admitted the usefulness of simple tools, instruments and any machinery that eased the drudgery of individual labour, he also acknowledged' that by virtue of inexperience the Ashram was unable to contribute anything substantial to the field of agricultural technology: "Whilst it is wrong to think that I dislike all machinery as such, I do feel that we are not competent judges of the usefulness or otherwise of machinery however small it may be for the toiling millions.... Let me tell you that in the Ashram we have a variety of simple machinery in the way of ploughs, grass-cutting machines, grinding-mills, etc. But I am sorry to inform you that not much of our investment in this line had proved profitable or promising. This has happened because we are all amateur farmers. And this is a judgement which I give you after an experience extending over a period of thirteen years."[164]

On the question of sanitation reform and the utilisation of human excreta for manure, both of which were linked to the removal of untouchability, his stance by the mid-1920s was that in addition to a sustained educational programme some form of governmental action would be necessary.[165] In view of Gandhi's opposition to State interference this appears defeatist, but perhaps better understood in the context of the failure of his propaganda to overcome public apathy towards the constructive work programme. A reason for the failure was his vociferous campaign for the removal of untouchability. Though many saw Gandhi as a saint, mixing with untouchables, scavenging excreta and using it as manure, all of which was practised at Sabarmati, were considered irreligious activities by orthodox caste-Hindus and aroused their ire.

By the end of the 1920s the removal of untouchability was given precedence in Gandhi's programme to alleviate the "triple malady" hampering village regeneration: insanitation, deficient diet and inertia. He conceived an exemplary role for the Ashrarn:

> The Ashram follows a kind of *dharma* appropriate to *sannyasis*. There a new caste or a new code of conduct suitable to the present age and in conformity with Hinduism is being formed. I look upon this effort as an experiment. If it succeeds, it will be treated as worthy of adoption. If it fails, it will have harmed no one.[166]

However to achieve genuine reform Gandhi became convinced that the most urgent need was a mass educational programme to awaken within the rural population a desire to help themselves.

The Educational Experiment

While the four-fold programme of 1920 remained the focal point of Gandhi's constructive work, he placed special emphasis on the role of education. In his view a total restructuring of the Indian educational system in terms of the national genius would ensure that uplift of the poor acquired a priority exceeding all other concerns. He believed the rejuvenation of Indian society would remain an impracticable objective while the middle classes and economic elites received a Western based education. Unless individual effort and social service were inextricably linked in the consciousness of India's youth, he feared his rallying cries would fall on deaf ears.

Under the prevailing system, which was structured on the basis of an institutional hierarchy, the students assimilated elitist, materialistic and career-oriented values. The type of work for which the students would be qualified ultimately was pre-determined according to the level they attained in the hierarchy. Competition was fierce and because of the acute shortage of seats in these institutions, the system of selection was open to abuse and corruption. In Gandhi's view the co-called "liberal" pattern of education introduced by the British reinforced the divisions and compounded the inequities which plagued Indian society:

> It has sapped the energy of the nation, it has shortened the lives of the pupils. It has estranged them from the masses, it has made education unnecessarily expensive. If this process is still persisted in, it bids fair to rob the nation of its soul.[167]

He was particularly concerned that an educational pattern develop which would impress upon youth the dignity of manual work, the necessity of respect for the individual, and awaken them to the plight of the disadvantaged classes.

During the early stages of the constructive work programme local action at the village level such as the revivification of spinning and weaving, was Gandhi's main concern. He appreciated its pedagogic and propaganda value, and though it fell far short of a comprehensive non-violent revolution he continued to believe in its efficacy. However, as the enormities of the task he had set himself and his followers unfolded, the conviction grew that a mass child and adult education programme oriented towards the needs of agrarian society was needed. The first target group of his programme was the urban middle classes, from whose ranks he hoped to attract sufficient numbers of community workers.

In many respects Gandhi's analysis of the prevailing system of education resembled the diagnosis of problems confronting Indian education made during the first stirrings of the National Education Movement in Bengal during the late 1890s and early 1900s. Satish Chandra Mukherjee, a luminary of the Bengali movement, argued that the fundamental weakness of the system was its failure to relate the curriculum content to the realities of the world the average Indian student would have to live in. "For that world is still the old Indian world of his forefathers," observed Valentine Chirol, "and it is far removed as the poles asunder from the Western world which claims his education." Mukherjee complained that education in India failed to develop men able to come to terms with the pressures of industrial change.[168]

The Bengali reformers were concerned with educating the people in preparation for something akin to Jawaharlal Nehru's later concept of national industrialisation, while resuscitating the religious and moral values of traditional society. Gandhi also accorded high priority to the latter objective, but he saw no benefits accruing to the rural population from universal industrialisation. It appeared to him more plausible to work towards transforming India into a co-operative and self-sufficient society, without the loss of regional identity and traditional areas of production which go hand-in-hand with social and economic centralisation.

The importance of universal education as a means of activating the various elements of national reconstruction had also been recognised by Gokhale. He had advocated compulsory primary education, but his stance on continuing adherence to Western education was diametrically opposite to Gandhi's view. Gandhi completely rejected the Western pattern in favour of a syllabus founded upon the ashramic method of ancient India. But Gokhale spoke for the great majority of the educated classes when he claimed that the advantages of Western education for India far outweighed its disadvantages: "The greatest work of Western education in the present state of India is ... the liberation of the Indian mind from the thraldom of old world ideas and the assimilation of all that is highest and best in the life and thought of the West. For this purpose not only the highest but all Western education is useful."[169] On the other hand Gandhi's belief was that India's salvation depended upon a resuscitation of traditional civilisation, a social and cultural continuity. On the subject of education the rift between Gandhi and the Western educated was most apparent. The educated classes had no intention of forsaking the system to which they owed their status in society and their livelihood. Their opposition to his concept of national education hardened over the years and their criticisms became more trenchant.

Gandhi's chief collaborator in his education scheme was "Kaka" Kalelkar, whom he had met at Shantiniketan in February 1915. Kalelkar had been educated at Fergusson College in Poona, where

The Satyagraha Ashram

he came under the influence of Gokhale, and later joined Lokmanya Tilak on the staff of the journal *Rashtra-mat*. From 1906 he had been involved in clandestine political activities, which included working through educational institutions to train young revolutionaries wedded to radical methods. As his reputation as a seditionist grew Kalelkar was forced to assume a false identity and wander the country. The meeting with Gandhi at Shantiniketan proved fortuitous for both parties. Long discussions with Gandhi convinced Kalelkar that non-violence should be the guiding principle of his life and that he had met his *guru* (teacher) in the person of Gandhi, who requested Tagore that he "loan" the services of Kalelkar to him. Accompanied by his eldest son he joined the Ashram at Kochrab soon after its establishment. In later years Tagore would light-heartedly chide Gandhi that Kalelkar was a loan he forgot to repay.[170]

Gandhi's plan was to establish a national school where boys and girls would be trained to serve their country. Surrounded by an atmosphere of simplicity, manual work and service, their training as potential *satyagrahis* would thus be inextricably bound up with Ashram life, just as it had been at Phoenix and Tolstoy Farm. Tagore and Gandhi shared a dislike of highly disciplined formal education, but their approach to the ashramic concept of education differed. The boys educated at Shantiniketan, in the words of a former pupil, "were a civilised, cultured type, showing innate good taste and keen interest in literature, music and art". However, he goes on to observe that the lack of formal serious education at Shantiniketan "frequently left its boys unprepared to meet the hard challenge of life".[171] The methodology employed by both Tagore and Gandhi was non-intellectual and non-professional, but while Tagore cultivated the higher pursuits of cultural learning, seemingly at the expense of his pupils' preparedness for the rigours of adult life, Gandhi believed that the social and economic conditions prevailing in India necessitated the education of youth to be efficient instruments of public service rather than cultured aesthetes.

Gandhi did not sympathise with Tagore's idea that art and other cultural pursuits were a vital element of an educational curriculum founded on the "unity of truth", and need have no other purpose than as a humanising influence upon the child.[172] Like Tolstoy, Gandhi argued that art should serve a distinctive social purpose as an instrument of moral rejuvenation, human integration and social organisation. In the face of abject poverty and starvation he saw little room for the pursuit and enjoyment of art in any form. In 1921, he wrote to Tagore: "I have found it impossible to soothe suffering patients with a song from Kabir. The hungry millions ask for one poem — invigorating food.... Whatever can be useful to those starving millions is beautiful to my mind. Let us give today first the vital things of life and all the graces and ornaments of life will follow."[173] He instructed the teachers at the Ashram school to teach drawing not as a fine art but with practical objectives such as drawing maps or improving handwriting. He received support for his approach from an unexpected direction. Tagore's brother, Dwijendranath, was also critical of the method employed at Shantiniketan: "Rabi is taking a wrong course. He is creating an atmosphere of mirth and music around him while India is travailing to give birth to her new child 'Swaraj'. He is unnecessarily pouring water on the widespread branches of universal brotherhood leaving its root to wither for want of water."[174]

From its modest beginnings Gandhi hoped to develop the Ashram project into a major scheme of education. He warned the leaders that the task would be difficult and might require many sacrifices on their part. Indeed, he asked them to be ready to turn themselves into beggars for the sake of the school. Including Kalelkar there were four teachers, the other three living in the neighbourhood of the Ashram and coming daily to give lessons in Sanskrit, Hindi and Tamil. Instructors were employed to teach manual skills such as carpentry and hand-weaving.

Just prior to the Champaran struggle in 1917 Gandhi outlined the objectives of the school, which he foresaw as being able to admit up to one hundred pupils, all of whom would be expected to pay their own expenses:

1. To adopt a new method of education.
2. To pay special attention to character-building, the aim being that ten per cent of the pupils at any rate got trained for national service.
3. To raise the status of the Gujarati language.
4. To work for the spread of the national language, Hindi.
5. To open schools of the new pattern in every place, and make this school a model for them, and for the Government as well, to copy. The aim is to have the teachers trained in this

school who will then go to the villages and run schools there.
6. To get the new pattern adopted by the Government.

Ideally, the teachers were required to have a knowledge of Hindi, Gujarati or Marathi, the latter because Maharashtra was contiguous to Gujarat. They were also expected to be proficient in agriculture and hand-weaving, since Gandhi believed instruction in productive skills was an essential factor in character-building. Another question he raised with the teachers was co-education. He reiterated his belief in its efficacy, but during the early years of the Ashram he was not in favour of common residence, arguing that girls should live under the constant supervision of their mothers.[175] His experiences at Phoenix and Tolstoy Farm had clearly left him wary of continuing the co-educational experiment. However, later he did admit girls to the Ashram. They boarded in the women's section under the supervision of an ashramite.

The evolution of Gandhi's educational philosophy was characterised throughout by his attitude to practical and theoretical research. His work involved observing and classifying certain facts, experimenting with them on a sufficiently large scale, objectively assessing the results and subsequently drawing conclusions from them. A good example of this was the discovery that children were usually adept at spinning, and that it enhanced their all-round development. With reference to the educational value of the *takli,* a simple spinning device, Gandhi wrote: "It develops in the spinner patience, persistence, concentration, self-control, calmness, realisation of importance and value of detail, ability to do more than one thing at a time, making one of them so habitual that its control and operation are almost unconscious, sensitiveness, sureness and delicacy of touch and of muscular control and co-ordination ... a realisation of the value of co-operative work, self-respect and self-reliance arising from recognition of one's ability to create something of economic value useful to oneself, one's family, to the school and to the village, province or nation."[176]

In 1920 Gandhi launched a major educational experiment by founding the Gujarat Vidyapith. As an outgrowth of the Ashram, the Vidyapith was established to serve a complementary function. Initially its aims and organisation were confused, but Gandhi persuaded Kalelkar and J. B. Kripalani to take charge of the project, and under their guidance it became a working proposition. Kalelkar set about making the students more village-minded by introducing spinning, weaving, carpentry and other manual crafts into the curriculum. To break down caste barriers a class for servants was begun. A Mahavidyalaya was established as a constituent college of the Vidyapith. Under the charter of this institution of higher learning a new academic degree was created equivalent to a "Bachelor of Rural Science". By establishing these schools Gandhi's idea was to institutionalise his protest against the career-oriented system of higher education introduced by the British: "It... hopes to build a new culture based on the traditions of the past, enriched by the experience of later times."[177] Over the years many educational centres were affiliated to or recognised by the Vidyapith.

However, the response of the educated classes to the aims and ideals of the Ashram and Vidyapith pattern of education was largely unenthusiastic. Moreover, many schools were later disaffiliated from the Vidyapith due to their inability to comply with the spinning and *khadi* conditions laid down by Gandhi.[178] It was his view that they either accept compulsory spinning or leave the scheme. From the mid 1920s attendance at the Mahavidyalaya also showed a steady decline. On occasion students were suddenly withdrawn from the Ashram school or the Vidyapith when their parents learnt to what extent their children were required to perform manual work. The patriotic cause espoused by Gandhi appealed to many parents, but few understood his use of autochthonous crafts to awaken their children to the dignity of labour and the importance of manual skills. He lamented the fact that many parents were inspired more by his charismatic role in national politics and his high standing as a man of religion than by his educational and developmental theories.

Yet Gandhi persisted. By 1921 he believed in the necessity of incorporating industrial training, particularly spinning and weaving, into the school curriculum, and that in the process every school could be made self-supporting.[179] His enthusiasm seemed boundless. Calling for schools which upheld the dignity of labour to be established all over India he cited an array of statistics and figures in support of his claims. His strategy involved a reconciliation of town and village and the elimination of factors alienating the urban worker from the peasant.

His approach to education was denigrated as "anachronistic" or "retrograde" by members of the educated classes. "In attacking

Western education and castigating lawyers and doctors, Gandhi was challenging the vested interests of his educated contemporaries, the very people who were the heart of the new politics, and controlled the Congress," observes Judith Brown. "It was hardly likely that they would find such an opponent congenial company."[180] The pedagogic principles underlying his ideas derived from the ancient ashramic system, in which the salient feature was the pervasive influence of religion upon the total configuration of ideals, practices and conduct. Education was a living expression of Hindu religious philosophy, a means of studying the fundamental truths of life, and an aid to detachment from worldly concerns and self-realisation. For Gandhi these were truths which permeated his educational theory, but to the bulk of India's Western-educated classes cast adrift from their traditional moorings, his ideas appeared obscurantist and irrational.

However, as with other areas of ashramic life at Sabarmati, reality did not approach the ideal. From the outset the misgivings of the educated classes towards the Ashram scheme had been known to Gandhi. Commenting on the draft prospectus of the Ashram in 1915, S. K. Rudra questioned the wisdom of following strictly the ancient *gurukul* model, thus preventing the children from any contact with their parents, and he suggested the necessity of including science and cultural activities in the curriculum. There was opposition to the separation of children and parents, particularly from Salima Tyabji, and S. G. Ranaday described the scheme as a "backward progress and suicidal to our nation".[181] Though Gandhi's criticisms of the prevailing education system were seemingly valid — i.e., not enough people were receiving education, there were great imbalances of a social and geographical nature, much of the education was irrelevant to India's needs, too many people were being educated to an unnecessarily high level at great cost to the country, and education was failing to produce attitudes conducive to the all-round development of the nation — as head of the Ashram it was his responsibility to fulfil effectively the role of the parent in the lives of the children entrusted to him. He found himself unable to do so and none of the teachers could be expected to substitute for him. Sabarmati could not realise its potential without Gandhi's undivided attention, and perhaps the clearest indication of the debilitating effect upon the community of his extended absences was Mira's description in 1929 of a number of

Ashram boys as being "selfish, bad mannered and wanting in a spirit of service".[182]

Conclusion

In South Africa Gandhi had attracted a group of people who agreed to follow a simple, essentially ascetic pattern of life. The majority of settlers at Phoenix, and later at Tolstoy Farm, contributed in some way to his political activities and ultimately to the success of the *satyagraha* campaigns; the communities provided a cadre of dedicated workers prepared to support him in whatever project he undertook. In the light of his South African experience Gandhi arrived in India in 1915 determined to apply the ideas and methodology that had won gains for the Indian community there.

The ashram concept was an essential part of this methodology, for it not merely provided a supportive community to develop and consolidate constructive activities, it also served as a training ground for *satyagrahis*. However, Gandhi realised that orthodox elements in Indian society would oppose his communal concept unless it could be organised on a strict ascetic basis; particularly so with regard to the important and revolutionary role he foresaw women would play in the running of his ashram and the freedom struggle in general. Thus the relative flexibility of the pattern followed at Phoenix and Tolstoy Farm was replaced at Sabarmati by a rigid ideology and code of conduct, which in many respects stifled individual initiative and creativity.

Gandhi's extended absences, and his delegation of responsibility to men and women lacking his charismatic authority and organisational ability, undermined the stability of the community. Throughout the 1920s the image of the Ashram conveyed to the public in the columns of *Young India* and *Navajivan* belied the petty jealousies and conflicts that severely handicapped its internal running and involvement with the construed veprogramme. Clearly, absolute vows were no assurance against human fallibility; the high incidence of rule violation indicates that few ashramites reached that level of detachment from worldly concerns required of them by Gandhi. He tried in vain to claim the failings of the Ashram as expressions of his own inadequacies, but his method of vicarious punishment won little sympathy from either his critics or supporters. Moreover, India was a caste-ridden society. Gandhi's efforts to imbue the Ashram and the constructive work programme with an egalitarianism alien to the Indian genius were frequently frustrated by a resurgence of caste mentality among the ashramites and other followers.

However, Sabarmati did provide Gandhi with a cadre of political and non-political workers, and in retrospect the high points of the Ashram correlate with the *satyagraha* and non-co-operation campaigns. During these periods ashramites were involved actively in political and constructive work beyond the confines of the Ashram. Detached from the day-to-day management of the community, ashramites involved in the *satyagraha* struggles worked independently in the villages; for example, during the Champaran and Bardoli campaigns. Without Sabarmati and its many offshoots the *satyagraha* campaigns would have been impossible. Ashram workers introduced, in the words of Pyarelal, "homoeopathic" doses of non-violence amongst millions of people in this fashion".[183]

The ashramic life fostered the discipline necessary to conduct a civil disobedience struggle at the grass-roots level, but the institution of the ashram in a sense "imprisoned" workers rather than released them for constructive work. In the case of Sabarmati, which depended on the donations of wealthy benefactors and other resources not produced within the Ashram, instead of the institution changing the environment it drew valuable resources from its surrounds. To run the Ashram became an end in itself, and it appears that this more than anything else convinced Gandhi that Sabarmati had outlived its usefulness.

Sabarmati provided Gandhi with a workshop in which he laid the ground-work for the social organisation and economics of his envisaged village community. However, as the different elements of the programme developed they became unwieldy and impossible to confine within the Ashram environment. The experience of South Africa led Gandhi to duplicate and thence expand the Phoenix pattern at Sabarmati; the experience of the 1920s led him to place less emphasis on the institution of the Ashram, and more upon the application of the ashramic ideal in the individual worker's interaction with village society.

NOTES

1. West, *op. cit.*
2. Interview to the *Madras Mail,* 23rd April, 1915, CWMG, Vol. 13, pp. 54-5.
3. Judith Brown, *Gandhi's Rise to Power, Indian Politics 1915-1922* (London: Cambridge University Press, 1972), p. 22.
4. See Gandhi's speech at Benares Hindu University, cited in D. G. Tendulkar, *Mahatma: Life of Mohandas Karamchand Gandhi,* 8 Vols. (Bombay Publications Division, Government of India, 1951), p. 223.
5. Gandhi to Maganlal Gandhi, 10 December 1914, CWMG, Vol. 12, pp. 559-61.
6. *Autobiography,* p. 318.
7. *Ibid.*
8. Cf. Sasadhar Sinha, *Social Thinking of Rabindranath Tagore* (Bombay : Asia Publishing House, 1962), pp. 74-85.
9. *Autobiography,* pp. 313-14.
10. Gandhi to Maganlal Gandhi, 27 January 1910, CWMG, Vol. 10, pp. 138-9.
11. Gandhi to V. S. Srinivasa Sastri, 13 January 1916, *Ibid.,* Vol. 13, p. 200.
12. *Autobiography, p.* 322.
13. *Ibid.,* p. 324.
14. *Ibid.,* pp. 328-9.
15. *Ibid.,* pp. 227-8.
16. *Ibid.,* p. 329.
17. Cf. R. Palme Dutt, *India Today* (Calcutta: Manisha, 1970), p. 629.
18. *Young India,* 3 December 1925.
19. Gandhi to G. D. Birla, 5 July 1932, CWMG, Vol. 50, p. 154.
20. *Autobiography,* p. 330.
21. *Ashram Observances in Action* (Ahmedabad: Navajivan Publishing House, 1955), p. 3.
22. B. R.Nanda, *Mahatma Gandhi* (Bombay: George Allen and Unwin, 1965), p. 91.
23. *Young India,* 4 October 1928.
24. *Harijan,* 7 September 1934.
25. *Ibid.,* 15 January 1938.
26. Cf. for a range of responses to the Ashram proposals; Letters to Gandhi from Sadhu Magalnath, 2 September 1915, S. N. 6228; S. Subramanian, 6 August 1915, S. N. 6219; S. K. Rudra, 2 July 1915, S. N. 6201; S. G. Ranaday, 25 August 1915, S. N. 226; K. V. Kukday, 10 September 1915, S. N. 6227; Sonja Schlesin, 3 November 1915, S. N. 6240; Herbet Turner, 8 November 1915, S. N. 6241; Salima Tyabji, 15 July 1915, S. N. 6203.
27. *Autobiography,* p. 330.
28. *Bombay Chronicle,* 15 May 1915.
29. Gandhi to V. S. S. Sastri, 23 September 1915, CWMG, Vol. 13, pp. 127-8.
30. *Autobiography,* p. 331.
31. *Ibid.,* pp. 331-2.
32. *Ibid.,* p. 333.
33. Cited in Tendulkar, *op. cit.*
34. CWMG, Vol. 13, pp. 455-8, 460-3.

The Satyagraha Ashram

35. Cited in D. G. Tendulkar, *Gandhi in Champaran* (New Delhi: The Publications Division, Government of India, 1957), p. 106; see also Rajendra Prasad, *Satyagraha in Champaran* (Ahmedabad: Navajivan Publishing House, 1949), p. 198.
36. *Autobiography,* p. 353.
37. Gandhi to Maganlal Gandhi, 16 October 1917, CWMG, Vol. 14, pp. 5-6.
38. See Gandhi to Maganlal Gandhi, 20 January 1918, *Ibid.,* pp. 160-1.
39. Address to Ashram inmates, 17 February 1919, *Ibid.,* Vol. 15, pp. 91-3.
40. *Ibid.*
41. *Ibid.*
42. Gandhi to Maganlal Gandhi, 1 June 1919, *Ibid.,* pp. 339-40.
43. Gandhi to Fulchand Shah, 9 August 1918, *Ibid.,* pp. 10-11.
44. *The Hindu,* 23 March 1925, CWMG, Vol. 26, p. 351. C. Rajagopalachari was a Brahmin lawyer from Madras, who dedicated himself to Gandhi's cause and later became the first Indian Governor-General of the Dominion of India; Cf. Rajmohan Gandhi, *The Rajaji Story,* 3 Vols. (Madras: Bharathan Publications, 1978).
45. *Navajivan,* 27 December 1925, *Ibid.,* Vol. 29, p. 340.
46. Gandhi to Mora, 27 July, 1927, *Ibid.,* Vol. 34, p. 245; sec also Gandhi to Ramniklal Modi, 15 December 1929, *Ibid.,* Vol. 42, p. 284. Vinoba Bhave had been converted to Gandhi's ideas upon hearing of his famous speech at Benares Hindu University in 1916. He joine the Kochrab Ashram and became Gandhi's most respected disciple. A Chittapavan Brahmin, from Maharashtra, Vinoba was devout and highly learned. He taught for a while at Kochrab, but poor health forced him to take one year's leave, during which he studied and taught in various places. He subsequently devoted himself to spiritual studies and village uplift in his Wardha Ashram, becoming involved in the *Satyagraha* campaign when his services were required by Gandhi. In the early 1950s Vinoba launched the Bhoodan Yajna movement which sought the redistribution of rural land and the reintegration of village society. For a thorough analysis of the Bhoodan movement see Geoffrey Ostergaard and Melville Currell, *The Gentle Anarchists* (London : Oxford University Press, 1971).
47. Mookerji, *op. cit.,* p. xxviii.
48. Gandhi to D. Hanumantrao, 16 March 1924, CWMG, Vol. 23, pp. 261-2.
49. *Navajivan,* 1 November 1925, CWMG., Vol. 28, pp. 405-8.
50. Gandhi to Prabhudas Gandhi, 2 Feb. 1918, *Ibid.,* Vol. 14, pp. 180-1.
51. Gandhi to Sonja Schlesin, 2 June 1919, S. N. 6635.
52. Gandhi to Maganlal Gandhi, 1 December 1924, CWMG, Vol. 25, p. 381.
53. *Navajivan,* 15 February 1925, CWMG, Vol. 26, p. 129.
54. See *Navajivan,* 29 April 1928, CWMG, Vol. 36, pp. 279-81; a Iso *Young India,* 26 April and 24 May 1928.
55. *Ibid.*
56. *Ibid.*
57. *Ibid.,* 24 May 1928.
58. *Navajivan,* 20 October 1921, CWMG, Vol. 21, pp. 322-3.
59. Speech at Gujarat Vidyapith, 28 January 1928, *Ibid.,* Vol. 35, pp. 503-4.
60. *Young India,* 8 November 1928.

61. *Navajivan, I* November 1925, CWMG, Vol. 28, pp. 405-8.
62. Gandhi to Chhaganlal Joshi, 11 April 1929, *Ibid.,* Vol. 40, pp. 231-2.
63. See Letters to Gandhi from Howard Harlehurst, 29 November 1928, S. N. 15100; Antoinette Mirbel, 26 January 1925, S. N. 10532; J. B. Spillemann, 20 October 1926, S. N. 10831.
64. *Navajivan,* 1 November 1925, CWMG, Vol. 28, pp. 405-8; see also Letters from Gandhi to Sharda, 22 August 1927, *Ibid.,* Vol. 34, pp. 384-5; K. G. Rekhade, 25 March 1924, *Ibid.,* Vol. 23, pp. 307-8; Harindranath Chattopadhyaya, 1 July 1927, *Ibid.,* Vol. 34, pp. 84-5.
65. Gandhi to Bechar Parmar, 23 June 1928, *Ibid.,* Vol. 36, p. 454.
66. Gandhi to Ramniklal Modi, 10 December 1929, *Ibid.,* Vol. 42, p. 257.
67. CWMG, Vol. 32, p. 485, cf. Gandhi to Esther Menon, 18 July 1932, *Ibid.,* Vol. 50, p. 259.
68. Gandhi to Mira, 20 July 1927, *Ibid.,* Vol. 34, p. 205.
69. Gandhi to Mrs. E. Bjerrum, 11 May 1928, *Ibid.,* Vol. 36, pp. 304-5.
70. 'Gandhi to Ashram Women', 13 December 1926, *Ibid.,* Vol. 32, pp. 429-30; see , also 'Gandhi's Talks to Ashram Women', *Ibid., p.* 495.
71. Pyarelal, Interview held in New Delhi, 30 November 1981.
72. *Women and Social justice* (Ahmedabad : Navajivan Publishing House, 1942), p. iv. Amrit Kaur held various offices in the AIWC from 1930 and acted as Gandhi's secretary for various periods from 1936 to 1946. She was a member of the Advisory Board of Education from inception to 1942 and again appointed in 1.946. She was a member of the Indian delegation to UNESCO in 1945 and 1946, and became Minister for Health in 1947. She became an intimate friend of Gandhi, and spent various periods with him at Sovagram.
73. *Speeches and Writings of Mahatma Gandhi* (Madras: Natesan and Co., 1918) p. xxiv; cf. Iyer, *op. cit.,* pp. 8, 73-81.
74. Cited in *Ibid.,* pp. 75-76; see also C. F. Andrews to Gandhi, April 1919, S. N. 6547.
75. In 1922 Gandhi overcame his inhibitions concerning co-education, beginning at Sabarmati what he called "a novel experiment". The girls resided in the Women's Section of the Ashram under the supervision of an ashramite; see Gandhi's speech to students of Satyagraha Ashram, S. N. 7195. For Gandhi's views on the rules of conduct to be followed by students at the Ashram see CWMG, Vol. 17, pp. 536-8.
76. See M. K. Gandhi, *From Yervada Mandir* (Ahmedabad: Navajivan Publishing House, 1932), pp. 6-10.
77. *Mahadevbhaini Dairy,* Vol. VII, pp. 202-5, CWMG, Vol. 26, p. 194; see also 'Gandhi to Bhagwanju', A. Mehta, n. d., *Ibid.,* Vol. 29, pp. 310-11.
78. *Young India,* 2 Feb. 1928; see also *Navajivan,* 29 March 1925, CWMG, Vol. 30, pp. 85-6.
79. Gandhi to Balwantrai Mehta, 2 September 1927, *Ibid.,* Vol. 34, p. 440.
80. Gandhi to Balkrishna Bhave, 10 September 1928, *Ibid.,* Vol. 37, p. 259; see also *Navajivan,* 28 July 1929, CWMG, Vol. 41, pp. 230-2.
81. *Ashram Observances in Action,* pp. 99-100.
82. Sarojini Naidu to Gandhi, 26 November 1925, S.N. 10665. Sarojini Naidu was a gifted poet who worked dosely with Gandhi during the freedom struggle and who became President of the Congress in 1926 and Governor of the

The Satyagraha Ashram

United Provinces in 1947.
83. Gandhi to J. P. Bhansali, 15 November 1929, CWMG, Vol. 42, pp. 168-9.
84. *Young India,* 8 November 1928; see also CWMG, Vol. 38, pp. 22-3; and letters from Gandhi to Kishorelal Mashruwala, 25 May 1928, *Ibid.,* Vol. 36, pp. 339-40, Mira, 31 October 1928, *Ibid.,* Vol. 37, p. 417.
85. *Young India,* 3 November 1928.
86. *Bombay Chronicle,* 8 April 1929, CWMG, Vol. 40, pp. 209-12.
87. *Ibid,* Gandhi wrote:" I have never claimed perfection for myself. Who knows my aberrations in the realm of thought have reacted on the environment around me. The epithet of 'Mahatma' has always galled me and now it almost sounds to me like a term of abuse... in spite of the full knowledge of the grave shortcomings and failures of the Udyoga Mandir, I still live on in the hope that it will one day justify its existence and reconvert itself into the Satyagraha Ashram"; see also Gandhi to Chaman, 27 February 1929, CWMG, Vol. 40, p. 42.
88. Gandhi to Chhaganlal Joshi, 6 May 1929, *Ibid.,* pp. 347-8.
89. *The Hindu,* 17 February 1930, CWMG, Vol. 42, pp. 477-8.
90. Gandhi to Motilal Nehru, 21 August 1928, *Ibid.,.* Vol. 37, p. 194.
91. Cited in Louis Fischer, *Gandhi: His Life and Message for the World* (New York: Mentor Books, 1954), p. 97.
92. Speech at prayer meeting on the eve of the Salt March, 11 March 1930, CWMG, Vol. 43, pp. 59-60.
93. Gandhi to Vasumati Pandit, 2 February 1931, *Ibid.,* Vol. 45, p. 142.
94. See Gandhi to Ganga Behn Vaidya, 2 February 1931, *Ibid., p.* 145. Gandhi wrote: "I got excited when I knew about this atrocity, but was not pained in the least. On the contrary, I felt happy. I would have certainly felt unhappy if none of you were among the victims of the assault. I know that there is ignorant attachment, even feeling in this, but I cannot conceal my attachment to the Ashram even if I tried to do so. The shortcomings of the inmates ... are intolerable to me. Likewise I feel happier when I see their virtues than when I see the virtues of others."
95. Gandhi to Chhaganlal Joshi, 2 February 1931, Ibid., p. 142.
96. Gandhi to Prema Behn Kantak, 28 July 1930, *Ibid.,* Vol. 44, p. 52.
97. The series was referred to as "Tuesday Morning Letters" written to Narandas Gandhi, the erstwhile director of the A.I.S.A. The letters were subsequently translated into English from the original Gujarati, and published in 1932 under the title of *From Yervada Mandir.*
98. *Bombay Chronicle,* 16 April 1931; see also *Navajivan,* 26 April 1931, CWMG, Vol. 46, pp. 36-7.
99. See Letters from Gandhi to Chhaganlal Joshi, 15 April and 2 June 1931, *Ibid.,* Vol. 45, p. 423, and Vol. 46, p. 284. In the second of these letters Gandhi outlined his views on the duties of the Dandi Marchers with regard to village work.
100. Gandhi to Chhaganlal Joshi, 25 July 1931, *Ibid.,* Vol. 47, p. 207.
101. Gandhi to M. G. Bhandari, 6 March 1932,/bid., Vol. 49, p. 182.
102. Gandhi to Prema Behn Kantak, 19 February 1932, *Ibid.,* p. 105.
103. See letters to Gandhi from Mira, n. *A.,* S.N. 16289, and 22 April 1933, S. N. 21035.

104. To recount all the unhappy incidents would serve no constructive purpose. Most noteworthy were the personality clashes bet ween Chhaganlal Joshi and Narandas Gandhi, between whom there appeared a deep-seated enmity. Prema Behn Kantak proved to be exceedingly temperamental and was inclined to behave imperiously towards other ashramites. Gandhi wrote concerning her attitude: "She should learn to control her tongue and restrain her obstinacy. She behaves in such a manner as to wipe out all that she does." Gandhi to Narandas Gandhi, 17 March 1933, CWMG, Vol. 54, p. 98. Balvant Singh, who joined the Ashram in 1931, described Prema Behn as being in temperament, bearing and habits, similar to a military officer. He recalls that there were a number of complaints against her harsh behaviour. After leaving Sabarmati she conducted an institution devoted to constructive work at Sasavad, Poona; see Balvantsinha Balwant Singh, *Under the Shelter of Bapu*, translated from the original in Hindi (Ahmedabad: Navajivan Publishing House, 1962), p. 15.
105. Gandhi to Narandas Gandhi, 23 October 1932, *Ibid.,* Vol. 51, p. 280; see also letters from Gandhi to Narandas Gandhi, 15/16 October 1932, *Ibid.,* p. 245; Ramaben Joshi, 5 January 1933, *Ibid.,* Vol. 52, p. 370.
106. Dr. B. R. Ambedkar to Gandhi, 7 February 1933, S. N. 19307.
107. Cited in Fischer, *op. tit.,* p. 118.
108. Gandhi to Narandas Gandhi, 21 November 1932, CWMG, Vol. 52, p. 34.
109. See Letters from Gandhi to Narayan M. Khare, 8 October 1932, *Ibid.,* Vol. 51, p. 109; Duncan Greenlees, 1 February 1933, *Ibid.,* Vol. 53, p. 206; and F. Mary Barn and Duncan Greenlees, 8 March 1933, *Ibid.*. Vol. 54, pp. 9-10.
110. Gandhi to Ashram Boys and Girls, n. d., *Ibid.,* Vol. 53, p. 425.
111. Gandhi to Prema Behn Kantak, 26 March 1933, *Ibid.,* Vol. 54, p. 213.
112. Gandhi to Ashram Boys and Girls, 26 March 1933, *Ibid.,* p. 210; see also Gandhi to Narandas Gandhi, 22 March 1933, *Ibid.,* pp. 159-60.
113. Gandhi to Mira, 24 March 1933, *Ibid.,* p. 175.
114. See Letters from Gandhi to Prema Behn Kantak, 27 November 1932, *Ibid.,* Vol. 52, p. 83; Narandas Gandhi, 5/6. May 1933, *Ibid.,* Vol. 55, pp. 126-7; and Duncan Greenlees, 9 May 1933, *Ibid.,* pp. 160-1.
115. See Letters from Gandhi to Narandas Gandhi and Hiralal Sharma, 9 May 1933, Ibid., pp. 162, 165. After the disbandment of Sabarmati Gandhi encouraged Sharma and his wife to settle at Wardha Ashram, which appears to vindicate Sharma's stance, and suggests that Gandhi dismissed the aspersions cast against him as groundless; see Gandhi to Hiralal Sharma, 9 April 1934, *Ibid.,* Vol. 57, p. 372.
116. Harijan, 6 May 1933.
117. Gandhi to Narandas Gandhi, 1 /2 May 1933, CWMG, Vol. 55, pp. 87-8.
118. Gandhi to Home Secretary, Government of Bombay, 26 July 1933, *Bombay Secret* Abstracts, Home Department Special Branch File No. 800 (40), pt. II, pp. 171-81; see also CWMG, Vol. 55, pp. 301-3.
119. *The Hindu, 27* July 1933, *Ibid.,* pp. 310-11.
120. See Letters from Gandhi to Vallabhbhai Patel, 24 September 1933, and G. D. Birla, 20 September 1933, *Ibid.,* Vol. 56, pp. 27, 41-2. Birla sympathised wholeheartedly with Gandhi's anti-untouchability campaign. The Harijan Sevak Sangh was launched with Birla as President and a governing body of

caste Hindus, but which later also included Harijans.
121. *Ibid.,* pp. 125-6.
122. The institutions and their respective activities included: 1. Harijan Ashram — Kanya Chhatralaya (Girl's Hostel) and Kanyalaya (Girl's School and Ladies Training Centre); 2. Harijan Sevak Sangh — to conduct Harijan Welfare programmes; 3. Ashram Goshala Trust — dairy etc. This institution has since been sold to a private concern; 4. Khadi and Gramodyog Kanyalaya — to operate *khadi* manufacture and weaving centre and *khadi* shops; 5. Ambar Experiment Committee—All India Khadi and Village Industries Commission runs this section, which conducts research in *khadi* production and the improvement of the ambar charkha, 6. Gandhi Smarak Sangrahalaya —Gandhi Museum and Library; 7. Gandhi Smarak Nidhi — Headquarters of Gujarat Branch is housed in the Ashram.
123. V. I. Pavlow, *Historical Premises for India's Transition to Capitalism* (Moscow: "Navka" Publishing House, 1979), p. 246.
124. *Hind Swaraj, p. 95.*
125. M. K. Gandhi, *India of My Dreams* (Ahmedabad: Navajivan Publishing House, 1947), pp. 120,124.
126. *Bombay Chronicle,* 8 April! 915.
127. *The Indian Review,* October 1917, CWMG, Vol. 13.
128. See Gandhi to Dr. Pranjivan Mehta.w, 2 July 1918, *Ibid.,* Vol. 14, p. 467,
129. Gandhi to Nirmala, 6 May 1919, *Ibid.,* Vol. 15, p. 281.
130. Gandhi to Maganlal Gandhi, 1 June 1919, *Ibid.,* p. 340.
131. For an account of the circumstances surrounding Gandhi's accession to the editorship of *Young India* and *Navajivan see Autobiography,* pp. 393-5.
132. See *Young India,* 21 July 1920 and 20 October 1921.
133. *Autobiography,* p. 418.
134. *Young India,* 11 August 1921.
135. Gandhi to Mahadev Desai, 25 September 1921, CWMG, Vol. 21. p. 207.
136. Cf. *Navajivan,* 1 February 1925, CWMC, Vol. 26, p. 62; also *Young India.* 3 June 1926.
137. *Ibid.,* 30 July 1926.
138. For Gandhi's concept of an ideal village see CWMG, Vol. 16, pp. 185-90.
139. *Navajivan,* 29 June 1924, CWMG, Vol. 24, p. 316.
140. Gandhi to Gangadharrao Deshpande, 27 July 1926, *Ibid.,* Vol. 31, pp. 200-1.
141. Indra Vidyalankar to Gandhi, 18 May 1926, S. N. 10729.
142. *Young India,* 1 October 1925.
143. *Ibid.,* 1 August 1929.
144. See Nanda, *op. cit.,* p. 168.
145. Cf. *Young India,* 20 November 1924.
146. The Hindu, 23 March 1925, CWMG, Vol. 26, p. 365.
147. Satyagraha Week marked the anniversary of the Jallianwalla Bagh incident in Amritsar in 1919. Brigadier General Reginald Dyer ordered troops to fire on over 10,000 unarmed people who had come together at Jallianwalla Bagh in contravention of Dyer's proclamation forbidding public gatherings. Over 1,500 casualties were inflicted, induding379 dead. The incident was followed by a series of atrocities against Indians in the Punjab, which revealed the depths to which racist elements in the Raj administration sank in order to

maintain Britain's grip on the sub-continent.
148. *Young India,* 5 May 1927.
149. *Ibid.,* 19 April 1928.
150. *Navajivan,* 3 July 1927, *CWMG,* Vol. 34, p. 100.
151. See Gandhi's speech to trainees at Khadi Vidyalaya, 13 April 1928, *Ibid.,* Vol. 36.
152. *Ibid.*
153. Jawaharlal Nehru to Gandhi, 11 January 1928, CWMG, Vol. 35, App. x, pp. 543-4;
154. Gandhi to Mahadev Desai, 30 November 1928, *Ibid.,* Vol. 38, p. 133.
155. See A. L. Basham, *The Wonder That Was India* (London : Fontana/Collins, 1971), pp.32, 196-7, 321.
156. Mookerji, *op. cit.,* p. xxix.
157. Gandhi to Maganlal Gandhi, 25 January 1927, CWMG, Vol. 33, p. 10. In reference to the expert advice Gandhi sought see his Letters to Sir Harold Mans (Director of Agriculture, Poona), 20 July 1926, *Ibid.,* Vol. 31, p. 168; Nilratan Sircar and Madhusadan Das (Research Tannery), 16 March 1928, *Ibid.,* Vol. 36, pp. 110-11; and Pratap S. Pundit, 26 March 1928, *Ibid.,* p. 144.
158. *Navajivan,* 22 May 1927, CWMG,Vol.33, p. 352.
159. See Gandhi to Chhaganlal Gandhi, 29 April 1929, *Ibid.,* Vol. 40. p. 306.
160. Gandhi to D. B. (Kakasaheb) Kalelkar, 4 August 1926, *Ibid.,* Vol. 31, p. 256.
161. D. W. Nagarkatia to Gandhi, 4 May 1917, S. N. 6353.
162. Cf. Gandhi's speech to trainees at Khadi Vidyaiaya, 13 April 1928, CWMG, Vol. 36, pp. 221-4.
163. See *Young India,* 9 June 1927.
164. Gandhi to B. C. Roy, 3 November 1928, CWMG, Vol. 38, pp. 7-8.
165. *Young India,* 27 August 1925.
166. *Navajivan,* 6 February 1921, CWMG, Vol. 19, p. 331.
167. *Young India,* 5 July 1928.
168. Cited in Haridas Mukherjee and Uma Mukherjee, *The Origins of the National Education Movement* (1905-1916) (Calcutta : Jadavpur University, 1957), p. 7.
169. Speech by Gokhale in Imperial Legislative Council, 18 December 1903, in D. G. Karve and D. V. Ambekar (eds.) : *Speeches and Writings of Copal Krishna Gokhale,* cited jn Brown, *op. cit.,* p. 45.
170. See "Kakasaheb Kalelkar", *The Illustrated Weekly of India,* 31 May 1959.
171. Sinha, *op. cit.,* pp. 72-3.
172. *Ibid.*
173. Cited in Madan G. Gandhi, *Gandhian Aesthetics* (Chandigarh and Delhi: Vikas Bharati, 1969), p. 67.
174. Dwijendranath Tagore to Gandhi, 1 September 1921, S. N. 7607.
175. Talk with teachers of the National School, 23 June 1917, CWMG, Vol. 13, pp. . 446-8.
176. *Young India,* 15 April 1926.
177. *Ibid.,* 17 November 1920.
178. *Navajivan,* 20 January 1921, CWMG, Vol. 19, pp. 258-9.
179. *Navajivan,* 8 May 1921, CWMG, Vol. 20, p. 78.
180. Brown, *op. cit.,* p. 45.
181. See Letters to Gandhi from S. K. Rudra, 2 July 1915, S. N. 6201; Srlima Tyabji,

15 July 1915, S. N. 6203; and S. G. Ranaday, 25 August 1915, S. N. 6226.
182. Mira to Gandhi, n. d., S. N. 16289.
183. Pyarelal, Interview held in New Delhi, 30 November 1981.

4

The Village of Service: "India in a Village"

Throughout the 1920s Gandhi persevered in his efforts to convince Congressmen of the value of the constructive work programme. They supported his schemes in so far as it enabled them to consolidate and improve their standing in Congress. Few agreed with his thesis that "political power is not an end but one of the means of enabling people to better their condition in every departments of life".[1] Congress work committees were formed to link constructive work at the village level to the aims of Congress politics. They proved to be largely ineffectual. Referring to these committees, Gandhi observed: "It became clear to me that the workers were in no mood to do any serious work of construction. The constructive programme provided no enchantment. They were not a social reform association.... They wanted to deliver "non-violent" blows. All this appeared so thoroughly unreal. They would not stop to think that even if they could defeat the Government by a childish display of rage, they could not conduct the Government of the country for a single day without serious and laborious organisation and construction."[2]

Though written in 1922 the comment is characteristic of Gandhi's attitude in general to Congress involvement in constructive work. In subsequent years he left the task of managing the Congress committees to Jawaharlal Nehru. The failings of the Congress, in this sense convinced Gandhi that the success of the constructive programme could not be dependent on the guidance and finance of central or regional organisations. By the early 1930s he was stressing the need for individual effort to achieve local reform and promote village-oriented activities.

Congressmen gave lip service to the constructive programme largely to take advantage of Gandhi's political acumen. The Congress committees forged links with the politically-minded

The Village of Service: "India in a Village"

"sub-contractors", or local power bases, which Gandhi utilised to promote social reform at the regional level. Through his constructive programme Gandhi had attracted more people than ever before into political activity, thus allowing Congress access to large political resources hitherto untapped. This revitalised the organisation during the 1920s and accounted for much of its strength during the period of direct action which followed the launching of civil disobedience in 1930. The regional power bases had been so constructed as to allow Gandhi's politically affiliated supporters to take control of the Congress organisation during the Salt *Satyagraha*. They simply moved from the cities back to their local areas, enabling the organisation to withstand civil martial laws.[3]

The formation of specialist social reform organisations had facilitated the decentralisation of the constructive work programme to some extent. Gandhi observed that "more effective work becomes possible through autonomous organisations created for specific activities".[4] Yet during the 1920s the community workdone at the village level by Gandhian activists was severely limited in most parts of India. His regional representatives came from a wide range of educational, political and social backgrounds. Often they represented the interests of landed peasants, urban money-lenders and professional intelligentsia, and were disinterested in constructive work among the really poor in the villages. There were instances of local grievances being voiced and selfish interests being pursued, factors primarily responsible for local civil disobedience actions being at variance to Gandhi's guidelines during the Salt *Satyagraha* and subsequent non-co-operation campaign.[5]

Disenchanted with Congress activities, and disappointed with the performance of the majority of his "subcontractors" in the early 1930s, Gandhi stepped up his vociferous campaign to focus attention on the plight of the poorest and weakest people in the villages. He began to depend more on colleagues capable of organising mass action without the need for political machinery. These men normally lacked real power within the Congress organisation but had the ability to sustain mass contacts outside their political roles. Such people lent credence to the social reform organisations when they showed a willingness to concentrate their efforts on village work.

The most influential was Jamnalal Bajaj, a wealthy *marwadi* industrialist, who had provided substantial monetary assistance to Sabarmati and other constructive work. He became a member of thirteen of the twenty social reform organisations established by Gandhi, often acting as a restraint on the political careerists and a link between the "sub-contractors" and the secondary level of mass contact workers. Gandhi wrote to Jamnalal's friends shortly after his death in 1942 :

> You are aware how intimate was the relationship between Jamnalal and myself. There was no work of mine in which I did not receive his fullest co-operation in body, mind and wealth. Neither he nor I had any attraction for what is called politics. He was drawn into it because I was in it. My real politics was constructive work, and so too was his.[6]

Gandhi argued that improvement in the living conditions of the poorest in the villages should be the true measure of India's development. In a speech to a social service organisation in 1931 he indicated the direction constructive work should take during the 1930s:

> Till today we worked in a wrong way—we did all our work in cities and formulated all our schemes keeping cities in view. We stayed away from village folk, hence they have so far regarded their privations as the result of divine wrath and could think of no other causes. Institutions of public service should be located among the people, be partners of their joys and sorrows and render service by spreading knowledge among them.[7]

This had always been Gandhi's intention, but during the 1920s few volunteers had met his exacting requirements and settled alone in a village. He had envisaged an important role for the ashramites in the village work programme, but he was exasperated by their "lack of faith .... their timidity and their false sense of shame". In response to a suggestion by a group member in 1919 that the Ashram assist the surrounding villages to counteract harassment by thieves, Gandhi replied that work promoted purely by self-interest was useless.[8]

The Village of Service: "India in a Village"

Gandhi was concerned to avoid a repetition of events in 1922 when enthusiasm ebbed with the cessation of civil disobedience. He exhorted his co-workers and the country as a whole to work for Hindu-Muslim unity, removal of untouchability, uplift of tribal people, and the uplift of women to their proper status in the home and society. The *Harijan Sevak Sangh* was founded in 1933 to promote and organise the service of untouchables by caste-Hindus.[9] Gandhi maintained that the sole aim of the organisation was the purification of religion, which left no room for those who approached the question from a political standpoint or for any selfish motive. He let it be known that anyone of this persuasion who came to his attention would be required to leave the service. The implication was that the organisation could not influence caste-Hindus if its credibility was undermined by the pursuit of any political aims apart from the attainment of *purna swaraj* (total independence). This had connotations far more sweeping than any narrow political objective: "Whatever meaning may be given to the word swaraj, removal of untouchability will be a fraud, if it does not carry with it the enjoyment by the freed Hindus of precisely the same rights as the other Hindus and all other communities may enjoy under it."[10]

Gandhi believed that human beings would cease to exploit each other if they recognised the essential unity of all religions and all mankind. In his view the task of the individual was to cultivate respect for all men, accept the creed of non-violence and work selflessly to achieve the brotherhood of man.[11] But he also realised that the superstition, ignorance and illiteracy of the villagers would handicap the programme. He directed his co-workers to conduct a rigorous propaganda against untouchability in the villages. While Dr. Ambedkar clamoured for more active participation by *harijans* in uplift programmes, Gandhi requested that they do nothing but cultivate self-reliance by leading a pure, hardworking life. In his view it was the duty of all caste-Hindus to see that they were given the opportunity to do so.

Harijan work could not be organised along the same lines as the *khadi* programme, because of the rigid opposition to socio-religious reform within orthodox communities. The *Harijan Sevak Sangh* trained scavengers in advanced sanitary methods, encouraged caste-Hindus to clean latrines and induced villagers to open temples, wells, roads and schools to *harijans*. The ultimate objective was the absorption of the *harijans* into the caste system. Reactionary opposition sprang up on all sides, but the rigorous propaganda had a measure of success.

Gandhi's promotion of the *harijan* cause throughout 1933 resulted in the movement spreading to many district towns through the establishment of local committees, and the placing of a significant number of full-time workers in the villages. Yet, as reported in *Harijan* by A. V. Thakkar, progress was on the whole slow: "The field is immensely vast and workers, especially whole-time workers, are very few and far between. I know of dozens of cases where whole districts are not touched, at least in an organised way, by this movement.... Even in many organised districts, very little work in purely rural areas has been attempted." *(Harijan,* 6 May 1933).

At the end of 1933 Gandhi undertook an extensive tour of India in an attempt to hasten the removal of untouchability. During nine months he addressed meetings, collected funds, visited temples and *harijan* colonies, guided workers engaged in *harijan* service, and inspired new hope *in harijans.* He awoke many caste-Hindus to their responsibility for the terrible conditions under which the *harijans* suffered. During the tour Gandhi Learnt of several factors inhibiting the progress of work in the villages. It became apparent that both *harijan* and caste-Hindu would be better served if, rather than concentrating all resources on *harijan* uplift, the village work programme had as its main object village reorganisation and reconstruction. In Gandhi's view it was vital to revive village industries and stimulate the economic and moral advancement of villagers as a whole.[12]

Many minor industries had supplemented the traditional rural income.[13] While in Gandhi's view *khadi* would remain the basis for village revival he sought to reintegrate these minor industries into the village economy. In addition he saw the need to promote research wherever possible into new products which could supply the needs of the villagers and had market potential. Gandhi's ideal was that the final article be used where it was produced, and preferably by the producers themselves. His thesis was that the circumstances of all villagers would be improved if the status of village crafts was raised. He appealed to the nation to support the village scheme by looking to the villages for the supply of daily needs. If it were discovered that certain needs could not be adequately supplied in this fashion, Gandhi claimed it was the responsibility of the buyer to channel his concern directly to the producers; insisting they improve and taking the trouble of organising them to do so.[14] He made it clear that self-sufficiency at the village level could not produce high standards of living, as judged from the standpoint of the educated and moneyed classes. It could only be sustained by a discipline of frugality and simplicity.

Before Gandhi withdrew from Congress in 1934 he gained approval to establish the All India Village Industries Association (AIVIA). Nehru was disappointed by his decision to dissociate himself from the Congress, but Gandhi argued that politicisation without reconstruction would not lead to the non-violent society of a self-reliant Indian Common wealth. The idea that mere transfer of power, without social renewal, would be an empty achievement was inherent in a statement to the press on his retirement from Congress in October 1934:

> If Congressmen forget the constructive programme and simply confine Congress activities to winning Assembly and Council elections and fruitless debates in the Assembly and Councils, they will soon find that I have taken with me the kernel of politics and they have kept for themselves only the outermost husk, without even the vitamins.[15]

When explaining the position the AIVIA would take with respect to Congress activities, Gandhi asserted that the role of the association was not to arouse political consciousness among the masses, but to revive industries and improve the method of work in villages.[16] He warned that political consciousness divorced from social consciousness would have disastrous consequences. Reports of corruption in the Congress seemed to confirm his view and reaffirmed his earlier disillusionment with the future "trustees of the nation". The *swaraj* was not a short-term political goal, but the ideal and guiding principle of a permanent social revolution.

Nehru and the increasingly popular Socialist Party, on the other hand, argued for the rapid politicisation of the masses. They stressed the importance of securing support for the socialist programme "among the workers and peasants. Gandhi found he could not reconcile policies such as the derecognition of private property and the complete socialisation of industry with his *sarvodaya* ideal. He criticised Congressmen for their lack of faith in the spinning wheel and their adherence to non-violence as an expedient policy rather than as a "fundamental creed".[17] Though his influence in Congress circles remained strong, the substantial differences between the Socialist programme and his own were a decisive factor in his decision to retire from active political life. The Congress leaders did not cease to consult him, and he would often reiterate his faith in Nehru as his "political heir", but the rift between the Socialists and himself widened.

The extent to which the Socialists established themselves as an influential force within Congress is mirrored in the Congress Presidential address at Lucknow in 1936: "The Congress should encourage the formation of peasant unions as well as workers' unions, and co-operate with such as already exist, so that the day-to-day struggle of the masses might be carried on, on the basis of their economic demands and other grievances. This identification of the Congress with the economic struggle of the masses will bring it nearer to them and nearer to freedom than anything else. The Congress would be in a position to co-ordinate all these vital activities and thus to base itself on the widest possible mass foundation."[18] The Socialist programme was firmly rooted in the concept of class struggle. They argued for propaganda programmes among the peasants to incite rebellion. For them the improvement of village conditions was dependent upon the dismantling, forcibly if necessary, of the *zamindari* system. Gandhi's reply was that change must proceed slowly in this direction. Any alienation of *zamindars'* sympathies would undermine current village work programmes.[19]

Though Gandhi acknowledged the selflessness of many Socialists, he felt they were essentially Western-minded. In his view their faith in the inevitability of class war and their belief in the innate selfishness of human nature were alien to the Indian genius. He referred to their ignorance of conditions in Indian villages and criticised their revolutionary haste. Radical elements of the leftist political groups accused Gandhi of supporting vested interests. By attempting to imbue the freedom struggle with religious ideas and promoting abstract goals, they claimed his aim was to obscure the central issue of capitalist exploitation.[20] Gandhi indicated he was indifferent about the time when the goal of freedom would be reached but not about the work to be done and the goal itself. Similarly, he felt that the issue of whether or not the wealthy shed their wealth was irrelevant. In his view correct means would ensure a more equitable society.[21]

He pressed forward with his village work programme. He put the choice simply. Either the programme was actively accepted and worked by a large number of young men and women prepared to devote themselves to a life of service, or the *sarvodaya* society would remain nothing more than an unrealisable ideal. For Gandhi the constructive work programme became the acid test for anyone claiming to be a fighter for freedom: "You will not tell me that this is an impossible programme, that you have not the qualifications for it. That you have not fulfilled it so far should be no impediment in your way. If it appeals to your reason and your heart, you must not hesitate. Do not fight shy of the experiment. The experiment will itself provide the momentum for more and more effort."[22] He argued that the cause of freedom would be lost unless young people from among the city-dwelling middle classes were willing to forego the frivolous pleasures of youth in favour of the simple, hard-working conditions of village life.

Candidates for village work were warned that to be a real villager is more difficult than to obtain a graduate degree".[23] Gandhi readily admitted that his requirements were exacting, but, as the object of village service was to open the villagers' minds to a better way of life, he deemed it essential that quality of work take precedence over quantity.[24] To encourage the villagers' interest in community development, it was important to communicate new ideas in terms they could understand. This necessitated the workers' personal identification with the villagers and the realities of village life.[25] Intellectual discourses on the doctrines of truth and non-violence would achieve little unless accompanied by an active display of love through personal service. In this sense Gandhi conceived of love as an active expression of non-violence. His argument was that if he and his co-workers took care of quality of work then quantity would naturally ensue.

Gandhi was not unaware of the problems involved in the village work scheme. He recognised that many workers would find their task frustrating and debilitating. The majority had spent their lives in towns and cities and had received a Western-based formal education. They frequently had little knowledge of village life, and the training received at various Gandhian institutions proved in many cases to be insufficient. Since the constructive programme had dispensed with the need for a large organisation and salaried staff, the workers were expected to serve the villagers with the aid of minimal capital and external support. Many developed what Gandhi referred to as a "fear complex": "Many workers are so frightened of village life that they fear that if they' are not paid by some agency they will not be able to earn their living by labouring in villages."[26] To reassure workers he explained that in the initial period of their service it was expected that they would of necessity adopt a higher standard of living than the villagers. He saw no harm in this so long as all needs could be satisfied within the village. In fact he optimistically believed that the villagers would not grudge the worker these necessary extras, and that it would not be "impossible for the villagers to obtain and live on the same articles of diet as the village workers and thus adopt the same standard of living".[27]

However, he ensured that the *gram sevaks* (village workers) had no false illusions concerning village reconstruction. After the initial period of adjustment it was expected that the worker would progressively renounce all material advantages. He warned that anyone who thought of privileges and rights would be disappointed. He reminded those who questioned the strict discipline that workers in positions of authority within the reform organisations were equal in every sense to the humblest of village workers. The strict observances at Sabarmati were now transformed into a code of conduct for the *gram sevak* settling alone in a village. Gandhi determined that independent and self-directed work achieved under the auspices of the social service organisations should be active expression of everything the constructive programme stood for. He called on new recruits to take inspiration from the work already under way.

After his withdrawal from Congress activities Gandhi was faced with the problem of counteracting the diminishing importance of self-discipline and individual action, which would accompany a waning of his charismatic role in national affairs. It was symptomatic of the nature of his leadership that for many village workers and the general public he was the embodiment of the constructive work programme. He recognised this unfortunate aspect of his leadership as a threat to the success of the work programme. The double-edged weapon of his own charisma had attracted national support for his political goals, but it severely hindered the quest for *sarvodaya* :

> It is a flattering thought that some people have derived their faith in non-violence from me. But I would warn them that I may prove a broken reed at a critical juncture, if they have not assimilated the spirit of non-violence and if it has not become an integral part of their lives. Faith in a man is a perishable quantity, for, it vanishes like smoke when their idol does not come up to their expectations; but what gives us hope and courage in the nick of time is undying faith in a cause or a principle, irrespective of persons from whom it is derived.[28]

The Harijan Tour of 1933 confirmed for Gandhi that a large proportion of village workers depended upon him for their inner strength, a dependency often expressed in their desire to have him visit their village. In the past he had received many complaints from ashramites at Sabarmati that the "soul" went out of Ashram activities in his absence. The problem as manifested in the microcosm of the Ashram assumed enormous dimensions when it began to undermine the effectiveness of the village work scheme. Another aspect was that despite all efforts to promote and foster local leadership, the village programme was planned and sustained by external leadersnip.[29]

The failings of the village scheme were due primarily to the difficulties the average man and women faced in attempting to reach the standard of service required by Gandhi, and to misconceptions among the workers as to the role they were expected to play in village life. To the various critics of Gandhian methods the volume of work done throughout India was insignificant when distributed over the respective provinces and considered in relation to the goals of the programme. Gandhi's usual response to criticism of this kind was to reiterate his belief that to sacrifice quality for the sake of quantity would be disastrous. "Village workers have to be found or made and, when once the fear of settling in villages is overcome, the response to the demand for a large number of workers will be much greater than it is today", he wrote to a worried Harijan worker.[30]

Despite Gandhi's call to strive with redoubled energies in return for past inaction, the village workers were not having the desired impact on village life. Their approach to issues such as untouchability and sanitation frequently induced either indifferent or angry reactions from the villagers. On occasion they became openly hostile to the intrusion of a *gram sevak* as he represented a threat to their own meagre resources. The promotion of *khadi* and other village industries simply bewildered those with no tradition of such work. Incidents also occurred where the workers' limited funds were squandered on useless buildings and other areas of low priority.

The problem essentially was that Gandhi and his co-workers had preconceived notions of the conditions prevailing in the villages and the work to be done. Rather than seek to familiarise themselves with the problems unique to each village as conceived by the villagers themselves, the *gram sevaks* would often impose Gandhi's experimental theories outright on illiterate people. By adopting an attitude of superiority in their dealings with the villagers, and by preaching a preconceived gospel of salvation, many *gram sevaks* merely succeeded in alienating those they were sent to serve. There was a growing number of critics, including village workers, who voiced dissatisfaction with Gandhi's concern for quality of work, purity of spirit, and the duty of bread labour. In an interview with Gandhi one disgruntled *gram sevak* called for a more radical approach to the problems of poverty and exploitation:

> You ask us to go and settle down in the villages, and work for our living like the villagers. I have done so, done all kinds of jobs, weaving, rope-making, hewing wood, etc., but I find it difficult to make ends meet. What are we to do? I think most of our ills are due to capitalism. The capitalists are relentless in their exploitation. Why should we spare them? Please do not fling at me your gospel of loving thy neighbour as thyself. It does not satisfy me.[31]

These remarks indicate the worker's sympathy for the Socialist programme. Confusion and frustration led many workers to question Gandhi's "gradualism". Much of their dissent was patently valid in terms of the *gram sevak* who was required to work for his livelihood for eight hours a day and then find time and

The Village of Service: "India in a Village"

energy to attend to the other multifarious concerns of the programme.[32] A member of an ashram that trained *gram sevaks* expressed concern that the ideal of bread labour unnecessarily limited the worker's capacity for social service.[33]

The fact remained that despite Gandhi's efforts to encourage a desire to serve the very poor amongst his predominantly middle class followers, the majority continued to regard the Mahatma as the embodiment of their ideals and sole source of inspiration. Yet Gandhi, thus far, had made no attempt to settle in a village, serve its people, attempt to solve its problems, and demonstrate the viability of non-violence as an alternative way of life.

To be sure, he had publicly expressed a desire to live and work in such a setting at the time of his withdrawal from Congress.[34] The failure of Congressmen to translate his ideals into practice had convinced him of the need to transform his role in national affairs from that of charismatic politician and leader to that of simple *gram sevak*. He wanted to set an example of selfless and diligent village service. However, he had shown no inclination to settle in a village in the past, devoting his energies primarily to political work. His attitude prior to 1934 is evident from a letter to his son Devadas in 1918: In the summer, living in a village appears grand indeed, but it is doubtful whether one would enjoy it in the monsoon. Personally, I think it would be very difficult for me to go to any place I like during the rainy season. My dislike of dirt is increasing, not diminishing. I feel suffocated if the lavatory, is the least bit unclean.... Those who are not particularly sensitive to lack of cleanliness are, I find, happy enough in a village."[35]

He could no longer answer criticisms and the anguished pleas of *gram sevaks* from a general theoretical position. "It is easier written than done, my friends will say, and I confess it is presurnptuous for one like me who has not yet sat down in a village to offer any advice", he wrote. "He jests at scars who never felt a wound."[36] To reassure village workers, to answer critics of the village scheme, and in response to whatever misgivings he held concerning the direction the constructive work programme was taking, Gandhi decided in 1936 to attempt his last major experiment in non-violence by settling alone in a small and backward central Indian village at the onset of monsoon. "We all know that conditions of life in a village are particularly hard in the monsoon," he said to a friend, "why, then should I not begin with that rich experience."[37]

The Establishment of Sevagram

After the closure of Sabarmati in 1933 Gandhi and a number of Ashramites took up residence in Vinoba Bhave's Satyagraha Ashram at Wardha. Gandhi was totally preoccupied with *harijan* service and the promotion of village industries. He encouraged his fellow inmates to take up village work, explaining that he had no intention of building another Ashram along the same lines as Sabarmati. Similarly, the teachers from the Gujarat Vidyapith were urged to adopt a village and educate the people. In 1934, acting on the advice of Jamnalal Bajaj, Gandhi selected Wardha as the headquarters of the AIVIA. It was a logical choice for a number of reasons. Apart from its central location, Jamnalal was a prominent figure in the district and the financial sponsor of the Wardha Ashram. In addition he made a donation to Gandhi of a large house, with twenty acres of orange orchards, in memory of Maganlal Gandhi. The property was renamed Maganwadi and became the administrative headquarters of the AIVIA, the management of which was taken over by J. C. Kumarappa, a successful economist converted to Gandhi's theories. His offices occupied part of Maganwadi, while Gandhi and a party of fifteen to twenty followers worked and lived in the remainder of the large house.

Ironically, the person most responsible for the choice of Sevagram[38] as the site for Gandhi's village experiment was the Englishwoman, Madeleine Slade (renamed Mirabehn by Gandhi). Living at Maganwadi with Gandhi, Mira found the conditions too confining. She began solitary walks which took her through a small village known as Sindi.[39] The insanitary living conditions of the village people appalled her. With the co-operation of Mahadev Desai, now editor of *Harijan* in addition to his secretarial duties, Mira began a sanitation programme in Sindi. Gandhi encouraged their work, but efforts to discourage the villagers from defiling the village environment went largely unrewarded.[40] Upon learning of this failure he instructed Mira to clean the roads of the village every morning with two or three volunteers enlisted from among the residents or visitors at Maganwadi.

To lend weight to these object lessons in elementary sanitation

Gandhi accompanied the cleaning party one morning and later offered to build the villagers simple earth latrines. He explained that the manure produced would not only enhance crop productivity but enable them to rotate suitable fodder or vegetable crops all the year round; this was a small but vital element in the cycle of self-sufficiency he sought to introduce on a national scale. "Your crops will be increased without any extra expenses or effort, your health will improve, for the flies will carry no disease germs, and your village will be turned into a clean spot", he told the villagers.[41]

In Sindi, as all over India, the primary task was to shake the people free of a deep-seated apathy to community development. They protected their caste interests and celebrated religious festivals with unbridled fervour, but were disinterested in any programme that threatened to disturb the *status quo* or which required additional work on their part. This was especially true of any activity traditionally associated with the role of the *bhangi* (scavenger). Each caste grouping clung to their ritual position in the hierarchy as a form of security and identification. Against this entrenched value system Gandhi opposed a christianised egalitarianism and work ethic, which was alien to the Hindu mentality. Even the presence of Gandhi in Sindi had little effect. Mira and her companions found that at most they occasionally received a negative form of co-operation. One man's contribution, for instance, was to discourage people from defiling a small area of road by scaring them away in the early hours of the morning.[42]

Toward the end of 1935 Gandhi's health relapsed due to high blood pressure. The cramped living conditions at Maganwadi and the lack of obvious progress at Sindi left him frustrated and contributed to his poor health. He wrote in a letter to a friend who had requested a message for his paper:

> I am really and literally drained dry. I have no gift for weaving messages to order. This village work is so taxing and so baffling that if I could help it, I would stop all writing and simply bury myself in a village and there work away for all I am worth, and that I should love to do in perfect silence.[43]

He now contemplated living in Sindi alone. By relying on

assistance only from the villagers he hoped to improve his rapport with them. Knowing the state of his health the workers at Maganwadi were shocked by this decision. To ensure that he remained where he could receive proper treatment in case of further illness, Mira offered to take his place in Sindi. Gandhi reluctantly agreed.[44]

Under Gandhi's instructions a small one-roomed brick cottage was constructed for her at Sindi. The population of the village were predominantly Mahars, an untouchable caste equivalent to the Chamars (leather workers) of north India. There were a number of other *harijan* households, considered ritually inferior to the Mahars, and one or two caste-Hindu families. Mira was soon faced with the problem of obtaining water in an Indian village. Each caste group utilised its own well. On the first day of her sojourn in Sindi Mira accepted water from a man of the lowest group, which resulted in her being refused permission to use the wells of the higher castes. She had failed to conform to the strict mores of the *jati* system and experienced the oppression and indignity of untouchability.[45]

Work in Sindi progressed slowly, but gradually Mira won the confidence of several villagers, who in turn encouraged other members of their caste to appreciate the value of sanitation and understand the discriminatory nature of untouchability. The Mangs were the first to co-operate. Ranked lower in *jati* hierarchy than the Mahars, a hereditary rivalry and enmity existed between the two groups.[46] The Mangs reconciled themselves to Mira using their well, but refused her colleagues permission to "pollute" the water. Yet it was a step in the right direction. Another breakthrough occurred when after nine months of scavenging in the village Mira and her co-workers discovered a man who recognised the value of manure produced from human excrement.[47] However, Mira was not wholly satisfied with these achievements because Sindi was considered little more than an outlying urban slum area of Wardha. She suggested to Gandhi that if someone would replace her in Sindi she would survey the area for a suitable village.

Gandhi accepted Mira's proposal, and she began a quest for a "typical village" within a radius of five miles. Mira describes her search:

It was a hard, dry, rather unresponsive country-side and the inhabitants were also rather dry in their temperament. In some places the Harijans were positively hostile. It was therefore difficult to find a suitable village. After walking day after day in all directions I finally decided that a village called Segaon (the future Sevagram), about five miles to the east of Wardha, would be the best, or rather the least unsatisfactory.[48]

Segaon proved to be an ideal choice. Not only was Jamnalal Bajaj a prominent businessman in the Wardha district, he was also *malguzar* (Maratha Revenue Manager) or *zamindar* of this village.

The division of land at Segaon followed the pattern established by the British in many parts of India during the nineteenth century. The government had promoted the vesting of land-ownership in indigenous revenue collectors or *zamindars,* transforming them into a new landlord class with obligations to their colonial patrons. In the Central Provinces the *zamindar,* or *malguzar* as he was known, was either sole proprietor or co-proprietor of a village, although with large reservations of rights to the original cultivators. B. H. Baden Powell observed "that there we have the peculiar feature of landlord villages, only that the landlords have no power of interference with the rent payments, or with the management of a considerable portion of their tenants".[49] If there were co-proprietors of a village, as in the case of Segaon, each had a defined share, most commonly a legal fractional share, on which the profits and burdens, though not the land itself, were divided. In Segaon the *malguzari* shares were divided between Jamnalal Bajaj (75 per cent) and Babasaheb Deshmukh (25 per cent). Of the total 1,550 acres of village land, 220 acres were owned by the *malguzars,* the remainder divided among sixty small landholders.[50]

Initially Mira took up residence at Segaon in an empty bullock shed which Jamnalal made available. She was replaced at Sindi by Gajanan Naik, a worker from Maganwadi. In contrast to her earlier impressions of Segaon and the surrounding area, Mira became romantically enthused with her new life-style. She described village life as "a vast and ever-varying array of priceless masterpieces"; and in a similar vein, "To me the city is the backwater, the village is the stream of life and beauty."[51] These visions of village life expressed an emotional contentment during her early days at Segaon, but it was short-lived. In the past her health had suffered during lengthy separations from Gandhi. As a longing to be with him increased she wrote that if living in the village meant perpetual separation from Gandhi she could not endure it. Her anxiety increased when Gandhi's blood pressure again rose sharply, causing another breakdown in his health. He was moved to an ashram closer to Segaon, but Jamnalal Bajaj refused visitors and residents any contact with him. When Mira found her way into Gandhi's room barred she became emotionally distraught. Eventually she was allowed to see him but received a further shock when informed that his blood pressure would become dangerously high if she did not remain in the village.[52]

Gandhi's health improved, but his blood pressure remained too high. On doctors' advice he moved to Ahmedabad for a short period. Mira was permitted several short visits to him before he left, but she observed that a "strange artificiality... had suddenly been raised between them."[53] She seemed unaware that her extreme possessiveness had placed a severe strain on their relationship. On the verge or a nervous breakdown she was forced to return to Maganwadi,

One of the requirements Gandhi expected of a village worker was that he or she "should not take any help from outside but should create his co-workers from the village itself". Mira had shown herself to be a stock example of *gram sevaks* who relied upon Gandhi for their inner strength and this greatly disappointed him. Though Mira's ambition was to live in a village with Gandhi and study his approach to the people and their problems, he would make no exception for her. Mira tried to justify her fear of the village by relating it to the distress she experienced at being barred during his sickness.[54]

Gandhi was now determined to replace Mira in Segaon. He had been dissatisfied with the progress at Sindi and felt the achievements there were piecemeal. "We have not yet mastered the art of living in a village", he wrote to a colleague.[55] He partly attributed the failings of the Sindi experiment to Mira's inconsistencies, which hardened his determination to settle in Segaon without her.[56] Though his decision upset her Mira took consolation from the belief that Segaon would be more suitable for him than Maganwadi. She returned to the village and began preparations for his arrival. She quickly found a suitable location to build a hut, and with the co-operation of Jamnalal's farm manager had it constructed from the same materials used by the villagers, but to her specifications. Gandhi was impressed with her efforts, saying of the hut that he saw "the villager's mentality about everything in it".[57]

During this period of several months Mira concentrated on the sanitation problem, which she knew was of particular concern to Gandhi. Initially she simply studied the villager's habits, allowing them to adjust to her presence. Subsequently she chose seven "squatting grounds" already in use by the villagers. Experience in Sindi had taught her the difficulty of changing the area habitually used. The grounds chosen were cleared, pits prepared and enclosures set up for men and women. A Bhangi family was engaged to keep the enclosures clean and daily sweep the lanes and open spaces. The latter were assured a bonus per cartload of manure, which would be produced within a few months of the pits being filled. It was proposed that the value of the manure should repay the cost of the enclosures and the Bhangi's wage.[58] Mira planned to extend this experiment to other villages, thereby creating jobs for unemployed Bhangis and generally enhancing the quality of rural life.

The response of the villagers was not encouraging. These uneducated people were ignorant of Mira's motives and understandably sceptical of the new system. Rumours circulated that those who used the latrines would be required to pay a monthly fee, that Mira was a government agent, and that some sort of taxation was the inevitable outcome. The people had learnt from experience that external agencies showed interest in the village usually for their own benefit. To allay doubts she would move around the village reassuring the people: "It is not money but manure that we want in return for our labours."[59] It soon became evident to Mira that to remould a belief system grown rigid over the centuries the innovator requires a reservoir of understanding and must be prepared to persevere and patiently instruct by example. Gandhi was aware that perhaps equally important was the willingness to accept that these methods by no means guaranteed rapid success. Sometime later in response to a colleague's concern that work in Segaon progressed very slowly, he said: "We have neglected the village folk for hundreds of years. How can we expect to transform their attitudes overnight? Even a Mahatma cannot work miracles. We must continue to serve the villagers with infinite patience, without expecting any spectacular results."[60]

By March 1936 Gandhi's health had improved sufficiently to enable him to resume normal activity. In a letter to Mira he reaffirmed his intention to settle in Segaon:

> Of course every intimate contact with the real villagers in their villages gives us new knowledge and new hope, though it also shows us the difficulties in our path. My heart is there. What my effort will end in I do not know.[61]

The report of the Gandhi Seva Sangh[62] meeting that took place just prior to his settling in Segaon mirrors the extent of his preoccupation with village work. He proclaimed that henceforth sessions of the Sangh would be held in obscure villages. Their task, he explained, was to explore the potentiality of reviving local industries and exhibiting their products. He stipulated that workers should only accept the minimum requirements to subsist in the village they served. Rajendra Prasad drew Gandhi's attention again to the question of excessive physical labour reducing the workers' capacity to perform educational and developmental tasks. Gandhi replied that "Every human being should maintain himself only through physical labour. I consider it a divine law."[63] Apart from the propaganda and pedagogical value of selfless manual labour carried out by workers whose caste rules forbade such work, he realised that poor villagers would be less sceptical of *gram sevaks* who managed to support themselves in the village through manual work. Surprisingly he did not preclude the possibility of a village worker opening a shop, provided it reduced the villagers' dependence on the towns, cities and unscrupulous businessmen.

The general tenor of discussions during this meeting of the Sangh revealed the misconceptions that persisted among the village workers. There was confusion concerning the dissociation of constructive work from political activity. Gandhi insisted that the two programmes complemented each other, but misunderstandings sprung up between political and non-political workers; factions formed with each regarding the other as inferior. Yet he was determined to distance village work from the machinations of power politics.

The Village of Service: "India in a Village"

The value of decentralisation was obvious, but several of Gandhi's colleagues questioned the wisdom of dissociating constructive work from the Congress power structure. They foresaw the tenuous link between the diverging programmes snapping if he withdrew from politics altogether, or worse, if he should die. Without effective political representation it would prove difficult to muster support for the constructive work programme. Just as Gandhi was unyielding in his belief that real freedom in India relied upon the removal of untouchability, Hindu-Muslim unity, and the revival of *khadi* and allied village industries, so too he was adamant that village work be kept separate from politics."[64]

Toward the end of March Gandhi notified Jamnalal Bajaj of his intention to settle in Segaon. Mira recollects that almost everyone in contact with him opposed the decision, and that she was criticised as being primarily responsible for it. In one sense this is true, but Gandhi had been waiting for such an opportunity to arise. The most influential opponent of the proposal was Jamnalal himself. An untiring and devoted friend, he feared for Gandhi's health in the harsh village conditions. To convince Jamnalal was all the more important to Gandhi because of his influential position in the village.

Gandhi was beginning to expound his concept of trusteeship. Just as the politicians were to be the "trustees of the nation", so the *zamindar* and other owners of wealth should be the trustees of India's poor. One of the principal designs of the Segaon experiment was to demonstrate the many instances where a little co-operation between the *zamindar,* community worker and villagers would lead to the wholesale enrichment of rural life. The economic elites would ultimately have to decide between class war or a voluntary conversion into trustees of their wealth. Under his plan they would be entitled to retain stewardship of their interests, but required to utilise their talents to increase the wealth of the nation rather than exploit its resources. With trusteeship Gandhi saw a means of counteracting the psychological and economic handicaps restricting the growth of social consciousness among the masses. To combat the resistance of recalcitrant *zamindar* profiteers, toward the end of 1936 Gandhi called upon villagers to withhold their labour until the landowner was forced to improve their living conditions; a non-violent exercise of the power inherent in their capacity as labourers.[65] It was another of Gandhi's ideal situations, far removed from reality. Caste divisions in the villages prevented any chance of the necessary co-operation and organisation coming into effect. The awakening of the masses would take time and a lot of effort.

Jamnalal Bajaj's stubborn opposition to the Segaon plan proved ultimately no match for Gandhi's arguments. He eventually acquiesced, financing many aspects of the village programme, and instructing his farm manager and workers to give their complete co-operation to Gandhi. By the time Gandhi returned to Maganwadi from Ahmedabad Jamnalal had given full authority to Mira to commence building a cottage for him at Segaon. According to Gandhi's instructions the foundations of the cottage were measured out on an acre of land donated by Jamnalal in an open field on the north side of the village. It was approximately one hundred and fifty metres from the outskirts of the village.

Among Gandhi's co-workers the general consensus concerning the village experiment was that life in Segaon would exacerbate his unstable blood pressure. They were keen to suggest alternatives. One argued that areas where village workers had been involved with rural reconstruction for some time would be more suitable. In this case, replied Gandhi, he would not be able to attend to work at Maganwadi. He added that he would not consider disturbing the work done through the initiative of dedicated village workers. Another asked that if he was determined to settle in Segaon why not have experienced workers to assist him? His answer simply was that he wanted to do himself what he expected of others, training villagers as community workers in their own village.

He refused to anticipate breakdowns in his health, but did promise to leave the village if physically unable to do the work, which was a general condition of village work. In answer to a co-worker who believed that the constructive work programme would be better served if Gandhi would undertake another promotional tour of the country, he replied with characteristic logic:

> In Harijan work the practical and theoretical aspects were combined. Here I cannot combine the two. I have been talking theory all these days.... without having personally come to

The Village of Service: "India in a Village"

grips with the difficulties of village work. If I undertook the tour say after passing three seasons in a village and among the villagers a year hence, I should be able to talk with knowledge and experience which I have not got today.[66]

In similar fashion he adroitly rebuffed all arguments to dissuade him from settling in the village, though he never remained there alone.

On 30 April 1936 Gandhi walked the five miles from Maganwadi to Segaon. Though his cottage was not completed he decided to accustom himself to village conditions by staying for a few days. He lived and worked under a temporary construction made of split bamboo matting and wickerwork. During this period the maximum daily temperature rose to 118 degrees Fahrenheit. As he had not fully recovered from high blood pressure his doctors insisted he move to a cooler climate until the monsoon arrived.

Before leaving for Nandi Hill in the south Gandhi arranged for Balwant Singh and Munnalal Shah to assist Mira in recruiting labourers and supervising the construction of the cottage. The former had been at Sabarmati and was the only worker at Maganwadi with knowledge of farming. He had begun making regular visits to Segaon to teach one of the village boys spinning with a *takli*. Since Gandhi had declared no meals would be available to visitors Balwant Singh assumed this also included him. He would leave after his work was concluded, taking his meal and sleeping at the Mahilashram[67] on the outskirts of Wardha. When Gandhi learnt the reason why he did this Balwant Singh was advised to remain in the village and earn his bread by teaching carding and spinning. He was given an additional student, a harijan boy Mira was training to render personal service to Gandhi. Munnalal Shah was a lawyer who had given up his practice to join Gandhi. After reading Mira's articles concerning the village experiment in *Harijan* he had asked Gandhi to allow him to join Mira in Segaon.[68]

During Gandhi's absence an ashram began to take shape. The hut known as the Adinivas (House of the First Quarter) had been completed. To the south-west of this were two small rooms, one of which was used as a latrine and the other as a bathroom. To the west they built a cattle-shed. A prayer ground was also prepared and Mira drew up a plan for a compound in which a variety of trees

- Neem, Olinda, Mango, Weeping Ashoka, Babul and Imlee - were to be planted. At the focal point of the prayer ground a sacred Pipal tree would be planted by Gandhi. On 16 June Gandhi's cottage was completed and during the night the monsoon began.

That same night Gandhi returned unexpectedly to commence his sojourn in Segaon, having walked the five miles in torrential rains. Balwant Singh recalls: "It was as if God had, through the storm, given him a glimpse of the hardships which he would have to undergo in living in the villages. The memories of that day are still vivid in my mind. Bapu lay covered by the rug provided by us. How he shivered. We felt very anxious about him. Had I been a painter I would have painted a picture of it and presented it to the readers."[69] It is unlikely that Gandhi would have relished the bedraggled image of him becoming public property.

He had come to Segaon for a number of reasons. A report appearing in the *Bombay Chronicle* (6 May 1936) inferred that he set out to realise and thence institutionalise a "model" solution to all the problems plaguing constructive work in the villages. If Segaon became an ideal centre of rural life Gandhi hoped the success of the village programme need no longer rely solely on his personal faith. Perhaps all India would consider the concept of *sarvodaya* a practical ideal if he could arouse the social awareness of the villagers. Beside converting the "unpromising village into a model one" and setting an example to fellow *gram sevaks*, he also hoped to detect flaws in his approach to village work.[70]

Gandhi was certainly aware of the symbolic importance of his decision to settle in Segaon, which would focus the public gaze on village work rather than his press image.[71] For him the true symbols of the village experiment would be the work done and the social awareness required to appreciate its value.

Gandhi had come to distrust the charismatic hold he exerted upon many of his colleagues. But in many respects the Segaon experiment revealed the extent to which he had become the victim of his own charisma. Within a short period Segaon had become Sevagram; another ashram was forming around Gandhi. He had longed to work quietly, secluded from the turbulent affairs of national politics and the excessive attention of his devotees, but as his secretary Mahadev Desai observed, how can a man who is known to and sought by men and women from all over the world hope to seclude himself from even his most devoted colleagues?[72]

The Village of Service: "India in a Village"

A ceaseless flow of people from all walks of life came to meet him, including poor villagers and the Viceroy of India, Lord Linlithgow. The visitors normally walked (sometimes through knee-deep mud) from Wardha as a road to Sevagram was not constructed until 1940. In the case of dignitaries like Jawaharlal Nehru, Jamnalal Bajaj made available the services of an ox-drawn cart. Uninvited visitors were discouraged from staying, as not even basic amenities such as food and water could be spared. Gandhi did not only discourage contact with the outside world during the experiment — his profuse correspondence and journalistic writings bear witness to this —but many people who sought to join the ashram or to meet him personally were warned of the harsh realities of village life.

In spite of Gandhi's wishes Sevagram developed into an ashram. He seemed powerless to discourage people from joining him. With the possible exception of Kasturba and Lilavati Asar, who had been at Sabarmati, Gandhi had maintained that he would stay alone in Sevagram. In deference to his wishes Mira had left one week after his arrival to live in a small cottage she had built a mile away near Veroda village. However Balwant Singh and Munnalal Shah were allowed to remain. Gandhi never achieved his object of living alone in the village; on the contrary his cottage became overcrowded.[73] Toward the end of 1936 Mira was forced to return to be nursed through an attack of typhoid. When her health improved Gandhi did not pressure her to leave, but allowed her to build a small cottage in the corner of his one-acre plot, with a room attached for teaching carding and spinning.

As Gandhi's blood pressure began to give him more trouble an experienced doctor advised it was imperative he moved to some quieter place than his cottage. He agreed to settle in Mira's small carding room, an arrangement which lasted until he left for a tour of South India in 1937. During his absence Mira and Jamnalal arranged for the small hut to be converted into a functional cottage for Gandhi, which became known as Bapu Kutir.

Jamnalal eventually had a small hut built for Kasturba, but even this she could hardly call her own. Pyarelal recalls that "when lady visitors came to see Gandhiji and sometimes to stay in the ashram she, with her characteristic generosity, put her hut at their disposal".[74] Over the years there were many additions to the original buildings. They included Akhari Nivas, the last residence of Gandhi, originally built by Jamnalal for his personal use and to accommodate guests. It was occupied for short periods by Gandhi's secretaries, Mahadev Desai and Pyarelal.

In the immediate vicinity of Bapu Kutir the Mahadev Kutir and the Kishorelal Nivas were constructed, which were the residences of Mahadev Desai and Kishorelal Mashruwala respectively. A short distance from these was the Parachure Kutir, a small hut built for the Sanskrit scholar Parachure Shastri. Imprisoned with Gandhi in Yervada Central Prison for his role in the civil disobedience movement of 1932, Parachure had been stricken with severe wet leprosy. Gandhi and Shriman Narayan found him lying on the roadside in a pit during an evening walk. He had come to Sevagram to die in peace and obscurity. The hut was constructed for him and Gandhi began massaging his wounds with oil. Coupled with fasting this treatment proved very effective; following Gandhi's example several inmates overcame their fear of the dreaded disease and took up the massage work. Subsequently Parachure's condition improved sufficiently to enable him to teach Sanskrit to a number of community children, and on occasion solemnise marriages in the Ashram, particularly between *harijans* and caste-Hindus.[75]

Another addition to the Ashram buildings was Rustom Bhavan, built in 1942 to accommodate the increasing number of visitors to Sevagram. It was donated by Jalbhai Rustomjee, the son of Gandhi's friend in South Africa, Parsee Rustomjee. As the number of residents increased a kitchen was built to the south-east of Adi Nivas, which was added to over the years. The kitchen was equipped with an oven for baking bread, a simple village-style steam cooker and a chimney to carry away smoke. J. C Kumarappa later described the sprawling colony that developed at Sevagram as "the *de facto* capital of India since service of the country is the function of a capital city".[76]

Community Life

Though Gandhi was resigned to live in the company of several co-workers at Sevagram, he by no means sought to establish another ashram. Clearly such a development would undermine the *raison d'etre* for the village experiment. During the early months of his life in the village he vainly sought to discourage

The Village of Service: "India in a Village"

attempts by his devotees to follow him. Lilavati Asar, for instance, was asked to remain at Maganwadi, since Gandhi feared she would be a disruptive influence.[77] Another follower was told that Sevagram was not an ashram and that those workers already there would subsequently be required either to work in other villages or return to Wardha.[78] In response to a colleague's query Gandhi explained that his efforts in Sevagram would be handicapped unless he maintained "a limited family".[79]

Gandhi also hoped to curtail correspondence, but this proved difficult. The mail continued to be inordinately heavy. As there was no post office at Sevagram, Mahadev Desai who had remained behind initially with his family at Maganwadi, handled the bulk of the post in his capacity as Gandhi's secretary and walked to Sevagram with whatever needed his personal attention. Gandhi's activities during an average week would include interviews of varying length with all of his visitors, the daily disposal of mail, and journalistic work to ensure the weekly "copy" for *Harijan* was completed in time to reach the publishers at Ahmedabad. He found that the demands of Mahatmaship becoming increasingly burdensome. As he became more involved with the village experiment work commitments to AIVIA and unavoidable engagements in Wardha and elsewhere caused him considerable anguish. He lamented not being able to perform more physical work in Sevagram and surrounding villages.[80] The multifarious administrative concerns of the constructive work programme and the changing political situation continued to demand his attention.

Gandhi was sixty-eight toward the end of 1936, and had been weakened by several bouts of high blood pressure; his myriad preoccupations left him little time or energy to tackle village work to his satisfaction. This in itself would have been a full-time undertaking for a strong, healthy man. In a letter to Mira on 20 January 1937, he rationalised his inability to devote more time to Sevagram: "I do not know that I shall be able to give more time to the village work than I am giving. My life has to be taken with its amazing limitations. It is enough that I live in the village and think out things in terms of the village."[81] However, the duration of Gandhi's sojourns at Sevagram became shorter, until the pressures of politics during the 1940s forced him to abandon work in the village completely.

A motley crowd of people gradually gathered at Sevagram, many of whom were motivated more by an ambition to associate with the Mahatma than by a desire to contribute their mite to village work. The growth of an ashram at Sevagram was inevitable. Notable among the unusual group of people attracted to Sevagram was Bhansali, an erstwhile professor at the Gujarat Vidyapith. For several years prior to joining Sevagram he had been a recluse, wandering naked and silent in forests, eating only raw wheat flour and *neem* leaves. He had sewn up his lips with a copper ring for a period to ensure he did not inadvertently speak. A chance meeting with Gandhi changed Bhansali's life.

Living at Sevagram under the Mahatma's influence, he renounced the path of extreme self-mortification. He occupied himself carding cotton, spinning and teaching. When on occasion he felt the urge to resume a life of penance, he would ask Gandhi for permission to hang upside down in the Ashram, but always accepted the tatter's firm refusal. Various religious men stayed at Sevagram from time to time, including Tukdoji Maharaj, a young *sadhu* who was a renowned *bhajani,* i.e., a singer of devotional songs of his own composition. Another was a Japanese monk, who worked very hard and each morning and evening could be heard beating his prayer drum and chanting Buddhist *mantras.*

A significant proportion of the group had spent time at Sabarmati. For instance, the manager of Sevagram from 1938 to 1966, Chimanlal Shah, lived at Sabarmati from 1919 until its closure. Commenting on the main difference between the two ashrams, Chimanlal observed that at Sabarmati Gandhi was the "father" of the community, but at Sevagram he was the "mother".[82] Evidently Gandhi's conception of an ashram underwent subtle changes. In the past the daily regimen of Sabarmati had been strictly regulated, and candidates 'for village work were expected to adhere to a strenuous time-table. At Sevagram permanent members were required to observe the ascetic code of eleven vows drawn up at Sabarmati, but apart from a skeletal time-table the only rules and regulations Gandhi expected the workers to observe during the early years of the village experiment were "such as grew out of the day-to-day experience of community living".[83] Their task was to set a good example, and to associate the villagers with the community life of the ashram in as many ways as possible. This was Gandhi's ideal but as the population of Sevagram swelled over the years and its management became more difficult, rules regulating every aspect of ashram life were laid down.[84] In fact many of the problems that beset Sabarmati similarly arose at Sevagram as the expanding colony became unwieldy.

The vow of *brahmacharya* and Gandhi's attitudes towards sexual relationships continued to be a source of much confusion and conflict among his co-workers. There were many instances at Sevagram and elsewhere of his colleagues falling prey to the natural desire to realise sexual fulfilment. He invariably expressed shock and disappointment at their failure to keep the vow of celibacy. Considering his overall objectives he appeared to place a disproportionate emphasis on the question of sexual continence.

By his own admission Gandhi found himself unable to repress sexual urges throughout his life. In 1936 during a period of rest in Bombay he was overcome with sexual desire. He rationalised the experience, claiming its origin lay in his pampering his body with food while doing no physical work.[85] Yet the failure to sublimate his sexuality and the misconceptions and confusion which arose as a result of revelations concerning his ongoing *brahmachari* "experiments" with young female devotees, caused Gandhi a great deal of anxiety.[86] He projected much of this anxiety on to his co-workers. Instances occurred where dedicated community workers were publicly shamed by Gandhi when he learnt of their failure to observe *brahmacharya*.[87] Others suffered through their efforts to please him.[88]

In the wake of revelations during 1938 concerning his experiments with young women at Sevagram, Gandhi found his position with regard to *brahmacharya* increasingly untenable. He believed that there was no harm in a *brahmachari* who had developed complete self-control mixing freely with women, and being bathed and massaged by them, provided the aspirant regarded every woman as a blood relative. Yet by his own admission Gandhi was an imperfect *brahmachari*. In terms of the strict rules set down in Hindu tradition to assist a *brahmachari* keep the vow, Gandhi's approach was extremely haphazard; and in the opinion of many people, including colleagues, his method was fraught with danger.[89] He claimed that incorrect diet was the source of his failure to realise perfect *brahmacharya*, but orthodox Hindus were sceptical of these claims and condemned his unorthodox practices. Gandhi always rejected their criticisms as invalid, but his refusal over the years to allow fellow ashramites the same liberties he enjoyed in this context placed him in an awkward and finally indefensible position. On 2 June 1938 he addressed the following confidential circular to inmates at Sevagram:

> Yesterday it became clear to me as day that it had been wrong on my part to forbid my co-workers to avail themselves during my lifetime of the freedom I had given myself. I cannot understand how I could have put up with it all these years. I feel my action was impelled by vanity and jealousy. If my experiment was dangerous I should not have undertaken it. And if it was worth trying I should have encouraged my co-workers to undertake it on my conditions. My experiment was a violation of the established norms of *brahmacharya*. Such a right can be enjoyed only by a saint like Sukadevji who can remain pure in thought, word and deed at all times of day. Having thus deliberated, I arrived at the decision yesterday. I feel that my experiments were responsible for the bitter experience of Dahyabhai and others at Sabarmati. Who can say how many more such moral lapses my conduct has not been responsible?[90]

Gandhi half-heartedly resolved to desist from touching women altogether,[91] but it was a short-lived resolution. Initially he made an exception of Kasturba and Dr. Sushila Nayar (Pyarelal's sister), both of whom administered to his daily needs, but before long he resumed the practice of bathing in the company of women, receiving massage from their hands, and resting his hands on the shoulders of young women during his daily walk. Gandhi explained that he could not bear the pain and anguish suffered by women devotees denied the opportunity to serve him in this fashion. The fact that he was prepared to face the consequences of allowing ashramites to follow his example,[92] but was unwilling to cease his experiments in *brahmacharya,* is a measure of his failure to sublimate the sexual instinct. The view is borne out by Gandhi's public disclosure shortly before his death in 1948 that he had been taking naked girls to bed with him for a number of years. To avoid public controversy he kept the practice secret, but admitted that

The Village of Service: "India in a Village"

this had been an error which stood in the way of his becoming a perfect *brahmachari*.[93] There have been a number of studies that attempt to explain Gandhi's *brahmacharya* experiments in psychological terms,[94] but the main point in the context of the Sevagram experiment appears to be that the emphasis placed by Gandhi on *brahmacharya* and related issues diverted attention unnecessarily from the main question of village uplift.

Many other problems faced by the small community that grew up at Sevagram were symptomatic in one way or another of Gandhi's charismatic authority. Members of the group vied with each other for his attention, and those deputised to organise and supervise activities within the Ashram often found it difficult to obtain the necessary co-operation from other residents. Munnalal Gandhi complained that Sevagram had become a *dharmashala* (resting place) for the weak-minded, and Gandhi himself remarked that the Ashram "was some kind of *shambhoomela*, consisting of all types of curious and abnormal persons who would ordinarily be regarded as 'cranks' in society.[95] Mahadev Desai believed that the greatest handicap to Gandhi's work in Sevagram was this unusual crowd of people who gathered about him. "each good in his own way but not fit to bear or even to share the burdens he has taken upon himself".[96]

The constant quarreling among the ashramites and their practice of complaining to Gandhi about one another's shortcomings had a destabilising effect upon the Ashram work programmes.[97] Mahadev clearly felt that these problems hampered the progress of village reconstruction. Shortly after an incident occurred, in which an inmate close to Gandhi was accused of theft.[98] Mahadev suggested that as the motley group were "utterly devoid of *ahimsa*" they should leave the Ashram. Gandhi's contribution to the discussion, which was subsequently reported in *Harijan*, was reminiscent of his response to crisis situations at Sabarmati:

> My *ahimsa* is imperfect and that is why my surroundings are not saturated with *ahimsa*. Sevagram is to me a laboratory for *ahimsa*. If my experiments here were successful and I could find a solution for the little problems that confront me here, I am sure the same formula would provide me a solution for the bigger issues that today face us in the country. That is why I am so reluctant to leave Sevagram. It is my laboratory for

satyagraha. It is there that I expect to discover the key to India's independence, not in Simla or New Delhi.[99]

In this sense Gandhi's communities reflected on a small scale the heterogeneity of the sub-continent and the difficulties of achieving unity within that diversity.

Stripped of stultifying caste and class attachments the *gram sevaks* ideally stood for the harmonious and balanced growth of the individual as the basis of a dynamic, evolutionary social system. In Gandhi's view the hierarchical nature of the caste system and the growth of the cities at the expense of the villages, precluded the development of social relationships on the basis of free association and co-operation between independent, fully integrated human beings. Communities founded on voluntary association and sustained by spontaneous organic growth were thus a prominent feature of his envisaged ideal society.[100]

Doubtless Gandhi looked upon the development of Sevagram as representative of this ideal but in reality the growth and stability of the Ashram were dependent upon his charismatic presence.[101] In 1936 he wrote in positive terms to Albert West concerning the establishment of the Ashram : "The Phoenix experiment for me was life-work. And so if you ever come to India, you will find me amid conditions simpler than in Phoenix. For the ideal has not only persisted but it bears today an ampler meaning."[102]

By 1941, however, he was considering the disbandment of Sevagram.[103] "I have experienced such disappointments regarding the Ashram that I have lost all interest in embarking on new ventures", he wrote to Kishorelal Mashruwala. "I do wish that some of you should set up a brotherhood during, or even after, my lifetime."[104]

Another factor which seriously handicapped constructive work at Sevagram was the high incidence of illness among members of the Ashram. Malaria, typhoid, enteric fever and dysentery were rife throughout the district, and the insanitary conditions prevailing in the village exacerbated the problem. Even the Ashram compound was not free of possible breeding grounds of disease. For instance, village children untutored in Gandhi's ways wandered freely in the Ashram. On one occasion during an outbreak of typhoid Dr. Sushila Nayar made an inspection of the

The Village of Service: "India in a Village"

Ashram premises. She found traces of human excrement on one of the grinding wheels.

The services provided for the sick were time-consuming. Each patient received careful nursing which included scrupulous attention to diet—the main ingredients were soya beans, unpolished hand-pounded rice, palm sugar and salads made from wild plants —and a regimen of enemas, sponge-baths, steam inhalations, wet-sheet and mud packs, together with a range of simple nature-cure treatments. Gandhi would not take medicines himself and was disinclined to prescribe them for others, but he would carefully administer and supervise the various dietetic and other nature-cure therapies in which he had utmost faith. When he went down with malaria he refused any treatment not available to villagers. Eventually he was rushed to the Civil Hospital at Wardha when he became so heavily infected that there was danger of his developing cerebral meningitis.[105] Frequently Gandhi was either bed-ridden, or convalescing away from Sevagram in more congenial climes, or preoccupied with the treatment of sick inmates. In 1940 he wrote good-humouredly of this adverse situation:

> I wanted to lead a solitary life at Segaon. But it has become an ashram without any rules and regulations. New buildings are springing up every day. I have made it into a hospital these days. I have humorously called Segaon a home for invalids. I am already an invalid in body and mind and I have collected quite a few invalids like myself. I have also compared Segaon to a madhouse. This too is an apt simile. The statement that *swaraj* can be achieved through the spinning wheel can come only from the mouth of a madman. But madmen are not aware of their madness and so I look upon myself as a wise man.[106]

Out of the hardships experienced by the inmates grew one of the most instructive and beneficial experiments carried out at Sevagram: a thorough examination and application of simple naturopathy and preventive medicine suitable to the needs of poor villagers. Gandhi's plan was to reconstruct Sevagram along the lines of his concept of a model village; that is, a village which lacked nothing in the way of hygienic comforts, proper food, proper sanitation, and, in the case of sickness, proper medical aid in keeping with the purchasing power of the poor. "Whilst talking of ideal conditions of cleanliness," recalls an inmate of Sevagram, "he often mentioned the latrine and the kitchen in the same breath, saying that there should not be a single fly in either of the places."[107]

As disease was linked to unhygienic conditions, the accent at Sevagram was on prevention rather than cure. Gandhi taught that the practice of cleanliness was inextricably bound up with self-reliance through economy and hard work. The inmates were instructed to conduct themselves in such a way as to provide object lessons to the villagers. They were required to clean their own eating utensils scrupulously, ensure that the latrines, kitchen and Ashram compound remained spotless, and to pay particular attention to their own personal hygiene. For instance, daily cleaning of teeth with twigs from *neem* or *babul* trees was compulsory. Initially the discarded twigs were thrown away as rubbish, but Gandhi directed they be collected, washed and, when dried, burnt as fuel. Peelings left over after cutting vegetables were put into a compost pit, but waste paper was burnt as it could not be converted into manure. The practice begun at Sabarmati of providing separate receptacles for solid and liquid excrement was continued at Sevagram; it facilitated the production of manure from the solid excrement. Gandhi insisted that workers forced to relieve themselves away from the proper latrines cover the excreta with earth to avoid odour and disease. The same applied to spitting. The minutest aspects of community life were thus attended to by Gandhi. He wrote instructive notices for the inmates in a notebook, which the manager of the Ashram, Chimanlal Shah, would circulate to the residents.[108] In all spheres the emphasis was upon self-discipline and self-reliance.

Like the rules and regulations of the Ashram, the activities too grew out of natural developments under changing circumstances. The rapid expansion of preventive and medical aid facilities at Sevagram followed Dr. Sushila Nayar's arrival in 1936. Though to begin with Gandhi had no intention of having a proper dispensary in the Ashram, the advent of the doctor led to the establishment of a small dispensary on the verandah of one of the buildings. In spite of Gandhi's reluctance to prescribe drugs he realised that in certain cases of severe illness there was no known substitute for allopathic drugs. On many occasions he had to take recourse to drugs such as quinine, sodium bicarbonate, potassium permanganate and iodine. Yet the fact that there was no equally

The Village of Service: "India in a Village"

effective alternative to these drugs in the Ayurvedic system continued to trouble him.

However, to ensure Sushila's services were fully utilised he supplied all the equipment and material she needed. The success of this service was no more apparent than during an outbreak of cholera in the district. Sevagram escaped with only three deaths due to Sushila having administered some four hundred inoculations. She also treated several cases successfully.[109] Before long a village health centre grew up at Sevagram. Over the years it developed into a fully equipped hospital attuned to the medical needs of the rural poor. Gandhi recruited local Harijan youths to work alongside himself and Sushila and be trained in his nursing methods. In this manner Gandhi and his co-workers demonstrated how great hardship can be transformed into a medium for imparting knowledge. The medical programme later expanded to include an extensive training scheme oriented toward the villages.

A medical breakthrough was made in the village by Dr. G. L. Batra, a retired Deputy Director of Public Health from Bengal, who came to stay with Gandhi. He discovered that nearly sixty per cent of the village children suffered from keratomalacia, a deficiency disease caused by lack of vitamin A. When Gandhi was informed of the problem he made available to Dr. Batra skim-milk and a canister of red palm oil. The latter collected all the village children together and gave each of them six ounces of skim-milk with palm *gud* (syrup) and a teaspoon of red palm oil. Within a few weeks of this treatment there was not a single case of keratomalacia left in Sevagram.[110]

In his determination to improve preventive facilities at Sevagram Gandhi resolved to study the question of making the village malaria-proof. Though its effects were not so devastating as those of cholera and plague, during the period he lived in the village malaria was by far the most prevalent of serious diseases in rural India, accounting for a quarter or more of the total sickness in the country. Using methods based on the research of noted experts in the field of malaria prevention, he launched a nation-wide campaign against the disease from Sevagram.

Permanent measures consisted of engineering efforts to deal with mosquito breeding grounds by draining the land, filling in pools and ponds, and the rectification of water courses. Weekly visits were made to village compounds in order to drain surface water or to apply a cover of kerosene or oil to prevent larvae breeding. In addition it was found necessary regularly to clear rubbish in which mosquitoes were likely to breed. Sulphur and other repellent substances were burned in the houses and sheds to drive the insects out and all water receptacles were mosquito-proofed where possible. The villagers were taught to recognise and destroy larvae in their breeding places.[111] Gandhi believed that apart from these preventive measures diet reform was the most important aspect of anti-malaria work. With regard to treatment he was convinced that in the long-term the adoption of a proper diet was more efficacious than constant drugging.

Self-sufficiency in food and improvement of diet were an integral part of village reconstruction. Gandhi was concerned that all village land be cultivated efficiently. He sought to reverse the apparent trend under the *zamindari* system of replacing a wide variety of relatively unremunerative food crops with "cash" crops. The strategy raised the income of the *zamindar,* but severely limited the nutritional sources available to the landless labourer and marginal farmer. To provide the people of Sevagram with a practical demonstration in various improved agricultural techniques designed to enhance the quality and output of crops, a section of the Ashram land was brought under cultivation. Crops such as sugarcane and papayas, which were ordinarily not extensively cultivated in the district, were introduced at Sevagram. At Gandhi's insistence colonies of bees were set up in the Ashram garden. Balwant Singh recalls that this development not only established a honey industry at Sevagram but also greatly enhanced the production of fruit and vegetables."[112]

Gandhi hoped the villagers would emulate the agricultural practices introduced in the Ashram, and subsequently take up the diet of the ashramites. It was the villagers' inability to do so that highlighted perhaps the greatest failings of the Sevagram experiment. In spite of the ideal of simplicity, the expenditure of the Ashram was far in excess of the collective means of the village. At Sabarmati Gandhi's wealthy benefactors had ensured that the Ashram did not have to support itself. Similarly, at Sevagram Jamnalal Bajaj placed all the *malguzari* and farm profits accruing to him from the village at Gandhi's disposal. The crowd of people drawn to Sevagram clearly benefited from this support more than the villagers, who resented the presence of the somewhat parasitic community. He was often forced to rationalise his inability to live without outside support.[113]

To counteract claims that the lifestyle of the ashramites was not commensurate with the poor villagers, Gandhi introduced various austerity measures. He insisted that only fruits and vegetables grown in the Ashram be used in the kitchen, and that as far as possible food should be eaten raw to conserve fuel. Yet the number of relatively non-productive persons at Sevagram continued to grow. "Whatever I do is for the poor," wrote Gandhi in 1941, "but today I am unable to prove it in Sevagram."[114]

Contrary to Balwant Singh's account of fruit and vegetable production at Sevagram, the evidence indicates there was a degree of mismanagement in the sphere of food production. On one occasion an entire wheat crop went bad due to carelessness, and it was feared that the Ashram would be forced to close due to insufficient production of vegetables. An amusing incident recalled by Gandhi's grandson Arun highlights the lack of initiative in this regard: "In 1946, our family were guests of the Sevagram Ashram. I was twelve and my sister was six years old. We were there for few months and every day for lunch and dinner we had nothing but boiled, saltless pumpkin and dry *bajra rotis*. After a few days of this, my sister Ela was fed up. She marched into Bapu's room and with child-like innocence suggested he change the name of the Ashram from Sevagram to Kohlagram (*kohla* is the Gujarathi word for pumpkin). Bapuji laughed and asked: "Why?" "Well, you serve nothing but pumpkin day and night", she explained. This was the first time that Bapuji heard of this and that evening at the prayer meeting he hauled up the people who were in charge of the kitchen and said: "When I spoke of living in simplicity it did not mean that you should cook pumpkin every day. Surely other vegetables can grow on our farms."[115]

Since the Ashram budget was subsidised by Jamnalal no amount of mismanagement could force the closure of Sevagram, but Gandhi's plan to turn the Ashram land into a model farm proved a difficult task. Toward the end of 1941 Gandhi decided not to purchase further land. By planting cash crops and marketing the surplus he realised that the Ashram laid itself open to the criticism that it merely exacerbated the exploitation of the village by the city.[116]

If I want, I can have the entire land in the village bought up but I have forbidden further purchase of land for the time being and, until I am able to distribute the entire proceeds among the tillers of the soil, I do not want to purchase more land. I must ask you for the present to set through the Ashram an example of ideal farming. They will then try to follow it of their own accord. At present farming in the Ashram is not as it should be and we are far behind the ideal. Our expenditure is too excessive and we must remedy this situation. We shall make steady progress only when we persistently direct all our experiments towards our ideal."[7]

Ideally a Gandhian ashram represented a small cadre of dedicated village workers, but the unruly crowd that gathered at Sevagram severely handicapped the efforts of those in the Ashram absorbed in constructive work. The majority of inmates did not set an example. On the contrary, their preoccupation with trivial matters and personal animosities destabilised the community. This undermined the tenuous rapport established between the Ashram and the villagers.

However a number of projects were relatively successful. The palm *jaggery* industry developed at Sevagram is a case in point. The *jaggery* experiment was started with twenty-five trees, but by April 1937 the Government had permitted the AIVIA to tap two hundred and twenty-five trees. Palm *jaggery* is a nourishing coarse brown sugar made from palm-sap. Initially he saw the necessity of employing a palm-tapper on his own terms, but as the industry developed he foresaw that the people would take it up on a co-operative basis. As the products of palm-sap were primarily for local consumption it was an ideal village industry. To some degree he was also able to supplant the notorious practice of toddy-making with the production of *nira*, a nourishing drink extracted from the palm-sap that can be refined into a sweet syrup. *Nira* and its by-product were immediately popular at Sevagram and sold in large quantities. When Gandhi learnt that Balwant Singh had cut down a number of palm trees in order to plant grass for the cattle, he wrote in the Ashram Notebook: "The Palm is a poor man's tree. Do I have to explain to you its usefulness? If all the palm-trees are cut down, life at Sevagram will be severely affected. The palm-tree is interwoven withour life."[118]

The promotion of *nira* faced staunch opposition from the Parsi community, many of whom were involved in the liquor industry. When three people at Sevagram died shortly after consuming *nira*, Parsis proclaimed that the drink produced cold, flatulence and diarrhoea, and could have fatal consequences. Subsequent investigations at Sevagram revealed that the deaths were due to cholera. Replying to the propaganda Gandhi was careful to point out that several people in the Ashram had drunk with impunity the same *nira* consumed by those who died.[119] No doubt serious diseases such as cholera contributed to the ruin of village life, but further studies revealed that *nira* in fact fortified the body against such diseases.

Another successful agricultural experiment at Sevagram was animal husbandry. Out of the small cowshed originally built for Gandhi's use developed one of the most efficient industries of the Ashram. New cow sheds were built when the expert in this field, Balwant Singh, began a project to develop the local breed of cattle. The farm manager and Mira were sent to the Allahabad Agricultural Institute to increase their knowledge of cattle. Initially milk had not been available at all in Sevagram, but Balwant Singh established and maintained a small dairy-farm. Milk was subsequently provided to the members of the Ashram and to the villagers. Gandhi's earlier misgivings about the consumption of milk were certainly dispelled at Sevagram. Its efficacy in the prevention and treatment of disease was very evident. Gandhi fully utilised Balwant Singh's ability to work with animals by encouraging him to become an expert in *goseva* (cow-service). He studied the uses of cow's milk and *ghee* (a machine was obtained to produce *ghee*), the economic use of hides, and all the activities that made cow protection, in Gandhi's view, a symbol of sound rural economics.

Gandhi acknowledged that the ineffectiveness of his cow-protection propaganda in the past had been due primarily to the failure of the previous experimentation undertaken at Sabarmati and elsewhere to produce startling results. At Sevagram and Maganwadi an integrated programme of cow protection work was instituted, including experiments in the proper use of hide and carcass, cattle-breeding to increase milk yield, the use of separated milk and other ways of economically utilising milk. Gandhi's ultimate aim was to develop a co-operative dairy in the village. However, when subsequently the cattle-breeding and farming departments of the Ashram were separated from the milk department, conflict sprang up between the responsible persons. It was virtually impossible to inculcate a spirit of co-operation in the village, riven as it was with caste factions, whilst members of the Ashram strove with one another over nonsensical issues.

Gandhi did not promote cow protection solely on an economic basis, but as a means to purify Hinduism. At Sevagram industries associated with the *goseva* programme were often linked to the removal of untouchability. When he learnt that *harijans* who skinned carcasses were not paid, but ate the carrion as their reward, he determined that the job be put on a cash basis. He arranged tanning classes where the skinners were taught improved methods and a variety of ways to use the flesh and bones. At this time the accepted value of a carcass was three rupees, either because the majority of caste-Hindus were ignorant of its real value or they superstitiously avoided anything to do with flaying of carcasses or the disposal of the flesh, fat, bones, intestines, etc. The *harijans* at Sevagram learnt to make much more money from this industry by studying the art and science of carcass disposal and utilisation. A tannery was opened a short distance from Wardha, and following Gandhi's request a skilled teacher for shoe-making and other leather manufacture was sent from the Radhaswami Sect in Agra to instruct the village tanners. Gandhi's thesis was that efficient organisation of the dairying industry, proper use of cowhide and carcass, and overall uplift of the tanner's profession, would establish the economic viability of the animal and thus reduce indiscriminate cow-slaughter. "This is not only a matter of economics," he told Balwant Singh, "it is also a matter of religion."[120] The reactionary opposition of orthodox Hindus, however, remained the greatest obstacle to the *goseva* programme.

From the beginning Gandhi expected *khadi* work to form the foundation of the various industries started at Sevagram. A *Charkha Parishramalafya* (spinning wheel work centre) was established in an attempt to popularise *khadi* in the village, and the *Charkha Sangh* (Spinning Wheel Association) shifted its headquarters to Sevagram. Gandhi reiterated his faith that *khadi* was the only village industry with the economic potential to serve as a permanent remedy and safeguard against unemployment and underemployment.

The Village of Service: "India in a Village"

Gradually the work in the Ashram developed to provide employment for a large number of people from Sevagram and the surrounding villages. The Ashram also started a centre in the village where young boys learnt weaving to supplement their earnings. The first *charkha* teacher at Sevagram was Balwant Singh. He recounts that many Sevagram boys subsequently became *khadi* teachers in other parts of the country, and that his first student demonstrated the benefits accruing from this work by being the first among the Harijans of the village to build a proper house for himself.[121]

In 1941 Gandhi inaugurated a *Khadi Vidyalaya* (Khadi Training College) established at Sevagram by the *Charkha Sangh*. He encouraged the students to devote themselves wholeheartedly to a scientific study of the spinning wheel and *khadi,* and to make improvements by new inventions and to serve the villagers. "Just as the sun is the centre of the planetary system, so is the *charkha* of our economic or village structure", he told them. "Without the sun, the world will perish; so without the *charkha,* which is our saviour and bread-giver, we shall lose."[122] Subsequently the *Hindustani Talimi Sangh* (All India Board of Education) which also had its headquarters at Sevapram (see last section of this chapter) also greatly enlarged its spinning and weaving activities. Both institutions attracted teachers from all over India.

Though the potential of *khadi* was never wholly realised at Sevagram, Gandhi did not give up hope that the village would eventually become a model *of khadi* and village economics. In an address to the *khadi yatra* Conference held at Sevagram in 1940 he said: "since the *yatra* had taken place here, I suggest that you draw up a programme for making the whole of the village of Sevagram khadi-clad within a year. The experiment will exercise you and your reason and may give you the key for making *khadi* universal."[123] Just before his assassination in 1948 Gandhi undertook a lengthy fast. Concerned that he might die as a result, Balwant Singh wrote from Sevagram seeking guidance. In his reply Gandhi expressed undying faith in *khadi* and the Sevagram experiment: "*charkha* ... can be further improved. It is for the Ashram to do so. The Ashram must stick to the *charkha* even if the entire country casts it away after my death. You have been in the Ashram from its inception. You must remain there till you die."[124]

During Gandhi's years at Sevagram the *khadi* programme in the village met with a degree of success, but he was far from content with the results. When Gandhi left Sevagram in 1946 not more than twenty per cent of the villagers wore *khadi*. The difficulties faced in breaking down the indifference of the villagers toward *khadi* vindicated his view that nothing but sustained, patient work of an educational nature would succeed in the villages.[125]

A problem was that villagers resisted the introduction of any activity that failed to attain "legitimacy" in terms of their own caste tradition. Gandhi realised that the conditioning of tradition and superstition could not be blithely dismissed by village workers in the quest for a more equable distribution of resources. The thesis underlying the *khadi* and village industry concept was that development cannot be imposed from above, i.e. under the aegis of an external agency, but would result from increased social consciousness. The Socialists favoured the redistribution of land as the solution to India's rural poverty; the Communists believed collectivisation to be the answer; but Gandhi argued that either proposal would ultimately lead to further exploitation whilst the rural poor were kept in a state of mediocrity through lack of educational opportunities, social services and proper diet. In his view an over-emphasis on centralised industrialisation would result in the extinction of a secure lifestyle for millions of village people forced to gravitate towards the towns and cities in search of work. His alternative was a decentralised pattern of work, whereby the worker retained his freedom, controlled his tools, his hours of labour and the nature and quality of his work. Given the opportunity to develop his creative powers, Gandhi believed the poor villager would realise his full potential in all areas of life. In these terms he sought to transform the mentality of the potential producers and users of village products.

Gandhi combated capitalist exploitation but was also thoroughly opposed to the socialisation of industry. While the Socialists and Communists cited the Russian Soviet model in support of their centralist theories, he sought to highlight the dehumanising effects of the factory system where workers are employed in monotonous jobs which afford none of the pleasures and satisfaction of creative work. He was prepared to adopt machinery and tools in so far as it reduced the drudgery of manual labour, but he regarded as retrograde any "development" that dehumanised production. Labour subservient to either capital or outside expertise was also anathema to him.[126]

The task of the village worker was to promote the village product at the expense of the factory product. For example, *khadi* in place of mill cloth, village earthen pots instead of factory-made china, reed pen instead of steel pen, handmade paper instead of ordinary paper, *babul* or *neem* twigs instead of the tooth-brush, leather goods made in villages out of village-flayed cattle instead of factory tanned hide, ordinary village *jaggery* (or *gur*) instead of factory sugar, and hand-pounded whole rice instead of mill-polished rice. In association with the AIVIA a number of these industries were introduced in Sevagram. Research into appropriate village technologies began under the auspices of AIVIA at Maganwadi, and in 1938 a museum to demonstrate the possible avenues of small-scale village industries was opened at Maganwadi by Gandhi in memory of Maganlal Gandhi. Gandhi believed that the economic uplift of the villagers depended on opening avenues of gainful occupation for all, which in turn he linked to all-round improvement in physical health, social reform and moral uplift.

Gandhi's ability to awaken the villagers to the intrinsic resources in their environment indelibly stamped his personality on the Sevagram experiment. An instance of this stemmed from his interest in the role of snakes in the agricultural economy. All of the communities he established were initially infested by poisonous snakes; over the years he had gleaned a great deal of knowledge from studying their habits. They performed a particularly useful function by reducing the numbers of rats, vermin and other pests. Before his arrival at Sevagram it had been common practice to kill all snakes, irrespective of whether they were poisonous or not. Since there are only four poisonous species out of over four hundred varieties identified in India, and since even these do not usually bite unless trodden upon or mishandled, Gandhi taught the villagers that indiscriminate killing was unnecessary. He made a further study of snake lore at Sevagram and then proceeded to teach ashramites and villagers to distinguish poisonous species. All were advised to wear shoes while walking in the dark and to make maximum use of lanterns. He arranged for an expert to instruct workers in the capture of snakes : one man mastering the technique of catching cobras and vipers with bare hands.

Another successful innovation resulted from Gandhi's

suggestion to use newspapers as insulation against cold and damp. He developed a quilt made out of old *saris*, newspapers and cotton waste. Old news-sheets were spread inside an envelope made of worn-out saris and thin cotton-waste padding was put in between this. The whole thing was then sewn up like an ordinary quilt. The *harijan* given the first quilt claimed he had never before felt so warm.

A primary object of the Sevagram experiment was to construct a model village built with the co-operation of *zamindar*, Ashram workers and villagers. Out of such co-operation Gandhi saw the growth of "a sort of republic," self-sufficient in the necessities of life and democratically governed: a non-violent community founded on harmony and co-operation between its members. To further this ideal Gandhi believed the programme of village regeneration could not be successfully implemented without giving precedence to the removal of untouchability. He maintained the *harijans* were the foundation of society; without their labour the rural economy would collapse, thus destroying Indian civilisation. He warned caste-Hindus that *harijans* would ultimately revolt against being kept deliberately in a state of poverty and mediocrity and might seek violent retribution for the centuries of exploitation and oppression.[127]

The *harijan* problem in Sevagram was illustrative of the oppression experienced by these people throughout India's villages. Differing from the myriad impoverished counterparts in no significant way, the village was an ideal laboratory for Gandhi's experiments. The majority of the population of six hundred and thirty-nine were *harijans,* including *Mahars, Mangs, Chamars* and *Bhangis,* of which the *Mahars* and *Mangs* were the most numerically important. These latter castes appeared very much alike except for occupational differences;. The *Mahars* were hereditary village servants, whose duties include cutting firewood, sweeping and cleaning the yards in front of houses, carrying cowdung cakes to cremation grounds, and digging graves. The traditional function of the *Mangs* was to supply ropes which were needed in the fields and houses.[128] The majority of caste-Hindus in the village were *Kunbis,* the remainder belonging to miscellaneous groups that included one family of *Brahmins*.

The *harijans* of Sevagram were denied access to the temples, the services of the priest, the barber, the tailor, the water carrier and

The Village of Service: "India in a Village"

their entry to schools, roads and wells was also forbidden. The *Mahars* were an exception as they exercised rights of possession over their own temples and wells. There were sixteen wells in the village, eleven belonging to caste-Hindus and five to the *Mahars*. The caste-Hindus had exclusive use of their wells, while the *Mangs, Chamars* and *Bhangis* received water from the *Mahars* but were not permitted to draw water themselves. As Mira learnt in Sindi, one of the most blatantly oppressive practices engaged in by the villagers to protect themselves from the pollution believed to be conveyed by lower castes was rigid adherence to the ritual system of obtaining water.

From the outset Gandhi made it clear to the villagers of Sevagram that the disabilities suffered by the *harijans* would be one of his major concerns. At his first meeting with the villagers in 1936 Gandhi explained his approach to the question :

> I should not think of coming here, except to serve you. But in many places my presence and the programme I stand for are viewed with considerable dread. At the back of this dread is the fact that I have made the removal of untouchability a life's mission.... But I may tell you that I should not think of imposing these convictions on you. I should try to do so by persuasion, above all by my own example. I shall try to serve you by cleaning your roads and your surroundings, by trying to render such help as I can if there is illness in the village, by teaching you self-help by way of helping you to revive your handicrafts. If you will co-operate with me I shall be happy, if you will not I shall be content to be absorbed among you as one among the few hundred who live here.[129]

After this brief speech the first ominous note of dissent was raised by the old *Kunbipatel* (headman) of the village. He welcomed Gandhi's proposition but pronounced that he would never co-operate in the *harijan* programme. He stated that he had never drunk water from the same well as a *harijan* or allowed *harijans* into caste-Hindu temples, and claimed that he had lived this way too long to accommodate any radical change. The old man's attitude indicated the staunch opposition within India's villages to any programme which sought to interfere with the hierarchical *status quo*. The *harijan* programme would require the greatest patience and perseverance.

Gandhi's first encounter with the villagers over the issue of opening wells to *harijans* revealed the extent of their opposition to the programme. After consultation with Jamnalal's farm manager he had decided to declare one of the farm wells open to all *harijans*. Initially they were fearful of the consequences and refused to use it. However, eventually one or two *Mahars* and a *Bhangi* plucked up courage and came forward. The ensuing uproar was so great that they were immediately forced to abandon the idea. Mahadev Desai likened the *calm* that followed to an "armed truce".[130]

For some time the villagers expressed their resentment towards the ashram's passive intrusion upon their life-style by a sort of social boycott. They resented the failure of the ashram members to observe their caste-rules and, moreover, mixing with *harijans,* scavenging excreta and using it as manure were considered irreligious activities by the caste-Hindus. The sanitation programme thus proved the most difficult to apply and maintain The problem was accentuated by Gandhi's belief that sanitation should be given priority in village uplift work.

> Lionel Curtis when he wrote that the Indian village consisted of dilapidated structures built on dung-heaps did not overdraw the picture. We have to remove the dung-heaps, turn them to good account and make the village site a smiling garden.[131]

The Ashram workers swept the village lanes and urged the people to use the common latrines set up earlier by Mira. The villagers refused to co-operate in carting manure, however, which meant they would not hire out their carts for this purpose. They also remained apathetic to the task of keeping the village clean. The ashramites worked and the villagers watched. Gandhi did obtain some positive response from a number of enlightened individuals, but he maintained that no claim of any substantial headway could be made until the people of Sevagram had made progress on all fronts.

In many respects the interrelated issues of untouchability and scavenging represented the watershed between the Ashram and the villagers, undermining progress in other areas of the programme. The antipathy of the villagers towards the removal of untouchability compounded their deep-rooted distrust of

The Village of Service: "India in a Village"

innovative schemes. The scepticism and apathy of India's poor, much of which related to their experience of exploitation under the *zamindari* system, was humorously but poignantly conveyed to Gandhi in the words of a village headman, whom Kishorelal Mashruwala met during the Sevagram experiment:

> We have only one difficulty; when there is famine in our parts, the crops die, the cattle die, human beings die, well-water dies but revenue and interest - these two never die. This is our only sorrow.[132]

Gandhi recognised the interconnectedness of the economic realities of village life and the oppressive social system. But it could be validly argued that he and his colleagues should not have taken up questions relating to untouchability until the people of Sevagram and elsewhere adjusted to the presence of village workers in their midst, and rapport was established. Describing the Sevagram experiment in 1940 Mahadev Desai wrote: "There is a hiatus between the villagers and us. There is yet no living link between us. We have our morning and evening prayers, but they touch not these simple folks. May be we have, with the best wishes in the world, not succeeded in coming down to their level and becoming one with them."[133] A reason for this "hiatus" was Gandhi's insistence that the village workers begin with scavenging and untouchability. These programmes offended the people and tended to alienate the workers from them.

There appear many instances where lack of co-operation from the Sevagram people can be traced to their discontent with the untouchability work of the Ashram. One exercise involved the construction of a road through the village to Gandhi's quarters, to link up with the road being built to connect Wardha and Sevagram at Jamnalal's expense. The village road scheme had in fact been proposed by the villagers themselves. They had given a written undertaking signed by seventy people, each of whom had agreed to collect cartloads of stones for three days. All other expenses were to be met by Gandhi. At the appointed time only fifteen to twenty people kept their pledge. It is difficult to gauge whether the villagers' response on this occasion was due to scepticism about the value of the road scheme or to a concerted boycott prompted by the Ashram *harijan* programme. Whatever the case, Gandhi disappointedly harangued the villagers on the issue:

> You must know that this work is for your own benefit, and not for the benefit of the *Malguzar*.... But I am told that you are indifferent to all that is happening, that you do not care whether you have the road here or not. I ask you to put your heads together and decide whether you should co-operate with us or not. I do not refer to untouchability. There is no untouchability involved in this work, nor in the revival of your handicrafts.[134]

But to the unsophisticated villagers everything related to the Ashram was imbued with the stigma of untouchability because its members contravened their caste-rules. Only with the active co-operation of the headman did Gandhi finally persuade the villagers to assist in the road scheme.

Undaunted by the villagers' hostility Gandhi set about overcoming their traditional prejudices in his inimitable fashion. One incident that attracted the attention of Mahadev Desai involved the old *Kunbi* headman. The situation developed when the village barber refused to cut the hair of a *harijan* boy, whom Gandhi had adopted as his sixth son. Gandhi responded by refusing the barber's services until he agreed to serve the *harijans*. "If someone could assure him that he would go straight to *swarga* if he were to cast off untouchability he would do so," commented Jamnalal Bajaj, "but he wants a reliable assurance, and he would not accept ours." The old headman was drawn into the controversy when the barber maintained that the *patel* would be one of the first to boycott him if he served the *harijans*. Initially the headman's attitude seemed to confirm the barber's fears. He told Gandhi that "everything is permissible to a Mahatma like you, but not to folks like us." However, Gandhi persuaded the old man to relent on this point-and to give an assurance that he was quite prepared to have a shave immediately after the barber had served the *harijan* boy. The barber remained unconvinced. He asked the headman, who was a member of a higher caste, to further demonstrate his removal of untouchability by dining with him. But the patel had gone far enough to his way of thinking and refused the offer. Yet Gandhi was satisfied since he never considered inter-caste dining a vital factor in the removal of untouchability. Eventually the

The Village of Service: "India in a Village"

headman became a daily visitor to Gandhi's house, which ordinarily he should have shunned because a *harijan* was employed there as a cook.[135]

The success of the *harijan* programme at Sevagram is difficult to gauge, but his conversion of the most influential man in the village was a tangible result of Gandhi's early endeavours. Progress was slow, however, and for several years the village response to the anti-untouchability work of the Ashram was almost wholly negative. On occasion not even the guidance and encouragement Gandhi gave his co-workers could temper their frustration with his methods. One worker went out each day to meet the villagers, talk to them, read to them and conduct a night school. He reported that gambling was rampant in the village, especially in the month of *shravana*, a devotional period for Hindus that includes a number of days of fasting. Fully aware of the extent of poverty in Sevagram this particular worker was appalled that the people would waste what little they earned after a lay's labour. He learnt that even the Harijans employed in the Ashram were no less involved. For days he watched them gambling, but was unable to wean them away from the habit. In an attempt to comfort this perplexed man Gandhi told him, "you must be thankful that they listen to you and do not contemptuously drive you away."[136]

At all times Gandhi persisted with persuasion and example as his only educational tools. Tolerating no distinction between the different *harijan* castes, he surrounded himself and the ashramites with as many as possible. In a departure from the approach he employed at Sabarmati, he manned the community kitchen with them so that they could be taught the art of conservative and hygienic cooking. Food was served to members and guests of the Ashram without heed to caste, creed, colour or sex. The *harijan* assistants also joined in the Ashram prayers and took part in all community activities.

Though the *harijans* came to the Ashram initially as servants, Gandhi soon put them at ease in their new surroundings by a process of gentle manipulation, largely based on a form of progressive and practical adult education. Gandhi never diverged from the principle that education should be "co-extensive with life itself. His aim was not to remove ignorance by imparting the knowledge of the alphabet but rather by providing villagers with object-lessons in sanitation, hygiene and the improvement of material conditions and social relationships. He came to believe that ashrams patterned on his ideals should train villagers to be community workers without alienating them from their own people. "Of course everywhere the difficulty is about workers," he told Amrit Kaur in 1937, "they have to be found or prepared locally. Importation is not possible for, nowhere is there a plethora of supply."[137]

Despite the vociferous opposition to his *harijan* programme, Gandhi never lost sight of the premise that a village worker must give first priority to anti-untouchability work and related activities. While on a trip to Gujarat in November 1936, he met a number of *harijan* workers at Sabarmati (by this time renamed *Harijan* Ashram). They questioned whether it would be wiser to promote village industries work if it was found impossible to persuade caste-Hindus to co-operate in anti-untouchability work. "That is a delusion", he replied, "you may be sure that he who gives up *harijan* work on a pretext like that will be able to do less for the village industries work."[138] Selflessness and fearlessness, essential attributes of a *satyagrahi,* were also fundamental qualifications for *harijan* work in Gandhi's view. Over the years the Sevagram Villagers' Association with Ashram activities gradually reformed then caltural and religious value sysem. Pyarelal recounts that the village temples of the caste-Hindus were eventually thrown open to the *harijans,* and the caste-Hindus began to attend the ceremonies and prayer meetings in the *Mahar* temple. According to him the caste-Hindus largely shed the prejudice against eating food handled by *harijans.* [139]

In many respects the time was not ripe for the far-reaching reforms Gandhi sought to introduce. In 1937 the Indian National Congress took up the responsibility of government in nine provinces. For the educated urban middle classes it was a time of high expectation and fevered political activity. The majority of Gandhi's colleagues, caught up in the excited atmosphere of the period, were sceptical of his view that *"swaraj* would come to India not through the Congress parliamentarians in the legislatures, but through efficient and conscientious discharge of their work by *Bhangis* and other workers without looking for reward or praise in municipal and public addresses."[140]

The Village of Service: "India in a Village"

The Politics of Constructive Work

Though they had utmost faith in his political judgment, many of Gandhi's politically-minded co-workers regarded his social theories as an aberration and were disinclined to seek the hardship of settling alone in a backward village. They argued that the dissociation of the constructive work programme from Congress politics allowed the Socialists free rein to propagate their brand of political education in the villages. In his speech at the Gandhi Seva Sangh Meeting held during April 1937 Gandhi dealt with this question: "The substance of the question is whether we should go to the villages to serve or for political awakening.... To me there is no political education apart from the constructive programme. Our aim is merely the propagation of the *charkha* and such other things. This does not mean that we do not wish to give the villagers political education. But there is no such thing as political education by itself. We should keep in touch with them without harbouring any motive. We have to develop their strength. I go to them with the eradication of untouchability and the like and give them education. Political education is just that. If I do something apart from this and go to the villagers seeking votes, I shall be doing exactly what we blame the missionaries for doing .... Take Segaon itself, where I live. It is in Maharashtra and people in Maharashtra are very political-minded. But even they don't ask for swaraj.... If I speak to them about the legislatures they may ask me if I would bring them a couple of bags of food-grains from there. What is the condition of India as a whole today? The talk of bread is all that the people understand. They have no use for politics."[141] During the Sevagram period the conviction grew that political activity divorced from constructive work was coercive and essentially exploitative.

He did his utmost at Sevagram to avoid political concerns. Whenever journalists attempted to draw him into political discussions he would adroitly evade their questions and instead focus attention on work in the village.[142] While Nehru and Congress were preoccupied with power, Gandhi devoted his energies to the realisation of the non-violent society. "About political matters I merely offer advice and then forget about it", he told the Gandhi Seva Sangh in 1937. "I do my writing for the constructive programme and for it I work."[143] Yet inexorably he was drawn back into the realm of power politics. Congress meetings were held at Sevagram and he continued to play a vital role in Congress decision-making. During the weeks of uncertainty following the election of Congress ministries in 1937, he served as an intermediary between the new Viceroy, Lord Linlithgow, and the Congress leaders. The confusion surrounding the exact status of the newly elected ministries was resolved when Gandhi extracted an undertaking that British governors would not interfere with the Congress administration.[144]

Even during the periods he was ensconced at Sevagram, he could find little peace from the tumultuous affairs of national politics. Ironically on one occasion he was the object of a *satyagraha* action. A group of *harijans* under the influence of Dr. Ambedkar's ideas marched to Sevagram and pronounced that they would remain until their demand that a *harijan* be appointed to the Congress cabinet was met. Unimpressed by Gandhi's helplessness on this issue, they occupied the living quarters of ashramites, delivered mocking speeches and fasted. They left after several days but doubtless their actions disturbed Gandhi.[145]

Notwithstanding Gandhi's objections a significant proportion of his co-workers did in some way become involved in politics. To many people the Gandhian movement was no more than a political faction vying with other factions for influence in the legislatures. It was evident that many members of the Gandhi Seva Sangh, for instance, took up membership as a means to enhance their political careers. Political opportunism was rife throughout India and the Gandhian organisations were no exception. In certain parts of India workers wearing Gandhi caps came to be regarded with contempt. Villagers in these areas had experienced the arrogance and attitude of superiority expressed by people wearing *khadi* and claiming to speak and act on behalf of Gandhi but who in reality sought to further their own careers. During the Gandhi Seva Sangh meeting held at Malikanda in February 1940 Gandhi repeated the words of a deputation from Noakhali that had just visited him, in order to highlight this problem: "We accept everything you say. But we are unable to understand what your followers here say....We can agree to what you say. Call it Gandhism, spinning, village industries — we would accept anything. We are your followers. But we are not followers of your followers. Your followers have nothing to offer."[146]

He was distressed that his name was being exploited in this fashion. Jamnalal Bajaj had set up the Sangh while Gandhi was in gaol during 1922-23 in order to propagate the constructive work programme, but he was adamant that members should not be associated with factional politics. Yet Gandhi himself had advised the Sangh in 1937 at Hubli to interest itself in parliamentary politics. He believed that the experience gained would be useful and that members of the Sangh would collectively exercise a constructive influence upon the legislatures. By the late 1930s the Congress Working Committee was dominated by Gandhians but members of the Gandhi Seva Sangh were feuding over political issues and contesting elections against one another. Gandhi denounced this trend: "This is hypocrisy. This is madness.... Such people make a laughing-stock of Gandhism."[147] He realised that the Sangh was a crutch for many of his colleagues, particularly those who thought of themselves as members of an elite association. Drawing a comparison between the decline of the Satyagraha Ashram and the unhealthy developments within the Sangh, Gandhi decided to disband the organisation in 1940.[148]

He was now determined to rid the constructive work organisations of workers who made a pretence of service but who were principally motivated by their aspirations to position and power. The fundamental re-structuring of the society he envisaged demanded community workers who were self-motivated, determined and willing to serve the poor without hope of gain.

Apart from disbanding the Gandhi Seva Sangh as an entity separate from the constructive work organisations, Gandhi resolved to enforce a rule preventing members of the latter organisations from becoming members of the Congress Working Committee. On one hand the constructive work programme was distanced from the political decision making process, but on the other hand a check upon the machinations of vested interests in political circles was removed. This created a dilemma for Gandhi, which was highlighted by Professor Kumarappa in 1947. "I am afraid most of the governments seem to be. concerned with vote catching programmes and schemes rather than real, solid, constructive work," he wrote to Gandhi.[149] At the time of this letter Kumarappa was contemplating whether to accept an invitation to join the Working Committee. Initially Gandhi's response was encouraging.[150] Within two weeks, however, he altered his view. He reminded Kumarappa of the rule concerning members of the constructive work organisations, and advised him to "resist this temptation". Gandhi's view was that members of the constructive work organisations should be invited to give advice on matters directly relating to then area of expertise, but should avoid political office.[151] Ultimately he left the decision to Kumarappa.[152]

Gandhi's ambivalent attitude to holding political office had been evident throughout his career as a public activist. His stature within India ensured that politicians sought his advice on a wide range of issues. Indeed, in many respects, they were obliged to do so in order to legitimise their own position. However, his influential status in national affairs was not shared by his colleagues in the constructive work organisations. By dissociating constructive work from political activity he sought to nullify the damaging effects of Congress careerism. But ironically the dissociation undermined whatever potential there existed for mass contact as a result of Congress association with the constructive work organisations, and considerably weakened the influence of genuine Gandhian activists in the legislatures. "In a very real way the death of Gandhi deprived the enthusiasts committed to his cause of their key to power, their vital piece on the political chessboard", observed Judith Brown. "In Independent India they became a group without leverage."[153]

During the 1930s Jawaharlal Nehru explained his differences with Gandhi on the question of linking constructive work to political activity. Gandhi had worked to establish and consolidate Congress influence over rural and small town elites through his methods of political subcontracting, but his appeal to the poor in the villages was predominately developmental. Nehru recognised the attendant problem in his Presidential Address to Congress at Lucknow in 1936:

> I have referred previously to the growing divorce between our organisation and the masses. Individually many of us still have influence with the masses and our word carries weight with them.... And yet organisationally we have lost that intimate touch we had. The social reform activities of the khadi and village industries and Harijan organisations keep large

numbers of our comrades in touch with the masses and those contacts bear fruit. But they are essentially non-political and so, politically, we have largely lost touch."[154]

Nehru acknowledged the vital nature of the work done at Sevagram and elsewhere under the auspices of the ashrams and constructive work organisations, but he questioned the wisdom of neglecting the political education of the villages. Ideologically sympathetic to the Socialist block in Congress, his concept of social revolution and state socialism was a significant departure from Gandhi's vision of a self-governing and self-sufficient village India.

Nehru described *khadi* and village industries as "temporary expedients of a transition stage rather than as a solution of our vital problem".[155] For Gandhi the spinning wheel remained a necessary foundation for all public corporate life. He saw it as the one visible link that indissolubly bound politicians to the lowest in the land. Nehru recognised this but maintained that it had little to do with the^ development of India's economy. "The khadi movement, hand-spinning and hand-weaving, which is Gandhiji's special favourite, is an intensification of individualism in production, and is thus a throw-back to the pre-industrial age", observed Nehru in his autobiography. "As a solution of any vital present-day problem it cannot be taken seriously, and it produces a mentality which may become an obstacle to growth in the right direction."[156]

By 1938 Congress membership had reached three million, but the election of Subhas Chandra Bose to the presidency signalled the changes that were taking place in the Congress structure. The spirit of sacrifice and selflessness which had been a hallmark of the Congress struggle for freedom was declining. The quest for power and position and the spread of corruption and ostentation aroused Gandhi's opposition and alienated him further from the bulk of the Congress membership. He did not share Nehru's conviction that political independence would remove the obstacles in the path of nation-building. "I am painfully conscious of the fact that a far greater and a far more solid awakening has to take place before we can confidently say that *swaraj* is ours for the asking", wrote Gandhi in 1938. "Any extraneous event may put power into our hands. I would not call that *swaraj* of the people."[157] He believed that only constructive activities could bring public activists in touch with the villagers in a way that was beneficial to the nation as a whole, but that this work demanded "constant vigilance, effort, study and diligence". In his view all citizens should take an interest in politics but the chief motivating force behind all organisations, political and non-political, should be the uplift of mankind as a whole. He refuted the claim that constructive work could only be sustained by political activity.[158]

During the the 1940s Gandhi's earlier misgivings as to the direction Congress would take in post-Independent India were brought into sharp focus. On the eve of his death he advocated the disbanding of the Congress as a political group, its transformation into a social service organisation, and the devolution of political authority to three tiers of elected national servants, of which the bottom tier should be the village *panchayat*. He observed that while India had won political independence, it still had to realise "social, moral and economic independence in terms of its seven hundred thousand villages."[159]

The late 1930s and early 1940s were an unsettled period in India's quest for nationhood, and Gandhi found himself increasingly drawn into the political imbroglio. Caught between his desire to remain at Sevagram and the demands placed upon him as a result of the developing political situation, it was an equally disturbed period in Gandhi's life. His health suffered and the inability to undertake more physical work left him dispirited on occasion. "I am after all a sinking ship," he told Mahadev Desai in September 1938, "who would choose to sail in such a ship?"[160] To ease his frustrations with the failings of the Ashram Gandhi extended his periods of silence. The internal and external struggles embroiling the Indian sub-continent were a constant source of worry to him, but he could find little peace at Sevagram. On the contrary, the internal situation of the Ashram became more confused. Despite continuous building operations the Ashram was crowded, increasing the problems of day-to-day management. Unable to stem the influx of inmates, Gandhi attempted to reduce his involvement with the internal affairs of the Ashram during 1940. "I do not want to insist on anything anymore and so beyond expressing my views on essential matters, I do not want to argue," he explained in an Ashram Note.[161] He broke his silence in order to discuss the political situation with members of the Congress

The Village of Service: "India in a Village"

Working Committee, but otherwise remained relatively detached from Ashram life. When his attention was drawn to a matter concerning the Ashram he would make his view known through the circulation of notes.

Though the distance between Gandhi and the Congress leadership had been growing during the late 1930s, in September 1940 the All India Congress Committee met in Bombay and sought Gandhi's guidance. In response to the Congress request for independence and the formation of a suitable government to hasten the process, the Viceroy Lord Linlithgow had introduced emergency orders curtailing freedom of speech and other liberties. Congress had offered to support the war effort if their proposal was accepted, but Churchill's war government was in no mood to bargain. Gandhi advised civil disobedience against the new measures. Individual *satyagrahis* from amongst Gandhi's close circle, including Vinoba Bhave, began the campaign by speaking out against the Government's war policy and deliberately courting arrest. During 1940-41 close to four hundred members of the legislatures were imprisoned and over twenty thousand protesters were convicted.

Yet despite Gandhi's preoccupation with the political situation, village work remained his main concern. "Lastly it is cruelty to animals to drag me from Sevagram except when duty makes a peremptory call", he wrote in February 1941.[162] In April of that year he described a village of his conception in a letter to Munnalal A Shah:

> That village may be regarded as reformed, where everybody wears *khadi,* which produces all the *khadi* it needs, in which every inhabitant spends some of his time in one or more processes relating to cotton, which uses only oil produced in indigenous oil-presses, which consumes only jaggery manufactured in the village itself or in its neighourhood and only hand-milled flour and hand-pounded rice; the village, in other words, where the largest possible number of village industries are flourishing, in which nobody is illiterate, where the roads are clean, there is a fixed place for evacuation, the wells are clean, there is harmony among the different communities, and untouchabiliry is completely absent, in which everybody gets cow's milk, ghee, etc. in moderate

quantities, in which nobody is without work, and which is free from quarrels and thefts, and in which the people abide by the sevaks' advice in all matters. This is possible in the existing conditions, I cannot of course say about the time required.[163]

Gandhi had sown the seeds with the intention of developing Sevagram into such a village, but it was left to his colleagues to nurture its growth. Many Ashram activities did bear fruit, but Sevagram did not develop into a model, healthy village in Gandhi's lifetime, and subsequently the work done was not consolidated in a way that would have pleased him. Like all Gandhi's communities Sevagram was a laboratory in which he experimented with ways and means to combat the poverty and oppression that pervaded village India. As with all experimentation there were successes and failures.

The difficulties faced at Sevagram were in many respects symptomatic of Gandhi's own ambivalence toward the relationship between politics and constructive work. He believed that the two fields of activity were inseparable provided one's spiritual integrity was not compromised by the day-to-day political struggle, and the means adopted remained commensurate with the conceived end. He attempted to elevate politics and community work to a spiritual plane, but his genuinely religious attitude was not shared by the majority of his followers. Martin Buber believed that in effect the expediences of the political situation had a corrupting influence upon Gandhi's overall programme: "The contradiction between the unconditionality of a spirit and the conditionally of a situation, to which situation, precisely, the masses of his followers, even of the youth, belong."[164]

Gandhi himself recognised that many people at Sevagram, and elsewhere, involved in the constructive work organisations, were inspired more by a desire to achieve some renown for themselves by association with him than by a wish to serve the really poor in the villages. In an interview with Ved Mehta during the 1970s one of Gandhi's grand-daughters - Sumitra, the eldest daughter of Ramdas and Nirmala Gandhi - summed up her impressions of the people who swarmed around Gandhi at Sevagram: "Everyone under the sun wanted to be known as a secretary to the Mahatma. The moment he died, they were all suddenly brought face to face with reality — without him they were nothing."[165] The tragic nature of Gandhi's involvement in politics was perhaps best expressed by Chakravarti Rajagopalachari, his friend, political associate and founder of an ashram in South India. Though clearly an exaggeration, his comments highlight the irony inherent in Gandhi's attitude to politics in India: "It may be that because of Gandhi we got our freedom before we were ready, before we had developed our character to match the responsibility. The handful of Gandhians who still believe in his philosophy of a simple life in a simple society are mostly cranks."[166]

True to the pattern of Gandhi's earlier communities inmates at Sevagram were in the forefront of the "Quit India" *satyagraha* campaign in 1942. Gandhi was arrested on the 9th of August, the day after he had delivered his famous "Do or Die" speech to the nation. A meeting was held in Wardha to condemn the Government action. During the police action to break it up a young boy was killed. As a direct challenge to the Government the Ashram became a centre of *satyagraha* housing intending *satyagrahis* from the surrounding villages and other Gandhian institutions. A committee was formed to co-ordinate activities in the Ashram. Many ashramites and young men from Sevagram and other villages broke the ban on meetings and processions, were imprisoned and suffered the abuses of the police. The majority of the women inmates, Chimanlal Shah, Kishorelal Mashruwala, Munnalal Shah, Balwant Singh and Bhansali were among those imprisoned on different occasions. After being arrested and released several times Bhansali fasted in order to draw attention to the oppressive measures adopted by the Government. His courageous actions focused attention on various police atrocities in the Wardha district, particularly cruelties perpetrated on women of Chimur, a village sixty-three miles from Sevagram. The Government finally conceded his demand for an inquiry into the Chimur atrocities and his fast ended successfully, coincidentally after an ordeal of sixty-three days.[167]

The political awakening that occurred among the villages surrounding Sevagram during the Quit India movement was perhaps on Pyarelal's mind when he observed that though the institution of the ashram was in many respects a hindrance to community work, i.e., in the sense that to run an ashram can become an end in itself, with regard to *satyagraha* there were infinite possibilities in the ashram concept.[168] Nehru saw the potential for arousing political consciousness among the villagers. Cadres of self-disciplined men and women could be utilised to impact political education. Yet Gandhi was unyielding in his belief that a harmonious, non-violent society and state would not proceed from political activity divorced from constructive work, and had warned of the dangers of contrary conditions which existed as far back as 1924:

> If we begin to use them (the masses) before they are ready we shall cease to represent them. We must first come in living touch with them by working for them and in their midst. We must share their sorrows, understand their difficulties and anticipate their wants.[169]

The excessive violence of the "Quit India" revolt, which the imprisoned leaders were powerless to contain, confirmed Gandhi's misgivings.

On 6 May 1944, Gandhi was released along with his companions from his last imprisonment. Mahadev Desai and Kasturba had both died in custody, leaving Gandhi bereft of two of his most loyal and dearest companions. After a month of convalescence, during which he observed long periods of silence, he returned to Sevagram. But the growing tension over the demand by the Muslim League leader, Mohammed Ali Jinnah, for the partition of India on religious grounds left Gandhi little opportunity to reabsorb himself in village work. In the pervading atmosphere of Hindu-Muslim confrontation it seemed to Gandhi that after exploiting his influence with the Indian people for the past twenty-five years he had now outlived his usefulness to the Congress leadership.

His frustration and disillusionment were evident during the Congress Working Committee meeting that took place at Sevagram during August 1946. At all hours of the day an unusual influx of visitors crowded into the Ashram, many of whom had come merely to see Gandhi. They surrounded his hut, forcing him to place curtains in the doorways in order to have privacy. In an address to these visitors he reiterated his belief that the root cause of India's woes was the failure to inculcate the self-help principle. It was the main reason why Sevagram was far from self-sufficiency arid the bane of constructive work generally. Lastly he condemned the senseless adoration of the visitors as symptomatic of the same ailment. "True admiration consisted in carrying out the wishes of the person one admired, not merely staring at him and thus wasting his time and one's own", writes Pyarelal in his account of the speech.[170]

Balwant Singh recounts that the death of Kasturba was a great loss to the Ashram. She performed all her tasks diligently and refused the service of others. Despite her failing health she was a source of strength among the inmates, attending to the sick, rendering personal service to Gandhi and maintaining a careful watch over the teenage boys and girls of the Ashram. "Since Bapu was much occupied with the affairs of the outside world, it was not he but Ba who constituted the centre of Ashram life", writes Balwant Singh. "When she was absent, the Ashrarn looked empty to us."[171] With Kasturba gone Gandhi seemed less able to tolerate the shortcomings of the Ashram. He upbraided the inmates for their failure to serve the villages in a spirit of love, and advised the sincere workers among them to leave Sevagram and settle down in the villages of their choice. The ideal of putting a *gram sevak* in each village remained Gandhi's ultimate objective. Pyarelal recalls that later in Noakhali, where Gandhi had gone to quell communal conflict in 1947, those that accompanied him were set up as village workers on their own. Pyarelal's own experiences with the villages under his purview at Noakhali were later recorded (and subsequently published in *The Last Phase*). Referring to Pyarelal's account of village work Gandhi commented, "This is what I dreamt about".[172]

It was Gandhi's intention to disband the Ashram towards the end of 1944, but he was subsequently dissuaded. Balwant Singh asserted that the problems at Sevagram were not due to the laxity of the ashramites *per se,* but were due to the concentration of various types of organisations that had grown up there: "... there was no unison among them, but rather a certain measure of conflict, with the result that work suffered. To add to the confusion, he had suggested new changes quite frequently. He had done the same in the Sabarmati Ashram and had repeated it here. I felt that if these institutions had been located in different villages and if they had worked independently, they would have served the villages much better." In terms of Gandhi's belief in the necessity of decentralisation and independent work, these criticisms should have been acceptable to him, but surprisingly he rejected them as revealing a "lack of intelligence". He argued that as the organisations were conceived and created by himself it was natural that they remain near him for guidance.[173] Yet he was unable to give neither these institutions nor the Ashram itself sufficient guidance because of his preoccupation with politics.

On the eve of Gandhi's final departure from Sevagram on 25 August 1946, his speech to the inmates underlined the flaws in his approach to politics and constructive work. In terms of the time he had spent in gaols for his political activism,[174] his words on the occasion not only proved prophetic but highlighted the inherent ambivalence towards politics that had undermined Gandhi's constructive work activities throughout his long career:

> When the Ashram was first started in Kochrab we set before us certain ideals. Same ideals are before us today. What is our duty in terms of these ideals in the face of the conflagration that is raging in the country today? Let us be humble and confess that we have not got the strength today to meet all the expectations that the people entertain of us. But we are sincerely striving for it. If we had fully realised the principles for which we stand, we should have rushed into the blaze and offered the purest sacrifices which might have conceivably quenched the flames .... The art of jail-going we have learnt with the rest. But jail-going is only the beginning, not the end of the *satyagraha*. The acme of *satyagraha* for us would be to lay down our lives for the defence of India's just cause. Let us then pray to God to give us the requisite purity and fearlessness in the true sense of the term, to make our sacrifice worthy of the altar. Then alone shall we be worthy of the name of the Ashram.[175]

On the one hand the Ashramites were told that selfless and silent service in the villages was the purest expression of non-violence, but on the other they were emboldened to lay down their lives as martyrs in the cause of peace. With his extraordinary capacity for work and sacrifice Gandhi was able to diminish the negative repercussions of his nationalistic activities upon the constructive work programme. But the truth of Gokhale's warning, i.e. that Gandhi made demands beyond the average person's capacity, was never more apparent.

As Gandhi had foreseen, very few inmates remained at Sevagram after his death. Several continued working in the spirit of the Ashram, while others took up careers unrelated to the Gandhian pattern. Though the many institutions that had sprung up during the active life of the Ashram continued their work, Sevagram itself was preserved in its original form "in order to give to posterity an exact idea of the Ashram as it functioned under the Mahatma".[176] In many respects, however, Gandhi's hope for the future lay not in the institution of the Ashram, but in the method of basic education developed at Sevagram. As J. C. Kumarappa wrote to Gandhi in February 1947: "...you realise this is the most uphill part of the work. This is so because we are dealing with adults. When the basic scheme has had its effect we shall have bent the bamboo while tender. What we are doing now is trying to bend the ripened, hardened poles. If it does not produce any results at least it gives us a training ground for ourselves which is also an essential part of our programme. So I never feel disheartened whatever difficulties we may meet."[177]

The Sevagram Method

The system of education developed at Sevagram and described by Gandhi as "Basic Education" or *Nai Talim* (New Way) indicated an awareness of the importance of education in achieving his aims. He believed that the reforms proposed under his programmes would have a limited effect unless there was a new approach, a complete restructuring of the Indian educational pattern. It was the integral factor through which all the interrelated and independent elements of national reconstruction would be linked: "Educational reform is so to speak more than educational reform ... it is also social reform and reconstruction in the widest sense of the work."[178] Seen in this context the introduction of *nai talim* in 1937 signalled the beginning of Gandhi's final and most crucial experiment in constructive work:

> Education has come last. Naturally, for education must follow practice. But it is there for the sake of all that has preceded, and for the sake of the entire scheme of life. It is to prepare the growing child for the place he will occupy in the future in this just and moral society, free from all exploitations. It is for the

formation of his character in the light of the requirements of such a society. It is the coping stone of Gandhiji's socio-political edifice.[179]

He believed in the principle of free and compulsory education for India. In his view this could only be realised by teaching children a useful vocation and utilising it as a means of cultivating their mental, physical and spiritual potentialities. The educational experiment at Sabarmati had convinced Gandhi that a vocation, preferably spinning, should have a central place in education, that education should be largely self-supporting and that it should be vitally related to India's rural heritage. The self-supporting principle underlay all his work, but after forty years of experimenting with education the catalyst which led to the refinement of the principle came from intimate contact with the people of Sevagram.[180]

In the midst of village reconstruction Gandhi formulated the idea that the "whole education should be imparted through some handicraft or industry", i.e., the adoption of a craft would be the means by which all the subjects of the education curriculum were correlated. Manual training would not merely supplement literary training, but in terms of individual wants and needs it would be the precursor to all levels of education.[181] There were two aspects to the self-supporting nature of his proposal. Firstly, that education should enable the recipient to be self-supporting in later life through vocational training, and secondly, that education should in itself be self-supporting. A child's education should be interrelated with training in a suitable craft and the product of the chosen craft should meet the expense of the teacher's salary. He emphasised that the only condition precedent to every school becoming self-supporting was "that the. State takes over the manufactures of these schools".[182]

To Gandhi's mind there was a fundamental opposition between education and violence. "If India has resolved to eschew violence, this system of education becomes an integral part of the discipline she has to go through", he observed. "We cannot, will not, think in terms of exploitation, and we have no alternative but this plan of education which is based on non-violence."[183] In his view the Sevagram method was conceived in such terms as to develop a co-operative and harmonious society of people aware of the social, economic, political and cultural needs of India. As the educational philosophy of Gandhi was inspired by the prevailing social, economic and political conditions in India, naturally it reflected the ideals upon which he based all the multifarious programmes of national reconstruction; "A national system of education is a reflection of a national system of ideals."[184] Mahadev Desai further clarified the vital role of non-violence in education during his speech to the Wardha Conference in 1937:

> The idea of self-supporting education cannot be divorced from the ideological background of non-violence, and unless we bear in mind that the new scheme is intended to bring into being a new age from which class and communal hatred is eliminated and exploitation is eschewed, we cannot make a success of it. We should, therefore, approach the task with firm faith in non-violence and in the faith that the new scheme is evolved by a mind that has conceived non-violence as the panacea for all evils.[185]

Gandhi wanted to reconstruct the villages which, he felt, were existing merely to be exploited by the cities and dependent on the latter's sufferance for survival. He believed that the strained and unnatural situation could only be alleviated when the city people realised their "duty of making an adequate return to the villages for the strength and sustenance which they derive from them, instead of selfishly exploiting them". To promote a healthy and moral relationship between the city and village Basic Education was necessary for city and village children alike.[186]

In Gandhi's estimation the potential wastage in vocational education could not even begin to compare with the tragedy of waste involved in capital-intensive production. He claimed that after one year of Basic Education the whole country would have benefited, provided the State absorbed much of the school produce for its own requirements and the nation bought with patriotic pride the remainder. He did not foresee any pressures being placed on indigenous manufacturers as very few were involved in the production of village handicrafts.

However, Gandhi did not promote manual work simply for the joy of creation or pursuit of knowledge, but recommended activities which he believed contributed towards the development of the individual as a member of a co-operative and democratic community.[187] The Sevagram method was conceived as a means of perpetuating the ideals of social service and citizenship through all the activities of children from the earliest formative years.[188] Basic Education was the constructive base upon which all the elements of Gandhi's proposed *sarvodaya* society were fused into an integrated concept.

In 1937 when the Indian National Congress was preparing to take up the responsibility of government in nine provinces, and popular representatives were going to share the responsibility for shaping the educational policy of the country, Gandhi wrote a series of articles in *Harijan* to herald the inception of the Sevagram Method.[189] The reaction of the public was generally unenthusiastic. There was a storm of protest from orthodox educationalists: "The new ideas were styled reactionary, anti-revolutionary, medieval, unpractical, faddist, spiritual...."[190] Many opponents of the scheme appeared to reach their conclusions by merely taking individual points and criticising them out of context, without trying to understand the full implications of Basic Education as an integrated scheme of social and educational reform.

The self-supporting aspect of Basic Education generated the greatest controversy among educationists and the public in general. One university professor believed the proposed system to be a short-sighted policy which would make the schools solvent and the nation bankrupt, and that it really amounted to nothing more than legalised child labour. His condemnation was based on an earlier article in support of Basic Education by a member of the Harijan Ashram at Sabarmati. The author wrote that "if each child is made to perform a certain amount of manual labour by way of this school fee, and the teachers are resourceful enough to make this labour fully productive, a considerable proportion of the running expenses of the school can be met from this source." To substantiate his claim he went on to cite figures of earnings through spinning of the girls at the Harijan Ashram. Each student was supposed to devote three hours daily to spinning, carding and weaving. On this basis twenty-five ten-year-old girls made an average of 12 annas each month (approximately 9 rupees per annum) which in the author's view, demonstrated "that a class of students of the age of ten years and above can be made very nearly, if not altogether, self-supporting through spinning."[191] The professor concluded from his analysis of the figures provided in the articles that even when a school had specialised in one occupation and had trained grown-up children, waste was considerable. His argument was that whilst a vocational school was a place for experimenting and wasting resources, India, with limited resources, could only afford to institute as few as necessary and only at important centres.[192] Gandhi realised that the figures provided from Sabarmati were not conclusive, but as the average earnings was arrived at after deducting the loss due to waste, it was certainly encouraging data. He was really asking the professor and the nation to take his educational experiment on trust.[193]

Groups such as Servants of India and the Theosophical Society were also critical of what they saw as an over-emphasis on craft. Dinkar Desai, of the Servants of India wrote that "the basic craft is given such a predominant place in the Wardha Scheme that it loses its real educational value. The predominance is so pronounced that craft teaching is sure to degenerate into the worst form of child labour." In his view handicraft should only have a limited scope in primary education, forming only a minor part of the curriculum.[194] Dr. George Arundale of the Theosophical Society criticised the Scheme for transforming the child into a wage making machine,[195] and S. N. Namle, a Montessorian sympathetic to Gandhi's ideals, believed that the presentation and co-ordination of subjects in the syllabus should not be restricted to craft, because this merely replaced the dominance of books by the dominance of crafts, without giving due consideration to the important part played by the unconscious or subconscious activities in the formation of human personality. Namle did not condemn the Wardha Scheme, but by retaining the mechanical divisions and restricted contents of the orthodox curriculum, he believed it was out of date from the outset. Instead of imposing craft on the child he opposed the Montessori idea of preparing an environment in which the cultural atmosphere of the society is presented to the child in such a way that full advantage is taken of the child's natural instincts and inclinations.[196]

Gandhi refuted the basic premise upon which the use of general terms like "child labour" to describe the Sevagram Method were founded, i.e., that regulated manual work is essentially harmful to the development of the child. In his view value judgments such as this conjured up images of oppression and exploitation, the removal of which was the aim rather than the product of Basic Education. J. B. Kripalani restated Gandhi's belief when he wrote, "to eliminate labour from child education and child life would be to cripple the growing faculties of the child". He felt it was superstition to believe that approximately three hours' vocational work a day would make education dull, or hamper the natural creativity of the child's mind. On the contrary, he believed vocational exercise would keep the mind of the student fresh and alert while providing at the same time a means of drawing out his or her intellect.[197]

In October 1937, a small conference of educationists met at Wardha to discuss the plan of education Gandhi had been propounding in the columns of *Harijan*. Under Gandhi's presidentship the conference adopted the following resolutions:

1. That free and compulsory education be provided for seven years on a national scale.
2. That the medium of instruction be the mother-tongue.
3. That the processes of education throughout this period should centre around some form of manual labour and productive work and all the other abilities to be developed or training to be given should, as far as possible, be integrally related to the central handicraft chosen with due regard to the environment of the child.
4. That this system of education would be gradually able to cover the remuneration of the teachers.

The conference also appointed a committee of educationists with Dr. Zakir Hussain as its Chairman, to prepare a detailed syllabus along these lines. Their report, which embodies what is known as the Wardha Scheme or "Basic National Education", was submitted to Gandhi on 2 December 1937.[198]

Gandhi realised that his function as an educationist was not to present a complete educational picture but only to suggest broad principles to be scrutinised, modified and implemented by other educationists. In answer to critics at the Wardha Conference, he said, "You should not accept anything out of your regard for me. I am near death's door and would not dream of thrusting anything

The Village of Service: "India in a Village" 241

down people's throats. The scheme should be accepted after full and mature consideration so that it may not have to be given up after a little while."[199] Though the Sevagram Method was the result of extensive experimental work in the field of education by Gandhi and his colleagues over a long period it remained necessary to have all the elements of Basic Education tested and corroborated by the Zakir Hussain Committee, which comprised a number of eminent and experienced educationists.[200] On the basis of the principles outlined in the Sevagram method the Committee prepared the main outline of the correlated programme of work for a period of seven years. It was expected that during this period (age seven - fourteen) the child would acquire "the essential modicum of social and civic training."[201]

It is the technique of correlation which signified the essence of the new pattern of education proposed by Gandhi. In this context the object of the Wardha Scheme was not primarily the production of craftsmen who could practise a craft mechanically, but the "exploitation for educative purposes of the resources implicit in craft work". Much of the criticism levelled at the Scheme was based on the argument that it is impossible to teach all subjects through a craft, and it is evident that Gandhi did", at first, think this was possible.[202] But he saw the difficulties of actually working the Scheme on this basis. He modified the principle to allow for knowledge imparted by craft to be supplemented by other processes.[203]

The greatest strength of the Wardha Scheme was the carefully designed curriculum prepared by the Zakir Hussain Committee. But regrettably the uniqueness of the new system proved to be its major handicap. The teaching profession of India was in such a dilapidated state as to severely limit the number of competent teachers capable of utilising its full potential. A critic of the proposal to conscript teachers to be trained in the new method declared:

> We have made far too many experiments with our young men and women, but this one bids fair in its results to land us in a ruin from which there will be no escape for at least half a century. The whole thing is based on the notion that teaching is one of those arts for which no adequate training is necessary and that everyone is a born teacher... The idea is a freak idea bound

to be tragic in results if applied. Again, how can each and everyone train children in handicrafts, etc.?[204]

The criticism was somewhat uninformed, but the author had a valid point in his general assessment of the teaching profession's inability to cope with the new method. However, Gandhi knew the only hope for success on a national level lay with the preparedness of teachers to undergo a short re-training course.[205] The Zakir Hussain Committee also recognised the need for properly trained teachers in their report. In this case it was a vital need because "when a radical reconstruction of the entire educational system is contemplated, the importance of the teachers who work out these changes is greatly accentuated."[206] The Committee required the teachers to have a good understanding of the educational and social ideology underlying the Scheme combined with an enthusiasm for working it out. Moreover, the teachers were expected to have an intelligent interest in the life and activities of their human environment and a thorough grasp of the intimate relationship between school and society.[207]

To enable the Scheme to begin as soon as possible a short emergency course of one year's training was provided for teachers specially selected from existing schools, national institutions and ashrams. The number of teachers to attend this abbreviated course was determined by the number of schools each province proposed to open. On the Committee's recommendation the next step was to set up a number of training schools in selected rural areas — at least one or two in each linguistic province—where teachers could learn the technique of correlation, and be trained to teach in the new basic schools. It was further planned to utilise existing training schools with the hope that the work of establishing basic schools for all the children in selected areas be completed within five years.[208]

To facilitate the rapid development of the Scheme it was necessary to involve the Education Department in conjunction with each province in a survey to establish the number of existing schools to be transformed, the number of new schools to be opened, the number of teachers required for them, and the cost involved. The department was also required to arrange to send all the teachers in the existing schools who could not attend the one year's course of training to specially organised refresher courses,

The Village of Service: "India in a Village"

where they would be instructed in the principles and methods of Basic Education. It was hoped that a scheme could be drawn up to ensure that all teachers in the service of the Department would attend such a course within five years from the beginning of 1938.[209]

It was proposed that when the first group of teachers had been trained new basic schools would be started in selected areas where all schools could accommodate the new scheme. The Committee recognised a situation developing where schools operating under the old system co-existed with the new basic schools in an atmosphere of false and unhealthy competition. Consequently they suggested that basic schools should initially be set up in areas where there were few schools and where, for that reason, the provision of educational facilities was more urgently required. Another recommendation was that every training school should have a demonstration school attached which "should be staffed by specially competent teachers who possess the necessary intellectual and practical disposition to work the scheme sympathetically". These would serve as model schools in each locality to provide inspiration and guidance for schools to be established later.[210]

Soon after the formulation of the syllabus the Scheme was brought for approval before the Indian National Congress at its Haripura session in February 1938. In a comprehensive resolution Congress endorsed the Scheme and initiated the formation of the *Hindustani Talimi Sangh* (All-India Board of Education).[211] However, though the scheme of Basic Education received support from many eminent educationists and the Congress, the Zakir Hussain Committee recommendations highlighted the need to promote interest in Government circles for a chance of complete success.

The Central Advisory Board of Education, which was attached to the Government of India Ministry of Education, and whose function it was to co-ordinate and guide the educational policy and programme of the Provincial Governments, appointed a committee to examine the new scheme in January 1938, with B. G. Kher (Minister for Education in Bombay) as its Chairman. The Kher Committee was instructed to "examine the scheme of educational reconstruction incorporated in the Wardha Scheme, in the light of the Abbott Wood Report on General and Vocational Education and other relevant documents."[212] The report by Abbott and Wood, two of India's leading educationists, vindicated the Sevagram Method by supporting the premise that manual work is the most satisfactory medium of instruction and the "key to a boy's serenity," On a national level much of the controversy over the new scheme ended with the acceptance by the Kher Committee of the basic principles underlying the Sevagram Method, and the general approval given to its conclusions by the Central Advisory Board of Education.

In pursuance of the resolution passed by the Congress at Haripura, the *Hindustani Talimi Sangh* was formed in April 1938, at Sevagram. The first object of the *Sangh* was to undertake extensive research work in the field of Basic Education and extend co-operation to Government and non-Government institutions already involved in experiments with the new scheme. The finalisation of the Scheme could not have come at a more fortuitous time for Congress, which was in office in seven out of the eleven provinces of India. Harking back to the first stirrings of the National Education Movement in Bengal during the early 1900s Congress was determined to get the maximum political mileage out of the Scheme.[213] However, it had taken extraordinary men such as Satish Chandra Mukherjee in 1906 and Gandhi in 1937 to stimulate the governing echelons into positive action, and the extent of actual reform was in fact limited to some extent by the amount of undivided attention these men were able to give their respective programmes.

The *Hindustani Talimi Sangh* began its efforts to put the Wardha Scheme into practice by requesting ihe Education Ministers in the seven Congress provinces to start basic schools and the national institutions to co-operate in the introduction and spread of Basic Education. It was understood that the first basic schools would serve as experimental models until the teacher training programme was firmly established. The Central Provinces' Government opened the first teacher training school at Wardha in conjunction with the *Hindustani Talimi Sangh* and the *Vidya Mandir* (Temple of Learning) scheme, under which every village where fifty or more school-going children were available was to have a *Vidyu Mandir*. It was proposed to attach a plot of land to each school, sufficient in area to provide the teacher with a living wage. Trust committees for each school were to be elected by the villagers on an adult franchise basis, and there was to be a reserve fund formed out of the net income of the trust, to be utilised in periods of famine and scarcity.

The Village of Service: "India in a Village"

In 1938 the Scheme had only been put into operation on a small scale but optimism in educational and governmental circles was high. There were over five thousand applicants for the first training course offered by the Vidya Mandir training school, out of which one hundred and sixty-six candidates were selected. Gandhi sought to impress upon these trainees the pioneering nature of their undertaking and the full implications of the Schemes.[214] He was conscious of two interrelated factors which might limit the success of the scheme. Firstly, the Sevagram Method had not been vindicated on a sufficiently large scale to warrant an automatic nation-wide adoption of the Wardha Scheme, and secondly, in the period in which Gandhi refined his educational approach there had been relatively little experimental work in its practical application at the national level.

The first twelve months of *nai talim* did appear to justify the high expectations of its creators. The Governments of Bombay, Bihar and Orissa constituted Boards of Basic Education and appointed officers with the object of supervising and promoting the programme,, Ten training centres were instituted by the Governments of Bombay, Bihar, Uttar Pradesh, Madhya Pradesh, Orissa and Kashmir. Among the national institutions, the Jamia Milia Islamia of Delhi and the Andhra Jateeya Kalashala of Masulipatam undertook the training of teachers, and the Maharashtra *Vidyapith* of Poona and the Gujarat *Vidyapith* of Ahmedabad started basic schools. The first basic schools established were the practising school at the *Vidya Mandir* training school, a voluntary school at Tagadur village in the Mysore State and the district board school at Sevagram.

The *Vidya Mandir* experiment was conducted by staff from the headquarters of the *Hindustani Talimi Sangh* (Sevagram) under the direction of Shrimati Ashadevi, who had been the first teacher to impart Basic Education to the children of Sevagram. Careful and complete records of the children's work and general development were kept to be used for further discussion or research on an individual and group basis. The experiment was conducted under no special conditions. The pupils were taken over from the municipal schools, mostly from the urban middle and lower middle classes, who had not been brought up in an atmosphere or tradition of craft work. The teachers were neither expert craftsmen nor specifically trained for the new system. They were from the old staff of the practising school and had received only a hasty training in spinning with *takli* and in the technique of correlated teaching. In the light of these conditions it was hoped that the experiment would be accepted as an average specimen.

At *Vidya Mandir* there was no fixed time table, as the teaching depended primarily on the opportunities arising from the craft work.[215] In terms of production and efficiency the experiment was so successful that the figures, when compared with the standard laid down in the detailed syllabus prepared by the Zakir Hussain Committee demonstrated that both in efficiency and production the attainment of the students at the end of two and a half months exceeded the standard fixed at the end of six months. The earning capacity as a group and per child was well above the highest expectations. However, the report of the experiment in *Harijan* does not indicate the success of the correlated method in realising the all-round development of the children.

On the other hand, the report of Gandhi's meeting with several of the first students to complete the Basic Education course at Sevagram was more encouraging:

> They were village lads from Sevagram and the neighbouring villages. Compared to those whom one sees working in the fields and who have never been to school, they were a heartening result of a first endeavour. They were clean, well-groomed, disciplined and well-mannered.[216]

Whilst it was difficult to gauge the success of the Scheme by the assessment of such an abstract variable as individual character development, it was possible to determine its real potential from the ease with which a large number of basic schools were begun within a relatively short period. M. S. Patel observed, with surprise, "the progress of Basic Education was not much adversely affected during the second year, even though the political situation had altered considerably."[217] The main reason was that the first All-India Basic Education Conference at Poona had resolved to safeguard the progress of the Scheme in spite of the war and subsequent resignation of the Congress Ministries. In 1939 the Bihar Government started thirty new basic schools in the district of Champaran, the Bombay Government introduced

The Village of Service: "India in a Village"

Basic Education in fifty-eight district board schools and twenty-eight other schools, in Gujarat, Maharashtra and Karnatak. With the addition of a few new training schools the total number in the country rose to fourteen.

Despite many encouraging results the optimism of 1938 had waned considerably by 1940-41. The Orissa Government decided to discontinue the scheme in the best interests of the province. Orders to take effect from March 1941 were passed to dissolve the Board of Basic Education, the Training School and fifteen basic schools. The fierce internal and external struggles embroiling the Indian sub-continent were taking their toll on the provincial governments, who found they could no longer afford to channel valuable resources into the education scheme. The situation highlighted the *raison d'etre* for Gandhi's idealistic emphasis on the self-supporting nature of his proposals. His message to the Second All-India Basic Education Conference in April 1941 appeared to foreshadow the principal reason for the decline of the Scheme :

> I hope that the Conference will realise that the success of the effort is dependent more on self-help than upon Government, which must necessarily be cautious even when it is well disposed. Our experiment to be thorough has to be at least somewhat made without alloy and without outside interference.[218]

The April Conference was attended by the representatives of the Departments of Education of Bombay. Uttar Pradesh, Bihar, Kashmir, and workers from non-Government basic schools. In their review of work progress they recognised certain problems but did not suggest that these were major obstacles:

> This Conference is happy to note that the reports of Government, non-Government and other basic schools lead to the conclusion that this education has greatly improved the health and behaviour of the children and promoted their mental development. The children attending the basic schools are full of energy and self-confidence, and can express themselves more clearly. They acquire the habit of co-operation and are free from social and other bonds. The Conference hopes that still better results will accrue from this education in future.[219]

The many general working problems mainly related to misconceptions held by teachers regarding the use of craft as the medium of correlation. An over-exuberant teacher would sacrifice the child's learning to achieve a synthesis at any cost. In cases such as these the only aim of the teacher was to prove that all knowledge could be imparted in a correlated way via the medium of the craft. On the other hand, some teachers did not use the craft process as a medium of learning, but simply as a means of academic instruction, i.e., the teacher merely changed the old teaching aids for craft materials or craft processes as a means of imparting academic knowledge.

Gandhi's plea remained that education be "coextensive with life itself". In an attempt to ensure that the Scheme progressed along these lines he conceived of a new framework which would extend the scope of Basic Education so that "it should include the education of everybody at every stage of life".[220] The third All-India Basic Education Conference was held at Sevagram in January 1945, to discuss this new interpretation of Basic Education, to assess its progress during the preceding five years and to plan the future programme.

Despite dwindling resources and a dearth of literature and trained teachers, the work continued. Experiments were begun in the fields of pre-Basic and post-Basic Education, and further research undertaken to work out the self-sufficiency aspect of the Scheme.[221] However, opposition to the Wardha Scheme in Government and Congress circles appeared to harden after Independence. Socialists and conservatives, who had earlier spoken with one voice in their condemnation of the emphasis placed on manual labour in the curriculum, pressured provincial governments into shortening the period of Basic Education and following it with a set period of formal academic education.[222]

The main areas of difference between the Government and the Gandhian educationists were the role craft should play in the curriculum and the importance of English, industrialism and urbanisation in the future development of India. The Government was prepared to give craft instruction merely a subsidiary role in its overall programme, and stressed the need to strengthen India through further urbanisation and industrialisation. Commenting on the ideological differences between the government and the

Gandhians, K.G. Mashruwala declared, "But that is exactly the reason why the Government should adopt a different terminology for their system of education and not call it Basic Education or the Wardha Scheme of Education, and should not use Gandhi's name in association with it."[223]

Nai talim was village-oriented to provide the majority of Indians with the minimum education necessary to understand the complexities of their environment and to be self-reliant within that environment. However, the failure to adopt a uniform system of education in the rural and urban areas exacerbated the old inequities. Urban areas adopted the orthodox Government curriculum, and whilst Gandhian institutions persevered for some time with Basic Education, increasing numbers of village people aspired to city life with its perceived material benefits, thus undermining their work. Kusum Nair identified this problem in her *Blossoms in the Dust,* in which she highlighted the attitude of the Sevagram villagers to the Basic Education programme of the Ashram:

> As for "basic education", of which Sevagram Ashram is the centre, they say with unconcealed contempt: "We do not send our children to the ashram school beyond the fourth class (i.e. primary), because those who pass out of "nai tailm" cannot get jobs. So our boys go to Wardha town; they walk the four miles to study in a conventional school.... We do not want to remain tillers of the soil forever. We also want to become lawyers and doctors. "Nai talim" is no good for that."[224]

Gunnar Myrdal has suggested that though any attempt to make primary schools basic would entail several modifications to Gandhi's original proposal, i.e., in the self-supporting and correlative aspects of the scheme, "basic-oriented" primary education none the less "could be the ideal solution to the much needed reform of the curriculum and teaching methods in Indian primary schools. The school would have local roots and its isolation from the community at large would be lessened; it would encourage the teacher to participate in the life of the community and exert his influence toward changing attitudes; and, most important for effective teaching, it would give all children the experience of performing purposeful work with their hands, which would also help to counteract prejudices against manual work.[225]

It is difficult to determine whether the failure of the reform was due to poor teachers, inadequate text-books, the reluctance of middle-class parents to send their children to schools which prescribed manual work, or a combination of all these factors. Perhaps those mainly responsible for implementing the scheme were not in tune with its ideals, or there was simply not enough sympathy for Gandhi's ideas among those in power after Independence. As Ram K. Vepa puts it, "Whatever the reason, the 'Basic Scheme of Education' of Gandhiji has for all practical purposes remained a dead letter even after Independence."[226]

Conclusion

The growth of Sevagram into an ashram was more an outcome of Gandhi's charismatic role in national affairs than of express design. However, the experiment brought into focus his ideas on the role of the concerned individual in village reconstruction. His was esssentially a humanist approach. Rather than refer to the villagers in terms of unwieldy, faceless statistics he spoke in terms of the needs of the lowliest in each village. He was concerned with the social, economic, spiritual and psychological needs of each individual, since for him individuals were the foundation-stone of the village. At the same time he placed the onus for village improvement on the shoulders of the individual. He believed that each person had the right to full spiritual, intellectual and moral development, but it was only possible through the service of fellow-men, which fulfilled the duty owed to society as stipulated in the *Bhagavad Gita*.[227]

In contrast to Gandhi's individualistic concept of social change Nehru and the Socialists expressed a collectivist mentality. Nehru believed that by collectivising the factors of production underlying the social and economic structures of the nation, and thereby amalgamating capital and labour under the power of a democratic socialist state, all basis for exploitation would be effectively removed. In the case of India he argued that all social wrongs would be redressed by dispossessing capital of its control over the factors of production, arid by progressively replacing agriculture as the mainstay of the economy with a strong industrial base controlled by the state. He maintained that India had been wedded far too long to past forms and modes of thought and action, and that any attempt to build up a country's economy largely on the basis of cottage and small-scale industries would be doomed to failure. He even went so far as to argue that just as a child's mind is stimulated by craft or manual activity, it is also stimulated by machines.[228]

Though Nehru gave assurances that the introduction of machinery on a large scale would absorb labour rather than create fresh unemployment, Gandhi could not conceive of a machine age developing in India at the expense of her 700,000 villages. To nullify the harmful effects of excessive institutionalisation he argued that the centralised economic and political system of the colonial regime must be replaced by a polity based on decentralisation. He conceived of his non-violent programme of positive action as the only viable means of combating the major problems he saw confronting Indian society: growing poverty and the rapidly increasing number of unemployed and underemployed; social dislocation and alienation on a large scale; a degeneration of spiritual and ethical values; and an increasing fear of real freedom.

During the latter part of his life Gandhi did focus more attention on the question of undermining the grip of the sub-strata of exploiters upon society, i.e., industrialists, wealthy merchants and bankers, and zamindars, but he never openly condoned forcibly dispossessing these groups. He always maintained that he was a socialist, but in his concept of socialism there was no place for violence, coercion, hatred and class conflict. He believed any attempt to invest absolute power in the state and uproot people from their traditional agricultural vocations would reduce them to automatons of a centralised factory system. In his view denial of individual freedom and creative activity would negate the duty of service to society and thus destroy genuine community.[229] Nehru and the Socialists found the ideal of non-violent *swaraj* too impractical, but Gandhi was unyielding in his view that disregard of non-violence would result in wholesale destruction.

The failure of Gandhi's followers to further develop his ashrams as vehicles of community activism stemmed from his inability to counteract the negative aspects of his charismatic authority. This is borne out by the fact that other Gandhian ashrams, which have been founded by men and women dedicated not only to Gandhi but to the ideals he stood for, have continued to serve people in various ways. But the Sabarmati and Sevagram Ashrams have been transformed into museums and national shrines.

Gandhi abhorred dogmatism for the same reason that he discouraged monuments to himself; it denied an interpretation of his philosophy as a dynamic and integrated evolutionary theory. He did not wish his ideas and practice to be "sanctified", such that any deviation from the historically "legitimate" methodology would be regarded as sacrilege. He knew this would petrify development and result in a sectarian approach to new problems: "There is no such thing as 'Gandhism', and I do not want to leave any sect after me. I have simply tried in my own way to apply the eternal truths to our daily life and problems." Today the facade of both Sabarmati and Sevagram stand as monuments to the inability of the Gandhian movement to keep abreast of changing situations and aspirations. On the twenty-eighth anniversary of Gandhi's death his grandson Arun wrote:

> The Ashrams where Bapu lived, worked and from where he gave inspiration to 400 million people have been turned into showpieces; there is nothing Gandhian about them.[230]

A detailed examination of the contemporary Gandhian ashram movement falls outside the parameters of this book. However, a number of observations need to be made. The so-called "heirs" of Gandhi who have sought to depoliticise the movement have misunderstood, or purposefully ignored, his intention in dissociating the constructive work programmes from power politics. He rejected the parliamentary programme of reform, which he saw being manipulated by vested interests, but he did not seek to purge *satyagraha* of its activating principle, the sanction of direct non-violent action. Rather he sought through the ashrams and constructive work organisations to provide dynamic outlets for the energies of the people, which he foresaw leading "to greater public participation, and, indirectly, to a greater control over the policies and actions of those who were in power."[231]

Non-violence has naturally been discarded by the architects of parliamentary democracy in India because the political leadership is only capable of operating within the neo-colonial framework it has created since Independence. On the other hand, non-violence remains the static symbol of a movement which tends to have few established bonds of organisation and hierarchy, and no rationally defined goals. Its members are primarily bound together by their loyalty to the memory of Gandhi and to Vinoba Bhave, a charismatic leader whose authority rested on his personification and exposition of an ideal stripped of its dynamism.[232] Today's exponents of selfless asceticism, daily spinning and fasting in the cause of truth and non-violence perhaps forget that the key to Gandhi's effectiveness as an activist was his ability to communicate with the people and co-ordinate activities to raise their consciousness.

Fumblings along Gandhian lines are recognisable in political and non-political developments since his death. Whether these will culminate in the realisation that a suitably modified concept of *sarvodaya* can provide a framework to realise the needs of modern India and ensure that independence means not only political freedom but freedom from hunger and want poses a largely unanswerable question. Today there is little indication that this will indeed be the case:

> In some of the ashrams there still are dynamic persons, but for some reason they have not been able to form a cadre of devoted and enlightened workers. Perhaps because of the present circumstances it may be more difficult today to find people who would want to be dedicated to Gandhian ideals. Even the villagers are today caught up in the vortex of economic and political whirlpools and appear to be running helter-skelter without knowing what they want or where they want to get to. In these circumstances to wean the people away from this mad scramble to something more constructive we need not just the Gandhian programme but a programme with more dynamism.[233]

It cannot be said that India has explored the possibilities offered by the Gandhian alternative. The direction the nation has taken since Independence is in no respect a reflection of his goals or activities.

NOTES

1. *Young India,* 17 November *1921.*
2. *Idib.,* 2 March 1922.
3. Gandhi suspended mass civil disobedience in May 1933, and all individual protest ceased after 7 April 1934. In October 1934 Congress reassembled again in Bombay.
4. CWMG, Vol. 42, p. 336.
5. Judith Brown refers to these regional supporters as having "entered the movement to defend or improve their position in their local power structure, and having served a remote apprenticeship under Gandhi they tended to become contractors in their own right for their particular group or interests, sliding beyond the reach of any central control", *op. cit.,* p. 327.
6. Cited in T. V. Parvate, *Jamnalal Bajaj A Brief Study of His Life and Character* (Ahmedabad : Navajivan Publishing House, 1962), pp. 160-1.
7. *Narvajivan,* 12 April 1931, *CWMG,* Vol. 45, p. 391.
8. Gandhi to Ramniklal Modi, 13 November 1929, *Ibid,* Vol. 42, pp. 139-40.
9. Cf. M. B. Verma, *History of the Harijan Sevak Sangh, 1932-1968* (Delhi: Udyogshala Press, 1971), p. 62.
10. *Harijan,* 30 November 1934.
11. Cf. *laid.,* 9 March 1934.
12. *Ibid.,* see also *Ibid.,* 21 December 1934.
13. Including hand-pounded rice, hand-pounded flour, village made gur, hand-made sugar, honey, hand-made paper and stationery, soap from indigenous materials. leather goods, tanning of bullock and cow hides, and pottery.
14. *Harijan,* 30 November 1934.
15. *CWMG,* Vol. 59, p. 264.
16. *Ibid.,* p. 222
17. *Bombay Chronicle,* 18 September 1934.
18. *Indian Annual Register,* 1936, Vol. I, p. 277.
19. See the report of a discussion between the leader of the Socialist Party, M. R. Masani, and Gandhi on 25 May 1934 in *Hindustan Times,* 4 August 1935; see also *Bombay Chronicle,* 11 January 1935.
20. Ashe notes that a communist party pamphlet of 1931 accused Gandhi of "posing as a saint in order to control the national movement and frustrate it, in the interests of the British and Indian plutocrats and princes". They eventually dropped the charge, but not before the seeds of doubt had been sown in the minds of many; *op. cit.,* p. 323.
21. Gandhi to Prema Behn Kantak, 10 September 1935, CWMG, Vol.61, p. 403; see also Gandhi to M. R. Masani, 14 June 1934, *Ibid.,* Vol. 58, pp. 75-6.
22. *Harijan,* 31 August 1934.
23. Cited in Vepa, op. cit., p. 81. The qualifications required for village work are outlined in *Harijan,* 31 August 1934, 29 February 1936, 18 August 1940 and 2 March 1947.
24. *Ibid.,* 19 August 1933.
25. *Ibid.,* January 1935.
26. *Indian Annual Register,* 1935, Vol. I, p. 79.

The Village of Service: "India in a Village" 255

27. *Harijan,* 24 August 1935.
28. *Ibid.,* 4 March 1933.
29. Attempts were made to decentralise the administration of the social reform organisations. For instance, the administration of the A.I.V.I.A. was decentralised to encourage individual initiative and to help the village worker establish his autonomy in rural areas. Yet Gandhi and his inner group of confidants remained the guiding force of the village programme.
30. *Harijan,* 16 September 1933.
31. *Ibid.,* 1 March'1935.
32. Cf. *Harijan,* 31 August 1934 & 29 February 1936.
33. *Ibid.,* 1 June 1935.
34. *Bombay Chronicle,* 18 September 1934, *CWMG,* Vol. 59, p. 9.
35. Gandhi to Devadas Gandhi, 29 July 1918, *Ibid.,* Vol. 14.
36. *Harijan,* 13 July 1935.
37. *Harijan,* 11 July 1936.
38. The name of the village was Segaon, but as it was often confused with a nearby village called Segaon; it was later renamed Sevagram or 'Village of Service'.
39. Madeleine Slade (Mira Behn), *The Spirit's Pilgrimage* (London : Longmans, l960), p. 192.
40. 15 March 1935.
41. *Ibid.,*
42. *Ibid.,* 22 March 1935.
43. *Ibid.,* 7 September 1935.
44. Mira Behn, *op. cit.,* p. 194.
45. *Ibid.*
46. Cf. R. E. Enthoven, *The Tribes and Castes of Bombay* (Bombay : Government Central Press, 1920-22).
47. *Harijan,* 30 November 1935.
48. Mira Behn, *op. cit.,* p. 196.
49. B. H. Baden - Powell, *The Indian Village Community* (New Haven : Hraf Press, 1957), p. 344; cf. Baden- Powell, *The Land Systems of British India,* 3 Vols. (Oxford: Clarendon Press, 1892).
50. *Harijan,* 1 February 1936.
51. *Ibid.,* 28 December 1935.
52. See *Bapu's Letters to Mira, 1924-1948* (Ahmedabad: Navajivan Publishing House, 1949), p. 291; see also *Harijan,* 25 January 1936 and Mira Behn, *op. cit.,* pp. 197-8.
53. *Ibid.,* p. 198.
54. *Ibid., p.* 199.
55. Gandhi to Surendra, 3 December 1935, CWMG, Vol. 62, p. 155.
56. *Bapu's Letters to Mira,* p. 293.
57. *Harijan,* 29 June 1935.
58. *Ibid., I* February 1936.
59. *Ibid.*
60. Narayan, *op. cit.,* p. 17.
61. *Bapu's Letters to Mira,* p. 294.
62. The Gandhi Seva Sangh was founded by Jamnalal Bajaj in 1923 to provide full-time workers for the non-co-operation programme and to promote Gandhi's ideas among the people. From 1924 to 1929 the workers were free to evolve their own programme of constructive work and implement it. In 1934

the Sangh's policy and programme were defined and it developed into a brotherhood of workers dedicated to the Gandhian cause. The Sangh was the parent body which supplied workers for the various social service organisations that arose throughout the 1920s and 1930s. By 1940 its members were mainly working under the auspices of these various organisations, thereby limiting the function of the Sangh.

63. CWMG, Vol. 62, p. 219.
64. *Ibid.*, pp. 227-8.
65. *Harijan*, 5 December 1936.
66. *Ibid.*, 9 May 1936.
67. The Mahila Seva Mandal was founded by Jamnalal Bajaj in 1924 to uplift the status of women in India. In 1933 the Kanya Ashram, conducted under the guidance of Vinoba Bhave to prepare women workers for community service was amalgamated with the Mahila Mandal, which included hostel buildings and about 8 acres of land donated by Jamnalal. The hostel was originally the Satyagraha Ashram of Vinoba Bhave, where he stayed for 12 years before establishing the Paramdham Ashram in Paunar, five miles north of Wardha. From 1948 the Mahilashram trained students under the Basic Education Scheme, and has since become a residential teachers training college affiliated to the Education Dept. of Maharashtra.
68. Mira Behn, *op. cit.*, p. 203.
69. Balwantsinha (Balwant Singh), *Under the Shelter of Bapu*, trans. from the original in Hindi (Ahmedabad: Navajivan Publishing House, 1962), p. 85.
70. Gandhi to Jamnalal Bajaj, 19 March 1936, CWMG, Vol. 62, p. 272.
71. *Harijan*, 12 December 1936.
72. Mahadev Desai, "At Sevagram", in D. G. Tendulkar *et al* (eds.) *Gandhiji, His Life and Work* (Bombay : Keshav Bhikaji Dhawale, 1944), p. 198.
73. Pyarelal described the living conditions of Gandhi and Kasturba in *The Illustrated Weekly of India*, 2 December 1962: "His new residence was an adobe structure with a tiled roof, supported by crossbeams resting on the mud walls. There was a running verandah in front and at the two ends, and another one at the rear with a kitchenette, and a small bathroom at the two ends of the back verandah. In this room he worked and rested along with eight other inmates, including Kasturba. She, poor lady, did not have a shred of privacy. The utmost concession that could be wrung for her was a small corner in one of the end verandahs curtained off to serve as a dressing room."
74. Pyarelal, *op. tit.*
75. Narayan, *op. tit.*, pp. 17-18.
76. Cited in R. V. Rao, *Sevagram, Gandhiji's Ashram and Other Institutions in Wardha* (Wardha : Sevagram Ashram Pratishthan, 1969), p. 1.
77. Gandhi to Lilavati Asar, 25 September 1936, CWMG, Vol. 63, p. 317.
78. Gandhi to Amrussalaam, 5 December 1936, *Ibid.*, Vol. 64, p. 107.
79. Gandhi to Chand Tyagi, 15 September 1936, *Ibid.*, Vol. 63, p. 288.
80. *Harijan*, 5 September 1936.
81. *Bapu's Letters to Mira*, p. 315.
82. Chimanlal Shah, interview held at Sevagram, Wardha, 24 March 1981.
83. Pyarelal, *op. tit.*
84. a. CWMG, Vol. 75, pp. 139-41; also *Harijan*, 31 October 1938, *and Ashram Observances in Action*, pp. 146-51.
85. Gandhi to Prema Behn Kantak, 21 May 1936, CWMG, Vol. 62, pp. 428-9.

86. Cf. Gandhi to Amritlal T. Nanavati, 2 May 1938, *Ibid.,* Vol. 67, p. 58.
87. *Ibid.,* Vol. 64, pp. 130-1,154-5; see also Letters from Gandhi to Ramnarayan and Narmada Pathak, 23 December 1936, *Ibid.,* pp. 167-8.
88. See Letters from Gandhi to MunnalalShah, 16 May 1936, 3 June l936 & 31 July 1940, *Ibid.,* Vol. 65, pp. 213, 269, & Vol. 72, p. 341.
89. Some of the orthodox rules in this context are: the *brahmachari* must not have contact with women in any sense, must not allow himself physical stimulants like milk, curds, ghee, hot baths, or massage oil. Gandhi felt that as his interpretation of *brahmacharya* was unique, these rules were inappropriate, though he did comply with dietetic restrictions. Among his colleagues, Mira, Amrit Kaur, Prema Behn Kantak and Chhaganlal Joshi were particularly outspoken in their questioning of Gandhi's *brahmacharya* experiments.
90. *CWMG,* Vol. 67, pp. 104-5; cf. Letters from Gandhi to Chhaganlal Joshi, 22 June & 1 July 1938, *Ibid.,* pp. 147-9.
91. Gandhi to Munnalal Shah, 4 June 1938, *Ibid., p.* 106.
92. Gandhi to Munnalal Shah, 13 September 1938, *Ibid.,* pp. 335-6.
93. The most authoritative account of the circumstances surrounding Gandhi's revelation appears in Nirmal Kumar Bose's *My Days With Gandhiji* (Calcutta: Nishana, 1953), pp. 131-7,154-60. Bose was Gandhi's secretary and Bengali interpreter during the period he spent in Noakhali during 1946; see also Mehta, *op. cit.,* pp. 193-7.
94. The most comprehensive of these is Erikson's *Gandhi's Truth.*
95. Narayan, *op. cit.,* p. 19; see also Gandhi to Munnalal Shah, 16 May 1937, CWMG,Vol. 65, p.213.
96. Desai, *op. cit.,* p. 206.
97 Gandhi to Munnalal Shah, 2 June 1937, CWMG, Vol. 65, p. 265-6.
98. Ibid, Vol. 72, pp. 124,151,153, 189. Gandhi planned a self-purificatory 'fast on this issue but was discouraged by the ashramites. Subsequently the inmate upon whom suspicion had fallen was cleared of the charge; see *Ibid.,* Vol. 73, p. 168.
99. *Harijan, 6* July 1940, CWMG, Vol. 72, p. 211.
100. Gandhi described his anarchistic vision of a decentralised society made up of villages, each of which is a little republic, economically self-sufficient and politically autonomous : "In this structure composed of innumerable villages there will be ever-widening, never ascending circles. Life will not be a pyramid with the apex sustained by the bottom. But it will be an oceanic circle whose centre will be the individual always ready to perish for the village, the latter ready to perish for the circle of villages, till at last the whole becomes one life composed of individuals, never aggressive in their arrogance but ever humble, sharing the majesty of the oceanic circle of which they are integral units." *Village Swaraj* (Ahmedabad : Navajivan Publishing House, 1962), p. 70.
101. See Gandhi to Krishnachandra, 22 March 1941, CWMG, Vol. 73, pp. 416-7. Gandhi has written : "I am in a delicate position. If in my presence only the will of the manager prevails, the order is maintained; if it does not prevail then there could be no order. If there were no order here then it would be nowhere, and then *satyagraha* would disappear."
102. Gandhi to A. H. West, 24 September 1936, *Ibid.,* Vol. 63, p. 313.
103. Gandhi to Mira, 13 May 1941, Ml, Vol. 74, p. 54.
104. Gandhi to Kishorelal Mashruwala, 13 May 1941, *Ibid., p.* 55.

105. Rajendra Prasad, *At the Feet of Mahatma Gandhi* (London : Asia Publishing House, 1961), pp. 262-3.
106. CWMG, Vol. 71, pp. 133-4.
107. Ramnarayan Chaudhary, *Bapu As I Saw Him,* translated from the original in Hindi (Ahmedabad : Navajivan Publishing House, 1959), p. 167.
108. Narayan, *op. cit.,* pp. 23-4.
109. Desai, *op.cit.,* p. 203.
110. Pyarelal, *op. cit.*
111. *Harijan,* 17 October 1936.
112. Balwantsinha, *op. cit.,* p. 150.
113. Gandhi to Munnalal Shah, 3 June 1937, CWMG, Vol. 65, p. 270.
114. Gandhi to Balwantsinha, 6 February 1941, ibid., Vol. 73, p. 317.
115. Arun Gandhi, "Whose Experiments with Untruth?", Mirror, November 1981, p. 102.
116. Gandhi to Krishnachandra, 27 November 1941, CWMG, Vol. 75, p. 119.
117. Speech at Prayer Meeting, 22 October 1941, *Ibid.,* pp. 43-4.
118. *Ibid.,* p. 216.
119. *Harijan,* 13 May 1939.
120. Balwantsinha, *op.cit.,* p. 148.
121. *Ibid.,* p. 154.
122. *Bombay Chronicle,* 2 August 1941, CWMG, Vol. 74, p. 203.
123. *Harijan,* 6 April 1940.
124. Balwantsinha, *op.cit.,* p. 155.
125. CWMG, Vol. 64, p. 407.
126. Gandhi to Dr. Fritz Michaelis, 13 August 1937, *Ibid.,* Vol. 66, p. 41.
127. Cf. *Ibid.,* Vol. 53, Appendix vii.
128. Sunanda Patwardhan, *Change Among India's Harijans,* (New Delhi : Orient Longmans, 1973), pp. 33-4; see also Enthoven, *op. cit.*
129. *Harijan,* 2 May 1936.
130. *Ibid.,* 25 July 1937.
131. *Ibid.,* 5 December 1936.
132. CWMG, Vol. 64, pp. 392-3.
133. Desai, *op. cit.,* p. 206.
134. *Harijan,* 19 June 1937.
135. *Ibid.,* land 15 August 1936,
136. *Ibid.,* 5 September 1936.
137. Gandhi to Amrit Kaur, 19 March 1937, CWMG, Vol. 65, pp. 7-8.
138. *Hurijan,* 28 November 1936.
139. Pyarelal, *op. cit.*
140. *Bombay Chronicle,* 22 December 1936, CWMG, Vol. 64, pp. 162-63.
141. *Harijan* 28 November 1936
142. See Gandhi's interview to Associated Press of India, 29 June 1937, and to *Hindu,* 8 July 1937, CWMG, pp. 329-30, 376-7.
143. CWMG, Vol. 65, p. 133.
144. Ashe, *op. cit.,* p. 337.
145. Payne, *op. cit.,* pp. 480-1.
146. CWMG, Vol. 71, pp. 257-68; see also *Ibid.,* Vol. 69, pp. 221-2.
147. *Ibid., pp. 237-9.*
148. *Ibid.,* Vol. 71, pp. 278-80.
149. J. C. Kumarappa to Gandhi, 1 February 1947, Gandhi Smarak Nidhi, New

The Village of Service: "India in a Village"

Delhi, hereinafter G. N. 10187.
150. Gandhi to J. C. Kumarappa, 16 March 1947, G. N. 10188.
151. Gandhi to J. C. Kumarappa, 29 March 1947, G. N. 10192.
152. Gandhi to J. C. Kumarappa, 4 June 1947, G. N. 10193.
153. Judith Brown, "Gandhi's Other Heirs", *South Asian Review,* Vol. 5, No. 3, April1972, p. 248.
154. *Indian Annual Register, Vol. 1, 1936.*
155. *Ibid.,*
156. Jawaharlal Nehru, *An Autobiography' (London* : John Lane, The Bodley Head, 1936), p. 523.
157. Gandhi to N. S. Hardikar, 24 February 1938, CWMG, Vol. 66, pp. 386-7.
158. *Ibid.,* pp. 23-4.
159. V. P. Varma, *The Political Philosophy of Mahatma Gandhi and Sarvodaya* (Agra: n. p., 1959), pp. 199-201; see also Pyarelal, *Mahatma Gandhi : The Last Phase, 2* vols. (Ahmedabad : Navajivan Pub. House, 1958), Vol. 2, App. B, p. 819.
160. Gandhi to Mahadev Desai, 10 September 1938, CWMG, Vol.67, pp. 326-7.
161. *Ibid., Vol.* 72, p. 91.
162. Gandhi to Rudandaroo, 11 February 1941, G. N. 6282.
163. Gandhi to Munnalal Shah, 4 April 1941, CWMG, Vol. 73, p. 421.
164. Buber, *Pointing the* Way. pp. 127-31, 136-7.
165. Mehta, *op. cit.,* p. 55.
166. Cited in *Ibid., p.* 49.
167. Balwantsinha, *op. cit.,* pp. 162-8.
168. Pyarelal, interview held in New Delhi, 30 November 1081.
169. *Young India,* September 1924, cited in Iyer, *op. cit.,* p. 144.
170. *Harijan,* 18 August 1946.
171. Balwantsinha, *op. cit.,* p. 172.
172. Pyarelal, interview held in New Delhi, 30 November 1981.
173. Balwantsingh, *op. cit.,* pp. 175-76.
174. He was imprisoned for 249 days in South Africa and 2089 days in India.
175. *Harijan,* 8 September 1946.
176. Narayan, *op. cit.,* p. 26.
177. J. C Kumarappa to Gandhi, 1 February 1947, G. N. 10187.
178. K. G. Saiyidain, *Problems of Educational Reconstruction* (Bombay : Asia Publishing House, 1 950), p. 16.
179. J. B. Kripalani, *The latest Fad,* cited in B. R. Garg, *Basic Education - Need of the Day* (Ambala Cantt: The Associated Publishers, 1975). 180.*Varijan,* 18 September 1937.
181. *Jbid.;3l* July 1937.
182. *Ibid., 18* September & 31 July 1937.
183. *Educational Reconstruction* (Sevagram: Hindustani Talimi Sangh, n.d.), p. 66.
184. H. Kabir, *Education in New India,* cited in Garg, *op. cit.,* p. 106.
185. *Educational Reconstruction, p. 116.*
186. *Harijan,* 9 October 1937.
187. Report of Dr. Zakir Hussain Committee, *Ibid.,* 11 December 1937.
188. See *Ibid.*
189. For a brief summary of the various points enunciated see Garg, *op. cit.,* pp. 78-9
190. M. S. Patel, *op. cit.,* p. 110
191. *Harijan,* 4 September 1937.

192. *Ibid.*
193. *Ibid.*, 18 September 1937.
194. Dinkar Desai, *Primary Education in India* (Bombay: Servants of India Society, 1938), pp. 78-81.
195. George S. Arundale, "Education Lecture Notes" (Adyar : Theosophical Publishing House, 1938).
196. S. N. Namle, "Basic Education and the Montessori Method", *The Montessori Magazine*, Nos. 2 & 3, March and June 1947.
197. See Garg, *op. cit.*, p. 60.
198. *Harijan*, 30 October & 11 December 1937.
199. *Educational Reconstruction*, p. 126.
200. The Committee included K. G. Saiyidain, Prof. K. T. Shah, Vinoba Bhave, Kaka Kalelkar, Kishorelal Mashfuwala, J. C Kumarappa, Krishna Das Jajoo, Mrs. Asha Devi and Sri Aryanayakam.
201. Report of Dr. Zakir Hussain Committee, *Harijan*, 11 December 1937 & 26 March 1938. The Report was published over two issues of *Harijan*.
202. See Gandhi's explanation of the system in *Harijan*, 11 September 1937.
203. *Ibid.*, 4 December 1937.
204. *Ibid.*, 16 October 1937.
205. See Gandhi's reply to this criticism in *Ibid*.
206. Report of Dr. Zakir Hussain Committee.
207. See *Ibid.*, for the curriculum laid down by the committee for a complete course of teachers' training over a period of three years.
208. *Ibid.*
209. *Ibid.*
210. *Ibid.*
211. *Ibid.*
212. Patel, *op. cit.*, p. 136.
213. *Harijan*, 30 April 1938.
214. See Gandhi's address to the candidates in *Ibid.*, 30 April 1938.
215. *Ibid.*, 26 November 1938.
216. M. K. Gandhi, Basic *Education*, cited in A. B. Solanki, *The Technique of Correlation in Basic Education* (Ahmedabad : Navajivan Publishing House, 1958), p. 46.
217. Patel, *op.cit.*, p. 143.
218. Cited in *Ibid.*, p. 144.
219. Cited in Ibid.
220. Cited in *Ibid.*, p. 145.
221. *Harijan*, 2 March 1947.
222. Outspoken opponents of the Wardha Scheme were the National Liberal Federation, who condemned the self-sufficiency aspect of the scheme and the proposal to change universities into merely examining bodies, and the socialists, who, though they acknowledged the importance of vocational' training, argued that India's future was bound up with machine production and the factory system; see *Indian Annual Register*, Vol. 2,1937, p. 376 & Vol. 1,1938, p. 413.
223. *Harijan*, 18 July 1948.
224. Kusum Nair, *Blossoms in the Dust* (London: Gerald Duckworth & Co., 1961), p. 187.
225. Gunnar Myrdal, *Asian Drama : An Enquiry into the Poverty of Nations*, 3 Vols.

(New York : The Twentieth Century Fund, 1968), Vol. 3, p. 1738.
226. Vepa, *op. cit.,* p. 253.
227. *Young India,* 8 January 1925.
228. Jawaharlal Nehru, *The Discovery of India* (New York : Anchor Books, 1960), pp. 328-30.
229. *Harijan,* 1 February 1942.
230. Arun Gandhi, "Gandhi Ashrams : No Gandhian Spirit", *The Illustrated Weekly of India,* 1 February 1976. It is a view shared by others. Evelyn Wood', writing on the failure of "neo-Gandhians" to communicate Gandhi's ideals to the people, wrote of his own attitude to Sabarmati and Sevagram : "To be frank, he must admit that the lunatic fringes of the Sabarmati and Sevagram Ashrams repelled him so intensely that, much as he loved, admired and enjoyed working with Gandhi, he avoided the ashrams as far as it was possible to do so", *Gandhi Marg,* Vol. 4, No. 2, 1960, p. 122.
231. Vishwanath Tandon, "Vinoba and Satyagraha", *Gandhi Marg,* Vol. 2, No. 7, October 1980, p. 393.
232. See Judith Brown, "Gandhi's Other Heirs", *South Asian Review,* Vol. 5, No. 3, April 1972, pp. 246-7.
233. Taraben Mashruwala reply to Questionnaire, 10 November 1981. Taraben, the renowned Gandhian worker and founder of the Kasturba Ashram at Madhan in Maharashtra, was one of the recipients of a Questionnaire sent by the author who agreed to reply. It is ironic that the Questionnaires sent to Sabarmati and Sevagram were unanswered, whilst those sent to Taraben and the Swaraj Ashrams at Vedchhi and Bardoli were answered. Kanakmal Gandhi, Secretary of the Sevagram Ashram, wrote by way of explanation: "I have discussed your questions with some of my colleagues here and we are unable to reply to your questions in the way they are framed. We feel, they are loaded and you may not be able to bring out the dynamics of Gandhi's Ashrams by means of such questions. Non-violence is a living force not only for individuals but also for the society. Those who wish to bring about a non-violent change in the society cannot do so just by preaching. Thoughts, actions and deeds should be in harmony with the ideal. Teaching is a lesser part of non-violent change." Kanakmal Gandhi to R. M. Thomson, 28 August 1981. The reply received from Vinoba Bhave's Paunar Ashram was as follows : "Vinobaji has received your letter of 16 August 1981. A few years back he had taken a vow not a write letters etc. Moreover he does not take any active part in the discussions also. Therefore, I cannot send his answers for your Questionnaire. I hope you will contact other prominent Gandhians also. You can get the detailed information from them as well as through the publications." Balajay (sic) to R. M. Thomson, 8 September 1981.

5

Conclusion

This book has sought to trace the genesis and progress of Gandhi's communitarianism and its role in the evolution of his non-violent alternative. His ideal of human development was radical and humanistic, but imbued with an asceticism which sought to cultivate simplicity, inner strength and detachment from worldly ambition. He believed in the perfectibility of man through self-realisation, which was a process evolved through birth and rebirth. His spiritual goal was to realise his individuality as an experience of universality, as an expression of the essential unity of all giving things. In his view those who sought the path of self-realisation through service to their fellow-men were sign-posts to a better future in which individuals, groups and nations would cease to maintain themselves at the expense of others.

Underlying Gandhi's humanism was the idea that man's nature and his relations with the external environment represent an organic whole which cannot be compartmentalised and understood in isolation. He believed that man's potentialities unfold through his experience of oneness and harmony with his fellow-man and nature. When he spoke of politics, he did not refer to the pursuit of narrow sectional interests, but the strengthening of democratic institutions that enabled the people as a whole to realise economic and political independence. By building character, by understanding moral values, and by being more self-reliant, he believed that the people would be better equipped to govern themselves. Right diet, right thought and right action strengthened the moral fibre of the individual, and laid the foundation for a righteous society that would, in Gandhi's view, enable man to satisfy his basic needs free of violence and coercion.

Against the centralist ethos of the modern state, which depended for its survival in his view, upon the increasing exploitation of human and natural resources, Gandhi opposed the ideal of humanity as a co-operative, harmonious entity, enabling man to develop his full potential as an integrated member of the human race. He recognised that modern man no longer experienced himself as a constituent part of his surroundings, but responded to society and nature as abstract entities from which he was largely estranged. He saw modern civilisation accepting technological progress, bureaucratisation, and social manipulation as vital ingredients of the historical process, without looking for the inherent and immediate value of any action or development. He saw alienation undermining social cohesion, leaving atomised individuals whose character and thought were increasingly shaped by the mass conglomerations that make up the bureaucratic industrial system. He saw the role of the individual in modern society becoming that of an unthinking automaton.

In London as a student, and later in South Africa, Gandhi was drawn to the ideas of humanists who challenged the Hobbesian doctrine of individualistic rationalism, which reduced man to a cog in the machine of state, and the utilitarian doctrine of the "greatest good for the greatest number", which he later described as a "heartless doctrine" that "has done harm to humanity".[1] To the radicals and reformists with whom he came into contact true freedom was not the satisfaction of individualistic wants and needs, but a collective experience of harmony between men and between man and nature. Violence and exploitation resulted, in their view, from man's failure to recognise the true nature of existence; the alienated man did not experience humanity as a whole but as a collection of individuals with narrow loyalties that prevented the growth of a humanism transcending clan, class, national and racial barriers. They sought a social pattern affording equal opportunity to all, based on mutual aid and a return to simple co-existence with nature.

Principles such as vegetarianism, the unity of religious tradition, non-attachment, self-renunciation and selfless service became inextricably bound up with the non-violent paradigm that Gandhi began to formulate under the influence of humanist thinkers and nonconformist Christianity. Moreover, through the eyes of Western intellectuals, he was introduced to the wisdom of the East, most particularly the traditions of Hinduism as a vehicle of self-purification and social renewal. He perceived little difference in the basic tenets of the major religions, and the conviction grew that Indians must revalue their own traditions in order to create a righteous society. He was impressed with alternative social philosophies and models that rejected the value system of the evolving capitalist order, but his desire to see India free of imperialist domination, and purged of its many inequities, led him to translate his thought into the language of Hindu tradition, the language of the great majority of India's heterogeneous people.

Throughout his early life Gandhi had shown a predilection for truth, moral teachings and renunciation. In South Africa, inspired by the writings of social philosophers such as Tolstoy, Ruskin and Thoreau and the practical example of a community of Trappist monks, be began to give his beliefs concrete expression. The problems faced by Indians in South Africa brought his concern for quality of life into sharp focus. He linked self-improvement with the struggle to win one's rights, and taught that only through self-suffering can one defeat and convert a more powerful opponent.

Gandhi's ideas and charismatic personality attracted a number of Europeans, who, along with Indian friends and relatives, helped him establish and maintain *Indian Opinion* and the Phoenix and Tolstoy Farm settlements as well as conduct a series on non-violent civil disobedience campaigns against repressive measures taken by the South African Government. The communal experiments crystallised his ideas on self-mastery as the basis for moral action. The courage shown by his *satyagrahis,* and the example of religious tolerance, racial harmony and voluntary poverty set by the Phoenix and Tolstoy Farm settlers, played a substantial role in mobilising support for the Indian cause in South Africa, enabling the community to win a short-lived but significant moral victory.

South Africa witnessed the genesis of Gandhi's *satyagraha* and ashram concepts, but he declared that his main objective was the uplift of India's downtrodden. This went beyond meeting the basic material needs of the people and envisaged a full-scale social revolution in a country sorely divided against itself. He couched his ideas in terminology comprehensible to India's Hindu masses, but his theories derived from a cross-cultural synthesis of ascetic and communal traditions, and were underpinned by a Christian egalitarianism alien to the bulk of his countrymen. A number of his ideas, such as the removal of untouchability, sanitation reform, uplift of women and co-education, challenged religious orthodoxy, and the fact that men and women lived together in his ashrams diminished the acceptability of his programmes to many Indians. Moreover, his indictment of modern civilisation as spiritually and morally bankrupt and harmful to the all-round development of India's people, alienated the educated elites who more often than not owed their economic and social status to Western education and the professional system transplanted from England.

Nevertheless, Gandhi's achievements in South Africa and the resulting patronage he received from prominent businessmen and intellectuals such as Gokhale and Tagore, assured him of a foothold, however tenuous, in the affairs of the nation. He fully exploited this advantage; and by the time of his controversial address at the opening ceremony of the Benares Hindu University in 1916 had founded the Satyagraha Ashram at Kochrab in Ahmedabad, and begun to propagate his ideas on the reform of the individual and society. *Satyagraha* had become for Gandhi not merely a technique of non-violent action to redress wrong-doing, but a means to return to the natural condition of man. By peripatetic teaching throughout India, he began to awaken people to the power of positive action as a means of building a new free society.

Though Gandhi's ashram concept was based on the principle of withdrawal and renewal common to Hindu and Christian ascetic tradition, he saw a dynamic role for his communities in the i application of *satyagraha*. In South Africa Phoenix Settlement and Tolstoy Farm had served as training grounds for *satyagrahis* and as a source of moral and economic support during the campaigns. Gandhi's idea was that ashram life would foster an active asceticism, and, while self-realisation remained the ultimate goal of the ashramite, active service to society was the means to that end. By imbuing the spiritual ideal of self-renunciation with a social conscience, he believed that religious values could be channelled through positive action to reform the individual and society. In his view the concerned individual who ordered his life around a refined asceticism, and yet remained active in society and politics, was an irrepressible agent of social change, immune from the corrupting influence of power.

In the tradition-bound, rigidly hierarchical society of India, Gandhi recognised the need for a moral or temporal sanction emanating from an organised group of activists capable of inspiring the masses to the necessary height of creativity and self-sacrifice. He conceived of *satyagraha* as that sanction. He saw Sabarmati and its many off shoots (ashrams and constructive work organisations) as a means of penetrating the barriers of ignorance and illiteracy and of arousing the masses out of their conditioned fatalism and inertia. In this context the role of the ashramites was educative.

Ideally free of caste and religious distinctions, they were expected to set an example of brotherhood and sisterhood, and selfless action which Gandhi hoped the nation as a whole would emulate. By breaking down caste ideology and inculcating a faith in sacrificial work, he sought to weaken the grip of divisive factors alienating the villager from the city-dweller and the manual labourer from the intelligentsia. He aimed to inculcate an awareness of the rights and responsibilities of citizenship, and to awaken the people to their innate power to change the social and physical environment.

However, the demands of the political struggle severely handicapped Gandhi's non-political work. His ability to exploit hitherto untapped political resources propelled him to the leadership of the freedom struggle. But whilst it was a relatively easy task to arouse people to an awareness of their rights, it was difficult to educate them to accept their responsibilities. In the atmosphere of fevered political activity and high expectation generated by the *satyagraha* and non-co-operation movements, Gandhi's plea that true freedom would not come from political independence alone but from sustained and constructive social change, fell on deaf ears. The majority of Congressmen had utmost faith in his political acumen, but many rejected his social theories as impractical and regarded the constructive work programme as an unnecessary drain on political resources.

Similarly, Gandhi's preoccupation with national affairs destabilised the Sabarmati Ashram. He soon discovered that absolute vows were no guarantee against human fallibility. The majority of ashramites were not sufficiently attuned to the de-mands of the ascetic discipline to which they agreed to submit. Men and women intermingling beyond the restrictions of

Conclusion

traditional obligation and custom were expected to sublimate their sexual urges merely by taking a vow, the observance of which was normally confined to male ascetics cut off from the company of women. Without the requisite detachment and commitment to chosen ideals the taking of absolute vows was shown to be self-defeating. Apart from incident after incident of vow-breaking, during Gandhi's extended absences the Ashram was beset with internal problems that only he, with his infinite patience and compassion, could resolve.

Yet Gandhi found himself unable to supervise either the internal workings or the external constructive activities of Sabarmati, with the result that he devolved responsibility on men and women who lacked his charismatic authority and organisational ability. The increasing institutionalisation of the Ashram and constructive work organisations led to the routinisation of Gandhi's ideas. This stifled individual initiative and creativity to a large degree and resulted in the growth of a rigid ideology and code of conduct that reduced his evolutionary theories to dogma. He recognised the problem but his energies were divided between such a multiplicity of roles as to leave him helpless. Though the Sabarmati ashramites displayed courage and endurance during the Salt Satyagraha and subsequent civil disobedience movement, Gandhi realised that the Ashram had outlived its usefulness and disbanded it in 1933.

Though Gandhi was never satisfied with the Sabarmati experiment, it did lay the foundation for a number of positive developments. Programmes of work undertaken in the villages were often the result of successful experiments in the Ashram. This was particularly true of the *khadi* industry and programmes such as child and adult education, sanitation reform, malaria prevention and cow protection. Another achievement of the Ashram experiment was its role in creating a new dimension for the participation of women in the affairs of the nation. Gandhi mapped out a vital role for women in the Ashram programmes, awakening many to a sense of their own strength and dignity as individuals. Women remained in the forefront of the Gandhian programmes as a result, and were often the mainstay of ashrams established after the Sabarmati pattern in rural areas.

The network of ashrams that developed was perhaps the major outcome of the Ashram experiment, for, though Sabarmati depended for its survival on wealthy benefactors, the smaller offshoots were managed more efficiently and economically and their work amongst disadvantaged groups proved to be more substantial. The experience of the 1920s encouraged Gandhi to shift the emphasis from the role of the ashram as an institution to that of the village worker who orders his life around the ashramic ideal. However, the ideal of placing a lone worker in each village was shown to be impractical. Ashrams were needed as supportive communities for the village worker. They were necessary to provide basic social services, to train villagers to be community workers and teachers among their own people, and to educate adults and children to be clean, healthy, independent-minded citizens, self-reliant and proud of their cultural and religious heritage. In the words of Taraben Mashruwala, the founder of the Kasturba Ashram at Madhan in the Amravati district of Maharashtra, "Just as one has a power generating station to cater to a particular area and this power is spread throughout this area and used for various purposes, so a social worker should become a source of enlightenment in a particular area radiating his or her influence over the surrounding areas."[2]

The Gandhian ashrams also played a supportive role in the *satyagraha* campaigns. In response to Gandhi's clarion call the ashram workers introduced and sustained programmes of self-improvement among the people of their area, many of whom were inspired to feats of self-sacrifice when the opportunity arose. Chimanbhai Bhatt, a member of Jugatram Dave's Swaraj Ashram at Vedchhi in southern Gujarat, recalls the substantial part played by the Ashram during the freedom struggle:

> In such an inspired atmosphere the Ashram played a very constructive and remarkable role.... During the freedom struggle the tribal people of this area also readily took to constructive activities such as spinning, weaving, giving up the drink habit and social reforms. Educationally also there has been steady and considerable progress. The great awakening was indeed astonishing because the tribal people, men as well as women, joined the freedom struggle, offered *satyagraha* and joyfully and courageously courted imprisonment. This greatly added to their moral, social and cultural stature. Even here in this small village of Vedchhi, with a population of 1,500 people, 13 men

and 7 women, who offered *satyagraha* were sentenced to various periods of imprisonment.³

The ashramic life cultivated the discipline and provided the support required to conduct civil disobedience at the grass-roots level. The possibilities in the ashram concept for rousing political awareness among the villagers were recognised by Nehru and Gandhi's politically-minded co-workers. Cadres of dedicated and highly disciplined men and women could effectively impart political education on a wide scale. But the idea of divorcing constructive work from political activity and arousing the masses to forcibly overthrow their overlords was repugnant to Gandhi. He believed that political consciousness devoid of social responsibility was destructive. To him freedom was not a narrow political objective, but the ideal and guiding principle of a sustained social revolution.

The rift between Gandhi and the socialist camp in Congress over the issue of political and social priorities widened during the 1930s. He could not reconcile concepts such as class struggle, violent dispossession and socialisation of industry with the *sarvodaya* ideal. Leftists accused him of supporting vested interests; he, in turn, whilst acknowledging the dedication of many socialists, criticised them for being Western-minded, and proclaimed their ignorance of human nature and conditions in the villages. He increasingly distanced the constructive work programme from the Congress organisation, which he believed was being manipulated by political careerists to further their own interests. Upon withdrawing from Congress in 1934 he buried himself in the village work programme.

The slow progress of the *gram sevak* scheme was due primarily to the difficulties faced by average men and women in sustaining independent and self-directed programmes of work in backward villages. They often had misconceptions as to the role they were expected to play in village life, and the strict code of conduct that Gandhi insisted upon sorely taxed their inner resources. Impatient for quick results, many *gram sevaks* attempted to impose precon-ceived work schemes, adopting an attitude of superiority towards the villagers and merely succeeding in alienating the people they were sent to serve. Though significant numbers of village workers adopted villages, and successfully lived amongst the people and served them, there was no indication that such individual action would flower into a broad-based programme reaching into every corner of rural India.

Yet Gandhi had utmost faith in the spirituality and non-violence of the village people, and their ability to survive the greatest hardship:

> The remote village life is in its way deeply spiritual in my opinion, more so than in the West. That is the permanent part of mass Hinduism. It will be finally judged by its influence on them. For ages the cult of violence has failed to produce any impression on them. History has no record of these villages having in a mass taken part in violence. Not therefore that they are totally non-violent. But they are comparatively so.[4]

He persevered, but the Sevagram experiment begun in 1936 by no means vindicated his faith in the *gram sevak* scheme. He found himself unable to tackle village work to his satisfaction and helpless to stop the flow of followers who gathered around him there. He had laid down the ideal that each ashramite settle in a village and inculcate ashramic values through service and example. Initially he saw the Sevagram experiment as an expression of the ideal, but in reality the growth of the Ashram was symptomatic of his followers' dependence upon him for their inspiration.

Though a number of programmes bore fruit, the overall experiment was weakened by excessive institutionalisation and the attendant increase in division of labour and conflict of interests. The community was racked with dissension, which, far from setting an example of harmonious and balanced social growth, undermined the tenuous rapport established between diligent ashramites and the villagers.

Another factor which severely handicapped the development of village work was the people's opposition to activities that were alien to their caste tradition, particularly those related to untouchability. Innovations that threatened the *status quo* met with resistance and, occasionally, outright hostility. The people protected their caste interests, enforced their caste rules and defended their ritual position in the hierarchy, because it afforded them security and identity. Against this entrenched value system

Conclusion 271

Gandhi opposed an egalitarianism and work ethic that was foreign to the caste mentality.

Gandhi recognised the educational value of selfless manual labour performed by *gram sevaks* whose caste-rules forbade such work, but he saw that the greatest need was for a mass education scheme to generate respect for the individual and awareness of the dignity of all types of work. The Wardha scheme was conceived for this purpose. Gandhi came to believe that ashrams patterned on his ideals should primarily serve a pedagogical function by tackling the problems of the villagers, showing them the way to develop self-confidence and thus self-reliance, and training children and adults alike to be community workers without alienating them from their own people. According to Chimanbhai Bhatt this remains the main concern of ashrams today:

> Ashram-based programmes generally mean that they are centres of post-Basic (secondary) educational institutions and primary teachers' training colleges. During the last thirty years such institutions have multiplied and are doing quite valuable work. Some of the Ashram institutions are generally helpful to the village society in various ways. Off and on, as need arises, batches of students led by teachers go out to the villages and help them in building roads, cleaning the village area, holding prayer assemblies and at times showing them good, instructive news-reels and film strips. In times of natural calamities such as droughts, tornadoes, floods, etc., also teachers and students, render very useful, devoted service.[5]

However, the scope of such activities appears limited. Uttamchand Shah, Secretary of the Swaraj Ashram at Bardoli, observes that though the ashrams have been successful in strengthening the character of their pupils and have assisted many disadvantaged groups to improve their condition, on the whole "they have been able to do very little in the field of education and social services".[6]

The work done by the Gandhian ashrams today is scattered and insufficient, and fails to make any dramatic impact upon the massive problems weakening the Indian body politic. Yet, in many areas the ashrams remain the only source of succour and hope to the poverty-stricken people they serve. An example is the *adivasi* areas of the Gujarat interior which are served by Gandhian ashrams. This is a stony, barren region where the water is brackish, the cattle emaciated and the people poor. In 1947 Narsibhai Baranda, an *adivasi* from Bharkota, founded the Shamlalji Ashram after receiving training in the correlated technique of Basic Education at the Swaraj Ashram, Bardoli. The Adivasi Ashramshala Scheme, as it came to be known, expanded over the years until today there are four ashramshalas in the area with a total of three hundred and forty *adivasi* students. In addition, the ashram programme, under the auspices of the Seva Samiti Tribal Scheme, runs hostels for boys and girls, adult education classes in the surrounding villages and a *balwadi* (pre-school) scheme incorporating Montessori and Gandhian methods. Due to the low productivity of the soil the ashrams are not self-supporting, though they cultivate fruit-trees, wheat, gram, maize and vegetables, and a small dairy programme provides milk.

But the scheme depends for its survival on donations from city voluntary agencies as Government subsidies do not cover expenses. While conditions prevailing in *adivasi* areas in Gujarat and elsewhere have improved considerably as a result of programmes such as the *ashramshala* scheme, the work done is not on a sufficiently large scale to influence the lives of the great majority of tribals in India, most of whom eke out a living in primitive conditions with little health care and sanitation.

Why have community development programmes in post-independent India failed to provide the vast numbers of rural and urban poor with even their basic needs ? Partly it is a legacy of Gandhi's efforts to dissociate the social reform programmes from the Congress organisation, which weakened the influence of Gandhian activists in the legislatures. He refuted the claim that constructive work could only be sustained by political activity of the type inherited from the colonial regime. He had forged a temporal sanction to check abuses of power, and in 1947, to ensure that the people would not be obliged to use the sanction against their own leaders, he advocated the disbanding of Congress as a political entity. He idealistically called for its transformation into a social service organisation, and the devolution of political authority to three tiers of elected national servants, of which the bottom tier would be the village *panchayat*. He sought thus to rid politics of careerists motivated by aspirations to position and power.

Gandhi outlined a role for politicians as "trustees of the nation", who should be models of simple living and ensure that the nation's wealth was utilised for the welfare of all. During the early years of Independence Congressmen preserved a facade of adherence to the ideals of *satyagraha* but "only the collusion of ideals with social and economic pressures can produce radical change in traditional societies: where the ideal alone is present, in practice it is either forgotten or distorted."[7] Gandhi believed that such pressures could only be effective if derived from individual effort tempered by self-control and motivated by the desire for self-improvement. However, for educated Indians caught up in the fervour of expectation surrounding independence his approach held no appeal.[8]

With Gandhi's influence in politics effectively removed Nehru forged ahead with his plans for large nationalised industries, elaborate controls, and ambitious government managed welfare schemes. He believed that these would establish a solid base upon which to "secure rapid economic growth and expansion of employment, reduction of disparities in income and wealth and prevention or concentration of economic power."[9] Congressmen and bureaucrats welcomed these policies, which enabled them to consolidate their new-found power by way of influence, prestige and patronage. The spirit of sacrifice, selflessness and unity which had permeated the freedom movement rapidly dried up. The new masters of India lost no time in adopting the ways of their erstwhile rulers. They were quick to ask the people to make sacrifices for economic progress but slow to set an example of co-operation and simple living. Gandhi had warned of a credibility gap opening if right means were not adhered to, but his political supporters had in the main accepted non-violence as a political expedient, not a philosophy of life. "The result is that India," wrote Jayaprakash Narayan, "instead of contributing something fresh to modern civilisation, is floundering in a welter of pale imitations of Western capitalism, socialism and communism."[10]

Gandhi's proposal to construct an Indian polity on the basis of the village unit was disregarded when it came to drafting a new constitution. Dr. Ambedkar, Chairman of the Drafting Committee, proclaimed:

The love of the intellectual Indian for the village community is of course infinite if not pathetic .... I hold that these village republics have been the ruination of India.... What is the village but a sink of localism, a den of ignorance, narrow-mindedness and communalism? I am glad the Draft Constitution has discarded the village and adopted the individual as its unit.[11]

The emphasis on the rights of the individual may appear laudable in a Western liberalistic sense, but Ambedkar's remarks held no practical relevance for the vast majority of Indians living in a rigidly structured village society, who were dependent on agriculture and the patronage of dominant caste groups, and denied equal opportunity. On the other hand, Gandhi recognised that unification of India would not be achieved by social uniformity on an individualistic basis, but by maintenance of the diversity inherent to the social system through respect for the dignity of the individual and provision of welfare for all. He called for a revaluation of the caste-idealism of the *varna* concept, infusing it with a flexibility that enabled the individual to develop his full potential, and ridding it of the inequities of caste ideology. He believed that the main task before an independent Indian government would be the humanisation of village society:

Man is not born to live in isolation but is essentially a social animal independent and interdependent. No one can or should ride on another's back. If we try to work out necessary conditions for such a life, we are forced to the conclusion that the unit of society should be a village or call it a manageable small group of people, who would in the ideal be self-sufficient (in the matter of their vital requirements) as a unit and bound together in bonds of mutual co-operation and interdependence.[12]

Amidst the growth of centralised state power in post-independent India, a development that appeared explicitly Gandhian in origin was the institution of *panchayat raj*. Article 40 of the Directive Principles of the Constitution, which was inserted well after the Constitution had been formulated, provided for the formation of village *panchayats* as units of self-government. The scheme resulted from the publication in 1957 of the *Report of the Team for the Study of Community Projects and National Extension*

Conclusion 275

Service. The chairman of the team, Balwantray Mehta, was a former Gandhian worker from Gujarat, but he insisted that it was not dogmatic adherence to Gandhian ideals that prompted the reform but, rather, administrative necessity.[13]

Panchayat raj entailed the devolution of much power over local concerns and substantial funds to a three-tiered structure of elected bodies at the levels of village, development block and district. The community development programme of the early 1950s had been based on American experience with the agricultural extension service, on quasi-Gandhian rhetoric concerning village uplift and on post-colonial paternalism.[14] The programme had been designed largely to increase food produc-tion but had failed to mobilise agrarian society towards significant social and economic growth. It was hoped that the devolution of some real power to local communities via *panchayat raj* would remedy the situation.[15]

However, rural democratisation did not proceed from *panchayat raj*. Gandhi had envisaged a harmonious, non-violent society and state as the basis for devolvement of central power to the localities and he warned of the dangers if contrary conditions existed. Taraben Mashruwala believes that community development in India today "is designed to cripple people, to make them weak and to make them more and more dependent upon the government" :

> It is a sad commentary on the nation's political history that so many years after independence the people are still not permitted to achieve economic or political understanding. Some crumbs of political or economic power are occasionally thrown by New Delhi into the begging bowl of villagers and for these crumbs the villagers are made to fight one another like cats and dogs. Because of this attitude the semblance of unity that existed in the villages prior to independence has now been totally crushed. Instead of progressing towards a more unified and responsible society the Indian villages are marching towards chaos and consternation. Any understanding and responsibility in the common man, most essential for a civilised society and good government, can only be instilled if the people are able to easily find and provide for themselves their basic needs.[16]

In summarising the effects of *panchayat raj,* Barratt concludes that "It is more realistic to characterise the three-tier system as an apparatus by which the government policy is transmitted to the villages than as' a mechanism of grassroots participation in fundamental planning for rural development."[17] In many cases the Gandhian ideal had been distorted by the magnification of existing social, economic and political divisions and rivalries. *"Panchayat raj* demonstrates at the local level how democracy can most cruelly divide in a complicated and diverse society," observes Judith Brown, "just as instalments of constitutional reform did at a higher level in the last forty years of the British *raj.*"[18]

Gandhi believed that village reconstruction must be accompanied by a deliberate policy of dismantling the centralised superstructure of control. In his view *sarvodaya* ultimately depended upon individual effort and self-reliance. The social revolution envisaged by him, aimed at developing a new relationship between man and his social, economic and physical environment, which required a transformation in existing institutions and techniques, and a radical change in the mentality of those who utilise them. He sought to demonstrate that the means adopted would determine the nature of the ends, i.e., ends would be determined by specific steps taken by individuals and groups, and by the nature of the institutions they established. His view was that *sarvodaya* could only be realised if planning came from the grassroots level because it was here that relevant programmes could be developed in terms of the day-to-day needs of the people.

His ashramic ideal was not limited to an institutional structure, but established a pattern for the individual based on service, self-reliance and creative activity. To live such a life, he believed, was to conserve and rejuvenate the fundamental ties that bind men and women together in organic communities. The service of the individual was seen by him as a visible link that indissolubly bound the worker to his or her human environment. His ashrams were living laboratories wherein he and his colleagues experimented with ways and means of enabling India's villagers to live in dignity and freedom. The essence of the communal experiment lay not in the institutional infrastructure that developed, but in the activities themselves and their heuristic value.

Today the ideals of *sarvodaya* and *satyagraha* remain alive in the thoughts and actions of many dynamic persons who have dedicated their lives to service. His legacy of the non-violent sanction is there to redress grievances, but the Gandhian methodology and its application is not "organised and coordinated by a central body so that whilst still remaining independent the efforts of the institutions are properly channelised."[19] In many respects the organisational infrastructure of the Gandhian movement is not utilised to its full potential because of the failure to modify itself in a dynamic way. "The processes of awareness-building which go on through the Gandhian ashrams and other organisations," observed Arun Chavan of the Verala Irrigation and Development Project Society, "are like rivulets in search of the mainstream."[20] Meanwhile the concentration of resources in the burgeoning cities further drains the village hinterland of its vitality, and the standard of living of the moneyed classes rises at the expense of the growing impoverishment of rural India. The gap between rich and poor can only widen, and the inappropriate structures of the centralised state become increasingly strained.

NOTES

1. Cited in Narayan, *op, cit.,* pp. 82-3.
2. Taraben Mashruwala, reply to Questionnaire, 10 November 1981.
3. Chimanbhai Bhatt, reply to Questionnaire, 29 October 1981.
4. Gandhi to Muriel Lester, 6 December 1926, *CWMG,* Vol. 32, pp. 391-2.
5. Chimanbhai Bhatt, reply to Questionnaire, 29 October 1981.
6. Uttamchand Shah, reply to Questionnaire, 30 October, 1981.
7. Judith Brown, "TheMahatma and Modern India", *Modern Asian Studies,* Vol. 3, No. 4, 1969.
8. P. Spratt, "Gandhi in Retrospect", *Modern Asian Studies,* Vol. 3, No. 4, 1969.
9. Cited in Kuldip Nayar, *India: The Critical Years* (Delhi : Vikas Publishing House, 1971), p. 91.
10. Jayaprakash Narayan, "Gandhi and the Politics of Decentralisation", in Ray, *op. cit.,* pp. 245-6.
11. Cited in Hugh Tinker, "The Village in the Framework of Development", in R. Braibanti & J. J. Spengler (eds.) *Administration and Economic, Development in India* (Durham: Duke University, 1963), p. 97; see also Brown *op. cit.*
12. Cited in Pyarelal, *Towards New Horizons* (Ahmedabad: Navajivan Publishing House, 1959), p. 8.

13. Hugh Tinkar, "Tradition and Experiment in Forms of Government", in C. H. Philips (ed.), *Politics and Society in India* (London: Alien and Unwiji, 1963),p. 183.
14. Barnaby B. Barratt, "The Alternative Village", *South Asian Review,* Vol. 7, No. 4, July 1974.
15. G. Rosen, *Democracy and Economic Change in India,* (Berkeley & Los Angeles: University of California Press, 1966), p. 93.
16. Taraben Mashruwala, reply to Questionnaire, 10 November 1981.
17. Barratt, *op. cit.*
18. Brown, *op. cit.*
19. Taraben Mashruwala, Reply to Questionnaire, 10 November 1981.
20. Arun Chavan, Reply to Questionnaire, 2 September 1981.

Postscripts

Introduction
– Mark Thomson

In 1979, I began a journey that was to take me to the true heart of India in so many ways. I lived in Mumbai for nearly five years, much of it spent with my wife who accompanied me for over two years. We joined the daily throng of busy Mumbai life; practiced yoga, which I still teach; travelled to tribal areas of Southern Gujarat to meet with community groups working with *adivasi* tribes; spent time in Gandhi's Sabarmati Ashram in Ahmedabad and Sevagram Ashram near Wardha; resided at the Gandhi Smarak Nidhi in Delhi to access the extensive archive. In Mumbai, my time was spent haunting the archives and libraries of the Asiatic Society, the University of Bombay, Maharashtra State Archives and Mani Bhavan Gandhi Sangrahalaya, poring over newspaper files, letters and the memoirs of those closest to Gandhi. We worked in the vegetable garden at Sevagram in high summer, bucket bathed with cold water at the Smarak Nidhi in Delhi's winter, ran the gauntlet of mosquito swarms at Sabarmati and had our lives changed forever.

The crowning experience of our journey was the warmth, hospitality, and encouragement received from members of the extended Gandhi family. Several of those we did not meet personally provided written insights into *ashram* life and those touched by these communities. Gandhi's grandson Arun, his wife Sunanda and their son Tushar spread a protective wing over us and made us feel at home in their home. Their kindness to us was a lasting gift that we have always cherished. Sushila Gandhi, the wife of Gandhi's son Manilal, provided invaluable written insights into the lives of the Gandhi family who remained in South Africa and the institutions Gandhi founded. The *ashrams* welcomed us and provided access to primary source material unavailable elsewhere. Two members of the Gandhi family have agreed to provide insights into the history and activities of the Phoenix Settlement and Sabarmati Ashram to embellish this Postscript and I am grateful to Ela, Gandhi's granddaughter, and Tushar (President, Mahatma Gandhi Foundation) for agreeing to participate. Who better than members of Gandhi's family to describe the legacy and potentialities of his communities?

As I was meandering through the extraordinary world of Gandhian *ashrams* and research institutions little did I know that another young Australian was charting a similar course, enthralled by the amazing life of Mohandas Karamchand Gandhi. It was to be many years before I met up with Tom Weber, who had cited this book in his excellent *Gandhi as Disciple and Mentor*[1] and who has continued to be a source of encouragement in the realisation of a new edition. Tom has agreed to provide an excerpt from a previously published article for this Postscript.

During 1992-96, I served as senior manager of the Australian development assistance programme at the Australian High Commission in New Delhi. This experience would have been largely unremarkable in the context of the Postscript, apart from several engagements. In 1994, National Press India awarded me the *Bharat Mitra Samman* for this book published the previous year. It was a surreal episode in that it was completely unexpected and such a magical event. I am fortunate to have the award and photographic evidence to prove to myself it actually happened.

Other engagements were equally profound in that they reinforced the enduring impact of Gandhi's work with marginalised and disenfranchised people. Among the many we supported financially, I had the great fortune to collaborate with organisations working with displaced *adivasis* in Rajasthan and landless *Rajputs* made redundant after careers in the disciplined forces; disparate communities forced to eke out survival in meagre circumstances. These organisations did not describe themselves as 'Gandhian' but his spirit was manifest in their focus on sustainable self-sufficiency and local empowerment. Such activities have left a lasting impression that Gandhi's influence continues to shape and inform community engagement around the world.

---

1. Thomas Weber, *Gandhi as Disciple and Mentor* , New Delhi: Cambridge University Press (2007)

As the new edition of the book is prepared for printing declaration of the Phoenix Settlement as a national heritage site has been gazetted by the Republic of South Africa. True to its mythical name the settlement has arisen from the ashes since its foundation to remain a beacon in the struggle against social injustice (see (III) "Phoenix rising" -Ela Gandhi). It is a place of pilgrimage and the original blueprint for Gandhi's communal experiments and a dynamic symbol of his philosophy of universal welfare, "guided by respect for all people, and as a challenge to colonial norms of segregation, languages and religions"[2].

The three contributors to the Postscript remind us that interest in Gandhian ideas and their extraordinary progenitor continues to burn bright. His legacy is not defined by museum artefacts and old *ashram* buildings, but the application of his ideas on human liberation and welfare for all. Gandhi's dynamic humanist approach to activism continues to influence the fortunes of many in a time of rapid change and uncertainty. The true custodians of his legacy are those who strive selflessly and non-violently to help those less fortunate than themselves.

---

2. See Appendix 1 "DECLARATION OF THE HISTORICAL PORTION OF THE PHOENIX SETTLEMENT, INANDA, ETHEKWINI, KWAZULU-NATAL AS A NATIONAL HERITAGE SITE", Republic of South Africa Government Gazette, No. 1017, 20 September 2020

"Gandhi Today"[1]
– Thomas Weber

During my most recent trip to India, I again had a chance to walk the hallowed ground of the Sabarmati Ashram in Ahmedabad and do some work in the archives. I have been a regular visitor to the Ashram since 1982 when I was preparing to re-walk Gandhi's Dandi *yatra*. And since then I have been there fairly frequently to catch up with Ashram friends and to do research work while completing writing projects. During these periods, as well as times spent visiting Sevagram Ashram and other Gandhian centres, I have often wondered as to their relevance and future in the 21st century.

Over the years I have imagined, in particular, what the Sabarmati Ashram might become and how it could play its role in spreading the message of Gandhi, how it could be ensured that the most effective use is made of this unique, world significant resource. Of course, as with Sevagram, it probably has a large role to play as one of India's most historical sites, as a museum and as a pilgrimage place (or even just a green oasis in the bustle of chaotic Ahmedabad). And it has just as important a role as an educational resource for school children, and as a place that fosters various educational programs and craft undertakings. My particular concern, however, is to think through ways that the Ashram could be made an even more satisfying venue for visiting researchers. Gandhi research needs more than universities.

For researchers such as me, and at least a few others who come from outside India each year, besides the historical atmosphere which in powerful ways supports the research experience, the heart of the

---

1. Thomas Weber, "Gandhi Today: In the Field and in the Academy (An Outsider's Observations)", *Gandhi Marg*, vol.34 (2/3): pp. 319-335.

Ashram is the archive. The Ashram probably has the best collection of Gandhi letters and other documents in existence, but the collection is not complete. If I am not mistaken, at the moment there are still important papers at the Nehru Memorial Library and the National Archives in New Delhi (when will the Pyarelal papers be released?) that the Ashram does not have copies of and vice versa. Is it possible for the institutions to get together to ensure that they each have as complete sets as possible. A "one stop shop" would greatly assist overseas scholars with limited time, and there is still something special about doing Gandhi research at the Ashram where the Mahatma walked and worked, and where one can still feel his spirit rather than in a museum/library in Delhi or Jalgaon.

Of course, in the fullness of time all the Gandhi documents will presumably be digitised and available to scholars from around the world via computers without them having to visit India at all. However, there will always be times when it will be important to see the actual documents to check margin notes, writings on the back, or to take care of missing information from incomplete scanning (which will always happen regardless of care—just have a look at problems introduced into the revised edition of Gandhi's Collected Works), or to provide perspective to scholarship by actually being at a Gandhian site that much of the material refers to.

This leads me to another possibly important issue. Of course, this may merely be the idle dreams of a far off scholar who does not understand the politics behind the management of Gandhi institutions, but could the Ashram be positioned so that it ensures that its outstanding collection is used by scholars in a way that helps to promote first-class Gandhi scholarship, and possibly to help to create a world-wide community of Gandhi scholars?

Some sort of international Gandhi research hub in India would be invaluable. And it seems to me that if it could be instituted at the Sabarmati Ashram, it could become the most important place in the world for scholars to come and work, to meet other scholars, to share information and discuss ideas. It could foster greater contact between various Gandhi experts and ensure that Gandhi scholarship is carried out at the highest level. I have long had a vision of there being a place in India where Gandhi scholars from around the world could come and work with the best of local scholars and inspire each other. Having access to documents, whether in hard copy or digital form, is not the same as having a group of like-minded people working in the one place. And if the place had a Gandhian atmosphere (such as the Ashram could provide, but simple academic libraries and archives, no matter how good they are, cannot) it would be a wonderful thing.

This dream may be worthy, but there is a problem. As with the Gandhi journals, there are now many Gandhi centres. Of course, it is important to enthuse young people with a sense of Gandhian activism and so universities should have Gandhi centres. But, at least from an outside view, the question arises as to how many quality Gandhi research centres the country can accommodate. I do not think that in this sense competition is productive. The materials and the scholars to work on them, like the articles in Gandhi journals, end up being spread too thin. No critical mass that could form into an international scholarly Gandhian community is likely to develop.

How much real Gandhi research is done at Gandhi research centres? How much of the time are they lying idle? All Gandhi researchers have friends they made serendipitously at the canteen of archives or Ashrams. Imagine the cross-fertilisation of ideas that could occur if there was one really good centre that attracted the best of Indian and overseas scholars. In short, perhaps one or two quality research centres may be of greater value than a proliferation of many largely unused ones. Less can be more.

"Phoenix Rising"
– Ela Gandhi

Much has happened at the Phoenix Settlement since this book was first published.

Gandhiji's constructive programme was and remains a great inspiration to all those who were managing the affairs of Phoenix Settlement.

The four ideals, viz sarvodaya or the welfare of all (this is the name given by my mother Sushila to the original Gandhi home rebuilt several times and stands as a heritage site at present on the Phoenix Settlement), satyagraha – the power of truth, swadeshi – made locally or an economic model based on self sufficiency and swaraj – control over one's self in order that all can be liberated, have been the guiding principles behind the work that has been done and is being done at Phoenix Settlement.

Responding to the need for medical facilities in the area, the Trustees of Phoenix Settlement in 1962 established a clinic in the vacant press building. One of the Trustees, Dr Rustomjee Jalbhai Rustomjee, a medical doctor took on the responsibility of running the clinic pro bono. It grew rapidly into a vibrant primary health care centre with the assistance of the Medical School in Durban, now known as the Nelson Mandela Medical School. This model was very much in line with Gandhiji's belief in preventive health care.

During 1969, many programmes were arranged to celebrate the centenary of Gandhi and Kasturba. Among the programmes was the building of a museum and library and a properly equipped clinic. These buildings were built and became functional in 1970.

The Press building then housed a crèche until 1984 serving the needs of the local community. There are two important principles in providing this facility.

1. That early childhood development is a crucial period in the life of a person and values and behaviour learned at this stage remain as habits throughout the life of a person;

2. That it serves as an important facility, which enables women to become economically active.

However, this was closed down and a training centre was started on the premises by Prof. Fatima Meer, teaching block printing, pottery and so on, to local residents. Presently we run a programme on values education.

Meanwhile, in the 70s the political situation in the country had become tense with the banning of the political organisations in 1960, the emergence of underground structures, the growing mass action and the government reaction with threats of security force action against any activity that could be regarded as political.

Within this situation, non-violent mass mobilisation of the community took place from the Phoenix Settlement, which became the meeting point for young activists. My husband and I were banned and house-arrested (1973-1982) and were forced to move out of the Settlement. My mother, Sushila reluctantly came with us to a nearby town, Verulam where we lived for over two decades and from where it was convenient for my children to attend school. We however maintained regular contact with the Settlement, where political and social activities continued.

In the 80s, a wave of unrest was instigated by the Government with political assassinations of leaders, detentions, torture, and ambushes. In August 1985, government orchestrated racial violence broke out in the Inanda area leading to the burning down of the buildings and the expulsion of the residents from the Phoenix Settlement. Within a few days after that the entire Settlement (100 acres) was occupied by families brought in from remote areas. Fruit trees, flowers, the entire landscape was vandalised together with all the buildings and its contents. Some articles were salvaged but a lot was stolen or destroyed.

After years of terrible carnage in the area, it was only in the early 90s that a peace accord was signed with the community. In 2000, after the government agreed to provide some funding the buildings were renovated and officially opened by the then President of South Africa, President Thabo Mbeki who said in an impassioned speech,

"Phoenix Settlement is an integral part of our history and our present, it is yours to preserve...Cherish it and thrive on this land. It is yours, it is mine, it belongs to all our children and grandchildren and those who have yet to enter the world."

Over 80 per cent of the land was given over to the City Council to house the people who had built temporary houses on the land and lived in squalid conditions.

A monthly newspaper named *Satyagraha* fashioned on the *Indian Opinion* model was being printed from the year 2000 and has now migrated to an electronic version, which can be accessed at www.gdt.org.za. More information on Phoenix Settlement can also be accessed from this website.

The challenge facing Phoenix is how to build a strong relationship with the surrounding community, to understand their plight and their aspirations so that a mutually dependent relationship can be built between the people and the Settlement and to develop a knowledge and interest in Gandhiji and Kasturba in the community.

At present, the following facilities are providing selected services:

A. Sarvodaya, the Gandhi home where there is a story of how Gandhiji's life and thinking transformed while in South Africa, what was the inspiration and how his thoughts and ideas have influenced various other movements around the world;

B. A museum where the "Seeds of Democracy" exhibition is displayed showing the various leaders of the liberation struggle, who lived in Inanda and who shared many common ideals such as shared spirituality, self-sufficiency, culture of non-violence and a passion for social justice;

C. A display on the life of Kasturba and her contribution with a focus on the marginalisation of women;

D. A display on the economy of *khadi* and the spinning wheel

E. An interactive wall on Gandhi and Mandela from which speeches made by these icons can be downloaded onto a smart phone;

F. A computer centre, an internet café and an education centre located in the Press building;

G. A drop-in centre in the clinic where the vulnerable can obtain a meal and support services;

H. A crèche and nursery school;
I. An activity centre in the home built by my father Manilal, named Kasturba Bhavan;
J. Government-run primary and secondary schools in this complex.

The Settlement is managed by eight Trustees.

The eThekwini City Council assists the Settlement to meet some of the needs in terms of basic maintenance of the place, and assistance is rendered by the Government of India as well as numerous individual donors.

There are no "Settlers" now, but the spirit of peace and Gandhian ideals continue to inspire all who enter the place. As my mother once said to my niece Uma,

> "This institution is a memorial to Gandhiji. It is a historical place. Phoenix, with its quiet atmosphere, trees and flowers, and even this very earth has always conveyed to me the message of that great man, who walked on this ground and lived amongst these things, I have never failed to experience the fragrance of Bapuji's sweet presence in Phoenix ... this land is sacred. It will always be a place of pilgrimage, for those who seek inspiration to better their lives and gain a little from the great men who have passed on."

The Settlement receives over 4000 visitors annually, both local and international. Regular activities are arranged to promote Gandhian values. Weekly children's activities are organised and faith based groups conduct various activities to promote values education.

The Trust has built partnerships with other faith based organisations and non-profit organisations. There is a strong initiative from the National Association of African American Studies (NAAAS) to have Phoenix Settlement declared a world heritage site.

So from manual individual alphabet setting to a computerised world, from a vibrant settlement to a densely populated area within which exists a heritage site and from *satyagraha* to a path leading to *sarvodaya*, which is the name given by the family to the original Gandhi home and it means the welfare of all. Phoenix is once again rising from its ashes!

"Sabarmati Ashram - A Fountain of Greatness?"
– Tushar Gandhi

Richard Quest of CNN International once invited me to a 'shoot' for an episode of his program 'Quest for Greatness' at Sabarmati Ashram. His question to me was, "Is this place the source of the fountain of greatness?" His question was of course because Bapu, Mohandas Karamchand Gandhi, had founded the Ashram and had from 1917 to 1930 lived here. Many great events in the history of the Indian freedom movement happened here and little wonder it came to be known as the *Satyagraha* Ashram. Bapu embarked on the Champaran *Satyagraha* from here. He and Sardar Patel led the Bardoli *Satyagraha* for the farmer's rights from here. It was from here that the first non-cooperation movement was launched and then withdrawn in the wake of the violence in Chauri Chaura.

While staying at the Ashram, Bapu established the Gujarat *Vidyapith* to provide nationalist education and instil a spirit of service in its students. In 2020, the Gujarat *Vidypith* will celebrate its centenary. It was here that Bapu was arrested and then prosecuted for sedition and sentenced to six years imprisonment. *Khadi* spinning and weaving was revived and the evolution of the *charkha* happened here. It was from here that Bapu embarked on the historic Dandi Kooch on 12 March 1930, vowing not to return to the Ashram until India gained independence.

After Bapu's departure in 1930, the Ashram continued to function and all the institutions established to carry forward the several objectives of Bapu's ideology continued their work and programs from its periphery. A few still function. In 1969, the year of the Gandhi Centenary, Sabarmati Ashram was refurbished and an iconic addition was made, a beautiful picture gallery and library designed by the iconic architect Charles Correa. 'Hriday Kunj', Ba and Bapu's abode in the Ashram were refurbished, but the rest of the Ashram was in decline. It was also changing from being a laboratory and showcase of Bapu's ideals and methods at work, into a stagnant monument; a place to visit, a place of pilgrimage.

Subsequently, the Ashram went into decline and was struggling. Many of the other residences of historic significance became dilapidated. Many of the precious artefacts, memorabilia, manuscripts and rare books suffered neglect, were destroyed or tragically lost. Sabarmati Ashram was barely surviving but it was attracting a steady number of visitors. A sound and light show was produced and every evening it would have two shows in Hindi and English narrating the history of the Ashram and of Bapu's life in the Ashram. It was popular with visitors but it became monotonous and jaded. New technology made it obsolete, people lost interest, and it was shut down. Infrequently and insufficiently, the Ashram would get grants from both State and Central Governments, which enabled it to limp along, but the Ashram was rapidly deteriorating.

A dark episode in the history of the Ashram happened in 2002, during an episode of communal violence in parts of Gujarat including the city of Ahmedabad. In the wake of a violent tragedy at nearby Godhra, fearing vandalism, the Ashram shut its gates to victims seeking refuge from murderous mobs. I think that day, if Bapu's spirit resided in 'Hriday Kunj', it would have wept and left. That blemish can never be erased. Driven by their desire to save a monument the Ashram management betrayed the man for whom the monument stood.

After 2002, Sabarmati Ashram witnessed resurgence. International visitors and VIPs started visiting as part of their India itinerary. As several heads of state and other dignitaries visited, the Ashram went through a period of renewed popularity, attracting new and significant funds and grants. A project of repairs and restoration commenced in earnest and the trustees and management took active interest in refurbishing the Ashram. Ahmedabad was also being transformed. Narmada river waters filled up the dried out riverbed of Sabarmati, and a riverfront project implemented; a grandiose scheme to beautify this part of the city. Arguably, it spoiled the simplicity, pristine surroundings, and environment of the Ashram. A natural setting had been replaced by a manmade concrete edifice. The riverbank that once formed the boundary of the Ashram was now separated from it by a concrete boulevard—the price of progress and development.

Things were also changing in the way the Ashram functioned. A new director, Tridip Suhrud, was appointed. He changed the way the Ashram was run and presented, restoring the picture galleries and refurbishing the displays, making them attractive and interesting, and, what was most commendable and something that was long overdue, making an inventory of all items of historic significance stored in the various neglected and dilapidated structures, cupboards and trunks in the Ashram. Not only were they inventoried but a serious effort was made to scientifically preserve them and a state of the art conservation archive was created to preserve what remained. All this was made available to research scholars; finally the Ashram was evolving from a monumental edifice into a research and conservation facility.

The Ashram campus was modernised, various structures which had been decaying due to neglect and disuse were repaired, restored and put to use. The Gandhi Heritage Portal Project awarded to the Ashram revitalised it, a team of scholars and technical persons started creating the Gandhi Heritage Portal, which is now online. Much required facilities for the convenience of the visitors were added, not only added but also maintained the standards of cleanliness Bapu would have demanded. It felt that the Ashram in one aspect was coming alive.

My father Arun would often lament the fate of the Ashrams, which had become what he called "lifeless monuments". After a recent visit, he said with joy that after a deep slumber Sabarmati Ashram had awakened and was in a small way alive and throbbing once again. Tridip had his detractors but he went about his work unmindful of those that finally brought about his downfall. Tridip was a person in a tearing hurry and due to his pace antagonised many of the 'status quo' loving Gandhians who felt threatened by what they termed "too much modernisation". They were happy to be caretakers of a cadaver; breathing life into it was something they were afraid of. Tridip's ambitions and impatience for change finally brought about his downfall. The 'statusquoists' and vested interests who had infiltrated the Ashram and captured parts of it forced Tridip to resign. Fortunately, what he had done during his tenure could not be undone and although things have stagnated after his exit, the Ashram, which remains primarily a monument, provides a much more interesting and pleasant experience for its visitors.

There is much that needs to be done. Sabarmati Ashram could provide a more immersive experience for its visitors; it must not only remain a monument to its founder but become a living showcase of the history of the Ashram and the ideology and philosophy of Bapu. Wise utilisation of technology would enable such an experience; mere photo displays and picture galleries are no longer interesting and sufficient.

The Sabarmati Ashram needs a further upgrade. 'Hriday Kunj' and the 'Vinoba-Mira Kutir' must be preserved as 'lived-in' memorials not just walls and empty rooms; this can easily be achieved. It is not enough to merely keep a small mattress, pillow, a low working desk, and charkha as displays in Bapu's day room, which was his office. It must look as if it is lived in; the visitor must feel as if the incumbent has just stepped out and would soon return and resume work. Ba's kitchen should be furnished as in her time to give the visitors a more realistic sense of their day-to-day life in the Ashram. All this is possible and can be done without trivialising the experience and its essence.

The Museum and Picture gallery must utilise technology to become interactive. A memorial of Bapu's departure from the Ashram on his pilgrimage to Dandi to win freedom should be installed, as that event is most significant to the history of the Ashram. This should be done by capable people who can retain authenticity. The organisations that are offshoots on the periphery of the Ashram need to be revived and made functional so that interested visitors can see Bapu's ideology and belief in practice. The Ashram needs to host more activities and events to attract not only visitors from outside the city but citizens of Ahmedabad more regularly, so that they too develop a feeling of involvement and attachment.

There is great potential and possibilities to make the Ashram more dynamic while preserving its identity as a monument, a part of our history. It must become more interesting and meaningful. All that is required is will, a vision and a dedicated dynamism. The Ashram should encourage and facilitate more scholastic activities designed to promote and modernise Bapu's ideals, methods, and vision. It must become a symbol of what was most dear to Bapu—communal amity and the oneness of humanity and the environment.

The fountain of greatness that once flowed here and inspired humanity must be restored and revived, to inspire present and future generations, as it did previously. With sufficient will and zeal there is much that Sabarmati Ashram can still offer.

Bibliography

PRIMARY SOURCES

1. Unpublished

a) Correspondence to and from Gandhi.

Letters from and to Gandhi at the Sabarmati Sangrahalaya, Ahmedabad.
Letters from and to Gandhi at the Gandhi Smarak Nidhi, New Delhi.

b) Interviews and correspondence

Uttamchand Shah, Swaraj Ashram, Bardoli, 30 September 1980
Ela Ramgobin, Post Box 331, Verulam, South Africa, 21 April 1981.
Arun Gandhi, 5 Shraddhanjali, Vithal Nagar, North Avenue, Santacruz, Bombay, 26 February 1981.
Kanakmal Gandhi, Sevagram Ashram, Wardha, 23 March 1981.
Chimanlal Shah, Sevagram Ashram, Wardha, 24 March 1981.
Pyarelal, Rat 25, New Central Market, Connaught Place, New Delhi, 30 November and 5 December 1981.
Kisan Trivedi, Harijan Ashram, Ahmedabad, 10 December 1981.

c) Questionnaire replies

Uttamchand D. Shah, Swaraj Ashram, Bardoli, 30 October 1981.
Chimanbhai Bhatt, Swaraj Ashram, Vedchhi, 29 October 1981.
Taraben Mashruwala, Kasturba Swaraj Mandal, Madhan, 10 November 1981.
Arun Chavan, Verala Irrigation & Development Project Society, Sangli, 2 September 1981.

Bibliography

2. Published

a) Newspapers and Journals

Indian Opinion, Natal, South Africa (1903-1914).
Young India, Ahmedabad, India (1919-1932).
Harijan Pune, India (1933-1941) & Ahmedabad India (1942-1948).
The Bombay Chronicle, Bombay, India (1914-1940).

b) Reference Works

The Indian Annual Register : An Annual Digest of Public Affairs of India, Calcutta : The Annual Register Office (1935-1938).

c) Gandhi's Works, Writings and Speeches (Books written by Gandhi and later compilations)

The Collected Works of Mahatma Gandhi, Delhi: The Publications Division, Government of India, in process of publication, 1958.
An Autobiography. The Story of My Experiments with Truth, Trans. by Mahadev Desai, London : Jonathan Cape (1966).
The Speeches and Writings of Mahatma Gandhi, Madras : Natesan (1934).
Ashram Observances in Action, Ahmedabad : Navajivan (1932).
Non-violent Resistance (Satyagraha), New York : Schocken Books (1961).
Mahatma Gandhi on Human Settlements, Ahmedabad : Navajivan (1977).
Socialism of My Conception, Bombay: Bharatiya Vidya Bhavan, n.d.
Satyagraha in South Africa, Ahmedabad : Navajivan (1938).
Unto This Last. A Paraphrase, Ahmedabad: Navajivan (1956).
Women and Social Injustice, Ahmedabad : Navajivan (1942).
Village Swaraj, Ahmedabad : Navajivan (1962).
India of My Dreams, Ahmedabad : Navajivan (1947).
Hind Swaraj or Indian Home Rule, Ahmedabad: Navajivan (1938).
From Yervada Mandir, Ahmedabad : Navajivan (1932).
Sarvodaya (Welfare for All), Ahmedabad : Navajivan (1954).
Industrialise and Perish, Ahmedabad : Navajivan (1966).
Basic Education, Ahmedabad : Navajivan (1951).

The Problem of Education, Ahmedabad, Navajivan (1962).
Key to Health, Ahmedabad : Navajivan (1948)
Nature Cure, Ahmedabad : Navajivan (1954).
Self-Restraint v. Self-Indulgence, Ahmedabad : Navajivan (1928).
Ethical Religion, Madras : Ganesan (1922).
Bapu 5 Letters to Mira 1924-1948, Ahmedabad : Navajivan (1949).
To Ashram Sisters, Ahmedabad : Navajivan (1952).

SECONDARY SOURCES

Published and Unpublished

a) Books

Andrews, Charles Freer, *Mahatma Gandhi's Ideas,* London : Alien and Unwin (1929).
Apter, David E. & Joll, James (eds.), *Anarchism Today,* London: The Macmillan Press (1971).
Ashe, Geoffrey, *Gandhi: A Study in Revolution,* London: Heinemann (1968).
Baden-Powell, B. H., *The Land Systems of British India,* 3 Vols., Oxford: Clarendon Press (1892).
————: *The Indian Village Community, New* Haven : Hraf Press (1957).
Balwantsinha (Balwant Singh), *Under the Shelter of Bapu,* trans. from the original in Hindi, Ahmedabad : Navajivan (1962).
Bandyopadhyaya, Jayantanuja, *Social and Political Thought of Gandhi,* Bombay : Allied Publishers (1969).
Basharri, A. L., *The Wonder That Was India,* London : Fontana/Collins, (1971).
Bhave, Vinoba & Narayan, Jayaprakash, *Gramdan for Gram s waraj,* Varanasi : Sarva Seva Sangh Prakashan (1967).
Birla, G. D., *In the Shadow of the Mahatma,* Bombay : Vakils, Feffer & Simons (1968).
Bolton, G., *Tragedy of Gandhi,* London : Alien & Unwin (1934).
Bondurant, Joan V., *The Conquest of Violence. The Gandhian Philosophy of Conflict.* Bombay: Oxford University Press (1959).
Bose, Nirmal Kumar, *My Days With Gandhi,* Calcutta, Nishana (1953).

—— : *Studies in Gandhism,* Ahmedabad : Navajivan (1972).
Braibanti, Ralph & Spengler, Joseph J. (eds.), *Administration and, Economic Development in India,* Durham : Duke University Press (1963).
Brown, Judith, M. *Gandhi's Rise to Power, Indian Politics, 1915-1922,* London : Cambridge University Press (1972).
—— : *Gandhi and Civil Disobedience. The Mahatma in Indian Politics, 1928-1934,* London : Cambridge Unrversity Press (1977).
Buber, Martin, *Paths in Utopia,* trans. by R. F. C. Hull, London : Routledge & Kegan Paul (1949).
—— : Martin, *Pointing the Way,* trans. and ed. by Maurice Friedman, London : Routledge & Kegan Paul. (1957).
Chaudhary, Ramnarayan, *Bapu as I Saw Him,* trans. from the original in Hindi, Ahmedabad : Navajivan (1959).
Chaudhary, P. C. R. *Gandhi and His Contemporaries,* Delhi : Sterling (1972).
Dange, S. A. *India: From Primitive Communism to Slavery,* Bombay; People's Publishing House (1949).
Datta, D. M., *The Philosophy of Mahatma Gandhi,* Madison : University of Wisconsin Press (1953).
Desai, A. R. *Rural Sociology in India,* Bombay : Popular Prakashan (1978).
Desai, Dinkar, *Primary Education in India,* Bombay: Servants of India Society (1938).
Desai, Mahadev, *The Gita According to Gandhi,* Ahmedabad : Navajivan (1946).
Dhawan, G., *The Political Philosophy of Mahatma Gandhi,* Ahmedabad : Navajivan (1951).
Diwakar, R. R. *Satyagraha — Its Technique and Theory,* Bombay : Hind Kitabs (1946).
Doctor, Adi H., *Sarvodaya : A Political and Economic Study,* Bombay: Asia Publishing House (1967).
Doke, Joseph J., *M. K. Gandhi-AnlndianPatriot,* Madras: Natesan (1909).
Dumont, Louis, *Homo Hierarchicus. The Caste System and Its Implications,* London : Paladin (1972).
Dutt, R. Palme, *India Today,* Calcutta : Manisha (1970).
Embree, A. T., *India's Search for a National Identity,* New York: Knopf (1972).

Enthoven, R. E., *The Tribes and Castes of Bombay,* Bombay : Government Central Press (1920-22).
Erikson, Erik H., *Gandhi's Truth,* London : Faber & Faber (1970).
Fisher, Louis, *Gandhi, His Life and Message for the World,* New York : The New American Library (1954).
——: *The Life of Mahatma Gandhi,* 2 Vols., Bombay : Bharatiya Vidya Bhavan (1955).
Fourier, Charles, *Design for Utopia,* New York: Schocken Books (1971).
Fraser, Kenneth C, "The Politics of Gandhi's Constructive Programme", Bachelor of Arts Thesis, La Trobe University (1976).
Friere, Paula, *The Pedagogy of the Oppressed,* Middlesex: Penguin Books (1972).
Fromm, Erich, *The Fear of Freedom,* London: Routledge and Kegan Paul (1960).
——: *Beyond the Chains of Illusion. My Encounter with Marx and Freud,* London : Abacus (1980).
Gandhi, Arun, "Kasturba", Bombay: Unpublished Manuscript (1981).
Gandhi, *Madan, Gandhian Aesthetics,* Chandigarh & Delhi : Vikas Bharati (1969).
Gandhi, Prabhudas, *My Childhood with Gandhi,* Ahmedabad : Navajivan (1957).
Garh, B. Rai, *Basic Education — Need of the Day,* Ambala Cantt: The Associated Publishers (1975).
Gerth, B. B. & Mills, C. Wright (eds.). *From Max Weber, Essays in Sociology,* London : Routledge & Kegan Paul (1948).
Hartog, Philip, *Some Aspects of Indian Education : Past and Present,* London : Oxford University Press (1939).
Hobbes, Aubrey, *Encounter with Martin Buber,* Middlesex : Penguin Books (1974).
Hunt, James D., *Gandhi in London,* New Delhi: Promilla and Co. (1978).
Hussain, S. Abid, *The Way of Gandhi and Nehru,* London : Asia Publishing House (1959).
Iyer, Raghavan N., *The Moral and Political Thought of Mahatma Gandhi,* New York : Oxford Univ. Press (1973).
James, William, *The Varieties of Religious Experience,* London : Longmans Green & Co. (1945).

Kalelkar, Kaka, *Stray Glimpses of Bapu,* Ahmedabad : Navajivan (1950).
Keer, D., *Mahatma Gandhi. Political Saint and Unarmed Prophet,* Bombay : Popular Prakashan (1973).
Kripalani, J. B. *The Latest Fad,* Wardha : Hindustani Talimi Sangh, (1946).
———: *GandhianThought,* New Delhi: Gandhi Smarak Nidhi (1961).
Krishnadas, *Seven Months with Mahatma Gandhi,* Ahmedabad : Navajivan (1951).
Kropotkin, P., *Mutual Aid : A Factor of Evolution,* London : W. Heinemann (1904).
Kumar, R. *(ed.), Essays on Gandhian Politics. The Rowlatt Satyagraha of 1919,* Oxford : Clarendon Press (1971).
Lewis, M. D. (ed.), *Gandhi. Maker of Modern India?,* Boston : D. C. Heath and Co. (1965).
Maine, Henry Summer, *Village Communities in the East and West,* London : John Murray (1881).
Mannheim, Karl, *Ideology and Utopia,* trans.by L. Wirth and E. Shils, London : Routledge & Kegan Paul (1936).
Mannin, Ethel, *Bread and Roses,* London: Macdonald & Co. (1944).
Marx, Karl, *Das Kapital,* ed. by Frederick Engels and trans. by Samuel Moore, Moscow : Progress Publishers (1954).
Mashruwala K. G., *Gandhi and Marx,* Ahmedabad : Navajivan (1951).
Mehta, Ashoka, *Studies in Socialism,* Bombay : Bharatiya Vidya Bhavan(1951).
Mehta, Ved, *Mahatma Gandhi and His Apostles,* Middlesex : Penguin Books (1977).
Mookerji, Radha Kumud, *Ancient Indian Education,* London : Macmillan & Co. (1951).
Moore, Barrington, Jr., *Social Origins of Dictatorship and Democracy,* Middlesex : Penguin Books (1969).
Mukherjee, Hiren, *Gandhiji. A Study,* New Delhi: People's Publish-ing House (1958).
Mukherjee, Haridas & Mukherjee, Uma, *The Origins of the National Education Movement* (1905-1916). Calcutta :Jadavpur Univer-sity (1957).
Myrdal, Gunnar, *Asian Drama; An Inquiry into the Poverty of Nations,* 3 Vols., New York: The Twentieth Century Fund (1968).

Nair, Kusum, *Blossoms in the Dust,* London : G. Duckworth and Co. (1962).
Nair, Sankaran, *Gandhi and Anarchy,* Madras : Tagore & Co. (1922).
Nambobdiripad, E. M. S., *The Mahatma and Theism,* New Delhi: People's Publishing House (1958).
Nanda, B. R., *Mahatma Gandhi,* London : Alien & Unwin (1965).
Narayan, Shriman, *Mahatma Gandhi. The Atomic Man,* Bombay: Somaiya Publications (1971).
Nayar, Kuldip, *India : The Critical Years,* Delhi : Vikas Publishing House (1971).
Nehru, Jawaharlal, *An Autobiography,* London : John Lane, The Bodley Head (1936).
———— : *The Discovery of India,* New York : Anchor Books (1960).
Nisbet, Robert, *The Quest for Community,* New York : Oxford University Press (1953).
———— : *The Social Philosophers,* St. Albans : Paladin (1976).
Ostergaard, Geoffrey & Currell, Melville, *The Gentle Anarchists,* London : Oxford University Press (1971).
Owen, Robert, *The Life of Robert Owen,* London : Charles Knight & Co. (1971).
Panikkar, K. M., *Hindu Society at Crossroads,* Bombay: Asia Publishing House (1967).
Parvate, T. V., *Jamnalal Bajaj. A Brief Study of His Life and Character,* Ahmedabad : Navajivan (1962).
Patel, M. S., *The Educational Philosophy of Mahatma Gandhi,* Ahmedabad : Navajivan (1953).
Patwardhan, Sunanda, *Change Among India's Harijans,* New Delhi: Orient Longmans (1973).
Pavlov, V. I., *Historical Premises for India's Transition to Capitalism,* Moscow : "Navka" Publishing House (1979).
Payne, Robert, *The Life and Death of Mahatma Gandhi,* London: The Bodley Head (1969).
Philips, C. H. (ed.), *Politics and Society in India,* London : Alien & Unwin (1969)
Philips, C. G. & Wainwright, M. D., *The Partition of India. Politics and Perspectives, 1935-1947,* Massachusetts : M. I. T. Press (1970).
Polak, H. S. L., *Mahatma Gandhi,* Madras : Natesan (1931).
Polak, H. S. L., Brailsford, H. N. & Lord Pethick-Lawrence, *Mahatma Gandhi,* London : Odhams Press (1949).

Polak, Millie Graham, *Mr. Gandhi : The Man,* Bombay : Vora and Co. (1949).

Popper, Karl, *The Open Society and Its Enemies,* 2 Vols., Routledge & Sons (1945).

Prabhu, R. K. & Rao, U. R., *The Mind of Mahatma Gandhi,* Ahmedabad: Navajivan (1967).

Prasad, Mahadev, *Social Philosophy of Mahatma Gandhi,* Gorakhpur: Vishwavidyalaya Prakashan (1958).

Prasad, Rajendra, *At the Feet of Mahatma Gandhi,* London : Asia Publishing House (1961).

————: *Satyagraha in Champamn,* Ahmedabad : Navajivan (1949).

Pyarelal, *Mahatma Gandhi. The Last Phase,* Ahmedabad: Navajivan (1956-58).

————: *Mahatma Gandhi. The Early Phase,* Ahmedabad : Navajivan (1965).

Radhakrishnan, S.(ed.), *Mahatma Gandhi : Essays and Reflections on His Life and Work,* London : Allen & Unwin (1939).

————: *Mahatma Gandhi — 100 Years,* New Delhi, Gandhi Peace Foundation (1968).

Ray, Sibnarayan (ed.), *Gandhi, India and the World,* Philadelphia: Temple University Press (1970).

Reynolds, Reginald, *To Live in Mankind — A Quest for Gandhi.* London: Andre Deutsch (1951).

Rolland, Romain, *Mahatma Gandhi,* London : Alien & Unvvin (1924).

Rosen, George, *Democracy and Economic Change in India.* Berkeley & Los Angeles (1966).

Rothermund, Indira, *The Philosophy of Restraint,* Bombay: Popular Prakashan (1963).

Rudolph, L. I. & Rudolph, S. H., *The Modernity of Tradition. Political Development in India,* Chicago: University of Chicago Press (1967).

Ruskin, John, *Unto This Last. The Political Economy of Art. Essays on Political Economy,* London : Everyman's Library (1968).

Saiyidain; K. G., *Problems of Educational Reconstruction,* Bombay: Asia Publishing House (1950).

Sarkar, Sunil Chandra, *Tagore's Educational Philosophy and Experiment,* Santiniketan : Visva-Bharati Research Publica-tion (1961).

Schumacher, E. F., *Small is Beautiful, A Study of Economics as if People Mattered,* London : Abacus (1974).
Sethi, J. D., *Gandhi Today,* Sahibabad: Vikas Publishing House (1979).
Shean, Vincent, *Lead Kindly Light,* New York : Random House (1949).
Shirer, William, *Gandhi, a Memoir,* London : Abacus (1979).
Shrimali, K. L., *The Wardha Scheme,* Udaipur : Vidya Bhavan Society (1949).
Shukla, Chandrashankar (ed.), *Gandhiji as We Know Him,* Bombay: Vora & Co. (1945).
——— : *Incidents of Gandhiji's Life,* Bombay : Vora and Co. (1949).
——— : *Reminiscences of Gandhiji,* Bombay : Vora and Co. (1951).
Simmons, Earnest J., *Tolstoy,* London : Routlcdge and Kcgan Paul (1973).
Sinha, Sasadhar, *Social Thinking of Rabindranath Tagore,* Bombay: Asia Publishing House (1962).
Sitaramayya, B. Pattabhi, *Gandhi and Gandhism (A Study),* Allahabad: Kitabstan Series (1942).
Slade, Madeleine (Mira Behn), *The Spirit's Pilgrimage,* London- : Longmans (1960).
Solanki, A. B., *Technique of Correlation in Basic Education,* Ahmedabad : Navajivan (1958).
Spratt, Philip, *Gandhism : An Analysis,* Madras : Huxley Press (1939).
Tawney, R. H., *Religion and the Rise of Capitalism,* New Delhi : Middlesex : Penguin Books (1938).
Tendulkar, D. G. *Gandhi in Champaran,* New Delhi: Publications Division, Government of India (1957).
——— : *Mahatma : Life of Mohandas Karamchand Gandhi,* 8 Vols., New Delhi : Publications Division, Government of India (1960).
Tendulkar, D.G. *et. al.* (eds.), *Gandhiji. His Life and Work.* Bombay: Keshav Bhikaji Dhawale (1944).
Thirtha, N. V., "A Comparative Study of Gandhiji's Educational Ideas and the Government of India's Basic Education Programmes — A Study in Values", Stanford University, Ph. D. Thesis (1959).
Thoreau, Henry David, *Walden,* New York : Thomas Y. Crowell (1966).
Tolstoy, Leo, *What Then Must We Do,* Trans. by Aylmer Maude, London : Oxford University Press (1934).

Unnithan, T. K. N., *Gandhi and Free India,* Amsterdam : J. B. Walters-Graningen (1956).
Varma, V. P., *The Political Philosophy of Mahatma Gandhi and Sarvodaya,* Agra (1959).
Vepa, Ram K., *New Technology. A Gandhian Concept,* New Delhi: Gandhi Book House (1975).
Verma, M. B., *History of the Harijan Sevak Sangh 1936-68.* New Delhi: Udyogshala Press (1971).
Weber, Max, *The Protestant Ethic and the Spirit of Capitalism,* Trans, by Talcott Parsons, London: Unwin University Books (1930).
——: *On Charisma and Institution Building,* Chicago : University of Chicago (1968).
Woodcock, George, *Anarchism,* Middlesex: Penguin Books (1963).
——: *Gandhi,* London : Fontana/Collins (1972).
Yagnik, Indulal K., *Gandhi as I Know Him,* Part I, Bombay : Advocate of India Press, 1933; and Part II, New Delhi: Danish Mahal (1943).
Zijderveld, Anton C., *The Abstract Society. A Cultural Analysis of Our Time,* Middlesex : Penguin Books (1974).

b) Periodical Material

Andrews, Charles Freer, "Mr. Gandhi at Phoenix", *Modern Review,* Vol. XV, No.5 (May 1914).
Barratt, Barnaby B., "The Alternative Village", *South Asian Review,* Vol. 7, No. 4 (July 1974).
Bhana, Surendra, "Tolstoy Farm. A Satyagrahi's Battleground", *Journal of Indian History,* Vol. LVII (August-December 1979).
Bharatiya L. K., "Gandhiji's Ashram. Institution and its Signifi-cance", *Lok Rajya* (16 October 1970).
Brown, Judith M., "Gandhi's Other Heirs", *South Asian Revieiv,* Vol. 5, No. 3 (April 1972).
——: "The Mahatma and Modern India", *Modern Asian Studies,* Vol. 3, No. 4 (1969).
Butler, Dom E. C., "Monasticism", *The Cambridge Medieval History,* Vol. 1, London : Cambridge University Press (1911).
Douglas, Dorothy W. & Lumpkin, Katherine Du Pre, "Communist Settlements", *Encyclopedia of the Social Sciences,* Vol. 4.
Gandhi, Arun, "Gandhi Ashrams — No Gandhian Spirit", *The Illustrated Weekly of India* (1 February 1976).

Goldie, Fay, "Last of the Gandhis in South Africa", *The Illustrated Weekly of India* (3 October 1971).

Groom, Donald G., "Impressions of Gandhi", *Gandhi Marg,* Vol. 13, No. 3 (July 1969).

Handa, Madan L., "The Existing World Order : A Gandhian Interpretation", *Gandhi Marg,* Vol. 2, No. 8 (November 1980).

Hunt, James D., "Thoreau and Gandhi: A Re-evaluation of the Legacy", *Gandhi Marg,* Vol. 14, No. 4 (October 1970).

Kalelkar, Kaka, "Gandhiji's Cottage in Sevagram", *Lok Rajya,* (1 October 1971).

Namle, S. N. "Basic Education and the Montessori Method", *The Montessori Magazine,* Nos. 2 & 3, (March & June 1947).

Narayan, Jayaprakash, "The Relevance of Gandhi", *Asian Studies,* Vol. 7, No. 3 (December 1969).

Patil, R. K., "Pattern for Rural Development", *Gandhi Marg,* Vol. 4, No. 3 (July 1960).

Pyarelal, "Gandhiji's Last Experiment: Sevagram Ashram", *The Illustrated Weekly of India (*2 December 1962).

Sharma, Sima, "Harijan Ashram. Sabarmati", *Link* (5 October 1969).

Spratt, P., "Gandhi in Retrospect", *Modern Asian Studies,* Vol. 3, No. 4 (1969).

Tandon, Vishwanath, "Vinoba and Satyagraha", *Gandhi Marg,* Vol.2, No. 7 (October 1980).

Thomson, R.M., "Gandhi at Sevagram: India in a Village," *Gandhi Marg,* Vol.2, No. 8 (November 1980).

———: "Gandhism : A Re-Examination", *Imprint* (October 1981).

———: "The Humanisation of Community — A Historical Perspective", *Gandhi Marg,* Vol. 3, No. 8 (November 1981).

Wellock, Wilfred, "Why Village Republics?" *Gandhi Marg,* Vol. 1, No. 2 (April 1957).

West, Albert, "In the Early Days with Gandhiji", *The Illustrated Weekly of India* (3, 17 & 31 October 1965).

Wood, Evelyn, "Bhudan as Communication", *Gandhi Marg,* Vol. 2, No. 1 (January 1958).

———: "Communications by Neo-Gandhians", *Gandhi Marg ,Vol. 4, No. 2 (April* 1960).

Workman, H. B., "Monasticism", *Encyclopedia of the Social Sciences,* Vol.10.

Appendix

DEPARTMENT OF SPORTS, ARTS AND CULTURE

NO. 1017   25 SEPTEMBER 2020

SOUTH AFRICAN HERITAGE RESOURCES AGENCY

DECLARATION OF THE HISTORICAL PORTION OF THE PHOENIX SETTLEMENT, INANDA, ETHEKWINI, KWAZULU-NATAL AS A NATIONAL HERITAGE SITE

By virtue of the powers vested in the South African Heritage Resources Agency, in terms of section 27 (5) of the National Heritage Resources Act (No. 25 of 1999) SAHRA hereby declares the historical portion of the Phoenix Settlement, including the Sarvodaya House, Kastur Bhuvan House, Printing Press Building, and Museum, on the remainder of Portion 498 of the Farm Piezang Revier FT, Indanda; eThekwini, KwaZulu-Natal as a National Heritage Site.

Statement of Significance

"The historical portion of the Phoenix Settlement is closely associated with Mahatma Gandhi's last decade in South Africa, his personal transformation (including race), his formulation of Satyagraha and his connection and understanding of liberation struggles in South Africa.

It is recognised that Gandhi was a product of the era in which he was raised, that his political concerns in South Africa focused primarily on the plight of British Indians, that he volunteered to serve the ambulance corps for the British as a demonstration of loyalty to the empire in two important anti-colonial events in South Africa and that, in the early years of his stay in South Africa, he used disparaging British colonial language in respect of Africans. However, it is also recognised that during the last decade of his stay in South Africa, Gandhi went through a personal transformation in his thinking regarding the colonial orientation of his youth. He posed many questions to himself as he experienced increased victimization by South African authorities. He tended to the wounded Zulu while he served in the ambulance corps and became interested in learning more about the racial discrimination endured by Africans and other people of colour. His early remarks about Africans were replaced by comments of admiration, support and a clearly expressed vision of a future South Africa that would be free of race. Gandhi's period in South Africa and his work within the South African Indian Congress, their alliance with South African Native National Congress (ANC), and the African People's Organization, was a political, and philosophical learning curve.

The Phoenix Settlement, devoted to Gandhi's philosophy of Sarvodaya (The Welfare of All) and the principles of Satyagraha, has played an important spiritual and political role throughout its long history by promoting social justice, peace, and equality. Gandhi established the settlement as an experimental communal farm, one guided by respect for all people, and as a challenge to colonial norms of segregation, languages and religions. He used a printing press and newspaper as a means to mobilize resistance and promote ethical and moral human development. He believed that communities like Phoenix advocating communal living would form a sound basis for decolonisation and the struggle against social injustice. These principles continue to be honoured through the work that the Phoenix Settlement does both within the surrounding community and abroad. Gandhi's own transformation, search for truth and enlightenment, principles of fairness, justice, non-violence and peace towards all people, continues to be a beacon of inspiration today and into the future."

Schedule

The demarcation of the site is as follows:

Site Name	Erf/Farm Number	Province	Town	Municipality	SG Diagram	Deeds
Historical Portion of the Phoenix Settlement	R/498 Piezang Revier 805 FT	KwaZulu-Natal	Inanda	eThekwini	2700/2005	2434/1913

Boundary Co-ordinates

Points	Latitude	Longitude
1	-29.70730419	30.9766849
10	-29.70763928	30.97636994
11	-29.70749601	30.97632419
12	-29.70743963	30.97633599
13	-29.70730419	30.9766849
2	-29.70768394	30.97695821
3	-29.70782184	30.97723399
4	-29.70808698	30.97725418
5	-29.7082763	30.97706792
6	-29.70833769	30.97681648
7	-29.70845373	30.97647213
8	-29.70776644	30.97611638
9	-29.7076822	30.97625274

Index

Abbott Wood Report 243
adivasi 272
Adivasi Ashramashala Scheme 272
Adyar 30
ahimsa 2, 6, 25, 99, 147, 203
Ahmedabad 93, 97, 101, 102, 107, 138, 139, 141, 144, 196, 199
All-India Cow Protection Association 153
All-India Village Industries Association (AIVIA) 179, 186, 199, 210, 215
Ambedkar (Dr) 134, 177, 273
America 13
Andrews Charles Freer 41, 83, 103, 118, 123
Andhra Jateeya Kalashala 245
anekantvada 6
Anti-Visisection Society 11
Arnold, Edwin 14
Arundale, Dr. George 239
Aryavarta 41
Asar, Lilavati 197, 199
Ashadevi, Shrimati 245
Ashe l, 34
Asiatic Registration Bill 71

Baden-Pawel, B H. 189
Bajaj, Jamnalal 117, 176, 186, 189, 193, 194, 197, 208, 225
Banerjee, Surendranath 139
bania 10
Bapu Kutir 198

Bardoli 130
Bardoli Satyagraha 129, 165
Barratt 276
Basic National Education 240
Basil 40
Batra, Dr. G. L. 207
Bawazeer Imam Saheb 109
Benares Hindu University 92, 103
Benedict 40
Besant, Annie 14
Bhagwad Gita 14, 20, 44, 55, 58, 63, 68, 74, 77, 91, 118, 124, 125, 250
Bhakti-yoga 19
Bhangis 216, 217, 218, 222
Bhansali 231
Bhatt, Chimanbhai 268, 271
Bhave, Vinoba 114, 121, 186, 229, 253
Bihar 104
Bihar Government 245, 246
Blavatsky, Madam 11, 13, 14
Blossoms in the Dust 249
Boer war 49, 59, 71
Bombay 19, 91, 229
Bombay Government 245, 246
Borsad 117
Bose, Subhas Chandra 227
brahmachary (celibacy) 32, 58, 84, 123, 124, 125, 126, 201, 202, 203
Briton 24
British 6
Brown, Judith 163
Buber, Martin 230
Burma 95

Index

Calcutta 95
Carpenter, 11, 13, 34
Chamars, 104, 105, 106, 122, 152, 165
Cha rka Sangh 212
Chavan 277
Christianys 15, 18, 24, 58, 73, 83
Christian Anarchism 26
Christianity 15, 20, 21, 34, 263
Communists 97, 214
Congress 174, 175, 179, 182, 193, 224, 226, 227, 228, 229, 232, 239, 243, 272
Cordes, John 52, 53, 82, 83
Curtis, Lionel 218
Dahyabhai 202
Dandi March 129, 130
Danibhen 102
Das, C. R. 148
Dave's Swaraj Ashram 268
Deccan Education Society 43, 81
Desai, Dinkar 239
Desai, Jivanlal 98
Desai, Mahadev 117, 152, 186, 196, 198, 199, 203, 218, 219, 220, 228, 232, 237
Desai, Pragji 85
Deshmukh, Babasaheb 189
Dharma 113, 156
Dhed l0l, 102
Dhoti 143
Doke, Rev. Joseph 46, 54, 62, 116
Dube, S. C. 8
Dudhabhai 102
Dumont, Louis 17, 18
Durban 37, 38, 44, 46, 47, 49, 53, 63, 79
Dwijendranath (Tagore) 160

Economic History of India 138
Elphinstone 17

Emerson 13, 78
England 11, 18, 23, 53, 80, 265
Ericson 5, 30, 72, 78
Esoteric Christian Union 20
Europeans 76

Fergusson College 43, 81
Fischer, Louis 31
Francis 40

Gandhi, Arun 9, 10, 69, 209
Gandhi, Chhaganlal 48, 59, 65, 82, 127
Gandhi-Irwin Settlement 133
Gandhi, Karamchand 5, 6
Gandhi, Maganlal 48, 59, 67, 77, 82, 93, 96, 107, 115, 117, 121, 141, 143, 153, 186
Gandhi, Maganlal 68, 69, 84
Gandhi, Mohandas Karamchand 1, 2, 4, 5, 6, 7, 8, 9, 10, 11, 12, 13, 14, 15, 16, 17, 18, 19, 20, 21, 22, 23, 24, 25, 26, 27, 28, 29, 30, 31, 32, 33, 34, 37, 38, 39, 40, 41, 42, 43, 44, 45, 46, 47, 48, 49, 50, 51, 52, 53, 54, 55, 56, 57, 58, 59, 60, 61, 62, 63, 64, 65, 66, 67, 68, 69, 70, 71, 72, 73, 74, 75, 76, 77, 78, 79, 80, 81, 82, 83, 84, 85, 86, 87, 91, 92, 93, 94, 95, 96, 97, 98, 99, 100, 102, 103, 104, 105, 106, 107, 108, 109, 110, 111, 112, 113, 114, 115, 116, 117, 118, 119, 120, 121, 122, 123, 124, 125, 126, 127, 128, 129, 130, 131, 132, 133, 134, 135, 136, 137, 138, 139, 140, 141, 142, 143, 144, 145, 146, 147, 148, 149, 150, 151, 152, 153, 154, 155, 156, 157, 158, 159, 160, 161, 162, 163, 164, 174, 175, 176, 177, 178, 179, 180, 181, 182, 183, 184, 185, 186, 187, 188, 189, 190, 191, 192, 193, 194, 195, 196, 197, 198, 199, 200,

201, 203, 204, 205, 206, 207, 208, 209, 210, 211, 212, 213, 214, 215, 216, 217, 218, 219, 220, 221, 222, 223, 224, 225, 226, 227, 228, 229, 230, 231, 232, 233, 234, 235, 236, 237, 238, 239, 240, 241, 242, 251, 252, 253, 263, 264, 265, 266, 268, 269, 270, 271, 272, 273, 274, 275, 276, 277.
Gandhi, Narandas 134, 135, 136
Gandhi, Nirmala 80, 133, 230
Gandhi, Ramdas 80, 230
Gandhi Seva Sangh 192, 223, 224, 225
Gandhi, Sumitra 230
Gandhi, Sushila 68, 69
Ganges 96
Germans 39
Ghose, Aurobindo 92
Gokhale, Gopal Krishna 43, 44, 65, 77, 81, 82, 91, 94, 95, 158, 265
Gokuldas 52
Go Seva Sangh 153
Govindswamy 48
Graham, Millie 52
Gram Sevaks 182, 184, 185, 270, 271
gram sevak scheme 270
Greenlees, Duncan 136
Gregg, Richard 155
Gujarat 6, 117, 129, 222
Gujarati 14, 161
Gujarat Vidyapith 150, 162, 200, 245
Gupta, Surendranath 109
gurukul 96

Hardvar 96, 97
Harijan 100, 178, 186, 203, 220, 238, 240, 246
Harijan Ashram 238
harijans 177, 186, 198, 212, 216, 217, 218, 222, 224
Harijan Sevak Sangh 138, 177
Harilal 80
Haripura 243
Harischandra 7
Hero & Hero Worship 18
Hindi 106, 134, 160, 161
Hind Swaraj 17, 25, 81, 86, 139, 143
Hinduism 14, 20, 30, 31, 34, 43, 97, 152, 263, 270
Hindus 5, 6, 96, 222
Hindustani Talimi Sangh 213, 243, 244, 245
Hrishikesh 96, 100
Hunt 18
Hussain, Dr. Zakir 240

India 34, 91
Indian National Congress 37, 222
Indian Opinion 45, 46, 49, 50, 52, 54, 55, 57, 61, 62, 64, 65, 66, 67, 68, 80, 264
Indians 73
Irwin Viceroy 130

J.B. Kripalani's Gandhi Ashram 113
Jainism 6
Jains 6
Jamia Milia Islamia, Delhi 245
Jesus 20
Jinnah, Mohammed Ali 232
Jnan-Yoga 20
Johannesburg 44, 54, 62
Joshi, Chhaganlal 115, 118, 128, 133
Jugatram Dave's Ashram 113

Kabir 160
Kaka Kalelkar 159, 160, 162
Kallenbach, Hermann 54, 71, 72, 73, 74, 75, 76, 77, 85
Kantak, Prema Behn 133, 136, 137
Karmayogi 33
Kasturba 9, 10, 52, 55, 56, 59, 60, 65,

Index

69, 93, 101, 102, 104, 107, 108, 128, 197, 202, 232, 233
Kasturba Ashram 268
Kathiawar Peninsula 4, 10, 11, 15, 18
Kaur, Amrit 122, 222
Khadi 68, 98, 117, 122, 139, 142, 143, 144, 145, 146, 147, 150, 151, 152, 162, 178, 193, 213, 214, 215, 224, 226, 227, 229
Khadi Seva Sangh 150
Khadi Vidyalay 155, 213
Khare, Pandit 109
Kher, B. G 243
Kher Committee 244
Kingdom of God is Within you 23
Kinsford, Anna 21, 39
Kitchen, Herbert 52, 62
Kochrab 98, 99, 100, 107
Kochrab Ashram 106, 141, 234
Kripalani, J. B. 162, 240
Kumarappa, J. C. 186, 198, 225, 226, 235
Kumbh Mela 95
kunbis 216, 220

Ladha 7
Lakshmi 102
Lathe, Professor 140
Light of Asia 18
Linlithgow, Lord 197, 224, 229
London 11, 15, 18, 22, 27, 39, 80, 91
London Vegetarian Society 12, 13, 20
Lucknow 180

Madhan 268
Madhya Pradesh Government 245
Madras 100, 101
Magalnath Sadhu 100
Maganlal 44, 95, 108, 110, 112, 116
Maganwadi 186, 187, 188, 189, 190, 194, 195, 199, 211, 215
Mahars 188, 216, 217, 218
Mahadev Kutir 198
Maharashtra 161
Maharashtra *Vidyapith* 245
Mahavir 6
Maine, Henry Summer 15, 16, 17, 18, 34
Maitland, Edward 20, 23, 55
Majmudar Ganga Behn 142
malguzar (Maratha Revenue Man-ager) 189, 208, 220
Malikanand 224
Mangs 188, 216, 217
Manilal 9, 68
Manusmriti 7
Marathi 161
Mariann, Hill 34, 38, 45
Mashruwala, Kishorelal 198, 204, 219, 231
Mashruwala, K.G 248
Mashruwala, Taraben 268, 275
Mehta, Balwantrai 275
Mehta, Sir Pherczeshah 19
Mehta, Ved 80, 230
Merton, Thomas 14
Metcalf 17
Mira Ben (Madeleine Slade) 119, 120, 133, 136, 164, 186, 188, 190, 191, 195, 197, 211, 217, 218
Modi, Ramniklal 113
Mookerji, R. D 41
Mukherjee, Satis Chandra 158, 244
Mukherjee, Sujit 32
Munshiramji, Mahatma 96
Muslim, League 92
Muslims 73, 83
Myrdal, Gunnar 249

Naidu, Sarojini 126
Naik, Gajanan 189

Nai Talim 235
Namle, S. N. 239
Nanda 1
Nanda, B, R 99
Nandi Hills 195
Narsibhai Baranda 272
Natal 17, 38, 47, 64, 65
Natal Indian Congress 37
National Education Movement 157
Navjivan 103, 125, 144, 150, 165
Nayar, Dr. Sushila 202, 204, 206, 207
Nazar, Mansukhalal 52
Nehru, Jawaharlal 144, 151, 152, 174, 180, 197, 226, 227, 231, 250, 251
Nehru, Motilal 148
Netherlands 24
New Delhi 204, 275
New Interpretation of the Bible 21
New Testament 15, 63
Noakhali 224, 233
North America 24

Olcott Memorial School 30
Orange Free State 20
Orissa Government 245, 247

Palestine 24
Panchayati raj 274, 275, 276
Parchure Kutir 198
Parchure, Shastri 198
Parker, Dr. Joseph 15
Parsee Rustoomji 48, 198
Parsi 6
Patel, M. S. 246
Patel, Vallabhbhai 117
Pavlov, V. I 139
Payne 1
Prefect Way in Diet 39
Perfect Way or the Finding of Christ 21
Phoenix 47, 48, 49, 50, 52, 53, 54, 57, 59, 60, 61, 62, 63, 64, 65, 66, 68, 70, 78, 80, 81, 82, 83, 84, 86, 92, 94, 96, 107, 115, 164, 204
Phoenix Settlement 2, 25, 27, 31, 45, 55, 57, 69, 70, 71, 85, 127
Phoenix & Tolstoy Farm 159, 161, 264
Piezang 47
Pinetown 39, 76, 124
Plea For Vegetarianism 12
Polak, Henry 46, 49, 52, 54, 62
Polak, Mrs. 62, 80, 110
Poona 43, 95
Porbandar 4, 9, 19
Prabhudas 115
pranamis 5
Prasad, Rajendra 192
Pretoria 20, 37
Pudupalayam 113
Punjabhai, Hirachand 107
punya 143
purdah 126
Plymouth Brethren 20
Pyarelal 1, 7, 8, 10, 86, 197, 198, 223
Pywell 53

Radhaswami Sect 212
Ragoo Govindoo 65
Rajachandra 22
Rajagopalachari 113, 230
Rajkot 9, 19, 97
Ramdevji, Acharya 96
Ramakrishna 42, 43
Ramanama 7
Ramayana 7, 118
Ramgobm, Ela 69
Ramzan 74
Ranaday, S. G. 163
Report of the Team for the Study of Community Projects and National Extension Service 275

Index

Rhodes, Cecil 30
Rhodesia 52, 53, 82
Rolland Remain 119
Round Table Conference 133, 134
Rowlat *Satyagrah* 80, 103, 145
Rudra, S. K 163
Ruskin, John 15, 26, 27, 28, 29, 30, 34, 47, 78, 140, 264
Russia 24

Sabarmati/Ashram 100, 107, 108, 110, 112, 113, 114, 116, 117, 118, 119, 120, 121, 122, 123, 124, 126, 129, 130, 131, 134, 135, 136, 137, 140, 141, 149, 154, 155, 163, 165, 176, 186, 200, 201, 202, 203, 208, 211, 221, 222, 233, 239, 252, 266, 267
Saivites 6
Salt, Henry 12, 13
Salt Satyagrah 132, 175, 267
Sam, 66
Sandhya Totaram 109
Sanatan dharma 101
Sanskrit 14, 160
Sanyasi 33
Sarabhai, Ambalal 102
Sastri V. S. Srinivas 95
Satyagraha 1, 2, 25, 26, 38, 50, 54, 57, 61, 63, 64, 71, 73, 77, 78, 82, 83, 86, 101, 102, 103, 104, 110, 122, 130, 204, 231, 234, 252, 264, 268, 269, 273, 276
Satyagraha Ashram 2, 68, 93, 97, 102, 103, 104, 105, 107, 110, 111, 115, 124, 125, 126, 127, 128, 129, 131, 134, 135, 136, 141, 142, 143, 164, 186, 225
Sarvodaya 110, 180, 183, 238, 253, 276
Seekers Club 44
Segaon 189, 190, 191, 193, 194, 195, 196, 205, 223
Sermon on the Mount 15, 18
Sevagram Ashram 2, 83, 196, 197, 198, 199, 200, 201, 202, 203, 204, 205, 206, 207, 208, 209, 210, 211, 212, 213, 214, 215, 216, 218, 219, 220, 221, 222, 223, 224, 228, 230, 231, 232, 233, 234, 236, 245, 246, 249, 250, 252, 265, 270,
Servants of India Society 94
Sevamandir 98
Sevashram 98
Shah, Chimanlal 206, 231
Shah, Munnalal 195, 197, 229, 231
Shah, Uttamchand 271
Shamlalji Ashram 272
Shantinikatan 60, 93, 94, 159
Sharma, Hiralal 136
Shriman Narayan 198
Shukla, Rajkumar 104
Shravan 7
Shudras 31, 100
Simla 204
Sindi 186, 187, 188, 190, 217
Singh Balwant 196, 197, 209, 211, 212, 213, 231, 233
Slade Madeleine 119
SobaniUmar 141, 142
Socialists 214, 223, 250, 251
Song Celestial 14
South Africa 2, 10, 13, 16, 19, 20, 23, 30, 34, 37, 38, 39, 41, 43, 45, 52, 54, 55, 57, 66, 67, 70, 71, 77, 78, 79, 80, 81, 82, 86, 92, 96, 98, 107, 108, 109, 110, 116, 118, 124, 127, 129, 130, 131, 134, 135, 136, 138, 164, 165, 198, 263, 264, 265
Sriniketan 94
Surgeon, Charles Hadden 15
Swadeshi 9, 8, 139, 140
Swaraj 139, 222, 227

Swaraj Ashram, Bardoli 271, 272

Tagore, Rabindranath 65, 93, 94, 159, 160, 265
Tamil 160
tapovan (abode of austerities) 41
Tapovan 98
Thakkar, A. V. 178
Theosophical Society 11, 13, 239
Theosophy 14, 22, 83
Third All India Basic Education Conference 248
Thoreau 12, 13, 26, 31, 32, 33, 264
Tilak, B.G 92
Tolstoy 12, 23, 24, 34, 47, 55, 78, 79
Tolstoy Farm 2, 54, 57, 70, 71, 72, 73, 74, 76, 77, 78, 85, 86, 107, 115, 164, 264
Transvaal 20, 64
Transvaal Critic 52
Trappist monastery 124
Trappists 39, 40, 45
Tukdoji, Maharaj 200
Tyabji, Salim 163

Udyog Mandir 127
Unto This Last 16, 27, 30, 34, 46, 52, 79, 140
Urdu 106
Uitar Pradesh Government 245

Vaidya, Gangabehn 131
Vaidyanathdhan 97
Vaishnava 101
Vaishnavas 7
Vaishnavites 6
Vallabhbhai Patel's Ashram 113
Vanaprastha (one retired from house-hold cares) 32
Varna (Colour) 29, 30

Vegetarian Society 11
Vepa, Ram K 250
Verala Irrigation and Development Project Society 277
Verulam 65
Vidya Mandir 244, 245, 246
Vijapur 142
Village Communities of the East and West 16
Vinoba Bhave's Satyagrah Ashram 113
Vishnu 5, 7
Vivekanand Swami 43
Vyavaharik 47

Walden Pond 31
Walden Pool 32
Wardha 113, 186, 188, 219, 231, 249
Wardha Ashram 114, 197, 199, 205
Wardha Scheme 241, 245, 249, 271
Weber, Max 57
West, Ada 53
West, Albert 46, 48, 49, 50, 53, 62, 63, 65, 66, 67, 80, 91
West, Roxbury 31
What Then Must We Do 24
Women and Social Justice 122
Woodcock, George 2, 38

Yajna 134
Yervada Gaol 103, 132
Yervada Central Prison 198
Young India 103, 125, 130, 144, 150, 164
Zakir Hussain Committee 241, 242, 243, 246
Zamindar 189, 193, 216
Zamindari 208, 219
Zaveri, Revashankar 117
Zulu/s 39, 50, 53, 62
Zulu Rebellion 54, 59